SPEAKING FOR THE DEAD

Medical Law and Ethics

Series Editor
Sheila McLean, Director of the Institute of Law and Ethics in Medicine,
School of Law, University of Glasgow

The 21st century seems likely to witness some of the most major developments in medicine and healthcare ever seen. At the same time, the debate about the extent to which science and/or medicine should lead the moral agenda continues, as do questions about the appropriate role for law.

This series brings together some of the best contemporary academic commentators to tackle these dilemmas in a challenging, informed and inquiring manner. The scope of the series is purposely wide, including contributions from a variety of disciplines such as law, philosophy and social sciences.

Other titles in the series

Law, Mind and Brain
Edited by Michael Freeman and Oliver R. Goodenough
ISBN 978-0-7546-7013-1

The Jurisdiction of Medical Law
Kenneth Veitch
ISBN 978-0-7546-4944-1

Medical Self-Regulation
Crisis and Change
Mark Davies
ISBN 978-0-7546-4459-0

Biotechnology and the Challenge of Property
Property Rights in Dead Bodies, Body Parts, and Genetic Information
Remigius N. Nwabueze
ISBN 978-0-7546-7168-8

Speaking for the Dead
The Human Body in Biology and Medicine

Second Edition

D. GARETH JONES and MAJA I. WHITAKER
University of Otago, New Zealand

ASHGATE

Published by
Ashgate Publishing Limited
Wey Court East
Union Road
Farnham
Surrey, GU9 7PT
England

Ashgate Publishing Company
Suite 420
101 Cherry Street
Burlington
VT 05401-4405
USA

www.ashgate.com

British Library Cataloguing in Publication Data
Jones, D. Gareth (David Gareth), 1940-
  Speaking for the dead : the human body in biology and
  medicine. - 2nd ed. - (Medical law and ethics)
  1. Dead - Moral and ethical aspects 2. Dead - Social
  aspects 3. Body, Human (Philosophy) 4. Medical ethics
  I. Title II. Whitaker, Maja I.
  174.2

Library of Congress Cataloging-in-Publication Data
Jones, D. Gareth (David Gareth), 1940-
  Speaking for the dead : the human body in biology and medicine / by D. Gareth Jones and Maja I. Whitaker. -- 2nd ed.
     p. cm. -- (Medical law and ethics)
  Includes bibliographical references and index.
  ISBN 978-0-7546-7452-8 (hardcover : alk. paper) 1. Human dissection--Moral and ethical aspects. 2. Human experimentation in medicine--Moral and ethical aspects. I. Whitaker, Maja I. II. Title. III. Series.
  [DNLM: 1. Cadaver. 2. Human Experimentation--ethics. 3. Death. 4. Human Body. W 20.55.H9 J76s 2008]

  QM33.5.J66 2008
  174'.2--dc22
                                                                              2008040010
ISBN 978-0-7546-7452-8

Mixed Sources
Product group from well-managed forests and other controlled sources
www.fsc.org Cert no. SGS-COC-2482
© 1996 Forest Stewardship Council
FSC

Printed and bound in Great Britain by
TJ International Ltd, Padstow, Cornwall

Contents

Notes on Contributors

D. Gareth Jones is Professor of Anatomy and Structural Biology at the University of Otago, Dunedin, New Zealand. He also serves as Deputy Vice-Chancellor (Academic and International) at that university. He is a neuroscientist, with considerable interests in bioethical issues as they relate to the human body.

Maja I. Whitaker is an Assistant Research Fellow in the Department of Anatomy and Structural Biology at the University of Otago.

Preface

The appearance of a second edition always requires justification. In this instance, events of enormous significance have taken place since the year 2000, with the result that about 50 per cent of the contents are new. Reflecting on these events, the ones of especial note include a motley assortment of retained body parts and organs scandals, and the flourishing of popular human body exhibitions, leading to the need for far more detailed analyses of these developments. Additionally, this edition extends much further beyond the confines of the dead body than did the first edition. This has resulted in largely new chapters on the developing body, neuroscience and modification of the body.

The introduction of this broader perspective in this edition has led to a rearrangement of much of the material, with the emphasis of each chapter being on 'the body', from the dead body to the plastinated body, and from the dissected body to the thinking body. In line with this change, 'cadavers' in the original subtitle has become 'the human body' in the present one.

Like the first edition, this edition proposes that the manner in which we respond to the dead, the use we make of their skeletal remains and their tissues, and the ways in which we learn about ourselves by studying them, raises ethical queries that go to the heart of what it means to be human. Hence, the apparently unfathomable gulf between them and us is far less unfathomable than we often imagine, and presses upon us the importance of understanding the many links between the living and the dead.

For many years, issues that anatomists would now consider to have ethical overtones were taken for granted. Indeed, most people failed to recognize that there are ethical issues in anatomy. The range of poignant ethical questions confronting those in clinical fields seemed to have passed anatomists by. Those in anatomy departments were spared having to confront issues like informed consent, or of deciding what to tell patients faced by imminent death, or when to turn off respirators. They simply dealt with dead people, and not unexpectedly, dead people did not seem to pose too many problems. The bodies had been obtained by legitimate means, as had the brains used in neuroanatomy classes and the skeletons that decorated the walls of the dissecting room, the anatomy museum, and sometimes the lecture theatre. Even histology slides were of dead, fixed pieces of tissue, sometimes from humans, sometimes from animals, that seemed to raise few if any ethical dilemmas. When the sections were of embryos, even these were often of pigs rather than human beings. When they were of humans, they had probably been obtained many years previously.

The use of human material in research had played an ever-decreasing role in recent years. While some devoted their time to studying human bones obtained from archeological digs, these were not generally seen as posing any especially difficult ethical problems. As long as they were treated with care and dignity, they could be kept indefinitely.

All this began to change as a revolutionary renaissance we now know as bioethics broadened and transformed what had been the much more confined domain of medical ethics. Ethical analysis that had been confined to specifically clinical realms, and to isolated topics such as abortion, began to be applied to reproductive technologies and organ transplantation, immediately raising profound ethical queries at both ends of life. These ethical queries concerned the status of the embryo at one end and brain death at the other, both of which can only be addressed by reference to the human body.

What is surprising is that, as the human body has been increasingly exposed to ethical assessment, anatomists have barely responded to the challenges this has posed for them. No longer is it possible for the world of anatomy to remain isolated from the world of ethics, or even the variety of social forces milling around it. In reality, of course, it never has been isolated, but anatomists have acted as though this were the case. The bodies being 'anatomized' in the dissecting room were obtained in a variety of ways, some deeply unethical. The skeletons purchased from reputable companies in the West came from what were probably far less reputable sources in India. Much of the skeletal material of indigenous peoples emanated from a scientific culture far removed from that of today's, in some instances characterized by racist attitudes anathema to today's scientific climate.

Any such exploration has to attempt to bring together the numerous strands of ethical discussion that are currently taking place on different facets of the human body, human tissue and human material. The results are surprising, since what has emerged is that, together, these constitute a common thread weaving its way through so many of the debates that constitute the medical side of bioethics. This is not a new finding, since as long ago as 1985, Kass commented in the following terms: 'How to treat dead bodies may seem to be a trivial moral question, compared with all the seemingly vital problems that confront the living. But, from a theoretical point of view, few are as illuminating of our self-conception and self-understanding'. This was the thrust of the first edition, and it is traced even more insistently in this second edition.

It is a truism to assert that anatomists need ethics. However, what is more important is that the ethical issues anatomists are confronted with are of concern to many others within society as well; hence this book is aimed at a general readership, that is, at anyone interested in ethical issues impinging upon the human body. However, this book differs from many others on bioethical issues, in that we have taken advantage of the interests of anatomists to view even well-known ethical issues from the perspective of those who are primarily concerned with the human body and human tissue. Responses to the first edition indicated that this approach has its merits, and hence is developed further in this one.

The need for another edition is demonstrated by the emergence of yet more ethical challenges associated with continuing uses and abuses of the human body. The formulation of new Human Tissue Acts in one legislature after another represents the need to keep abreast of scientific developments. Nevertheless, reactions to some of these developments, including on occasion by anatomists and the general public are surprisingly ill informed. It is our hope that this new edition will rectify to some extent gaps that currently exist in what is a vitally important debate.

In this edition I have been joined by Maja Whitaker as co-author. This is in recognition of Maja's input into every facet of the writing and researching of this edition, and in ensuring that the book is as up to date and broadly informed as it can possibly be.

D. Gareth Jones
Dunedin, New Zealand

Acknowledgements

We would like to thank Dr Mike King for his invaluable assistance in helping to bring this book to fruition. He diligently read through every chapter, bringing his ethical expertise to bear on all facets of the book, thereby serving as a helpful critic and adviser. He also provided enormous assistance in rationalizing the numerous references. We would also like to thank Kristina Buch for her contribution to Chapter 8. The financial support provided by the Department of Anatomy and Structural Biology at the University of Otago is acknowledged in providing Fellowships for Maja Whitaker and Dr Mike King.

Chapter 1
The Dead Body

Introduction

In the eyes of most people anatomy and cadavers are inseparable. Talk to practising doctors about their experiences as medical students in anatomy, and their thoughts will drift instinctively to the dissecting room and the dead bodies, the cadavers, they encountered there. One of the most vivid accounts of a first acquaintance with a dissecting room is provided by the composer Hector Berlioz. In his *Memoirs* (1969, 46), he writes:

> … I gave myself up wholly to studying for the career which had been thrust upon me. It was soon put to a somewhat severe test when Robert, having announced one morning that he had bought a 'subject' (a corpse), took me for the first time to the dissecting room … at the sight of that terrible charnel-house – fragments of limbs, the grinning heads and gaping skulls, the bloody quagmire underfoot and the atrocious smell it gave off, the swarms of sparrows wrangling over scraps of lung, the rats in their corner gnawing the bleeding vertebrae – such a feeling of revulsion possessed me that I leapt through the window of the dissecting-room and fled for home as though Death and all his hideous train were at my heels. The shock of that first impression lasted for twenty-four hours. I did not want to hear another word about anatomy, dissection or medicine, and I meditated a hundred mad schemes of escape from the future that hung over me.

It is not clear how accurate was this description of the dissecting room Berlioz encountered in the Paris of 1822. Regardless of the excessive repulsive feelings that may have coloured his account, and of the rebellion against his father that was so much a part of his unhappy encounter with the world of medicine, it is a highly evocative picture that lingers in the memory. This is not all there is to know about anatomy, but it is a facet of the anatomist's world that cannot be entirely dismissed.

Almost invariably the dissecting room is seen as the place where anatomy begins and ends. This is a travesty, as unhelpful as it is misleading. The suggestion that the world of the anatomist is nothing more than that of dead bodies lying on slabs in the dissecting room is a caricature, missing as it does anything that can be seen and understood using microscopes. The other world of cells, let alone everything that can be studied at the subcellular or molecular levels, is tragically lost. While this misapprehension is of greater interest to anatomists than to anyone else, it needs to be borne in mind throughout this book as we move seamlessly from the macroscopic to the microscopic and back again. A second unfortunate implication is the impression that dead bodies are of little concern to anyone other than anatomists (and in a parallel clinical context, pathologists). From the perspective of this book, this is an even more serious misconception than the first, since anatomy has a great deal to contribute to the world of clinical medicine, providing as it does entry to an appreciation of the significance of the dead body. This, in turn, has another consequence, namely, that it is impossible to approach the dead body in an ethical vacuum, whether it is within the context of anatomy or of clinical medicine. One point that we hope will emerge is that the ethical context developed to understand the uses and abuses of the dead body in the dissecting room is relevant to the development of appropriate ethical contexts within clinical medicine. The reason for this is that, since the dead body was once a living human body, there is a strand between the two, with mutual connections leading in both directions.

In more recent times, the significance of the dead body for the world beyond academia and clinical medicine has become readily apparent in two quite different domains. The dead body has moved into the public domain in dramatic fashion with the unprecedented popularity of plastination exhibitions (Chapter 4). These are neither anatomy in a strict sense, nor are they clinical medicine. We shall examine how they can best be categorized in due course, but there is no doubt that they extend the boundaries of conventional perspectives in ethically challenging ways. The other domain is that of research using the human body and human tissue. While research projects utilize human material in a variety of contexts, the most striking is the use of human embryos (Chapter 7). The ethical debate here is probably more vociferous than in any of the other areas we shall encounter, and it is not generally approached from the perspective of a dead human body. However, we consider that the approach we shall adopt is a potentially fruitful one.

We shall also explore two even more surprising areas with their respective emphases upon the nervous system (Chapter 8) and human enhancement (Chapter 9). While many of the topics covered in these chapters do not deal with dead human material, we consider they are natural extensions of what may be regarded as the core themes in the earlier chapters.

Anatomy and the Culture of Dissection

'Anatomy' is generally defined as 'the science of the structure of the bodies of humans, animals and plants; a treatise in this field; the artificial separation of the parts of a human, animal or vegetable body, in order to discover their position, structure and relations; dissection' (*Shorter Oxford English Dictionary* 2002). 'Anatomy' can also refer to a detailed analysis of a particular topic (for instance, 'the anatomy of a crime') and, in a non-technical sense, the human body (*Collins English Dictionary & Thesaurus* 2006). Quite clearly, 'anatomy' in the sense in which it is used in anatomy departments is far more specific than many of these definitions.

Anatomy departments as discussed here limit their attention to human anatomy. They are departments of human anatomy, even though much research within them concentrates more on rats and mice than on humans. Central to their *raison d'être* is the structure of the human body. This is particularly the case for teaching, in which dissection of the human body constitutes a central activity. For medical students in particular, anatomy is largely defined as what can be learned from dissection of the human body. Gross anatomy, with its dissection and macroscopic study of the regions and systems of the human body, is the closest we come to a public image of anatomy, regardless of how members of an anatomy department may view the scope of their discipline. Anatomy, in this sense, is replete with nineteenth-century connotations that sit uneasily alongside the activities conducted in many contemporary anatomy departments.

It is impossible to move beyond this elementary point without enquiring into the culture of dissection, with its roots in the sixteenth and seventeenth centuries. No matter how anatomy is defined in the twenty-first century, there is no debate as to its position within the spectrum of academic disciplines: it is a biological science. What debate there is, concerns whether it belongs mainly within the domain of medicine, as a science serving medical education, or as one of the biomedical sciences.

In other words, were we to use the verb 'anatomize' or the noun 'anatomization' today, we would use it in a scientific sense. When a body is anatomized, or dissected, a complete body is reduced to its component parts in an attempt to build up a new body of knowledge. More specifically, the body of one individual is dissected so that a profession's understanding of the morphology and function of bodies in general can be increased. In the light of that which is learned about specific bodies, the intention is to strengthen and broaden the science of anatomy in general.

But what do we mean by such an obvious term as 'the body'? According to Kass (1985), the term in Old English referred to the living body, and only later in Middle English was the same term used for the dead body or corpse. Later, it was used to refer to the person or individual being.

Kass argues that, although the term 'body', in its primary usage, refers to the body of human beings or of animals, it is an abstraction. The body is always *some* body, it is *somebody's* body. This, in turn, raises questions such as: is my body mine or is it me? Can it be alienated from me, like other property of mine, such as my car or my dog? On what basis do I claim property rights over my body? Do I hold my body as a gift? If so, is it mine to dispose of as I wish? However we wish to answer questions such as these, we find we are moving continually between a particular body, *somebody's* body, and the body in general. Whether or not Kass is correct, we have to agree with him that we cannot limit our horizons and interests to a generalized 'body'. Cadavers, body parts, tissues and bony remains always come from particular individuals, and even when these individuals lived in the distant past, they can never be completely dehumanized. They still remind us that they were once one of us.

However, the scientific ethos within which anatomy has functioned for two hundred years (see Chapter 2) arose out of a bewildering array of competing cultural forces. These provide a much broader appreciation of anatomy than that obtained by viewing it solely as the science of dissection.

Developing a Vision of the Interior of the Body

Prior to the modern, dispassionate, scientific approach to the human body, anatomy was part of a popular culture enamoured with the interior of the body but experiencing great difficulty in coming to terms with this largely hidden domain. In the Early Modern period in Europe, particularly the sixteenth and seventeenth centuries, there existed a fascination with the body that led inevitably to a morbid curiosity with dissection – the only known way of exploring this tantalizing and exotic territory. Dissection was not carried out in a sanitized environment as in the modern dissecting room, but in anatomy theatres with bodies straight from the gallows. It was carried out in a manner imbued with a prescientific understanding of the body, and in close association with playwrights and poets, a world far removed from modern conceptions. Jonathan Sawday in his elegant book, *The Body Emblazoned* (1995), brings to light the culture of dissection in the Early Modern period, with the morbid eroticism of some Renaissance poetry and theatre, the longing of writers to explore the unknown mysteries of the body's interior, and the surprisingly close connection between the respective theatres of playwrights and anatomists.

In sixteenth- and seventeenth-century Europe, the body was considered taboo, was viewed as capricious, and was talked of in the language of treason, treachery, duplicity and secrecy (as in the writings of John Donne). According to Sawday (1995, 43), this was an 'intangible world of imaginative and symbolic desire, where ritual, intellectual curiosity, and the sovereign rites of justice and punishment, merge into a fascination with the human interior'.

Contributing to the flourishing of anatomy during this period was a fascination for matters of sexuality and pain, which in turn were closely associated with dissection. Of considerable surprise is the conjunction between the anatomy lecture theatre *cum* dissecting room, and the playhouse. In analyzing the play *The Anatomist*, by the seventeenth-century writer Edward Ravenscroft, Sawday (1995, 46) finds that 'the role of the corpse ... conceals criminality, duplicity, and licence'. In the play, the corpse serves as a focus of attention, a place for demonstrating technical skill and a refuge from the outraged guardians of sexual morality. Sawday further argues that in order to obtain the delights of the flesh, the play suggests that we first have to be willing to become flesh. 'And once we are flesh, what happens when the anatomist catches our eye?' (Sawday 1995, 47).

Earlier, in 1594, Thomas Nashe writes in *The Unfortunate Traveller*, of his narrator being examined and then locked up to await dissection. At this point, the character meditates:

> Oh, the cold sweating cares which I conceived after I knew I should be cut like a French summer doublet! Methought already the blood began to gush out at my nose. If a flea on the arm had bit me, I deemed the instrument had pricked me. Well, well, I may scoff at a shrewd turn, but there's no such ready way to make a man a true Christian as to persuade himself he is taken up for an anatomy … Not a drop of sweat trickled down my breast and my sides, but I dreamt it was a smooth-edged razor tenderly slicing down my breast and my sides. If any knocked at the door, I supposed it was the beadle of Surgeon's Hall come for me. (quoted in Sawday 1995, 49)

Even stranger to us are the accounts of poets and writers outlining their dreams of dissection, feeling the hand of the dissector with its associated shiver of erotic anticipation. Such erotic dreams of partition were present in poetic texts until well into the seventeenth century. Being dissected was seen as the most complete form of physical surrender. An illustration of this is a poem dating from 1659 by Richard Lovelace, who, addressing his mistress, makes his poetic persona surrender to her:

> Ah my fair Murdresse! Dost thou cruelly heal,
>
> With Various pains to make me well?
>
> Then let me be
>
> Thy cut Anatomie,
>
> And in each mangled part my heart you'l see (quoted in Sawday 1995, 51)

Sawday argues that, by accepting the most complete form of physical surrender, namely dissection, the poem is able to express the extent of the poet's desire for his beloved.

The fascination and horror of dissection stemmed, in part, from its close liaison with public executions (Hildebrandt 2008). In the sixteenth and seventeenth centuries, the felon, executioner, anatomist, plus various advisers and assistants each played a carefully orchestrated part in the spectacle that made up the culture of dissection: these were two acts in a single drama. It was not until the eighteenth century that clinical detachment emerged. Prior to William Harvey's time (1578–1657):

> … anatomies were performed in public … as ritualistic expressions of often contradictory layers of meaning, rather than as scientific investigations in any

modern sense … In the age of Vesalius … the centrality of the public anatomical
demonstration rested as much on the dignity invested in the anatomist, as on its
utility as a branch of natural science. (quoted in Sawday 1995, 63)

The Renaissance anatomy theatre contained outlines of judicial court, dramatic
stage, and basilica-style church or temple. It was a place of symbolic confrontation:
between the naked cadaver and the anatomist; between the old text-based and the
new observational approach to knowledge. Anatomy represented the symbolic
power of knowledge over the body of the individual criminal, the anatomist
gradually emerging as the living embodiment of a progressive technological
regime. Anatomists were active participants in the execution process, thereby
demonstrating the conjunction between science and the executioner's skills
(see also Richardson 1988). The result was that, if anatomists were to be able to
continue their investigations on the human body, they had to be seen to be more
than the executioners' accomplices. One means of doing this was by viewing their
activities as having some divine significance, with the remains of the dissected
body providing a medium with which to understand the creative intent of God.
As anatomists peered into the interior of the body, they were peering into a sacred
temple. In the Early Modern period it was these overtones that legitimized anatomy,
a situation that remained unchanged until Descartes and Rembrandt, when the
body became no more than an abandoned ruin.

Of particular fascination was the genre of self-dissection, in which the body is
depicted as an accomplice to the dissection process. An example of this is found
in the work of Andreas Vesalius, where anatomy appears to animate the body and
endow it with a life of its own, enabling it, in effect, to assist in its own dissection.
This genre gave the impression that knowledge of the (dead) body was actually
knowledge of the living, thereby stressing the naturalness of dissection. The need
for this may have been the ambivalent and emotionally charged spectacle of
public dissection. Nevertheless, this failed to completely rehabilitate dissection.
The dissection of cadavers still existed on the edge of living society, and hence
dissected cadavers constituted an uneasy community of the dead. In depicting
cadavers in this manner, anatomists like Vesalius and their illustrators provided a
commentary on human destiny, just as much as on human anatomy. They appear
to be saying that the anatomist was not disrupting the body, as much as the body
was willingly allowing the anatomist to assist the general process of decay and
dissolution. This provided a context for dissection, which prior to the sixteenth
century, was far from self-justifying.

However much our contemporary cultures appear radically different from these
early European ones, it would be foolhardy to overlook this important message:
anatomy, and especially gross anatomy, is not a self-justifying regime. It is not
carried out in a cultural and philosophical vacuum, but neither is any procedure
that invades the human body, living or dead. This social, cultural and philosophical
dimension impinges on many of the projects of contemporary medicine, let alone
across the whole gamut of human anatomy. It also comes to the fore in contemporary

debates over what can be done to, and with, human embryos. Research on human embryos may be regarded as the face of this debate today. Subjecting human embryos to research procedures requires the assent of the communities in which they are being conducted. This work is no more self-justifying than is the use of human cadavers as a source of organs (see Chapter 5).

Anatomy, History and Society

As illustrated above, the history of human anatomy is closely linked to the history of dissection of the human body, simply because the development of anatomical concepts has been heavily dependent upon access to human bodies. Herein has lain a plethora of problems. The initial problems, which spanned many centuries, stemmed from difficulties in obtaining human material for dissection. Such difficulties arose from cultural perceptions, and will be discussed only briefly, since they belong to the domain of the historian and have been explored at length by others (Lassek 1958; Richardson 1988). What emerges from these discussions is that little serious human anatomical work is possible apart from study of the human body itself. Obvious as this may sound, it has many repercussions in areas far removed from dissection, such as organ transplantation and the grafting of fetal material into patients (see Chapter 5). Rarely is this crucial link made.

Human anatomy as a discipline concentrates on the human body in order to throw light on human structure. The concern in this book is with a complementary emphasis, one that starts from the discipline of anatomy in an attempt to throw light on numerous issues surrounding the living human body as well as the cadaver. The approach of the human anatomist can provide a framework for understanding the human body, including its significance for current ethical and social debate. Just as the history of human anatomy posed innumerable questions for the societies in which those developments took place, so contemporary human anatomy in its broadest context provides an important forum for the consideration of ethical and social questions emanating from the uses society makes of human bodies, including organs and tissues.

Greek and Roman Influences

Aristotle is sometimes considered to be the first anatomist in the modern sense of the term, possessing a keen observational skill which aided his precise description of body parts and the formulation of an objective nomenclature for the positions and relationship of each part (Crivellato and Ribatti 2007). However, he never dissected an adult human cadaver, confining himself to examining human fetal material and various animals. As a result, while he made a significant contribution to comparative anatomy and proved a huge influence on Galen and the Renaissance anatomists, many of his physiological concepts turned out to be wrong.

Herophilus (350–280 BC) is the first person recorded as having opened the human body after death, his aim being to understand more about the body's structure and about disease processes (Lassek 1958). It is claimed that Herophilus dissected between 200 and 600 human bodies, his major contributions lying in the description of various aspects of brain anatomy, including the meninges and cerebellum, and also the misleading *rete mirabile*, which will be discussed below. He also developed a complex theory of the pulse related to musical theory (Lloyd 1973). The dissections were predominantly of the bodies of condemned criminals, and although both Celsus (42 BC–37 AD) and Tertullian (155–222 AD) later accused him of dissecting living humans, the evidence for this is inconclusive (Singer 1957).

Erasistratus (310–250 BC) also dissected human bodies, his major interests being the sensory and motor nerves associated with the brain and spinal cord, and on the heart and circulation. He correctly identified the heart as a pump and appreciated the role of the four main heart valves. However, he was mistaken in claiming that only the veins and right side of the heart carried blood whereas the left side and arteries carried air (*pneuma*). Lloyd describes his work as 'an extraordinary combination of careful observation and bold, sometimes wild, speculation' (Lloyd 1973, 84). Between them, Herophilus and Erasistratus assembled two complete human skeletons, which for many years served as an epitaph to the Alexandrian School, whose anatomical advances are testimony not only to the brilliance of these ambitious scientists but also to the broadminded patronage of the ruling Ptolemies. In spite of their extensive experience with human dissection, their worldview, with its dependence upon animal and vital spirits for an understanding of the functioning of the human body, was far removed from what is accepted today.

Following these pioneering investigations, dissection of the human body declined, finally coming to a halt by the middle of the second century AD. Some writers were skeptical about the value of studying a dead body to aid in healing the living, and while others held that dissection was valuable they contended that animals, particularly apes, were a sufficient guide (Lloyd 1973). Nevertheless, the intervening years witnessed the emergence of various anatomy texts, as well as the pivotal if enigmatic figure of Galen (130–200 AD). Like Herophilus, Galen was a practical investigator. He was responsible for carrying out public dissections of animals, and was also physician to the gladiators. Galen was prepared to criticize the views of his predecessors, and reinvestigate their claims for himself. Nevertheless, important as these attitudes were, he made few personal contributions to the knowledge of human anatomy. Contradictory as this seems, it stems from his lack of access to human bodies, the dissection of which was denied him within the Roman Empire. Consequently, his investigations were confined to the study of animals, a limitation that had unfortunate repercussions for the interpretation of some of his writings.

By the end of his life, Galen had restructured the whole body of medical knowledge, leaving knowledge and concepts that would pass unchallenged for the next 1,300 years. His enormous influence stemmed from his prolific writings, and from the wide range of scientific findings and medical ideas inherent within them. Galen's writings covered every branch of medicine, including anatomy, physiology, pathology and therapeutics (Hunter 1931), and these alone accounted for about 50 per cent of all surviving Greek writings in these areas.

Unfortunately, he appears to have attributed to the human subject structural peculiarities found only in certain non-human animals, of which the *rete mirabile* arrangement of blood vessels at the base of the brain was a classic example (the *rete mirabile* is found in pigs but not humans). The example of the *rete* is instructive, since it provides a good illustration of Galen's influence. Although the *rete* was first described by Herophilus, it was incorporated by Galen into his general theory of human bodily function, according to which 'vital spirits' were produced in the heart from where they were distributed to all parts of the body. On reaching the cranial cavity, the blood was thought to enter this network of fine blood vessels at the base of the brain, at which point the vital spirits were converted into 'animal spirits'. Thus, the *rete mirabile*, as the structure responsible for the generation of animal spirits, constituted one of the fundamental underpinnings of bodily (and brain) function formulated during classical antiquity. The others were the location of the soul in the brain, the existence of nerves associated with the brain, and the cell doctrine of brain function (Clarke and Dewhurst 1972).

Such developments were not entirely surprising, since Galen's philosophical system constrained him to develop an anatomical basis for the action of natural, vital and animal spirits. His anatomy was also dominated by an attempt to demonstrate that every organ was perfectly adapted to its function, a viewpoint based on his philosophy that all parts of the human body reveal perfectly the design of an all-wise creator (Lassek 1958).

Galen's knowledge of human anatomy was restricted to the skeleton and muscles, and to what he had seen in wounded gladiators. His knowledge of the large internal organs of the body was derived mainly from studies of a wide range of animals, including pigs, sheep, dogs, fish, birds and apes. Since it was generally assumed that animal and human bodies were fundamentally alike in their structure, no problem was foreseen in examining the bodies of animals in order to understand human anatomy. These were serious limitations, but in spite of them Galen was a formidable experimentalist and his use of living animals enabled him to tackle a diversity of questions. A notable feature of his work was his highly detailed descriptions of certain body regions, such as the hand with its intricate musculature. Nevertheless, errors are common within his writings, such as his failure to distinguish nerves from tendons, with additional confusion arising from his study of animals, leading to a lack of clarity regarding which anatomy he was describing.

Galen occupied an important place within the philosophical ethos of his time as well as for many centuries afterwards. His spirit doctrine complemented contemporary Christian thinking on the soul, while his philosophical position was further enhanced by the notion that 'form' determines 'function', and that the complexity and beauty of organic structure are due to a divine providence (Lassek 1958). These viewpoints ensured for him a central place in anatomical and philosophical thinking, aided and abetted by two additional factors: the assumption by others that he had actually dissected human bodies, and the universal dependence on authoritative texts (including Galen's). Unfortunately, the problems and pitfalls that inevitably ensued were many and had long-lasting and serious repercussions.

In the long term, therefore, his influence was to cast a pall over the development of anatomical concepts. The disappearance of human dissection for many centuries after his time ensured there was no way in which this influence, as misleading as some of it was, could be countered. Ultimately, Galen, the supreme experimenter, was to turn his successors away from observation of the natural world, because his particular philosophical system made people content with the solutions only he had put forward. Galen's views became immutable, being transformed into an orthodoxy that, in the eyes of the Medieval scientists, supplanted the need to carry out further investigations.

Medieval Developments

Many centuries were to elapse before further significant developments took place in understanding the human body. For these, it is necessary to move on to 1315 and to Italy, when Mondino di Luzzi (1276–1326) revived the practice of human dissection in Bologna (although there is evidence that a prior postmortem had been performed in 1286; see Park 1995). The pressures against this reawakening of human dissection in Italy were considerable, including popular prejudice, and superstitious respect for the dead. However, permission was given by the Church; for instance, Pope Clement VI (1291–1352) mandated autopsies of victims of bubonic plague (Rodning 1989). Germany, England and France presented a different picture, with little evidence of autopsies or dissection before the late fifteenth century. Despite this, there appear to have been no signs of a generalized taboo against dismembering the human corpse. Members of the aristocracy travelling abroad commonly requested that, should they die while away, their body be dismembered and their bones boiled in either water or wine. With the flesh and entrails buried locally, the bones would then be transported hygienically to their chosen resting place (Park 1995). The Christian cult of relics (often severed body parts) had also normalized the practice of dismemberment (Park 1995).

The dissections conducted in fourteenth century Italy were of executed criminals and were held in public; inevitably, they were hurried. Typically, the actual dissections were carried out by a barber, with Mondino reading out the instructions from a high professorial chair, and a demonstrator, using a rod, pointing out the various structures of interest. Of greater importance from the perspective of the present book is the reason behind these dissections, namely, to illustrate Galen's texts, and to serve as an integral part of medical education, since medical students sat and watched. No attempt was made to analyze the structures dissected, nor to advance anatomical understanding. A dissection of this type was carried out in about four sessions, probably one each day, covering in turn digestive, respiratory and circulatory systems, plus superficial muscles. Despite many limitations, Mondino was the first of the modern human anatomists, in that he was principally interested in bodily structure rather than disease. His book *Anatomy* became the standard text for medical schools for 200 years, and more importantly established dissection as an accepted part of the medical curriculum.

Recognition of the place of human dissection in medical curricula quickly spread, with the result that one or more dissections annually were made obligatory in a number of universities and colleges of surgeons (for example, at Bologna and Padua). However, these dissections had a limited influence, since most students could do no more than observe and those outside the main centres were excluded from even attending. Moreover, when viewed as an isolated phenomenon, the dissected cadaver added relatively little new anatomical information (Siraisi 1990). Such dissections were essentially visual aids to an appreciation of those anatomical (and physiological) ideas already found in the standard texts such as Mondino's *Anatomy*.

Consequently, in spite of the revolutionary nature of these developments, human anatomy as a science failed to advance to any significant degree. With Mondino's death, there was no successor to carry on his developments, and the spirit of enquiry lapsed. Even worse, translation of Galen's texts into Latin served to elevate these as *the* texts to be adhered to: progress towards understanding human anatomy had once again been stultified.

Still prevalent at this time was the widespread belief that dissection of the human body was an act of desecration. In a celebrated formal proclamation of 1299, *Detestande Feritatis*, Pope Boniface VIII declared that whoever cut up a body, or boiled it, would fall under the ban of the Church (Park 1995). Although this was not aimed at stopping dissection in medical schools (but against the practice of the Crusaders of cutting up their dead, boiling the separate parts, and transporting the skeletal remains back to Europe), it inevitably had a dampening effect on dissection until the fifteenth century (Rodning 1989).

Not surprisingly, any human dissection carried out after Mondino's time was carried out in secret and occurred spasmodically. In spite of this hostile atmosphere, it was becoming increasingly clear that few advances in human anatomy could be made without dissection, and gradually permission for dissection was given by various European universities and medical schools. Further advances were subsequently made by people such as Berengario da Carpi (c1470–1530) and Leonardo da Vinci (1452–1519). Berengario da Carpi's influence arose from his exploitation of the possibilities afforded by anatomical illustrations. Anatomical terminology at the time was sparse and it was much easier to describe structures diagrammatically than linguistically. Da Carpi's other contribution arose from his skill as an independent critical investigator, in particular his forthright criticism of the two established authorities, Galen and Mondino.

In spite of this contribution, a major revolution in human anatomical understanding had to await the advent of Andreas Vesalius (1514–1564), who finally cast off all vestiges of the Galenic tradition through his assiduous dissections of human bodies (many obtained from graveyards). He generally carried out these dissections himself, and although he initially attempted to accommodate what he observed to what Galen had written, he finally dropped the reading of Galen entirely. By moving away in this radical manner from reliance upon the interpretation of a text, he directed attention at the human body itself. His reliance upon accurate illustrations opened the way to new discoveries, overturned the understanding of human structure, and thereby succeeded in neutralizing the authority of Galen (Lassek 1958). This approach destroyed long-standing superstitions and ill-founded tenets, and ushered in what we would regard as foundational scientific research in anatomy and related disciplines.

One of the most striking aspects of Vesalius' work, as epitomized in his book *On the Fabric of the Human Body* (1543), was the trouble he took to consider the relationship between individual organs and the body as a whole and his concern to relate structure and function. His aim was to achieve integration, and it was this that lifted his work above that of his predecessors.

Of crucial significance for everything Vesalius did was his insistence on actual dissection and on first-hand practical experience of human dissection. In the preface to his major work, he wrote of:

> ... that detestable procedure by which some conduct the dissection of the human body and others present the account of its parts, the latter like jackdaws aloft in their high chair, with egregious arrogance croaking things they have never investigated but merely committed to memory from the books of others, or reading what has already been described. The former are so ignorant of language that they are unable to explain the dissections to the spectators and muddle what ought to be displayed according to the instructions of the physician who, since he has never applied his hand to the dissection of the body, haughtily governs the ship from a manual. Thus everything is wrongly taught in the schools, and days are wasted in ridiculous questions so that in such confusion less is presented to the spectators than a butcher in a stall could teach a physician. (quoted in O'Malley 1964, 50)

Before leaving these developments, a number of additional points should be made. The first of these is that, while the initial goal of anatomical study in Medieval times was a better understanding of traditional texts (Siraisi 1990), there appears to have been a degree of tolerance for deviations between textual descriptions and physical appearances. Consequently, Mondino's *Anatomy* repeats various erroneous descriptions found in authoritative texts. This may have arisen because dissection alone was unlikely to have been sufficiently influential to overturn dominant philosophical ideas or astrological theories. Siraisi (1990) backs up this assertion by reference to the concept of the seven-celled uterus.

During the twelfth century the ancient concept of a seven-celled uterus became common. This theory suggested that the human uterus had seven divisions, three warm divisions of the right engendering males, and three cold ones on the left engendering females, and a seventh division, in the middle, capable of producing hermaphrodites. At some time during the thirteenth century, the idea became falsely attributed to Galen and was subsequently accepted by Mondino and numerous other medical and non-medical writers. The seven-celled uterus theory actually gained in popularity with the resurgence of human dissection, even though some surgeons and human anatomists acknowledged the existence of differences between the authoritative textual accounts of the uterus and the appearances actually found in cadavers. With time, questioning of the texts was supported by increasing emphasis on anatomical writings based on actual dissections, by increasing numbers of medical personnel performing dissections, by increasingly detailed attention to the full range of Galen's works in Greek, and by the advent of printing (Siraisi 1990).

Another point to note concerns the extent to which leading Italian Renaissance artists advanced the cause of dissection-based anatomy. This was probably limited in scope, even for those artists who themselves dissected, including someone of the calibre of Leonardo da Vinci. Nevertheless, he and others probably did help create a climate of attentiveness to detail, particularly concerning surface and skeletal anatomy (Siraisi 1990). Leonardo's early anatomical studies (carried out between 1487 and 1493) were strongly influenced by traditional views. For instance, he depicted the ventricles of the brain as interconnected spheres, that is, he drew what he thought he *should* be seeing, rather than what he *actually* saw. Later in life when Leonardo returned to his anatomical investigations, he laid great stress on dissections themselves (both human and ox). Dissecting at least 30 human bodies, he devised ingenious solutions for particular anatomical problems, including demonstrating the ventricles of the brain by the injection of melted wax. Although the resulting wax cast was slightly distorted, it had a far more realistic shape than his earlier depiction. This signifies that Leonardo, along with other leading artists and anatomists at the time, was coming to depend far more on what he could observe and describe, and far less on what he thought structures should represent. Observation was gradually overtaking the stultifying tradition embedded in Galen.

An interesting aside to this commentary is the situation that prevailed in late eighteenth century Japan. Like Vesalius' *On the Fabric of the Human Body* (1543), the publication in 1774 by Sugita Gempaku (1733–1817) of *Kaitai Shinsho*, a translation of a Dutch medical text, introduced the notion of anatomical dissection as the primary, essential way of understanding the nature of the human body (Kuriyama 1992). Although dissection had been performed before this time (references to dissection appear in China as early as the Han dynasty – 206 BC–221 AD), traditional medical beliefs caused physicians to see what they thought they *ought* to see, rather than what was actually apparent. Of preceding generations of Chinese physicians, Gempaku wrote: 'even though they looked at the difference between accepted beliefs and the actual structure of the organs and skeleton, they wavered haplessly in suspicions and doubts' (Kuriyama 1992). The attitude towards anatomical dissection in traditional Japan, as well as the manner in which it was conducted (actual dissections were performed by non-physicians with an audience of doctors looking on), are both highly reminiscent of pre-Vesalian Europe.

A final point of note is that the Church did not attempt to prevent human dissection, at least from the fifteenth century onwards. In fact, a postmortem was performed on the body of Pope Alexander V in 1410 (Shultz 1992). Both Pope Sixtus IV (1414–1484) and Pope Clement VII (1478–1534) sanctioned dissection for educational purposes. As a consequence of these attitudes, Rome later became one of the main centres for the study of human anatomy.

One crucial practical issue threads its way through any account of the early conflicts in attitudes towards the human body and its dissection, namely, the immense difficulties encountered in obtaining adequate supplies of human bodies. While the use of condemned criminals was sanctioned early on, this provided no more than a limited supply, and recourse was made to robbing graveyards. It is with this development that we encounter the first of many ethical conflicts connected with the medical and scientific treatment of the human body, and which we will take up in Chapter 2.

The World of the Dead Body

Even in the modern world, the process of dissection requires justification. Those societies that allow dissection still protect the dead human body from the forays of clinical teachers, adventurers and entertainers. Although examples of some of these will be thoroughly assessed later (see Chapters 3 and 4), it is useful at this juncture to illustrate the range of possibilities. These represent the outer limits of anatomy, even though most of them would be shunned by the vast majority of anatomists. Before tackling these, however, consider the following relatively innocuous incident, which sets useful boundaries for further discussion of treatment of the dead body.

> A newborn baby's body was sent more than 200 kilometres in a cardboard box from one hospital to another for a special postmortem examination. A stores worker discovered the body in the parcel delivered by a courier when the bottom of the small box broke open. The baby should have been transported either by ambulance or by funeral director. All involved, from health chiefs to the baby's parents were shocked at the blunder. Although the body was still inside a plastic box, the incident was generally described as disgraceful.

In this case, nothing amiss was done to the body, nor was its transportation a distance of 200 kilometres the issue. It was simply that the container was inadequate, thereby jeopardizing the dignity of the dead body, and the sensitivies of the family and the worker who discovered it. This provides a signal to all who would transgress the limits presumed to govern society's approach to the cadaver that powerful regulatory forces are at work. An understanding of these is urgently required if the body's potential in therapy and research is to be utilized to the full.

Many societies allow dead bodies to be used in anatomy departments and medical schools for purposes of teaching and research. However unusual it is by normally accepted social standards, this use of cadavers is deemed to fit within the constraints of moral and civil behaviour. In general, the public is allowed to view such human material only under severely circumscribed conditions, to ensure that it is not treated merely as a means of gratuitous satisfaction. Despite this, there are exceptions. Consider the following illustration.

> Cadavers have been exhibited in macabre public peep shows at a Department of Forensic Medicine for many years. A member of the laboratory staff was arranging regular after-hours shows, including slides and films of suicides and cadavers. In the mortuary visitors were allowed to see and touch the dead bodies. During these visits, no attempt was made to educate visitors in the basics of human structure and function, nor were visitors helped to understand clinical diseases. The money from the entry fee was pocketed by the staff member.

In this instance, bodies being kept for legitimate clinical reasons were exposed to the public gaze for commercial gain, without any foundation in serious science or clinical research. In the absence of either informed consent or any educational rationale, the individuals whose bodies were being displayed in this manner were being exploited. Although this incident is a contemporary one, its overtones of taboo and mystery have much in common with sixteenth and seventeenth century Europe. Dispensing with an objective approach to the cadaver entails a return to a radically different worldview, which, from today's perspective, results in a degrading view of the dead body. The similarities between this illustration and the popular human body plastination exhibitions of recent times are troubling (see Chapter 4).

What about the sale of body parts? Consider the following:

> An American non-profit organization selling human body parts for research can provide almost anything, including brains, hearts, knees and spines, diseased or healthy. Slivers of tissue can be supplied from at least 75 body parts, including appendices, testicles and toenails, with a choice of donor ages, diseases and ethnic backgrounds. Bodies are provided by hospitals, mostly from brain dead donors who have previously given consent for their bodies to be used for medical research. In other cases, bodies donated to anatomy departments for dissection have been dissected, but with body parts being sold to other organisations for therapeutic and research purposes.

The uses to which these body parts are put are, ostensibly, good ones, namely research and therapy. But the transactions are purely commercial and the bodies are being treated as property. Issues of exploitation must be faced, although these do not automatically invalidate the sales. What they do is shift the boundaries of the discussion, raising questions about the nature of the consent required for these procedures to take place, and the nature of the altruism undergirding the procedures. For instance, what are the criteria for determining whether an organization set up to distribute body parts is acting in an altruistic manner? Is the notion of altruism metamorphosed when employed in this way? Does the sale of body parts transform society's view of the dead body, making it into a commodity to be bartered and traded as if we, the living, own the remains of those no longer alive? Any movement in this direction takes society a step closer to objectifying the cadaver, removing it from being *somebody's* body to being a body: *nobody's* body.

The Estranged World of Autopsies

Implicit within the modern approach to cadavers is society's willingness to allow them to be dissected after death, in order to determine more accurately than possible during life the cause or causes of death (see Chapter 2). The autopsy or postmortem has a close association with the dissection carried out in dissecting rooms. But are there limits even to this activity? Consider the following:

> The pathologists who took her dead son's brain during a coronial autopsy left Wendy Stride with an awful legacy. Although the brain's removal was beyond her control, it meant she could not honour the last wishes of her 19-year-old son, Timothy. A month before his death in a road accident, Wendy and her son had a discussion about donating one's organs for transplantation. At that time, Timothy clearly expressed his feelings that he wanted to leave this world intact, and by cremation.
>
> At the time of his cremation, the family believed Timothy's body was indeed intact, but two years later they learnt to their horror that his brain had been removed following the accident. Mrs Stride says the family was outraged about not being told of the removal of the brain, since this denied them the chance to honour Timothy's last wishes. For the family, this is a hurt that will remain with them for the rest of their lives. Mrs Stride said: 'It was my son's heart and brain that made him what he was and I am sure most parents would feel the same'.

At first glance, the reaction of the mother may appear extreme, since the majority of her son's body was intact. It is true that his particular preference had been overlooked, but the nature of his beliefs are not known. Should society be concerned about the removal of an organ or two, when the body is to be cremated anyway a few days later? In this illustration, the perspective of the pathologists is ignored, but there is every likelihood that the brain would have been valuable in diagnosing the cause of death, in training pathologists, and possibly in research.

Nevertheless, Mrs Stride's response cannot be readily dismissed, since it tells us that both she and her son felt there was something special about the body –

certainly the dead body, and one assumes about the living body as well. They obviously did not believe that one should dispose of human bodies in the same way that we dispose of the bodies of rats or mice. The disrespectful treatment perceived by Mrs Stride made her extremely angry and upset. This points to the depth of our moral intuitions, and to the value we generally place on other human beings like ourselves. This suggests that pathologists are not free to keep whatever organs they wish, without specifying their reasons and without gaining the agreement from relatives on the length of time they are kept. Strictures of this nature stem from an overriding concern to maintain the dignity of the cadaver, and ensure that relatives are included within the sphere of decision-making. Once ethical considerations are brought into play, tension may be created between these and both therapy and research, so that opportunities for the latter become constrained. This is inevitable once ethical decision-making is incorporated into scientific and clinical decision-making.

Additional issues arise when the cultural mores of indigenous peoples are ignored. The following incident from New Zealand illustrates this.

> Māori elders complained about the treatment of human remains after the body of a man was returned to his family minus his brain. This is because in Māoridom it is very hurtful and emotionally stressful for pathologists to hold on to someone else's brain. In one case, a funeral was delayed for two weeks until the deceased's brain was returned to the family. This highlights the differing perspectives of coroners with their emphasis on the importance of forensic investigation, and overriding cultural perceptions that all parts of the intact body should be buried.

This incident brings into conflict, not simply ethical and scientific considerations, but the expectations and customs of diverse cultural groups. Dissection and autopsy are based on the underlying presumption that, under certain circumstances and with certain strictures, the body can, and should, be reduced to its component parts. Alongside this goes another frequent presumption, that the body does not have to be buried complete. In many societies, incompleteness is not regarded as threatening the dignity of the person who has died and is now to be buried or cremated. However, this is far from universally the case, and cultural sensitivity requires that where the two attitudes co-exist within a society, both are treated with deference. This will have consequences for what can and cannot be done to dead bodies, it will influence postmortem procedures, and it may even result in considerable rethinking of their role in such societies. The interrelationship between science and ethics is a very close one, but so are the competing demands of contrasting cultures (see Chapter 6). Autopsies belong to one culture and their role in scientific medicine is legitimized by this particular culture; for another culture no such legitimization may occur.

Disputed Cadavers

The domain of disputed cadavers takes us much further away from conventional practice, into realms where ethical concerns are clearly highly contentious areas, where people have been unjustly treated when alive, and decisions are required about what to do with their bodies. Two examples of this nature will be highlighted. In the first, ethical decisions are required to deal with the aftermath of the Nazi regime.

In the late 1980s it came to light that tissue samples and skeletons from the cadavers of victims of Nazi-era executions were being used for teaching purposes at German medical schools. The Israeli religion minister demanded that all body parts from Nazi victims be returned to Israel for proper burial. This, in turn, led to a demand within Germany that the universities stop using any such remains. It had been known for many years that, during the Nazi era, cadavers for medical education were procured by universities from nearby execution sites, but the origins of the slides and skeletons being used in anatomy classes had never been questioned.

The practice of using the cadavers of executed criminals began before the Nazis gained power, but the number of executions rose dramatically after 1933. Accompanying this rise was an expansion of the crimes which warranted execution, to include not only serious crimes such as murder but also political opposition (Hildebrandt 2008). The Anatomy Institute at Tübingen alone received 1,077 bodies from the execution site in Stuttgart between 1933 and 1945. The Anatomy Department at Humboldt University received most of the bodies executed at Plötzensee from 1939 to 1945, numbering nearly 3,000 people, mostly political prisoners (Hildebrandt 2008).

Officials at Tübingen found four slides that had been prepared from two cadavers of Nazi victims who had been executed for political reasons. One was a woman of Polish extraction, the other a man presumed to be German. In Heidelberg, three slides (out of a collection of 1,500) were found dating back to the early 1940s. The names of the people from whose cadavers they were taken were not listed on the slides, but the indication 'decapitatus' suggests that the people may have been victims of Nazi persecution. A skull was also found that had been preserved by the 'preparator' of skeletons employed in the anatomy department from 1937 to 1946. All four items were removed from the Institute's collection and were buried.

In a follow-up incident in 1990, unknown persons desecrated the graves where body parts and tissue samples taken from the corpses of Nazi victims had been buried. The samples had been part of a collection in the Anatomy Institute of the University of Tübingen. A number of years previously, the University removed from their collection the remains of anyone who was known or even suspected to have been killed by the Nazi regime and a commemorative ceremony in honour of these (approximately 400) people had been held.

These incidents direct attention in a more poignant way than previously encountered to the close relationship between the living and the dead. Not only was no consent provided for the uses to which the dead body was to be put, but the living body had been treated in unscrupulous ways. If the living body had been treated in these ways, what are the repercussions for any uses to which the dead body is put? The concerns raised here appear to suggest that the body of a dead person who was treated unethically during life, should not be further exploited by being used for teaching or research. Once the unethical treatment is recognized, the most ethical way forward for that person's remains is to treat them in a highly respectful manner, namely by burial or cremation. Whether or not this is inevitably the case will be discussed in subsequent chapters. The thrust of these incidents for now is the thread linking what happens during life with what happens after death. This has repercussions for those wishing to study body parts, even when the contemporary scientists or teachers have had no connection whatsoever with those responsible for the original unethical treatment. This link between the present and the past is also brought out by the following.

A number of British universities and museums have returned their collections of Aboriginal bones to Australia. This follows concerted efforts by Aboriginal civil rights campaigners to have the bones returned to their ancestral homes. The universities decided to return human remains from their collections on request, provided that the remains were deemed to have cultural or religious significance to the group concerned. These collections were largely amassed during the late nineteenth century, when interest in evolutionary lineages and in concepts like phrenology were at their height. There is evidence that some bones and skulls came into collections as a consequence of massacres of Aboriginal populations. The return of remains has disappointed some physical anthropologists, who use these collections to study the interrelationships between Aboriginal tribes. They regard this as a move that will endanger the very existence of their discipline.

This illustration raises similar issues to those above, even if the historical criminal elements are not as prominent. In this scenario, injustice was frequently present, and differing cultural perspectives on the significance of ancestral remains, the legitimacy of the scientific investigation of such remains, and even the worth of science itself all play a part. This constitutes a powerful mix, demonstrating that the study of human remains is not a simple objective scientific procedure. While the parameters of this debate are far removed from those of the sixteenth and seventeenth centuries, what does emerge is that anatomy (or biological anthropology in this last illustration) is only acceptable when it fits within the expectations of a particular culture. To dissect human bodies or study human bones is an intrusion into the intimacy and privacy normally reserved for the dead, and where societies tolerate these activities, they do so only within given parameters. These vary between societies, and a society's acceptance of a given activity should not be taken for granted.

Changing Perspectives with Time and Culture

Central to a number of discussions in this book will be the changing ethical standards and expectations over time. These, in turn, may be closely linked with changing social outlooks and cultural aspirations. What was once unacceptable can become acceptable, and *vice versa*. This raises problems for ethicists and scientists alike, when the object of study (or data emanating from it) stems from a period characterized by different expectations. As hinted at in the last illustration, human material (and data) obtained in ways once considered acceptable poses problems for contemporary societies where ethical constraints render that same human material (and data) unobtainable today. Even within today's societies, populations differ on what is ethically acceptable, a pluralism that is remarkably similar to the variety of expectations encountered between successive generations.

The approach adopted depends on whether it is that of scientists, ethicists or policy makers (anyone outside the immediate field of study and therefore unaffected professionally by the decisions made). There is little doubt that personal involvement can affect one's appreciation of the issues at stake. Scientists find it difficult to close their eyes to data obtained unethically when those same data could prove of immediate relevance to their own work. It is much easier for those not affected by such a dilemma to condemn use of certain data on the ground that it involves a lowering of ethical standards.

It may be helpful to stand aside from ethics for a moment and take account of a parallel situation in science: changes that take place in technical standards and expectations. This is a well-known phenomenon, for instance, as one technique and its capabilities are replaced by another technique opening up radically different possibilities. These changes may be accompanied by dramatic shifts in concepts and outlook. Within science such changes may be accepted without demur – even when a favourite idea is overturned. Changes in direction stemming from technical advances are the essence of science.

To illustrate, consider the procedures used to count the number of nerve cells, which have undergone a profound revolution over the past 20 years (Gundersen 1986). 'Biased' ways of counting nerve cells have been replaced by 'unbiased' means. The significance of this is that estimates of nerve cell numbers in nervous tissue (using 'biased' methods) in many early studies may be wrong and supposed trends thought to be associated with the effects of, say, malnutrition or alcohol on the brain may be misleading. What can be done in this circumstance?

The easy part of an answer is to ensure that no current studies are carried out using 'biased' procedures, or that if they are, the results are not accepted for publication in reputable journals. However, it would be unhelpful to argue that all previous studies should be retrospectively banned by preventing them being quoted in current publications. Such a policy would not wipe them from the communal memory, forming as they do the basis of much current thinking. Furthermore, they are not universally wrong. Some trends based on biased methods may still have validity, but where this is not the case that part of the work will have to be repeated using 'unbiased' techniques.

Scientific and ethical standards today will often be different from those in the past and care is needed in deciding what use is made of the earlier, less satisfactory work. There are no short cuts either scientifically or ethically, but neither is it possible to completely isolate contemporary thinking and approaches from the previous studies and attitudes on which they are based.

The Ethical Significance of the Dead Body

Before returning to historical developments in the next chapter, a preliminary exploration of why the human body might have ethical significance is essential. If it has no such significance, why be concerned about dissection?

> Imagine a society with a view of the human body totally different from any we now have. This hypothetical society views dead human bodies as insignificant. Cadavers have neither monetary nor sentimental value, and are regarded simply as garbage. When someone dies, instead of going to the expense and trouble of arranging a funeral with funeral directors, the members of this society do what they like with the bodies, since it is a matter of individual choice and taste. Death certificates are not issued as the cause of death is of no consequence to society at large.

> Understandably, there are certain restrictions, since bodies deteriorate, which is socially embarrassing and distinctly unpleasant. The poorer members of society sometimes simply throw the cadaver away, placing it in a cardboard 'body box' available from supermarkets, and putting it out with the garbage to be picked up with the next collection. Alternatively, those with gardens might burn the body. This is a bit more difficult, and there are certain restrictions, all of which cost money. But this is a far cheaper option than engaging the services of funeral directors.

> The richer members of the society often decide to get their loved-one preserved, just as anatomy departments and funeral directors preserve bodies. Once this has been done the preserved corpse is sometimes placed in the clothes the person liked to wear, and put in a position of honour in the lounge room. Others choose to have a large case erected with doors, which can be opened whenever required; yet others have the flesh removed and only keep the skeleton.

> The research-minded often donate the body to some worthy cause, such as a research group experimenting on the effects of car crashes on the occupants, since it is far more realistic to use real human bodies than artificial models.

For some in the society this is regarded as preferable to disposing of them
immediately.

What does a society such as this tell us about attitudes towards the dead body?
Does it matter how the dead body is treated? Is it right to act in certain ways, and
wrong to act in contrary ways? Does it matter if one person arranges for a funeral
director to bury her mother, while the other throws his mother's body on the local
tip? Is it simply a matter of personal preference?

We could only act as described in the above scenario if we placed no value on
the human body. We could only dispose of it as we do of rats or mice, if human
beings were considered to be disposable. But do we actually think like this? When
our favourite pet dies we do not throw it away without a second thought. We
may not treat it exactly like the remains of our grandmother, but if it has meant
something to us, we are aware of our loss. We treat the remains of the pet in a way
we consider appropriate to our priorities and values during its life. Most people
have deep moral intuitions that prompt them to bestow value on other human
beings like themselves (whatever the precise nature and level of this value). This is
why most people are horrified by pictures of corpses being dumped in mass graves
after a holocaust. It touches something very deep in their sense of what is right
and wrong; they recognize this as a form of indignity, and would be even more
distressed if one of the bodies was that of someone known to them.

In attempting to unravel this moral intuition, an initial component is the close
identification of people and their bodies. Our recognition of each other depends
upon a recognition of an array of physical characteristics which are distinctive
features during life and are not extinguished immediately on death. Hence, what is
done to a dead body has relevance for our feelings about that person when alive:
the cadaver and the person cannot be totally separated.

A second component concerns other people's responses to the cadaver. Those
who knew the person when alive have memories of that person: what he or she was
like, his or her personality, attitudes, beliefs and hobbies. In a sense, the cadaver
represents an array of built-in memories that can never be completely separated
from it. For most people these memories lead to a sense of respect for a cadaver
and its enshrined associations.

A third related component emphasizes the deceased person's relationships: he
or she was someone's relative or friend, and that person is now grieving the death.
Respect for the cadaver is respect for the relatives' grief. Although the depth of
grief will decrease as time passes, the reality of the cadaver may play a substantial
role during the grieving process.

Taken together, these components of moral intuition suggest that there are
certain ways in which cadavers are and are not to be treated, even if unfettered value
is not bestowed upon them. However, even with rough guidelines, unanswered
questions remain about precisely what can or cannot be done to cadavers in the
dissecting rooms of anatomy departments.

By themselves, recognition of the intrinsic and instrumental value of cadavers does not provide a rationale for why bodies can be dismembered during dissection in ways society does not ordinarily allow. In similar vein, they fail to provide definitive reasons why we do not allow economics students to dissect bodies, nor why it is appropriate for health science students to dissect bodies in a university laboratory but inappropriate in their homes. The framework is provided by what any society will and will not tolerate. Many contemporary societies allow dissection under stringent and well-defined conditions, but what is allowed varies from one society to another, and as we have seen attitudes have changed momentously in Western societies down through the centuries. Moreover, changes in attitudes reveal nothing about the correctness or otherwise of the attitudes themselves.

In searching for a basis to societies' attitudes and also to changes in these attitudes, an important ethical consideration stems from the manner in which bodies for dissection are obtained. For instance, we need to ask whether it matters if we use unclaimed as opposed to bequeathed bodies. This issue will be explored further in Chapter 2. The rationale behind this distinction is that bequeathed bodies have been donated for the purpose of dissection, by those who have made an appropriate free and informed decision prior to their death. They wanted this for their bodies after death. By freely willing their cadavers to be used for educational purposes, they have acted altruistically by, quite literally, giving themselves. When the bodies are unclaimed, they are unwanted, signifying the lack of meaningful relationships between the deceased and those around them. No decision was made to bequeath their bodies at death; they were taken and used by others. We shall argue that the differences between these two situations are ethically significant.

Nevertheless, it has to be conceded that it is relatively easy to argue in this way in many contemporary Western societies, and ignore the tortuous path that has made this conclusion possible. In order to traverse this ground, it is necessary to go back two to three centuries and follow the conflicts and dilemmas so closely associated with obtaining bodies for dissection in Britain, the United States, Australia and New Zealand.

Chapter 2
The Dissected Body

Obtaining Bodies for Dissection

Historical Developments in Britain

The major morbid elements in the history of human anatomical study in Britain are well known, revolving as these did around body snatching and murder. However, unless placed within a broader context, they remain little more than gory episodes illustrating an unsavoury past. If left as such, they fail to provide any input into serious contemporary ethical debate. In order to do this, it is imperative to break down the barriers so often set up around these events.

Considerable help in this regard has been provided by Ruth Richardson who, in her 1988 book, *Death, Dissection and the Destitute*, set forth with great clarity and poignancy the thesis that the Second Anatomy Act of 1832 made poverty the sole criterion for dissection in Britain (Richardson 1988). In order to understand this thesis, however, some appreciation of the various sources of cadavers in Britain prior to 1832 is required, and it is here that we encounter the use of murderers' bodies, grave robbing (body snatching), and murder. It is relevant, therefore, to enquire further into the circumstances surrounding these uses of human bodies, and to follow the developments that ensued over a period of 150 years or so.

From the sixteenth century onward dissections in Britain were of criminals executed for murder. Dissection was regarded as a punishment, since it was something *over and above* execution itself. In 1752 an Act of Parliament gave judges discretion in issuing death sentences for murder, allowing the substitution of dissection instead of gibbeting in chains (the gibbet was a structure resembling a gallows, from which the bodies of executed criminals were publicly hung as a warning to others). Dissection acquired the reputation of being at least as bad as gibbeting, since both had the same intention – to deny the wrongdoer a decent burial.

Regardless of these considerations, this means of acquiring bodies could not match the ever-increasing demand, and another means of supply, namely grave robbing, emerged. With the passage of time this became by far the most prolific, if not the most notorious, means of obtaining bodies. The earliest grave robbers were surgeon-anatomists and their pupils, and by the 1720s the stealing of bodies from London graveyards had become commonplace. Later, professional body snatchers (resurrectionists) emerged, often working in gangs. In order to facilitate the body trade, there was usually a close liaison between the surgeon-anatomists (or medical schools) and the resurrectionists, who provided several thousand bodies annually.

Astley Cooper, the popular royal surgeon of the early nineteenth century, began robbing graves himself until he could pay others for the service. He was known to have a particularly close and generous relationship with the resurrectionists he employed, paying for legal representation if they were charged and supporting them and their families if jailed (Burch 2007). In this way, the overall needs of the medical schools for bodies were amply met (Richardson 1988). The majority of the bodies stolen from graveyards, known as *resurrected corpses*, were predominantly (if not entirely) those of the poor. This was undoubtedly a result of pragmatism, since the poor were ill equipped to protect the bodies of their deceased from the ravages of the resurrectionists. On the other hand, the well off buried their loved ones in church vaults or used multiple coffins or other protective devices. And so it transpired that amongst its many transgressions, grave robbing was grossly inequitable.

The Scottish surgeon John Hunter (1728–1793), sometimes called the father of modern surgery, began his career obtaining and dissecting bodies for his brother's medical school, from which the demand for fresh bodies helped transform grave robbing into a 'carefully orchestrated, highly managed and increasingly lucrative industry' (Moore 2005, 56). Despite his unusually close association with the resurrectionists, Hunter never faced legal action. He claimed to have dissected thousands of bodies over the years (Cornelius 1978), an unprecedented number. It was his ensuing unrivalled knowledge of human anatomy combined with his unconventionally modern scientific methods that made him an enterprising and expert surgeon of public renown (Moore 2005). Of his original collection of 14,000 human and animal preparations only 3,500 specimens remain, including the illicitly obtained skeleton of Charles Byrne, the Irish giant. These are stored in the recently redeveloped Hunterian Museum at the Royal College of Surgeons of England in London.

It is hardly surprising that, by the beginning of the nineteenth century, grave robbing was frowned upon by many within society, who expressed disquiet about the moral and social acceptability of both this practice and the subsequent mutilation of the dead. In response, the legitimacy of dissection was defended by the medical establishment, on the basis of its ultimate medical benefits – the training of doctors and advances in human anatomical knowledge. However, the medical profession's defence did not address the legitimacy (or otherwise) of the means by which bodies were obtained. Astley Cooper testified to an 1828 Select Committee that 'there is no person, let his situation in life be what it may, whom, if I were disposed to dissect, I could not obtain. The law only enhances the price, and does not prevent the exhumation' (Burch 2007, 235–6). Failure to attend to these legal issues evoked concern in some quarters, an excellent example of which was provided by a forthright editorial in the medical journal the *Lancet*: 'It is disgusting to talk of anatomy as a science, whilst it is cultivated by means of practices which would disgrace a nation of cannibals' (*Lancet* 1832).

The seriousness of the situation was aggravated by activities taking place inside dissecting rooms, treating cadavers violently and even disrespectfully by committing acts of sexual indecency on them. Not surprisingly, during the late eighteenth and early nineteenth centuries, it became widely accepted that anatomists allowed human remains to be treated as offal (Richardson 1988).

By 1829, there was a pressing public desire to stop the resurrectionists, and this led to the first Anatomy Bill that recommended the use of cadavers from hospitals and workhouses. Whenever patients had no relatives to bury them, or the relatives were too poor to do so, these cadavers were used for dissection. This recommendation had an inevitable consequence: the poor were classed alongside the worst of criminals as potential subjects for dissection. It was this socially divisive aspect of the Bill that led to its rejection by the House of Lords.

At much the same time, the situation was aggravated by another development, the commissioning of murders as a means of providing cadavers for dissection. The infamous Burke and Hare murders in Edinburgh, and similar ones by Bishop and Williams in London, proved of crucial significance for the history of anatomy in Britain.

It appears that the deaths in Edinburgh were actually committed at the request of the proprietor of an Edinburgh medical school, Dr Knox, prompting the nursery rhyme, 'Burke's the butcher, Hare's the Thief, Knox the man who buys the beef' (Burch 2007, 80). Yet Knox was never investigated in connection with the Burke and Hare murders. To this proprietor the receipt of murdered bodies was a 'mere misfortune', which would almost certainly have occurred to anybody else in his situation; he was the blameless object of misguided prejudice. But this was not how the public perceived the murders – in the public arena they only served to worsen the already dubious reputation of anatomy.

How, then, were bodies to be obtained? One possibility was their bequest, not an unexpected source of bodies, since there had been a steady stream of bequests between 1828 and 1831. With hindsight it is very surprising that this option was bypassed, but bypassed it was, in favour of the use of unclaimed bodies. The medical profession of the time considered this the most uncontroversial source of bodies, and so it was that the 1832 Act sanctioned this source of cadavers for dissection. By abolishing the use of dissection as a punishment for murder, the inevitable, if unintended, consequence was that poverty became the sole criterion for dissection (Richardson 1988).

The major contrast between the 1832 Act and the unsuccessful Bill of 1829 was removal of any reference to hospitals and workhouses. The social status of the proposed subjects of dissection had been deleted, although the intentions of the Act remained exactly as before. As a result, in the 100 years up to the early 1930s, 57,000 bodies were dissected in the London anatomy schools. Of these, 99.5 per cent came from institutions housing the poor, that is, workhouses and asylums.

Up to the 1940s few bodies used for dissection in Britain were bequeathed, and it was not until the 1960s that bequests exceeded 70 per cent of all cadavers dissected. Richardson (1988) has suggested that the reasons for this slow, but dramatic, change probably include changes in the social meaning of the cadaver as demonstrated by a parallel rise in the popularity of cremation, growing disbelief in the spiritual significance of the dead body, a growing awareness of the role and value of scientific medicine, and changing attitudes towards poverty.

The unethical nature of these historical practices is self-evident, ranging from murder to exploitation of the poor, and from complicity in murder and stealing to the lack of informed consent for the use of cadavers (Campbell et al. 2005). Historical atrocities like these can never be bypassed or ignored, since they *did* happen and many of the gains of the past were built on these unethical foundations.

Since the Anatomy Act of 1832, British legislation governing the dissection of cadavers has continued to emphasize the importance of consent given by the individual prior to death. This is evident in the subsequent Anatomy Act of 1984, and its replacement, the Human Tissue Act 2004, which applies in England, Wales and Northern Ireland, which requires written and witnessed consent by any donor of a body to be used for anatomical dissection or public display (British Medical Association 2006). Interestingly, Scotland is governed by its own legislation in this area, the Human Tissue Act 2006. This is notable particularly for its use of the term 'authorization' in place of consent. Although the terms are legally equivalent, the use of authorization is intended to strengthen the ethical significance of an individual's wishes for the treatment of his or her body after death (Department of Health 2005). The term 'authorization' replaces 'lack of objection' in Scotland's Human Tissue Act 1961, which the 2006 Act repeals. Given the history of cadaver use in Britain, and the rise in popular and academic interest in medical ethics, these legal responses are fitting.

Historical Developments in the United States

Essentially the same events and struggles took place in the eighteenth and early nineteenth centuries in the United States. The American situation was characterized, not only by body snatching, indictments, high emotion, riots and occasionally murder, but also by a hesitancy in developing adequate dissection laws (Lassek 1958). Anatomy laws varied from state to state. In the 1880s human dissection was still illegal in some states, and even into the 1910s there was no legal way to obtain a cadaver in some places (Warner and Rizzolo 2006). As in Britain, those most vulnerable to unethical practices such as grave robbing were the disadvantaged and the disenfranchised – the poor and, often, African Americans (Blakely and Harrington 1997; Halperin 2007).

In the United States, the first dissection of a human subject was performed in 1638 in Massachusetts. A very early legal code in Massachusetts was *The Body of Liberties*, and this mentioned no penalty for the disinterment of human cadavers. A Massachusetts resolution of 1647 allowed students studying medicine and surgery to have the liberty once every four years to 'anatomize' (dissect) the body of a criminal, providing it was made available by a decision of the court (Lassek 1958). However, this was not the case in some other states, for instance, in Georgia where dissection was illegal until 1887 (Blakely 1997).

As the number of medical schools increased during the late eighteenth and nineteenth centuries, all legal means of obtaining bodies proved inadequate, and body snatching came into its own. This dubious activity was largely carried out by anatomists and their students. For the physicians and medical students engaged in it, detection and arrest were distinct possibilities. For instance, when Dr Joseph McDowell, a respected anatomist, resurrected the body of a young girl who had died of an unusual disease, he only narrowly escaped being caught by her relatives and friends by pulling a sheet over himself and pretending to be a cadaver in the dissecting room (Shultz 1992).

Compared with Britain, professional resurrectionists played a minor role in the United States, and relatively few murders were committed for the purpose of selling bodies for anatomical study (sometimes referred to as *burkism*, after the Edinburgh Burke). Two notorious exceptions to this were the Cincinnati Burking of 1884 and the Baltimore Burking of 1886 (Shultz 1992).

The practice of body snatching, whether by medical practitioners and their students for educational purposes, or by professional resurrectionists for profit, elicited a great deal of public resentment, and at least 13 resurrection riots occurred between 1765 and 1852 (Lassek 1958). Legislation to prevent body snatching was attempted in a number of states. As early as 1796, the general assembly of New Hampshire imposed a $1,000 fine, imprisonment for not more than one year, and public whipping as the penalty for grave robbing. Other states followed, though relatively few people were brought to trial. However, no efforts were made to provide a more adequate legal supply of cadavers for dissection. The first and probably only national law concerned with human dissection was passed by the US Congress in 1797. This gave federal judges the right to add dissection to imposition of the death penalty for murder.

African Americans and the poor provided a disproportionately large number of bodies for dissections. Though disinterment remained illegal, grave robbings from pauper and African American cemeteries were usually ignored by the authorities unless an incensed white citizen complained (Halperin 2007). It was only when white bodies were discovered to have been stolen that riots began. Southern medical schools frequently used the bodies of African American slaves, whose social status as chattel persisted from life to death. Medical schools would even advertise to purchase African American slaves terminally ill with interesting diseases. The South Carolina Medical College touted one of the benefits of the school as being the ready availability of African American bodies for dissections 'without offending any individuals in the community' (Weld 1968 quoted in Halperin 2007). The English travel writer Harriet Martineau accurately assessed the situation, reporting, 'in Baltimore the bodies of coloured people exclusively are taken for dissection because the whites do not like it, and the coloured people cannot resist' (Martineau 1838 quoted in Halperin 2007).

In Massachusetts, duelling provided an additional legal source of bodies. This was not intended to 'legalize' human dissection, rather it was to make duelling as unattractive as possible (Shultz 1992). But neither the bodies of executed murderers nor those of duellists provided sufficient cadavers for dissection during the first three decades of the 1800s.

These factors led to the Massachusetts Anatomy Act of 1831, which permitted civil officials to surrender for anatomical purposes bodies that would otherwise have to be buried at public expense. However, problems remained, since it was not mandatory for civil officials to release bodies for dissection. Furthermore, it forbade the use of the bodies of any who during life had signified the burial of their remains, or individuals whose relatives or friends requested that the bodies be interred (Lassek 1958). Consequently, a shortage of anatomical material continued after passage of the Act. Other states passed Anatomy Acts in subsequent years, such as Pennsylvania in 1867, and Maryland in 1882, but these did not abolish grave robbing in its entirety as they failed to provide sufficient cadavers.

The ill repute of anatomists, medical schools and their students was legendary in many places in mid-nineteenth-century United States. Medical students were usually looked upon as a disreputable, vulgar and possibly depraved group (Shultz 1992). This is well illustrated by an 1845 resolution in an Ohio township, to the effect that:

> ... the depredation of morals consequent upon the disinterment of bodies, and the annihilation of the better feelings and sentiments that usually follow a long familiarity with the horrid dissecting-room, renders it no doubtful question, whether medical colleges are not productive of more mischief than benefit to the country. (quoted in Edwards 1952, 179)

Even this brief survey demonstrates that early American history had much in common with events in Britain. However, the American Anatomy Acts were less decisive on the use of unclaimed bodies than they had been in Britain. This, combined with the fact that American legislation failed to provide a legal means of obtaining an adequate supply of human cadavers, meant that throughout the first half of the twentieth century the majority of American medical schools still depended primarily on unclaimed bodies for anatomical study.

It was at this point that social welfare legislation, with accompanying death benefits, began to intrude. In the 1930s legislators responded to public calls for decent burials for the indigent by providing government-funded death benefits (Davidson 1995). Local welfare authorities, instead of relinquishing unclaimed bodies to medical schools, entered into profitable arrangements with undertakers or cemeteries. This both bestowed commercial value upon the dead body, and precipitated the need for bequest laws. These were brought together in the first Uniform Anatomical Gift Act of 1968, enshrining a right of donation, and with a moral basis of free choice and volunteerism. A second Uniform Anatomical Gift Act in 1987 followed and built on this foundation, clarifying the process of donation and making irrevocable the donor's intentions (Dalley et al. 1993). This move towards widespread use of, and subsequent dependence upon, bequeathed bodies has included a large element of pragmatism (Jones 1994).

Currently in the United States, it is legal for medical schools to receive unclaimed bodies for dissection. In general the bodies must be held for some time before beginning dissection, should a family come forth to claim the body. This delay varies between states from 10 days to 6 months. In some states a body may not be touched during this time, and the ensuing deterioration makes the body unsuitable for preservation and dissection. As a result, the number of unclaimed cadavers that medical schools receive is actually very small (Davidson 1995), though in some larger cities unclaimed bodies can constitute the major source of cadavers for dissection. By far the majority of schools (around 80 per cent) run donor programmes, although for a small number these do not prove sufficient (Davidson 1995). In this case, schools with surplus cadavers are often asked to bridge the shortfall. Similarly, in South Africa at one medical school, unclaimed bodies sourced from government mortuaries provide 77.8 per cent of all bodies used for dissection (Labuschagne and Mathey 2000).

Experience and Legislation in Australia and New Zealand

At this point, it is worth noting a lesser-known example, namely, New Zealand. Developments in New Zealand stem from the beginnings of the University of Otago Medical School (based in Dunedin) in 1875. The New Zealand experience owed almost everything to the British one. The unclaimed poor provided practically the entire supply of bodies from 1889–1902, and an average of 50 per cent from then until 1915. They remained a significant element until the Benevolent Institutions (poor houses) were dismantled. The potential interruption to supply was readily filled by the local mental hospitals, so much so that it was the outcast of society languishing in mental hospitals that provided most bodies in the first half of this century (Jones and Fennell 1991). The significant feature of these historical developments is that, until the 1950s, the bodies used were of those who had not provided any form of consent.

The first record of a bequest in New Zealand was in 1943, but these became more frequent only during the 1950s and eventually became the major means of supply in the early 1960s. Accompanying this trend was a dramatic decrease in the importance of mental hospitals as a supply source.

In Australia the establishment of medical schools and the necessary supply of cadavers developed in a similar vein. For much of the nineteenth and early twentieth centuries bodies were routinely obtained without consent from the poorest classes of society.

The first dissection class at the University of Melbourne was held in 1863, and from the very beginning the medical school was hampered by a shortage of cadavers to dissect (Jones, R. L. 2007). In 1862 a bill very similar to the English 1832 Anatomy Act was proposed, forbidding the dissection of executed criminals, but it failed to designate any legitimate source of cadavers, raising fears that body snatching would arise.

In popular thinking the dissection room was repulsive, it was thought of as 'a kind of cannibal sausage establishment, where human mince-meat is continually being produced' (Jones, R. L. 2007, 85). Public aversion to dissection was not entirely ill-founded, particularly considering that the students were not well supervised, leading to misdemeanours, such as 'meat fights', that today would be considered grossly inappropriate and offensive.

R. L. Jones (2007) suggests that there had been some trouble with grave robbing at the Melbourne colony. There had certainly been a dearth of bodies to supply early anatomy classes. A number of attempts were made to convince the Melbourne Benevolent Asylum to provide the university with bodies, but the inmates of the asylum organized a petition opposing this and the proposal was summarily rejected in 1869.

Enrolments at the medical school grew through the 1870s and 1880s and the shortage of cadavers for dissection grew more urgent (Jones, R. L. 2007). As students protested the lack of cadavers and many failed the course because of a lack of practical experience, the course itself was at risk, and better-equipped courses at UK universities beckoned. The problem was alleviated somewhat by the alcoholic preservation of corpses made available during the non-dissecting summer months, and the provision of corpses from county hospitals. Numerous and insistent approaches were made to charitable institutions throughout the state, with some success. The Immigrants Home, a benevolent institution for homeless itinerants, provided a good proportion of the corpses, as did the two Victorian Houses for the Aged and Destitute in the area. Additionally, the introduction of the preservative formaldehyde, and possibly also the use of Aboriginal corpses, upped the supply of cadavers, quieting the students' complaints.

New Zealand's legislation concerning dead human bodies commenced with the Anatomy Act of 1875, which itself followed the pattern of the British Acts of 1832 and 1871 (Jones and Fennell 1991). Besides setting up licensed schools of anatomy and providing for licensed anatomists, the 1875 Act stipulated that any party having lawful possession of the body of a deceased person could permit that cadaver to undergo anatomical examination (that is, dissection) unless it was known that the deceased had objected to this during his or her lifetime, or a surviving spouse did so. For the purposes of the Act, those authorized to have lawful possession of dead bodies were 'the surgeon of any hospital, the keeper of any lunatic asylum, and the keeper of any gaol ...'. Provision was also made for living persons to bequeath their bodies voluntarily, unless a surviving husband, wife or known relative objected. An important stipulation was that the body could not be removed from the place of death for 36 hours.

Dissection was to be carried out in such a way as to avoid unnecessary mutilation of the cadaver, and anatomical examinations were to be conducted in an 'orderly, quiet and decent manner'. The body, before and after anatomical examination, was to be transported in a decent coffin or shell, and after dissection was to be decently interred in consecrated ground or in an appropriate public burial ground within eight weeks of death.

It is interesting that this early piece of legislation recognized the place of bequeathing bodies, although this appears not to have been acted on. Another point of interest is that the use of unclaimed bodies in the 1875 Act is a restricted usage, since there is an 'opt out' clause: any objection registered during life by the deceased or after death by the surviving spouse was sufficient to prevent use of the body. Such an 'opt out' clause renders untenable the notion of an unclaimed body, as there was no way of being certain that an objection had not been lodged. In spite of this, it must be assumed that this clause was not implemented, or even widely known about.

This Act was amended in 1884 to extend the list of authorized people having lawful possession of a body, by including police officers and the keepers of asylums and public establishments housing destitute persons. The other amendment was to lengthen the period before interment from eight weeks to six months.

Further developments accompanied the Medical Act of 1908, the inclusion of another clause in 1946, and the Medical Amendment Act of 1954. As a result of these, additional people were stipulated as being entitled to the possession of a cadaver. Provisions were made for cremation of the remains, and also for the removal of healthy tissue for therapeutic purposes, and postmortem examinations for research and medical education.

Legislation in New Zealand revolves around the Human Tissue Act 2008, which recently replaced the Human Tissue Act 1964. The 1964 Act was far from comprehensive, and contained a number of points of interest. The first is that, while the voluntary donation of bodies was paramount, there remained the possibility that the medical superintendents of mental hospitals and superintendents of penal institutions could authorize the use of bodies for dissection unless the deceased person had previously expressed an objection to this or a surviving spouse or relative did so. A second point is that the deceased person's wishes regarding donating his or her body could be overridden by the objections of a surviving spouse or relative. Third, there was no reference to the length of time the remains may be kept prior to burial or cremation, and it is explicitly stated that 'any part of the body may be retained indefinitely for further study'. The emphasis on avoiding unnecessary mutilation of the body was still present, as was the emphasis on carrying out the examination in 'an orderly, quiet and decent manner'.

Even the 1964 Act, therefore, had elements of the macabre British history reflected within it. Although donations were paramount, there was still room for the involuntary use of the bodies of the criminal, hospitalized or insane if the body was unclaimed by relatives and the deceased had expressed no wish against this while alive. The emphasis on decency probably had its roots in the abuse of bodies in dissecting rooms in the early nineteenth century in British anatomy schools. The stipulation to wait 36 hours after death provides a glimpse into the undue haste with which unclaimed bodies were taken from hospitals and workhouses for immediate dissection 200 years ago.

The new Human Tissue Act 2008 makes informed consent the fundamental principle governing the legal collection and use of human tissue. This replaces the 'lack of objection' required by the Human Tissue Act 1964. The primary consent or objection comes from the deceased person before death or someone nominated by that person to consent on their behalf. In the absence of this, the immediate family or another close relative can consent. There are a number of situations where informed consent is not required, including tissue used for criminal justice purposes, quality assurance, external audits, or research approved by an ethics committee, for example, research relating to a major public health risk. In addition, consent to a postmortem explicitly includes consent to retain tissue where it is required for the purposes of the postmortem. Details of the reason for retention, and the length of time tissue will be retained, must be provided. If tissue is to be retained for any other reason (such as ongoing research or education), separate and specific consent will be required. The Act also requires that decision-makers and others involved in collecting tissue take into account the cultural and spiritual needs, values and beliefs of the individual and their immediate family.

In Australia, each state has separate legislation on the removal and use of human tissue, however, they are all broadly similar. In Victoria the Human Tissue Act 1982, and the more recently amended Human Tissue Regulations 2006, govern the use of human tissue. In New South Wales the relevant legislation is the Human Tissue Act 1983, which was amended in 2003 and 2006. Both states give precedence to informed consent as the fundamental principle underlying the removal and use of human tissue. Tissue can be removed for the purpose of therapy or research if the deceased person had, during their lifetime, given consent in writing to the removal of tissues from their body, and that consent had not been revoked. If this is not the case, tissue can also be removed if the deceased had not expressed an objection to the removal of tissue and the senior available next of kin consents. In addition, in Victoria, oral consent is also recognized if the deceased person gave consent during their last illness in the presence of two witnesses.

Small tissue samples which have been lawfully removed from living or deceased persons may be used without consent for the purposes of carrying out analyses or tests that are part of quality assurance programs, audits, or that are necessary for the delivery of services carried out at a hospital, laboratory or similar institution. The Australian Acts also make provision for registered schools of anatomy and tissue banks, and prohibit commercial trading in human tissue, whilst allowing the recovery of reasonable costs associated with the processing and storage of tissue.

Why People Bequeath Their Bodies for Dissection

In an attempt to gain information on the motives of donors, Fennell and Jones (1992) undertook a survey of some of those who had bequeathed their bodies to the Department of Anatomy and Structural Biology at the University of Otago. At the time of this study the information sent to all who enquired about bequeathing their bodies stressed that the role of cadavers was almost exclusively in teaching anatomy to medical and health science students. It also made clear that bodies bequeathed in this way were not used for organ transplantation. It explained that, despite the wishes of the deceased, the objection of any near relative at the time of death will preclude the Department accepting a body. Hence, donors were urged to discuss their intentions with close relatives before making the bequest.

By far the most common reason for making a bequest was found to be providing an aid to medical science and teaching. Two-thirds of all respondents submitted this reason, and both men and women placed it well ahead of the next most common reason, namely, gratitude to the medical profession. These reasons are dependent on the perceived status of medical science in the eyes of the general public, and on its perceived value for the welfare of the population. A desire to avoid funeral expenses featured occasionally (in about ten per cent of responses) and for some, a dislike of funerals and unnecessary ritual was a factor. Other reasons included family brain illness, the spouse already having made a bequest, abhorrence of cemeteries, and a distrust of funeral directors. A number of respondents commented that their physical peculiarities or illnesses might be of interest to students.

The option of organ donation had not been considered by many of the respondents. Generally they knew little about it, or thought they were too old for their organs to be of any value. In a few cases, opposition towards transplantation or scepticism regarding it was quite marked. In particular, respondents raised queries about whether 'brain dead' people are actually dead, and about psychological trauma associated with organ transplants.

A significant finding to come from the Otago study was the overwhelming misapprehension that cadavers are generally used for medical research purposes (Fennell and Jones 1992). Only four per cent were aware that their bodies would not be used for research – in spite of the fact that the information they received prior to completing the bequest explicitly stated that bodies received by bequest are not used in research. The respondents appeared either to make no distinction between research and teaching, or were unclear of the difference.

This raises the question of the public's perception of medical research. It may be that, for many in the general community, teaching students is classed as research. If this is the case, does this apparent confusion have any implications for informed consent? After undertaking a similar study, Richardson and Hurwitz (1995) did not perceive this confusion to be problematic, since in their view, it is sufficient that donors consistently articulate a 'manifold desire to contribute to medical progress'.

The question of unclaimed bodies played no part in the Fennell and Jones (1992) study. However, Hafferty, in his book *Into the Valley* (1991), studied medical students' reactions to death. He noted that the students, who were not informed of the source of the bodies (whether donated, purchased or unclaimed), strongly wished to believe that they were dissecting donated bodies. For them, it was much more comforting to imagine that the person, when alive, had given permission for his or her own dissection, rather than that it had been authorized by the medical establishment.

In contrast, the thought that cadavers had the status of unclaimed bodies was very disturbing for many students. As one student phrased it: 'Being an unclaimed cadaver is an indignity … the only reason most of these cadavers are here is because they were too poor to pay for a funeral or nobody cared for them enough to bury them' (Hafferty 1991, 84). In responding in this way, students were forced to confront the cadavers' status as formerly living humans.

Medical schools cannot afford to overlook the close interrelationship between their dependence upon bodies and body parts for teaching purposes and sympathetic or unsympathetic cultural attitudes that are crucial factors in their availability.

Is it Ethical to Use Unclaimed Bodies?

As we have seen, while the bequeathing of bodies is now very common in many countries, this was not the primary source of bodies in previous centuries: back then, and even now in some countries, many dissections are performed on unclaimed bodies. This discrepancy raises a number of questions. Is there any moral benefit from using bequeathed rather than unclaimed bodies? Since the switch to the use of bequeathed bodies appears to have often occurred for primarily pragmatic reasons, does this indicate there is no ethical difference between the two?

Why Cadavers Have Ethical Significance

In an attempt to address such questions, a starting point is provided by asking why the treatment of cadavers is considered to be of ethical significance. One answer is that the cadaver has *intrinsic* value: it is an end in and of itself. Alternatively, the cadaver may have *instrumental* value: it can be used as a means to an end.

The closest we come to recognizing a cadaver's *intrinsic value* is when we bestow a person's intrinsic value upon their dead body at death. We do this because we consider that a person and his or her body are inseparable. We recognize each other because we recognize each other's bodies, and while this applies supremely during life, some very important aspects of this identity continue following death. May (1985, 39) has expressed it like this: '… while the body retains a recognizable form, even in death, it commands the respect of identity. No longer a human presence, it still reminds us of the presence that once was utterly inseparable from it'.

When we turn to a cadaver's *instrumental value* we recognize that it serves as a vital source of memories and responses. This leads to the conviction that a cadaver should be respected and treated in a 'decent' manner. As we remember a person who has died, we respect the person who *was*. All that remains of the person is the cadaver, and yet our respect for that person, and for the memory of that person, leads to respect for the person's remains, a link that is not readily broken. Not only this, but relatives and friends of the deceased grieve the death, and the dead body is an integral part of the initial grieving process. A cadaver may also prove of instrumental value when it serves as a source of organs, and when it is used for teaching purposes or clinical practice.

The most helpful way forward recognizes these two sets of values: intrinsic *and* instrumental, since both contribute to societies' recognition of the cadaver's significance (Jones 1994). Consequently, the manner in which cadavers are treated *is* of moral interest. We respect a person-now-dead when account is taken of that person's wishes when alive. Only in this way do we recognize a continuum between the two, and hence the cadaver's intrinsic value. Similarly, when serious note is taken of the wishes and feelings of still-living relatives and friends, we are recognizing the relationships of the deceased as well as the cadaver's instrumental value. On the negative side, we show disrespect to a person-now-dead when we allow that person's body to be dissected in the absence of any consent on the person's part prior to death, and/or in the absence of any close friends and relatives to argue the case for the deceased. In other words, dissection of an unclaimed body may be a form of exploitation, since those with greater rights and opportunities pre-mortem are protected from this. But is the use of unclaimed bodies accompanied by consequences such as these?

To answer this, it is helpful to deviate from the dissecting room and consider the moral values governing organ donation (Vawter et al. 1990). The first value normally used is that of *autonomy*, according to which, each individual should have autonomous control over the disposition of his or her body after death, regardless of social need or the public interest. Donation implies that the people concerned made a *free and informed decision* prior to their death, to allow their bodies to be used as the source of transplanted organs.

The individual also has sets of relationships, and this brings into focus a second set of moral values, that of the *interests of family members*, who can in certain jurisdictions override the wishes of the deceased, even when the latter has specified that his or her body is to be donated for teaching, research, or therapeutic purposes. Whenever this occurs, it brings with it an apparent clash of moral values – between the prior autonomy and interests of the deceased, and the actual autonomy and interests of the living. To focus on the interests of living relatives over those of the deceased is to imply that family members have greater interests, and are more susceptible to harms or wrongs than is a dead person. This appears to emphasize the instrumental value of the cadaver at the expense of its intrinsic value, leading to an imbalance which may have detrimental consequences in other areas of decision-making.

Underlying the previous values is a premise that the giving of one's body is preferable to being coerced into doing it. This is the value of *altruism*, according to which it is better to give than to receive, and the good of others is better than self-interest (May 1985). The gift element is central to this value, and from this perspective an opt-in scheme for organ donation is preferable to an opt-out scheme that lacks altruistic intentions (see Chapter 5).

A further value stems from a common response, namely, that death, especially when premature or unexpected, is tragic. Some people may find solace and meaning in the use of body parts to assist others, sometimes referred to as the *redemptive aspect* of organ donations. The death of one person confers life on another. Out of a tragedy can come new life and hope, a transformation that stems from one person freely giving organs to another person in desperate need of them.

The Centrality of Altruism

The crucial problem with the use of unclaimed bodies revolves around the *absence of altruism*. The 'unclaimedness' of these bodies stems from the weakness, vulnerability, and frequently dereliction of the people when alive, and it is this unclaimedness that mirrors their 'unwantedness'. This may be warranted if cadavers are assigned instrumental value alone. The result is that, rather than protecting the interests of such people, their interests have become subservient to other interests.

The inevitable query from which we cannot escape is a dual one, stemming from a lack of consent on the part of anyone in the situation of becoming an unclaimed body, and from the fact that such people often come from disadvantaged sectors of society. Taken together, these considerations provide forthright hints that the process may be unfair, and that it may allow the exploitation of one individual by another, or one group by another.

Two arguments are sometimes brought to bear against the emphasis placed here on altruism. The first is that, in reality, altruism may not be an individual's only motive. Desperate people may seek money for their bodies to help their relatives pay the funeral expenses. Hence, rather than seeking the good of others, they are looking after those close to them. This is not altruism, but neither is donation under these circumstances devoid of goodness. To assist relations is altruistic, even though bequeathing one's body for dissection is a by-product of this. At least this is an autonomous choice of the donor unlike the use of unclaimed and unwanted bodies.

This raises a second objection, that the use of unclaimed bodies in countries such as India actually bestows meaning upon an otherwise worthless life. The argument here is that a person considered value-less during life may actually acquire value at death through the use of his or her body for dissection. This argument stands or falls on a living person's status within society, where an elevation in value *after* death is made possible by the very limited value placed on these individuals *before* death. In our estimation this is an untenable view of human life and not one that should be contemplated as a basis for decision-making.

But are the benefits of dissection for medical students are so great, either in terms of anatomical knowledge gained or as a means of self-discovery about death and dying (Bertman and Marks 1989; Marks and Bertman 1980), that society is morally justified in potentially jeopardizing the autonomy of a limited number of disadvantaged individuals?

It may be argued that what is done to a few disadvantaged individuals has no repercussions for the far greater number of individuals who are not likely to end their lives as unclaimed cadavers. It may be possible to assess these few (by and large) elderly individuals in isolation from the very much larger number of young individuals who are killed in road accidents, and who may be candidates for organ transplantation. How bodies come to be in dissecting rooms cannot be isolated in ethical terms (and should not be isolated procedurally) from how human bodies come to be in operating theatres as organ donors, or how human tissue comes to be in research laboratories. There is a delicate ethical thread linking all three areas, and it is the continuity of this thread that is a fundamental concern of this book.

It may also be argued that unclaimed bodies have *no family interests*. Hence, these interests are not susceptible to being infringed by use of the bodies of the deceased without prior consent, perhaps justifying employing unclaimed bodies. But does a willingness to ignore the previous interests of those who have now died signify a neglect of the autonomy of similar individuals when alive? It is arguable that there is a connection, since both reflect the treatment of living people: ignoring the previous interests of those who have now died parallels neglect of the autonomy of the living. At the other extreme, if the value of people after death is perceived as being greater than prior to death, there ought to be a moral compulsion to improve conditions when alive: a relevant consideration in those countries where such situations apply.

The final value referred to in relation to organ transplantation was its *redemptive element*. The force of this value is weakened when bodies are donated at the end of a long life rather than following a premature or unexpected death; death in the former case is often less of a tragedy (it may have been expected; it may be seen as a natural conclusion to a long, fulfilled life; it may even be viewed as a release from prolonged suffering). Although bodies being dissected do not directly give new life or new hope to individual patients or even to groups of patients, this may ultimately come when the medical students become practising doctors. The case for transformation and redemption as ethical imperatives, while not as compelling as that for organ transplants, cannot be entirely dismissed.

A long way removed from these uncertainties are the memorial services held prior to burial or cremation of dissected remains, for those who have bequeathed their bodies, as a means of signifying respect (Bertman and Marks 1989). While these services take a variety of forms, their aim is to honour those who have donated their bodies to an anatomy department for the purposes of teaching and research. This serves as a formal and public demonstration of anatomy departments' appreciation for such bequests. Whether secular or ecumenical, such services bring together the altruism of the donors, the gratitude of the students and faculty, and the memories of close relatives and friends. Such services are fitting symbols of the positive use to which bodies can be put after death.

Putting these considerations together, it would seem preferable to err on the side of using bequests. Teaching departments may have to accept some educational inconvenience in terms of having fewer bodies available for teaching if the more significant matter of the value of individual free choice (on the part of an individual prior to death and the family at the time of death) is to be retained.

Cadavers as a Teaching Tool

The logical consequence of the preceding discussions is an examination of the use made today of cadavers within a medical school dissecting room environment. Once cadavers are obtained, what use is made of them? How do students respond? Are cadavers really necessary as teaching and learning tools?

Perceptions of the Cadaver

How do those, such as medical students, who actually utilize cadavers, perceive them? In particular, how do medical students view cadavers in the dissecting room, since this is one of the traditional arenas in which human anatomists function?

It has long been recognized that dissection can have a peculiarly hardening effect on the dispositions of students, and an appropriately balancing development of professional values and character is necessary (Warner and Rizzolo 2006). An American medical professor in 1847 cautioned his students, 'anatomy, however indispensable it may be, tends certainly to freeze up the springs of human feeling, and destroy our sympathy for human suffering' (Miller 1847, quoted in Warner and Rizzolo 2006, 404). This posed significant problems for those advocating the medical education of women, whose delicate moral constitutions would surely be defiled by dissection. The affective components of human dissection were ultimately seen as a crucial part of medical education, as a transformative moment that shaped the doctor's identity.

Leon Kass (1985, 21), following the sudden death of an extraordinary man, wrote:

> There he lay, peacefully, a frail figure ... as if in a pleasant dream ... I asked myself, "Where *is* he? Where did he go? Where is that mind, that learning and understanding, those unwritten books that no one will now write?" ... The body, the still warm and undisfigured body, identical in looks to what I had seen the day before, mocked me with its unintentional dissembling and camouflage of extinction. Here, there was vastly *less* than meets the eye. The dead body may be more than what our science teaches, but it is also less than what it appears to us to be. The body may be more than stuff, but the man seems to be more than his body.

Reflecting on this episode, and contrasting it with a dissecting room scene, Kass emerges with two opposing views of the human body, and he is uneasy with both. The first is that we are only physical beings; we are our bodies and nothing more. The second is that we are more than our physical beings; we are more than embodied matter, having some intangible and unseen dimension.

This particular paradox is beyond the scope of this book, although its existence is surprisingly helpful for an understanding of cadavers. This is because we cannot escape the general notion that dead bodies are both very much like us, and also very different from us. They are sufficiently like us to be recognizable, both as human beings and as individuals. And yet they are sufficiently unlike us to leave the distinct impression that they now belong to a category of being different from the one to which we, as living subjects, belong. After all, they cannot respond to us, neither can they speak, move or communicate. We expect them to be the sort of beings we are, but they fail us and in a sense let us down. What, then, is the relationship between the dead body and the person who was once associated with that body? This is an issue that permeates all thinking about the significance of the human body, and the view that we adopt has important repercussions for the way in which we respond to dead bodies, both of someone we have known and also of others. This is of relevance when making decisions about, for example, the use of organs from those killed in road accidents.

Against this background, let us think further about the cadavers medical students study and dissect in the dissecting room. Unfortunately, the literature available is relatively limited. Hafferty (1991) has conducted the most extensive study in this area, on what he terms 'death and the socialization of medical students'. He noted that students are upset to varying degrees by the dissection of different parts of the body. To some students, dissection provokes anxiety, since it reminds them of human beings, of people just like themselves. This 'human referent' aspect of dissection is most prominent during the study of head, face, and arm, as well as during dissection of the neck, pelvic and perineal regions. Hafferty concluded that the greater the emphasis on regarding cadavers as formerly living human beings, the greater the emotional upset. To other students the dead body is an aesthetically repulsive object, the death, formalin and smell all conspiring to repel the sensitive. Taken together, these negative influences constitute a substantial barrier to academic learning.

Why, then, struggle to come to terms with the distress of the dissecting room, with its threatening cadavers, when anatomy can be learned from clean, aseptic books with glossy colour pictures, from simulation models, or from computers? A detailed educational answer to this question is not relevant in the present context, except to make the comment that the study of dead human bodies is a far more relevant introduction to the study of living patients than is the study of inanimate diagrams or photographs (no matter how these are presented). Even the complex models and virtual reality simulations that have been developed for surgical training and practice have not proved adequate without additional cadaveric dissection (McDougall 2007; Thompson 2001). For health professionals, the study of *somebody's* body is more appropriate than study of *the* body.

However, it must be noted that the practice of dissection is not the most emotionally traumatic experience that medical students face. In the 1950s medical students at the University of Kansas reported that the stress of anatomical study came from the vast amount of detail they were expected to master, rather than the dissection experience (Becker et al. 1961). More recently, in Ireland, students rated the dissecting room as far less stressful than their exams and work load (McGarvey et al. 2001).

It became evident during Hafferty's study that cadavers can be viewed in various ways, and these are crucial to individuals' responses to cadavers and to the task of dissecting them. The possibilities include viewing dead human bodies as biological specimens, as formerly living human beings, or as an amalgamation of features – formerly living human beings, learning tools, and of value for future clinical situations. These perceptions demonstrate that, for most students, cadavers are ambiguous entities; not only is their identity unclear, but it even changes in character in different situations. Those for whom the cadaver reminded them of human beings could be further subdivided, into those who viewed cadavers as surrogate future patients, or as a future 'me'. Few of the students were prepared to experience cadavers as a 'future me' and, therefore, as relevant to their own personal concerns. Hafferty (1991, 123) writes:

> Dissection, as a literal process of destruction and dehumanization, had become a disturbingly personal reality for these students. In this meeting with death as a future self, even those students who maintained a formerly-living-human-being perspective of their cadavers retreated from the cadaver as a personal referent.

Hafferty noted an inconsistency in the students' reactions to issues such as the possibility of donating their own bodies for dissection, regardless of the group into which they fitted. This, he considered, stemmed from the potentially haunting presence of the cadaver as a 'future me'.

A complementary approach is that of Howard Carter (1997) who, in his book *First Cut*, spent 16 weeks following a medical class in a traditional anatomy dissecting course in an American medical school. This unusual book, written by a professor of comparative literature and humanities, is an outsider's account of this strange process, driven by a fascination at what might have happened a few years previously to the body of his father following its donation to a medical school.

Carter hones in on the good working relationship between students and 'their' cadavers: 'One way or another, the students are slowly creating a functional relationship between themselves and these bodies, or, wider still, between themselves and any human bodies, dead or alive. This is no small shift in orientation; while it goes by tiny steps in the lab ... it is a heroic jump' (Carter 1997, 57). It is this relationship that constitutes for Carter the basis of the loyalty and honour bestowed by the students on their cadavers.

Like Hafferty (1991), Carter recognizes a variety of approaches to cadavers on the part of the students. The first response he detected was that of disgust and aversion, which, in his experience, usually fades away; the second, a consequence of focusing on localized regions and structures, is the reduction of the cadavers to biological exhibits. This desensitizing progression is well documented, and some conclude that it can have negative consequences for how the student will relate to future patients (Francis and Lewis 2001). A physician and writer, Dannie Abse, described his experience in the dissecting room thus: 'Our first disgust weakened to distaste, and our distaste was usurped by numbness, by an apathetic neutrality'

(Abse 1974, 69). Frank Huyler (1999, quoted in Francis and Lewis 2001, 5), an American doctor, evokes the internal conflict he experienced between appreciating the cadaver as a person and as a resource for scientific study:

> It was strong and frightening, because even as we reduced him to pieces I knew that he was real, that he had stories to tell, that he had looked out at the sea from the decks of ships. I could feel it when I chose to. Mostly I chose not to. Mostly it was anatomy.

Carter (1997), however, recognizes a third response, a reassertion by the students of the humanity of the cadavers, dependent on an awareness of variations and 'oddities'. In Carter's eyes, dissection is not a form of dehumanization, since the students make connections between the implied personhood of the cadavers, the students' own bodies, and future patients.

Carter's discussion of what he perceives to be an 'intimacy' between the students and their cadavers is remarkably enlightening, discussing as he does the importance of knowledge of the innermost part of our being, or the inner workings of our bodies, knowledge rarely valued in our culture. This, together with our avoidance of death, amounts to a 'denial of corporality that touches both the living body and the dead' (Carter 1997, 199). For him, this is an enormous loss, compensated to some degree for these students, who as they 'work their way into the body come to know its textures and qualities through direct sensory apprehension in a way that our touch-aversive society otherwise avoids or even forbids' (Carter 1997, 199). Carter comments: 'This cut is a specialized kind of touch, one that destroys in order to promote understanding' (Carter 1997, 199). Going further, he sees the course as an 'extended lovemaking to one human body – an anatomical necrophilia in the most positive sense – and, by symbolic extension, to all human bodies' (Carter 1997, 205).

For Carter the anatomy course is a clear rite of passage, as it prepares students for the intimacies of the consulting room. This stems from an acknowledgement that they are working with a gift, that of a body to take apart, thereby engendering in the students a sense of reverence and responsibility with regard to future encounters with the living bodies of patients. In a personal vein, he recognizes in his father's bequest, the opportunity for his body to serve as a passive teacher after his death, allowing students to make their own discoveries among his tissues and bones.

Even as cadavers are 'anatomized', that is, divided and shredded, the anatomy lab serves as a maieutic place, in his words, 'a womb where knowledge is birthed' and the students are midwives for a learning of their own (Carter 1997, 104). For him, anatomy represents an intellectual approach that leads to comprehensive and synthetic wisdom, providing 'order, validation, and affirmation, even as the bodies slowly come apart, disintegrating toward chaos' (Carter 1997, 105). We are left with the unique (or almost unique) status of the dissecting room situation, since it conveys vistas of humanity and perplexing questions lying well beyond the strictures of students learning an anatomical vocabulary.

Contemporary Ethical Quandaries

The foundation laid thus far has involved exploring the use of cadavers in anatomy departments. Important as this is, cadavers are not confined to the dissecting rooms of anatomy departments. They are examined during postmortem procedures, by researchers attempting to come to a better understanding of the functioning of our bodies, and by anthropologists focusing on skeletal remains from the recent and distant past seeking to throw light on how people lived and died in other cultures and civilizations. Regrettably, a considerable range of these investigations has involved what amounts to the mistreatment and abuse of dead bodies.

This raises at least two areas of concern: the manner in which dead human bodies are treated, and our dependence on human bodies and tissue for medical research. These, in turn, bring to the fore our moral obligation towards cadavers, and the research imperative, without which much current knowledge of the human body would not exist.

Body Parts Scandals

In recent years a number of scandals involving human body parts have been uncovered. As media reports have publicized the appalling details, the often-ignored tissue bank industry has come under scrutiny, revealing a furtive demand-driven market reminiscent of Burke and Hare. The majority of these scandals originate in the United States, where the tissue industry is most developed, and are generally associated with one of three institutions, university willed body programs, funeral homes or crematoria, or autopsies.

Universities often find themselves with more bodies donated than they require for their own teaching or research. These surplus bodies are then sold on to other medical schools and research companies, or for medical training seminars, often through a middle man, the body broker. This income is not technically 'profit', which would be illegal, but is ploughed back into the program to cover processing and storage costs and salaries. However, demand is often greater than supply and, with no limit on what can be charged, prices are inflated. The litany of instances of malpractice is extensive, with a succession of scandals hitting the headlines every year.

At the University of California, Irvine in 1999, the director of the Willed Body Program sold six spines to a research company for US$5,000 (Warren 1999). In another instance, in 2002, the director of the cadaver laboratory at the University of Texas Medical Branch, was charged with taking toenails and fingernails from cadavers without consent and selling them to a pharmaceutical company for personal profit (Vine 2003). In 2003 an autopsy assistant at the University of

California, Davis was charged with stealing various body parts, including bones, fetuses, organs and even heads, over several years. He is alleged to have stored them at his home in order to conduct his own research (Morin 2003). In 2004 it was revealed that seven cadavers that had been donated to Tulane University in New Orleans and subsequently sold on to the US Army via a body broker, were blown up in land mine tests. The University believed the cadavers were going to other medical schools (Burdeau 2004). Also in 2004, it was revealed that bodies willed to the University of California, Los Angeles medical school had been sold on to a body broker at considerable profit. This followed revelations in 1996 that the University had mishandled donor remains, mixing ashes with medical waste and dumping them in the city landfill (Ornstein and Zarembo 2004).

Outside universities a number of scandals have been revealed involving funeral homes and coroner's offices. In 1997 it was revealed that the corneas from patients being autopsied at the Los Angeles County coroner's office were routinely removed, without the knowledge or consent of the decedent's family. Under a little-known state law, which was instituted to combat transplant shortages, the corneas of a cadaver can legally be removed when there is no known objection from relatives (Alta Charo 2004). However, it appears that the relatives would have been available to discuss donation. The corneas were resold with a considerable mark-up (Frammolino 1997).

In 2003 an undertaker in California was arrested for illegally removing and selling body parts from cadavers he was supposed to cremate (Hall 2003). Phillip Guyett, a long-time tissue broker associated with funeral homes, was shut down by the Food and Drug Administration (FDA) in 2006, citing deficiencies in tissue practice, donor screening and record-keeping (Associated Press 2006).

The most recent body parts scandal involving funeral homes involves Biomedical Tissue Services based in New Jersey. A number of undertakers were involved in removing tissue from cadavers under their care. They are alleged to have falsified consent documents and doctored medical records eliminating references to diseases which would normally disqualify the tissue from use (Charatan 2006). The undertakers removed bones, as they did from the cadaver of radio personality Alistair Cooke, and replaced them with PVC pipes to ensure the removal was not visible externally. Cooke's medical records were altered, changing his age from 95 to 85, and his cause of death from bone cancer to a heart attack. The tissue products have been recalled, but some were transplanted in 2004 and 2005 in the United States and beyond, generating fears of contamination (BBC News 2006b).

Underlying Problems in the American Tissue Donation System

These scandals serve to undermine public trust in the tissue donation system, threatening the present support of legitimate organ and tissue donations and willed body programs. They also demonstrate a serious lack of respect for the human body. The scandals raise a number of issues that point to underlying problems with current tissue donation procedures and particularly the nature of the tissue bank industry in the United States.

Donation of cadavers is precisely that; there is no financial reward apart from incidentals. It is a 'not for profit' transaction, with altruism as a guiding ethical principle. However, the close alliance of 'for profit' companies with 'not for profit' institutions enables body parts to be traded for profit by these companies. If this practice is not divulged to the original donors, it is taking unfair advantage of their altruism. It can be argued that pro-rata payment should be made to their families unless they have already agreed to this arrangement. However, even if this were to occur, patients ultimately receiving the body parts or tissues are being denied the benefits of the original altruistic gesture. This is not to argue against payment for 'added value' when considerable costs have been incurred in modifying the tissue in some way, but this is quite different from blatant profiteering.

One of the chief prerequisites for the ethical acceptability of any kind of body donation is informed consent. The decedent and/or their family must have given permission for the procedure, understanding what it will entail. This raises the question of what qualifies as fully or adequately informed consent. Donation of one's body to 'science' or as a 'gift of life' does not justify the range of previously listed practices. Precision of definition is required. Openness is essential with its call for integrity and respect for those who have freely given of their body in the first place. Without this original gift, there would be no bodies to broker.

Tissue banks often contend that most donors or their families do not want to know all the information that could be made available (Katches et al. 2000), and to a certain extent this is probably the case. But the fact that families are often shocked or grieved when revelations are later made indicates that more information is needed initially, and this can be tailored to the individual situation (Gottmann Kulik 2004). Ethically judicious practice errs on the side of too much rather than too little information. Only in this way is respect shown to those contemplating donating their bodies.

Tissue banking is estimated to be a US$1 billion industry today (Charatan 2006), and many find the lucrativeness of the trade and the commercialization of human tissue inherently contrary to the very ethos of body donation. Many of the voluntary non-profit organizations that administered tissue donation in the early years have been replaced by professional organizations selling their 'product' in glossy catalogues (Gottmann Kulik 2004). In the search for profit, tissue often goes to the highest bidder, which unfortunately may not be the greatest need. Donated skin is often preferentially processed into products for cosmetic surgery, leaving burns units struggling to find sufficient skin products for those in desperate need of them (Heisel et al. 2000).

Whose responsibility is it to ensure the tissue is safe and is ethically acquired? Legislation generally plays a major role in regulating such activities, but in many situations the policing required is lacking. In the United States the tissue bank industry has been poorly regulated at both federal and state levels. While organ transplantation is well regulated, there is virtually no regulation of the interstate traffic of tissue (Alta Charo 2004). The Uniform Anatomical Gift Act 1987 (section 10) prohibits the sale or purchase of bodies or their parts, but it allows a 'reasonable' charge for removal, processing, storage, transportation, quality control or disposal. There is no limit on these charges.

The American Association of Tissue Banks (AATB) issues its own strict standards and accredits companies, but this is not mandatory. The majority of tissue banks are not accredited, with only 119 listed on the AATB website whereas around 2,800 are registered with the FDA. The FDA issued new regulations on human tissue in 2005, but these are still not well enforced with very few inspections occurring. In light of recent scandals, in 2006 the FDA issued guidelines reminding companies of the new regulations (Food and Drug Administration 2006b) and has formed a task force to address the present shortcomings (Food and Drug Administration 2006a). The proposals require licensing and training of all those who deal with human tissue, more funding for FDA staff and inspections, compulsory accreditation by the AATB, limiting profits on donated tissue and regulating or banning tissue recovery in funeral homes (Marchione 2006).

However, some commentators claim that what the industry needs is not more government supervision, but increased internal responsibility and transparency (Waltz 2006). They contend that the organizations that purchase bodies should require documentation to show that they have been acquired, stored and handled in an appropriate way. The AATB has recently advised its members to police their business partners (Marchione 2006), and the FDA has explicitly stated that each person who receives tissue is responsible for ensuring that the establishment they deal with has adhered to the current good tissue practices requirements (Food and Drug Administration 2006c). It remains to be seen whether these approaches will turn around an embarrassingly dubious industry.

The United States is certainly not the only country experiencing problems with an illicit trade in human body parts. From the 1850s India has been the centre of an international trade in human remains, supplying human bones to Western medical schools (Carney 2007). While this trade was once legal, the requirements of informed consent were probably never met. A long chain of supply involving both Indian and Western companies helped disguise the corrupt nature of the industry; as the former president of the Indian Association of Exporters of Anatomical Specimens said, 'No one advertised, but everyone knew it was going on' (quoted in Carney 2007). However, when it became apparent to Indian authorities in 1985 that grave robbing and possibly even murder were occurring to supply this trade, the Indian government prohibited the export of human remains and the skeleton market collapsed. While other countries such as China and Thailand could also supply human bones, they were not of the quality or quantity of India's. As a result the price of human skeletons sky-rocketed, and inferior plastic replicas became the norm.

However, the Indian ban was not fully enforced. In 2006, Indian police arrested Mukti Biswas, the head of an underground grave-robbing ring, and closed his bone processing facility. He had been operating successfully under the ban until public complaints about thefts from burial grounds and the smell from his factory forced the police to take action. Mukti's business links were traced to Canada (Carney 2007), illustrating the burden incumbent upon Western dealers and suppliers in human material to ensure that their products are acquired legally and ethically.

The Place of Autopsies in the World of Medicine

The most commonly encountered procedure affecting cadavers is that of autopsy (also known as postmortem examination or necropsy). In past years, in many countries a sizeable proportion of those who died in hospitals underwent a postmortem examination. More recently, however, the proportion has dropped dramatically, so that figures of the order of 5 to 10 per cent of hospital deaths autopsied are now common (Burton et al. 2004).

In the modern autopsy, pathologists remove and inspect major organs, and use sophisticated tools to analyze body fluids, tissues and cellular components. As a consequence, autopsy entails disfigurement of a cadaver, even if this is a matter of *internal* disfigurement. As such, it is important to consider the reasons used to justify such destruction. It also raises issues of consent – before death by the person now dead, and after death by next of kin. Do the issues of consent vary depending on the reasons for the autopsy, or because of cultural factors?

Justifying Autopsies

Autopsies have been considered of value in five areas: as a means of establishing truth, detecting change, providing information, instructing learners and promoting justice (Lundberg 1984).

In most instances the major reason for performing an autopsy is to establish truth; that is, to identify definitively the basis of the disease process(es), and to determine the cause and manner of death (Emson 1992). Angrist (1971, 758) has written:

> ... the autopsy is the moment of truth for all medical care and the time of reckoning to improve the care of the patient ... it becomes a stimulus and incentive for care and increases both empathy and science in medicine.

When someone dies unattended, or without having been under medical supervision, an autopsy is the only way of categorically establishing how the death occurred (Geller 1983). For deaths occurring in a hospital setting, or in cases where the person was under the care of a medical practitioner, autopsies serve as an important quality control device, checking the accuracy both of the pre-mortem diagnosis and treatment decisions. In the case of autopsies in late fetal, neonatal, and infant deaths (the percentage of which is also declining) an additional function is served, that of assisting in parental counselling should there be implications for future pregnancies (Cartlidge et al. 1995).

With the development of modern diagnostic tools, doubt has been cast on many of the traditional reasons for autopsy. However, the data from a number of studies challenge this assertion. In 11 to 17 per cent of cases, there is a major discrepancy between the cause of death, as stated on the death certificate, and that determined at autopsy (McKelvie and Rode 1992). Maclaine and co-workers (1992) found the death certificate error rate in their sample to be 23 per cent, while Nichols et al. (1998) noted the detection of an undiagnosed cause of death in 45 per cent of their cases. Approximately two-thirds of the undiagnosed causes of death were judged to be treatable conditions.

Autopsies also have a role in detecting change and providing data on public health issues. Without them, some suicides, homicides, and cases of contagious disease could go undetected (in this sense, the autopsy promotes the interests of legal justice). Johnson (1969) reported that over one five-year period in London, more than five per cent of all unnatural deaths had been unsuspected prior to postmortem examination, including cases of poisoning, head injury, child abuse and suffocation. Autopsies are also useful tools in discovering and investigating new diseases, particularly those due to environmental or occupational factors (Iserson 1994).

Autopsies are traditionally considered to be important teaching tools in the study of pathology and medicine. Surveys of medical students have shown that by far the majority of medical students regard autopsy as a valuable means of obtaining new information about disease processes, and of improving future patient management (Botega et al. 1997).

Reasons given for the decline in the number of autopsies vary. Brown (1984, 447) has outlined some public beliefs that may interfere with gaining consent for autopsy. These include the belief that medical diagnosis is sufficient; that the clinician's job finishes at death; that the deceased has suffered enough; that body mutilation will be visible at the funeral, or that autopsy arrangements will delay the funeral; and religious and quasi-religious beliefs.

However, there is evidence that the decline in autopsy rates is not due to the public's unwillingness to agree to the procedure. Sanner (1994b) found that 84 per cent of people questioned would accept an autopsy being performed on themselves, and 80 per cent would give consent for the procedure to be carried out on a close relative. The suggestion has been made that physicians are not requesting as many autopsies as previously because of concern that errors in their diagnosis or treatment might be uncovered, with the possibility that legal action will ensue (Lundberg 1984). Alternatively, physicians may be reluctant to accept the death of patients, regarding them as failures (Geller 1983), or may be unwilling to approach grieving family members for permission to carry out an autopsy (Smith and Zumwalt 1984).

Why Should Consent be Required for Autopsies?

One of the most contentious aspects of autopsies is removal (and retention) of organs, particularly the brain. Quite apart from forensic reasons for doing this, human tissue plays a crucial role in the teaching of neuroanatomy to health science and allied students, and in scientific research (Cordner 1992). In 1991 in the United States, a public outcry arose when it was discovered that brains were being removed by the medical examiner at the time of autopsy and given to the University of Pennsylvania medical school for use in their teaching, without the knowledge or consent of the deceased's next of kin. Officials from the coroner's office defended this practice on the basis that the medical school gained much needed human organs for their teaching and research, and the coroner received free dissection reports from the medical school pathologists. The families of the deceased, however, did not view the practice with favour and it was halted (Anderson 1991).

In 1999 in the UK it was revealed that a large number of organs had been retained from children's bodies after postmortem at the Royal Liverpool Children's Hospital (Alder Hey). This elicited a considerable public outcry from parents, a protest that increased as the subsequent inquiry released its findings, and the extent of the scandal was revealed (Royal Liverpool Children's Inquiry 2001). It was discovered that the pathologist, Professor Dick van Velzen, had ordered the systematic retention of almost every organ in every pediatric postmortem case for the overriding purpose of research. Parents had been deliberately misled into thinking they were burying their deceased children intact. The tragedy is magnified by the fact that the vast majority of the stockpiled organs were never used for medical education or research. Professor van Velzen's misconduct was not limited to this, since he had lied, fabricated postmortem reports, abdicated his clinical duties, falsified statistics, and encouraged other staff to do so. Unfortunately, managerial inadequacy and poor administration had allowed these misdemeanors to go unhindered for some time. The inquiry found that while the situation at Alder Hey was not unique, it constituted a 'considerable exaggeration of the national picture' because of the misconduct of Professor van Velzen (Royal Liverpool Children's Inquiry 2001).

The Alder Hey scandal was first uncovered during an inquiry into the major failings in the pediatric cardiac surgery unit at the Bristol Royal Infirmary (Bristol Royal Infirmary Inquiry 2001), which also revealed the large-scale retention of organs at Bristol (Bristol Royal Infirmary Inquiry 2000). Tissue was systematically taken at or after the postmortem of children who died following pediatric cardiac surgery. However shocking this was to the public at the time, it was not exceptional.

Following the Alder Hey and Bristol scandals the Chief Medical Officer conducted a census of retained organs throughout the UK (Department of Health 2001b). This found that there were 54,300 organs, body parts, still-births and fetuses in storage that had been retained since 1970. The majority of these were kept at a small number of specialist centres and medical schools. Around half of the organs were brains, and a sixth hearts. There were an additional 50,000 organs and body parts in museum or archived collections from before 1970. Retained tissue was often disposed of as medical waste. The census also revealed that around 16,000 organs and body parts had been retained illegally after coroner's postmortems. While a coroner's postmortem does not require consent from the next of kin, tissues can only be retained when necessary to determine the cause of death. Any further retention of tissue requires consent as for hospital postmortems. However, it was a long-standing and widespread practice for tissue to be retained without consent. The Alder Hey Report concluded that this practice 'arose from a sense of paternalism on the part of the medical profession which served to conceal retention in the supposed best interest of the parents. Such practice was misconceived and was bound to cause upset and distress when, inevitably, it came to light' (Royal Liverpool Children's Inquiry 2001, 444).

While many of the organs had been retained after relatives had signed consent forms, these forms were vague and were signed at a time of great distress without adequate support or advice. This failed to constitute adequately informed consent. A major flaw was the lack of definition of the word 'tissue', which could include organs and body parts, contrary to lay understanding of the word as only very small pieces of organs. The consent forms were generally consistent with the terminology of the Human Tissue Act (1961), which only required that relatives 'did not object' to tissue retention. This fell well short of the positive agreement required by today's ethical standards.

The Alder Hey report concluded that 'a weak and poorly understood legal framework has allowed bad practice to flourish' (Ramsay 2001, 357). A major review of UK law was demanded, and the resulting Human Tissue Act (2004) has much stricter requirements concerning informed consent and procedures for retaining tissue.

The UK scandals and ensuing inquiries prompted an internal review at Green Lane Hospital in Auckland, New Zealand of its own 'heart library' (Cole and McCabe 2002). Established in 1950, this collection contained more than 1,300 hearts from aborted fetuses, infants and children with congenital heart defects, and had proved invaluable in enabling New Zealand surgeons to make major advances in cardiac surgery. The internal review discovered that many parents were unaware that organs had been retained from their deceased children, and in February 2002 the hospital initiated a process of informing parents and returning hearts. Many of the hearts had been obtained without consent from the parents, although a consent procedure had been in place in more recent years. Despite a public outcry from shocked and grieving parents, the hospital had acted entirely within the law. New Zealand's Human Tissue Act (1964) did not require parental consent for organs to be retained after postmortem (Skegg 2003). Since detailed pathological examination of organs required to establish the cause of death could require a delay of up to six weeks, it was not considered appropriate to return the organs to the family this long after the child's funeral.

The Cartwright Inquiry of 1988 had raised greater awareness of consumer rights and consent issues in New Zealand, which was reinforced in the Health and Disability Services Consumers' Rights Code (Office of the Health and Disability Commissioner 1996). This code stated that no body part could be retained for research or education without informed consent (clauses 7[9] and 7[10]). However, this stipulation applies only to health procedures carried out on living persons, not autopsies (Skegg 2003). It was not until the Human Tissue Act 2008 that informed consent was required for the retention of tissue after postmortem. Though the law was slow to change (Cole and McCabe 2002), the ethical and social climate was much quicker and normal hospital procedures were generally modified in delayed response to this before the Human Tissue Act 2008 was passed.

In Australia in 2001 it was revealed that a number of long bones and joints had been obtained from cadavers at postmortem at the New South Wales Institute of Forensic Medicine and distributed to researchers. These bones were removed without consent and in addition to any justified intervention or examination of the body as a part of autopsy to determine the manner of death. At the time staff thought they were acting in accordance with the law and no prosecutions were made. The ignorance of the law was attributed to a 'systemic failure by the profession in its education and training' and poor administration (Walker 2001).

These are far from isolated incidents, and have caused much anguish to members of the public. The double tragedy of death and the unknown retention of body parts, often separated by a number of years, reawakens and compounds the grief first experienced (Jones and Galvin 2002). The scandals have highlighted the need for clarification of existing legislation and greater regulation regarding acquiring and storing human biological material. In Australia new guidelines were widely instututed in 2002 following the UK organ retention scandals and the subsequent revelations and outrage at home. As in the UK it had been standard practice to retain tissue after autopsy for further research, and this was legal under the various Human Tissue Acts, though it was no longer publicly acceptable. The National Code of Ethical Autopsy Practice emphasized the importance of open and honest communication between health professionals and family and developed a model for requesting consent for non-coronial postmortems that details the possible retention of organs or tissue (Australian Health Ministers' Advisory Council Subcommittee on Ethical Autopsy Practice 2002).

The problem underlying the various scandals is a lack of ethical awareness as to why we should treat the human body or human tissue with dignity and respect and what such treatment entails. If this is understood, the significance of informed consent is automatically embraced, and the emphasis shifts from 'taking' and 'retaining' to 'donating' (Department of Health 2001a). These, and other ethical principles, have been outlined in various UK reports (Department of Health 2001a; Retained Organs Commission 2002), which propose the following guidelines in relation to the retention of human tissue:

- *Respect*: treating the person who has died and their families with respect.
- *Understanding*: for many parents and families their love and feelings of responsibility for the dead person are as strong as they were during life.
- *Informed consent*: permission is sought and given on the basis of fully informed consent.
- *Time and space*: families need time to consider agreeing to a postmortem and donation of tissue and organs.
- *Skill and sensitivity*: toward the needs of the relatives.
- *Cultural competence*: awareness of differing attitudes towards postmortem, burial, and the use of organs.
- *Gift relationship*: balance should move from 'taking' and 'retaining' of organs to 'donation'.

These principles protect the interests of both the deceased and the grieving families. However, they fail to address those of medical professionals and researchers. From their perspective, retained organs are useful not only to ascertain the cause of death, but also to train other medical professionals and possibly in research. Conflict can occur between the needs of medical research and efforts to protect the dignity of human beings and demonstrate respect for human tissue. Account needs to be taken of the dual importance of scientific and clinical research on the one hand, and informed consent and allied ethical considerations on the other (Jones 2002b).

The potential value of human tissue for an understanding of human disease is so great that an intensive effort must be made to seek informed consent for the retention of organs and tissues at postmortem, for both teaching and research purposes. This could either be obtained from the patient prior to death or the next of kin after death. The details of the procedure must be plainly specified, including the organs and tissues to be removed, and the future uses to which they will be put.

Additionally, any discussion of postmortems must take into account cultural factors. A postmortem is abhorrent to some cultures, such as the Chinese and New Zealand Māori, who place especial significance on the integrity of the body (and especially the brain) when buried. Tongan cultural belief states that if the brain is not buried with the body, madness can descend upon surviving relatives (Reid 1992). When cultural factors such as these exist, pathologists, by and large, attempt to accommodate them by carrying out studies on the brain within a short time frame. In this way, the medical and cultural needs can be met in most cases. This, however, leaves no place for the removal of brains for teaching or research purposes from the cadavers of those belonging to these groups.

The Human Tissue Act 2004, which applies in England, Wales and Northern Ireland, allows for the removal of parts of the body for therapeutic purposes or for the purposes of medical education or research only when consent has been given by the person while alive, their nominated representative, or by a qualifying relative. The nature of the consent required to carry out autopsies for audit and teaching/research purposes is different from that required for coronial purposes when sudden, unexplained death has occurred. In the former situation, justification for the autopsy stems far more from the needs of the biomedical profession than from those of the deceased's relatives, whereas in the latter the reverse holds. Consent must be far more stringent in the former than in the latter situation, although this alone should not prevent extensive use of postmortem tissue. In seeking consent for an autopsy on the grounds of teaching or research, the requirements should be clearly specified. These include the organs or tissues required, and the use to which they will be put. Without detailed specification, the consent will be less than adequately informed.

The problem all too often is that paltry efforts are made to obtain consent for hospital autopsies, even when the need for human tissue is compelling. In our view there is no virtue in allowing human tissue to go to waste. Educational and scientific causes constitute a good, and, when this can be done ethically, human tissue should be provided for these causes.

The decline in the rate of autopsies has been precipitated by myriad ill-defined factors, which in turn highlight the lack of serious discussion of the rationale behind postmortems. While many good reasons exist for carrying out autopsies, and while justification for the procedure in general is not difficult to find, a lack of convincing reasons in some cases and a lack of effort in obtaining consent from next-of-kin have placed the procedure in jeopardy. The instances in which eyes, hearts and brains have been removed without consent, only to be followed by public outcry and private distress, epitomize the tragedy of unethical attitudes. In the final analysis, the loser will be the medical profession and patients.

Tissues of the Body

Discussion up to this point has centred on human cadavers, on bodies as a whole. Even in discussing the dissection of bodies, our attention has been mainly confined to relatively large body parts, such as arms, legs and the brain. Whenever anatomists think of the body, they move readily from the overview provided by gross anatomy, to the next level represented by the systems of the body, then to the organs which constitute much of the systems, and finally to tissues that are found within and between the organs. This gradation from the largest and most obvious to the smallest and least obvious is important descriptively, and is also an important reminder that we should never confuse these various levels.

When we think of the systems of the body, we think of systems such as the digestive, cardiovascular, muscular, nervous or skeletal systems. The organs are obvious – heart, lungs, kidneys, bladder and brain. Tissues are not so well known, but include the general connective tissues, along with fascial tissues, blood, and mucous and serous membranes (lining organs and the cavities of the body). And then there are muscles, nerves, glands, ligaments, tendons, cartilage and bone.

If internal organs are removed from a cadaver, when that person prior to death had expressed a wish that this be done for therapeutic or research purposes, and/or when living relatives agree with this action at the time of death, we can argue that the intrinsic value of that cadaver has been respected. The person's wishes and expectations have been kept. Conversely, when consent for such actions has not been given, the cadaver has been desecrated. Biologically, the two cadavers are identical, but there is an ethical difference between them.

How far can this ethical difference be taken? The removal of the brain without consent is very troublesome to many relatives, but what about the removal of a few sebaceous glands or a sliver of bone, or even mucous membrane from the lining of the mouth? Is size important? The remaining cadaver is 99 per cent complete. Is it taking the ideas of integrity and autonomy too far to insist that consent is always required to remove connective tissues, cells like fibroblasts and epithelial tissues lining the gut? Organs, or substantial parts thereof, have a much greater emotional and cultural significance than small tissue samples. In the case of histological slides much of the human material has been replaced with chemicals – a situation which is taken to the extreme with plastination (Chapter 4). As tissue is increasingly fragmented, does consent become irrelevant? In our view, we should err on the side of seeking consent, thereby retaining the centrality of consent for anything done on or to the human body, and leaving it to the individual to determine the importance they place on different parts of their body.

In examining these issues further we first need to consider the circumstances in which these tissues might be taken. The most likely situation is for this to happen during surgery.

Use of Biopsies from Surgical Operations

The removal of organs or tissues at operation is for the benefit of the patient, the material that is removed being unwanted by the patient. Under normal circumstances, this material will be incinerated. But what if researchers want to use it? Is consent required? If so, is this of the same nature as consent to bequeath one's body, or consent to remove material from a body at postmortem?

The bequest of a body makes that body available for teaching and research purposes, (as we have seen) often to assist, or out of gratitude for, the medical profession. Once consent has been given in these general terms, material is available for use. The interests of the deceased are served by the acceptance of the bequest. A postmortem is carried out in the interests of the patient only in a very marginal sense; the most it can do for the deceased is throw light on reasons for the death – primarily it will assist the medical profession in improving its diagnostic abilities. Consent for a postmortem is, therefore, consent only for those procedures required to establish cause of death, and not for the removal of additional organs or tissues that might be useful for other teaching or research purposes.

An operation is aimed at benefiting the patient now, and at providing either extended quantity or improved quality of life, or possibly both. Consent for the operation is consent for the surgical procedure itself and for medical procedures associated with it that will benefit the patient. It does not cover what is to be done with any material removed from the body, unless this is specifically included. But does it matter what is done to tissues removed at operation, since they have been removed with the goal of benefiting the patient? Does the tissue become the property of the hospital? Similar comments can be made about biopsy material, since this is removed with the aim of providing the patient with an accurate diagnosis of a suspected ailment.

In the case of operations and biopsies, the object of interest is material unwanted or not needed by the patient. Does this alter the consent required to use it for research purposes? Should any consent be required? Since the tissue has been removed in an attempt to improve the quality of the patient's life, it might be argued either that the patient has no interests in any unwanted tissue, or if there are some interests in it, these should lead to use of such tissue for research purposes as a form of gratitude for the treatment received. The tissue removed was part of a disease process, and is of no value to the patient. Whichever of these two views is adopted, any form of consent that might be required is of a very weak variety. In general the potential benefits that may emanate from the research should outweigh the consent required to use the patient's tissue.

The Human Tissue Act 2004, which applies in England, Wales and Northern Ireland, does not require consent for the use of tissue left over from diagnostic or surgical procedures for the purpose of clinical audit, education, performance assessment, public health monitoring or quality assurance. This surplus tissue may only be used in research if the tissue is irreversibly anonymized so that the researcher cannot identify the tissue donor (Department of Health 2005).

It would be a fairly simple solution to routinely ask the patient for consent for the use of surplus tissue at the time that they agree to a given surgical or diagnostic procedure (Ashcroft 2000). This consent could not normally be specific to a project, but the patient could be informed of broad principles regarding type of research, access and commercial development.

Stored Biological Material

The scandals over the retention of organs at postmortem have led to the close scrutiny of the collections of human material stored in various archives and museums. This so-called 'archival material' refers to any human material that has been taken during postmortem or medical treatment (such as diagnosis or surgery), and stored for future reference. It includes material in pathological archives, such as histological slides of various tissues like blood and bone marrow. These archives are essential for quality control and assurance, reviewing diagnoses, and for establishing the natural history of diseases, and so their storage is governed by the reasons for their initial retention.

Tissue may also be stored for use in future research projects, whether foreseen or as yet unknown. It is crucial that the consent given at the time the tissue is removed covers the possibility of storage for further use. The donor must be informed whether the tissue will be anonymized and what kind of research, if known, the tissue may be used for.

A number of databases of biological material, often known as biobanks, have sprung up worldwide in Iceland, Japan, Estonia, Canada, the United States and Sweden (Kaiser 2002; Kaye 2006). The biological material is linked with information on lifestyle factors and environmental exposure and the subjects' medical records to trace the interplay of genes and the environment in the causes and course of many common severe illnesses. The power of such databases lies in their prospective nature and the large number of participants, and biobanks are increasingly considered to be an essential research tool.

The UK Biobank project (www.ukbiobank.ac.uk) is the largest yet. Launched in 2006, it aims to collect information and biological samples from 500,000 participants aged 40–69. As thousands of cases of diseases emerge amongst the participant cohort over time, researchers will be able to search the databases for important information on a range of diseases. The rules of the UK Biobank state that only scientifically and ethically reviewed projects will be allowed and only anonymized (coded) data will be made available to researchers.

It is impossible to foresee all potential research uses of a biobank, and so when participants are recruited they cannot give truly informed consent to all possible research, challenging established legal and ethical norms. The counterargument often claims that individual interests must be balanced against the public good of biobanks (*Lancet* 2006) and that public opinion generally accepts blanket consent (Wendler 2006). However, these rationales may not be sufficient to satisfy the demands of autonomy (Caulfield 2007). Others consider that broad consent to biomedical research, the specifically stated purposes of the biobank and to the standards enforced by the biobank, plus the option of withdrawing consent at any time, may satisfy the requirements of general informed consent (Hansson et al. 2006).

The Council of Europe (2006) has issued a recommendation to member states on the use of human biological material in research in an effort to create a common international framework. This has become ever more important as cross-border flow of biological material and international collaboration increases. The primary goal of the guidelines is to protect the fundamental dignity and freedom of people whose biological material could be used, but this is balanced against the need to facilitate biomedical research as a potentially powerful tool to improve human health care. Informed consent again features as the crucial principle regarding any use of human biological material. Because blanket consent may fall short of the ethical requirements for informed consent (Caulfield 2007; Wertz 1999), consent at the time of storage should be as specific as possible with regard to foreseen research uses, and an individual should be allowed to place restrictions on the types of research for which their tissue may be used. If future research is not within the scope of original consent, it has been suggested that reasonable efforts should be made to contact the donor, although this may breach anonymity. However, if this is not possible, research may continue if it is of significant scientific interest, cannot be carried out in any other way, and if there is no evidence that the person has expressly opposed such research use.

Any storage of tissue for use in future research must have a convincing scientific rationale. Though not all research uses are foreseeable at the time of storage, there must be some clear reason for considering that the tissue will be useful in the future and will be able to be used. Stockpiling material without a research paradigm is ethically unacceptable (Jones et al. 2003).

The Council of Europe's recommendations permit researchers to use human tissue without consent once it has been irreversibly anonymized. This is in line with the 1999 report by the National Bioethics Advisory Council in the United States, which concluded that informed consent is not required for the subsequent use of stored tissue that has been anonymized (National Bioethics Advisory Commission 1999). Any such restrictions could seriously hinder potentially valuable scientific research on existing collections. While this exemption to the usual consent requirements is particularly useful in allowing the continued use of existing collections, it could be abused if researchers obtaining tissue in the future were to anonymize it instead of requesting consent (Trouet 2004).

Anonymization is crucial ethically because it provides confidentiality for the donor. Without this, the donor could be subject to discrimination and stigmatization, and this is of particular concern in the areas of employment and insurance. It is important to note that even if an individual's material is anonymized, the group to which the donor belongs may still be identifiable, and thus subject to discrimination or stigmatization based on the research results. The protocol should be prepared in such a way as to minimize such foreseeable risks (Council of Europe 2006).

The anonymization of tissue and associated data can be carried out to varying degrees. A specific code can be assigned to the material that is not accessible to the user, but is under the control of a third party. Such linked anonymized material remains ultimately identifiable (Council of Europe 2006). Tissue can be rendered unidentifiable by the irreversible removal of any identifying information (unlinked anonymized material).

It is not always appropriate to completely anonymize biological material as it may compromise the scientific quality of the research in question. Specific data, whether health-related or more generally personal, may need to be linked to the tissue in order to provide information pertinent to the research. In addition, the research might uncover information relevant to the current or future health of the individual, in which case anonymization would impede the possibility of giving health-related feedback to the donor. These instances can generally be identified in advance and consent tailored as appropriate.

In these ways every effort is being made to protect the interests of all involved, both directly and indirectly. At the same time the legitimate needs of research and of an increased understanding of basic biological and disease processes are also kept in view. These ongoing tensions demonstrate the crucial importance of well-informed ethical debate.

Pulling the Threads Together

This chapter has covered a large amount of diverse material, and has moved from the historical to the contemporary. However, the central thrust of all the topics has been the dissected body. The scene set by the historical section of the chapter has been crucial, since if the principle of informed consent and the ethics of bequests had not emerged, the current debate would have assumed a very different character from the one we have encountered. Additionally, asking basic questions about why cadavers have ethical significance is crucial. Delving into the centrality of altruism as an ethical guide point has also emerged as a major determinant for subsequent ethical debate.

In view of these considerations, it is all the more troubling to be faced with the number of scandals involving body parts and the retention of organs. These did not take place in the first part of the nineteenth century, but in the latter part of the twentieth century. We still have a great deal to learn and complacency is certainly not justified.

Alongside these developments are the challenges raised by increasing technological sophistication. No longer is the 'dissected body' confined to large-scale dissection, but it involves taking even smaller tissue sections for uses both now and perhaps well into the future. No mention has been made here of genetic analysis, but this of course is a possibility on any stored tissue, with all the additional ethical dimensions raised by this form of analysis.

Chapter 3
The Abused Body

Introduction

There is rarely any question that the abuse of living people is wrong, although, as we shall see, a consensus is lacking concerning ways of dealing with the present day results of past abuse. But can cadavers be mistreated? In what sense can a dead person, someone who is no longer with us, be abused? Is it the memory others have of that person that is being defiled? Maybe the human race is demeaned when one of their kind (even though now dead) is treated in a less than human way. But what is a 'less than human' way, and what does this mean when thinking about a dead person?

These are not easy questions. Can we expect to provide clear rational answers or do we rely on intuitive feelings alone? Will our intuition on this matter prove to be an important pointer to the sort of treatment we think should or should not be inflicted on the bodies of those who were once like us?

These are far from new questions. One only has to think of the minor prophets in the Old Testament, all of whom were deeply concerned with justice within their societies. Of these, Amos specifically separated out for condemnation the crimes of one group of people who, not content with marauding, pillaging and killing, directed their venom at the body of one of their enemies. Having killed a particular king, they burnt his bones to ash (in those times this was a hideously denigrating practice, unlike today when cremation is widely accepted) since killing him by itself was inadequate. Their hatred could only be assuaged by desecrating his dead body, thereby undermining his integrity as an individual. In its negative way, this highlights a crucial strand in Hebraic thinking: the importance of the dead body. This is an emphasis that persists in present day society, even though the reasoning behind it and its practical repercussions may prove elusive.

These questions highlight the emphasis one places on the intrinsic as opposed to the instrumental value of cadavers (see Chapter 2). However, no matter where the emphasis is placed, the possibility of abuse of a cadaver has to be treated seriously.

Teaching on the Clinically Dead

The clinically dead have for many years been used by students and clinicians alike to learn a variety of clinical procedures. Those health professionals involved in emergency care often use fresh cadavers to practise and teach certain non-invasive or minimally invasive techniques. Endotracheal intubation, where an incision is made enabling a tube to be inserted through the trachea (throat) to allow a person to breathe, is the procedure that has been found to be most commonly practised, but many other techniques are carried out on the newly dead by those in training (Burns et al. 1994). This training normally occurs immediately after the patient's death without gaining the consent of, or even notifying, the deceased's relatives. The long history of this practice suggests that its place in clinical medicine is widely supported, or at the very least has not raised undue concern within the medical profession. Iserson (1993) argues that using the newly dead for education is not disrespectful, but is in fact a way of showing increased respect because: 'it promotes the real value that the dead body symbolizes rather than the sanctity of the symbol for its own sake'. Iserson contends that the postmortem practice and teaching of lifesaving procedures, such as endotracheal intubation, is morally and ethically justified because there are no effective alternatives to using clinically dead patients. Additionally, the practice does not disfigure the body, is carried out with an attitude of respect, even awe, and it is essential for clinicians to become competent at performing the procedures (Iserson 2005).

It is argued that the use of the newly dead patient affords physicians and other health care workers the opportunity to perfect techniques that are either difficult or impossible to learn any other way. Burns and co-workers (1994) suggest that, provided other means for learning are inadequate, this can be justified given certain provisos. Firstly, the institution must evaluate carefully who has a legitimate need to master the technique. Secondly, only non-mutilating procedures should be permitted. Thirdly, the use of the newly dead must be the culmination of a structured training program, and candidates should be required to master the basic techniques on models, computer simulations, and other teaching aids, only using the newly dead to refine their skill. However, these writers consider that permission for the procedure must be obtained in advance, and they propose that a failure to do so would cause a further deterioration in the public's trust of the medical profession.

Many of the training programs that make use of newly deceased patients for teaching purposes do not require either verbal or written consent from the patient's families – the proportion is as high as 80–90 per cent (Burns et al. 1994; Fourre 2002). In a study of hospital departments in Australia and New Zealand, 46 per cent of departments used the newly dead in teaching but none required consent to be obtained from relatives and in only one instance was there a written policy guiding the practice (Ginifer and Kelly 1996).

A major argument used in support of using the newly dead in teaching without prior consent is that the necessity of obtaining permission from relatives would raise a significant emotional barrier for clinicians who are often hesitant to approach distraught relatives with requests of this nature. Waiting for consent would result in a delay, thereby conflicting with the need to complete the procedures before the onset of *rigor mortis*. Iserson (1993) contends that the newly dead's consent for the procedure should be presumed, without regard to relatives' wishes. Others also advocate an exception to the requirement for informed consent in this instance because of the substantial social benefit that can be gained, the fact that the dead person is not at risk of harm, and because the family should not be burdened at this time (Orlowski et al. 1990).

Pragmatic arguments of this type rely almost entirely on the *benefit* expected from the procedures, this benefit overshadowing the desirability of obtaining consent from interested parties. However, even when the nature of the benefit is not in doubt, the ease with which the value of the cadaver and interests of the relatives are overlooked is of concern. The arguments against use of unclaimed bodies noted in Chapter 2 are also relevant in this context, and should not be lightly dismissed. Similarly, caution is urged by the connections linking these procedures with those necessary for the removal of organs from cadavers for transplantation purposes (see Chapter 5).

The seemingly innocuous nature of non-invasive procedures may be deceptive, since what is done to dead bodies in the teaching of endotracheal intubation and what is done to other bodies in complete body dissection may amount to an indignity in both instances. Neither benefits the people now dead, although they both help society in general. Nevertheless, it would appear that the gulf between the procedures *is* of ethical relevance (see Chapter 2). This is the gulf between a body that remains intact, and one that will cease to exist as a recognizable entity. It is also likely that, given the opportunity to consent, far more people would be prepared to allow their bodies to be subjected to a minor procedure like endotracheal intubation than a major destructive one like dissection. An example of this is a study by Benfield et al. (1991) which found that a number of parents consented to their newly dead children being used in teaching intubation skills but not to an autopsy. One survey of older adults found that 54 per cent thought it acceptable to practise or teach life-saving skills on the newly dead, though 80 per cent considered that consent would be necessary for such a procedure (Oman et al. 2002).

Consequently, the use of cadavers for purposes like endotracheal intubation is probably acceptable to many people, although this does not convert the procedure into a routine one. A failure to obtain consent ensures that the procedures remain private, and the absence of public scrutiny and audit is never the course of choice.

Ethical concerns over teaching on the newly deceased are probably due, in part, to a closer scrutiny of how dead bodies are treated as a result of the very public scandals over organ retention at postmortems (Chapter 2). It is generally agreed that informed consent must be given for any procedure to be carried out on the newly deceased. The American Medical Association's Council of Ethical and Judicial Affairs (2002) has recommended the following guidelines:

1. Institutional policies must be in place that address training procedures on the newly dead. These policies must respect the interests of all parties involved (patients, relatives, hospital staff, trainees and society).
2. The teaching of life-saving techniques should only be carried out as a 'structured training session', and be closely supervised.
3. Physicians must make every attempt to obtain the preferences of patients prior to death, or failing this, informed consent from the next-of-kin after death. In the absence of this, the procedure must not be carried out.

Similarly, the Society for Academic Emergency Medicine has recommended that families be asked for consent prior to practising procedures such as endotracheal intubation (Schmidt et al. 2004). In the final analysis, failure to consult patients and families ensures that these procedures remain private, making them readily open to exploitation. Furthermore, the public should have a right to know if the newly dead are being used for training procedures in hospitals without consent, regardless of the repercussions for the medical profession. Secrecy will only undermine public trust in the medical profession when exposed (Schmidt et al. 2004; Wicclair 2002). Public trust must be preserved if future appeals to the public, in terms of body and organ donation for teaching and research, are to be successful.

Putting these considerations together, the judicious handling of these possibilities suggests that obtaining consent from patients prior to death is the best option, even if it does limit the extent of clinical experience available, and obtaining consent from the next of kin is a second best option.

Research on the Clinically Dead

These considerations are also relevant in the research arena. In France in 1988 there were public revelations regarding a series of medical experiments conducted on the body of a car crash victim who, although clinically dead, was being kept in a deep coma by artificial means (Dickson 1988). The doctor involved had wanted to determine whether the inhalation of nitrous oxide gas necessarily led to cyanosis (a bluish discoloration of the skin caused by lack of oxygen), and had administered potentially lethal doses of the gas to the clinically dead patient without previously informing either the patient's family or the hospital's ethics committee. The doctor behind these experiments described such patients as 'almost perfect human models, who constitute intermediaries between animal and man' (Dickson 1988, 1370).

The experiments led to storms of protest in France, and to the doctor's suspension from duties. Objections to these and other experiments on dead people were based principally on the lack of informed consent by the patient or, alternatively, the failure to consult with the patient's family. In the view of some, the patient had been treated as an object rather than a human subject, thereby exemplifying medical imperialism. The French National Association of Medical

School Teachers defended the doctor's actions, stating that experiments on the body had always constituted a necessary element of medical progress and that, in their estimation, the doctor had only been 'carrying out his duty' as a research worker (Dickson 1988, 1370). The doctor himself argued that experiments on individuals certified as clinically dead but being kept artificially alive were little different from those carried out on cadavers.

Another 1988 study involving the use of brain dead subjects tested the efficacy of monoclonal antibodies to prevent blood clotting (Coller et al. 1988). In this case the ethical issues surrounding research on the brain dead were well thought out (Coller 1989). Little research on clinically dead subjects was openly conducted after this, and it was not until 2002 that the issue was again publicly raised (Guterman 2003). Since then brain dead patients have been used to test an experimental blood oxygenating system and also for research on the differential homing of peptides to tumour blood vessels for the purpose of developing targeted cancer drugs (Arap et al. 2002). The latter research groups have also used nearly dead cancer patients whose life-supporting equipment and drugs are to be imminently withdrawn, giving a life expectancy of only a few hours. This research group and another specially established ethics committee have articulated guidelines for research on the clinically dead (DeVita et al. 2003; Pentz et al. 2003). These guidelines emphasize informed consent by either the decedent or next of kin, respectful treatment of the dead including limited duration of the intervention, the priority of organ transplantation over research, the scientific merit of the research, and the unequivocal and independent declaration of brain death or imminent death.

Issues of consent after the individual in question has died have much in common with those already discussed in relation to unclaimed bodies (see Chapter 2). What would the recently deceased have wanted? Would they have approved? Were their wishes known? In the case of car crash victims, it is more than likely that their views were not known, although if they were an organ donor this would provide valuable clues regarding their preferences. In the case of cancer research subjects, participation was seen by the family as honouring the patients' articulated values regarding altruistically contributing to medical research and treatment (Pentz et al. 2003). If no attempt is made to establish these preferences, the only conclusion to be drawn is that the deceased's wishes, whatever they might have been, are considered of no consequence. Their autonomy has been ignored.

Then there are the interests of the living – the deceased's relatives and friends. They are susceptible to harms and wrongs; they are mourning the loss of a loved one in tragic circumstances. Experimentation on the clinically dead body of that loved one, without first gaining consent, is only possible by ignoring the grief of the mourners. Failure to consult them, and the infliction of what may be perceived as an indignity on the body of someone they have respected and cared for, amounts to a disregard for their interests and autonomy.

In view of these considerations, experimentation on the clinically dead, in the absence of any consent, ignores important moral values governing the treatment of dead bodies. Although research using the clinically dead is conducted with the best of intentions, it is difficult to see how an opt-out scheme (automatic use of a person's cadaver if that person had not registered an objection prior to death) could work satisfactorily here. This system will be discussed further in Chapter 5 in connection with organ donation.

There still remains the possibility that research of this kind has a redemptive aspect. The knowledge gained from the experiments, and the impossibility of carrying out such research ethically on living human beings, may itself constitute sufficient justification – even in the absence of consent. However, the problems already noted with lack of consent remain, and if experimentation in the absence of consent is regarded as wrong, there is no way possible clinical benefits can circumvent this, no matter how alluring they appear to be.

Experiments using the recently deceased without consent cannot be supported. But what if informed consent for this type of experimentation had been given prior to death? Is there a distinction between this experimentation and dissecting a cadaver? If the patient is dead it is difficult to see that there is any difference.

But even normal consent may be inadequate. Some could argue that the recent occurrence of death distinguishes the two situations, since bodies used in dissection have been dead several months. An additional difference is that the body has not been fixed with preservatives, as have medical school cadavers, a procedure that helps depersonalize the body. One also imagines that these experiments took place before a normally timed funeral or cremation, whereas there is no immediate funeral or cremation in the case of cadavers used in anatomy departments. Interesting as these differences are, they are mainly of social significance, and should not be interpreted as ethically significant.

Finally, how does this situation stand alongside endotracheal intubation of the newly deceased? If consent is preferable for that procedure, the same surely is the case in this situation. In both instances, consent is the determinative factor, since it serves to protect the interests of all parties concerned.

Trauma Research

In 1978 the Department of Transportation in California contracted with several university laboratories to test designs for automobile air bags in actual crashes of cars at varying velocities. Since dummies had proved unsatisfactory for measuring the degree of protection for living passengers, some researchers had, with the consent of next of kin, substituted human cadavers. One congressman wrote to the Secretary of Transportation charging that: 'the use of human cadavers for vehicle safety research violates fundamental notions of morality and human dignity, and must therefore permanently be stopped' (Wade 1978). As a result, testing was temporarily abandoned despite the Department's protest that prohibition of the use of cadavers would set back progress on vehicle safety for many years (Feinberg 1985). Similar crash test research using cadavers has also been conducted for many years in France (Nau 1988) and Germany (Fedarko 1993). One series of experiments carried out in Germany was reported in the *Times Higher Education Supplement* in 1994:

> Since 1975 the Heidelberg University Clinic used over 200 human corpses for crash test research, including children's corpses. Their aim was to examine the reliability of dummies by simulating the effects of car crashes on human beings. The automobile association in Germany condemned the tests on ethical grounds. Representatives of the Catholic Church consider that they call in question reverence for the dead. There was no exterior disfigurement, and parents had given permission for the tests to be carried out.

Information from cadavers has been crucial in the design of safer steering columns, windshields, safety belts, dashboards, airbags and head restraints (Crandall et al. 1995; King et al. 1995; Mattern et al. 2004; Viano and Lau 1988). More recently, the risk of wrist and neck injuries from side airbag deployment has been assessed using prosections and whole body cadavers (Duma et al. 2003a; Duma et al. 2003b). The data obtained from cadaver experiments such as these are used to assess and inform the design of anthropomorphic dummies (see also Sances and Kumaresan 2001). Researchers must first determine the mechanical properties and injury limits of the human body under varying degrees of impact to obtain anatomically significant information by which force measurements on dummies can be interpreted (King et al. 1995; Mattern et al. 2004). Cadaver research is also necessary to determine why certain combinations of forces, such as those from side-impact collisions, cause greater degrees of injury, especially to the brain (Roach 2003). It has been estimated that the use of cadavers to optimize safety systems has saved more than 60 lives and lessened uncountable injuries per utilized cadaver (King et al. 1995). This is what Roach (2003) terms the 'ghastly necessary science of impact tolerance'.

In assessing these experiments, it is useful to use the experience of dissection as a baseline. What is the nature of the differences, if any, between experiments of this type and dissection? Next of kin had given their consent for the experiments, and no attempt was made to carry them out in a secretive way. Hence, the objections raised to some of the studies on the clinically dead do not apply here. Is the outcry, then, made on ethical or emotional grounds?

The collision experiments and dissection differ in the means employed to destroy once whole cadavers: in the former it is thought that they are violently smashed to pieces, whereas in dissection they are carefully reduced to their constituent parts in laboratories by medical technicians or students. Smashing bodies is violent and destructive, whereas dissection is analytical and scientific. The end result in both situations is destruction: generally far greater destruction in dissection than in the case of the collision experiments, which rarely produce any mutilation or gross disfigurement (King et al. 1995). On the other hand, there may be a symbolic difference (Feinberg 1985) suggesting that what is significant is the manner in which the destruction is brought about, with the violent form of destruction being regarded as offensive by many within today's societies. This is interesting, since what societies will tolerate at any particular time is relative. This emerged clearly in Chapters 1 and 2, where dissection itself was not tolerated by most societies a few hundred years ago.

Even allowing for this relativity, a symbol may be important in a world fraught with domestic and social violence, nationalistic wars, and mass starvation. Smashing cadavers, even with consent and with the object of saving lives in the future, may appear too high a price to pay for the resulting benefits. The violent destruction of dead people may in turn condone the violent destruction of living people, although this is unlikely as long as the two procedures are kept procedurally and conceptually separate.

The nature of the destruction inflicted on the cadavers in trauma research raises the question of whether truly informed consent is feasible. Is it possible for the experimental subject prior to death or relatives after death to apprehend the extent of the procedures and the consequences these will have for the cadaver? By the same token, is it possible for those bequeathing their bodies to realize what dissection involves? The simple answer is no, and yet this does not invalidate the consent that is given. Frequently, the person consenting does not want to know detailed information (Roach 2003). What is required is the provision of adequate information to make an informed decision about the general direction in which to proceed.

It is only against this background that one can turn to examine the expected safety benefits of experiments such as these, and balance these against the offence experienced by some people. Undoubtedly, there are those who are offended by dissection, but they are able to steer clear of it. The same applies to trauma experiments. There are no grounds for thinking that human dignity is placed in jeopardy by destructive experiments, but not by dissection.

In terms of the anticipated benefits of these experiments, the comparison is between considerable possible benefits in the case of the airbag experiments, but potentially only marginal educational benefits in the case of dissection. Hence, the airbag experiments may serve to enhance human value and welfare (in terms of safety issues) more than dissection ever can. This argues in favour of such experiments, especially in those societies that permit the use of cadavers for dissection.

A further illustration of what may be termed trauma research is provided by a criminal investigation in France in 1987. Following the discovery of a local woman's body at the bottom of a well, covered with quicklime and buried beneath a thick layer of concrete, a forensic pathologist ordered that bullets be fired into the heads of five cadavers in an attempt to establish the exact circumstances surrounding the woman's death. There was evidence to suggest that the victim had been shot, but the experiments were conducted to eliminate the possibility that the quicklime in which the body had been resting for many months may have been capable of causing the bullet-like holes found in the victim's skull (Nau 1988).

More recently, cadaveric specimens have been used in ballistics research to examine the damage caused by 'less lethal' weapons, which involves firing shots at unembalmed human specimens (Bir and Viano 2004; Bir et al. 2005; Voiglio et al. 2004). Cadavers have also been used in researching blast injuries, including the effectiveness of anti-mine footwear and helmets (Hayda et al. 2004). Ballistic gelatin is often used instead of human tissue (Jussila 2004), but it is not an accurate simulant of all characteristics (Boyer et al. 2005). As with automotive collision research, the data produced from cadaveric ballistics research is additionally used to assess simulants and optimize test surrogates (Hayda et al. 2004).

The bodies used in these experiments were obtained according to required national standards, and were of people who, before their death, donated their bodies to medical science. Despite this, the public reaction to reports of the French experiment, for example, was indignant (Nau 1988). Some believed that, since the bodies were donated, there were no legal or ethical issues to answer. Others questioned the scientific value of the experiment, and believed that the prior approval of an ethics committee was essential before any procedure such as this was conducted. However, there is a further consideration, and this is whether or not the ballistics experiment qualifies as the type of science to which the people involved had donated their bodies during their lifetime. Would those involved have altruistically left their bodies to medical science had they been aware of the possible use to which their remains may be put?

This scenario revolves around the extent of the 'informed' consent previously given. If it included specific reference to the type of experiment undertaken, even in general forensic terms, there appear to be no consent problems. On the other hand, if those bequeathing their bodies to an anatomy department could reasonably have believed that their remains would only be dissected by medical students, the use of the bodies in ballistic experiments appears unjustified.

However, as pointed out in Chapter 2, Fennell and Jones (1992) noted that most of those bequeathing their bodies were confused about differences between research and teaching. Therefore, consent for forensic experiments of this type may be of only limited value. What should be insisted upon is consent by next of kin to the specific experiment being contemplated, in addition to the general consent implicit in bequeathing one's body to an anatomy department. In the absence of this additional consent, the experiments are fraught with ethical uncertainty.

The 'Body Farm'

Another controversial research use of human bodies is that carried out at facilities like the University of Tennessee's Anthropological Research Facility (ARF), better known as the 'Body Farm' (Bass and Jefferson 2003). The ARF was established in 1971 by forensic anthropologist Bill Bass to conduct ground-breaking empirical research on human decomposition rates and features, information on which had previously been only anecdotal. At the ARF bodies are left to decompose in various environmental settings: in deep and shallow graves, inside cars, under water, encased in concrete, clothed vs. nude, summer vs. winter and so on. The bodies are observed undergoing the various stages of decomposition (Mann et al. 1990; Rodriguez and Bass 1985), samples are taken for biochemical research on time-dependent decay chemicals (Vass et al. 1992), insect populations are studied (Rodriguez and Bass 1983), and even odour analysis can be explored. Such studies have proved crucial in solving numerous crimes and also in investigations in conflict regions such as Rwanda and Kosovo.

The grisly use of bodies at the ARF may disgust many, but the bodies are still treated with respect – professional conduct is imperative, the specific wishes of the decedent or family are carried out where possible, and memorial services are held. The decomposition process studied at the ARF is not unnatural, although it would normally occur out of sight underground. More intrusive studies have also been conducted, including burning cadavers and amputated limbs, and sawing long bones to detect the marks left by differing saw types.

A similar facility has recently opened at Western Carolina University in North Carolina, where the mountain environment provides a contrasting climate. Plans for a facility at Texas State University have been hampered by nearby residents' complaints and fears that circling vultures could endanger a nearby airport (BBC News 2007b). A similar 'Investigative, Scientific and Anthropological Analysis Facility' has been proposed in India. However, this appears to be of an entirely different calibre. Its advertising website (www.insaaf.co.in) with its salacious and sensationalist design is inappropriate for a proposed academic facility.

The main source of bodies used at the Tennessee ARF today are those donated by either the decedent or family. Historically however, the ARF has used mostly unclaimed bodies and was established with only limited ethical discourse on the acquisition, treatment and disposition of human remains (Christensen 2006). The extreme nature of the research conducted at the ARF makes informed consent even more important than usual; the vague decision to donate one's body to 'research' is insufficient.

Dead Mothers and Living Babies

In February 1981, a 24-year-old woman was admitted to hospital with suspected meningoencephalitis (a disease causing swelling of the brain). She was 23 weeks pregnant and the fetus was still alive and healthy. When, 19 days later, the woman was declared brain dead, the decision was taken to maintain her vital organs on life-support in an attempt to save the fetus. After five days, a 26-week-old infant was delivered by Caesarean section, and the woman's life support was discontinued (Dillon et al. 1982). This case was the first successful attempt to maintain a maternal cadaver in order to incubate a fetus until viability. In August 1993, a baby boy was delivered by Caesarean section 105 days after his mother was declared brain dead (Lindemann Nelson 1994). In a more recent instance, in May 2005, Susan Torres was declared brain dead after long-dormant melanoma had metastasized to her brain; she was 15 weeks pregnant. Her husband and parents, certain that she would have wanted to save the baby, decided to keep Susan on life support and 13 weeks later a healthy baby girl was delivered (McCrummen 2005). Such successful cases are rare, however, and some of the unsuccessful ones have proved even more contentious. The following case taken from Anstötz (1993, 340–1) is one such example:

> At noon on 5 October 1992, Marion Ploch, a dental assistant, was on her way home from work. She was 13 weeks pregnant. On the road … she crashed her car against a tree. Because she was suffering from a fractured skull, the young woman was taken by helicopter to the university hospital in Erlangen. There she was treated at the intensive care unit. Her parents were informed that Marion had no chance of survival. On the evidence of comparable cases in the literature the doctors thought the fetus would have a real chance of survival … [and] sought the parents' agreement to keeping Marion coupled to the apparatus that was maintaining her bodily functions.
>
> On 8 October the doctors confirmed that brain death had occurred, but did not turn off the respirator. On 9 October, Marion's parents sent a cry for help to a newspaper. Amid emotional public discussion, the doctors did everything possible to keep the fetus alive. On 16 November, almost six weeks after the diagnosis of brain death, the fetus was spontaneously aborted.

Regardless of whether the outcome of such a case is a living infant, we need to enquire to what extent benefit is gained by any of the parties involved. It appears not to be in the interests of the cadaver to be maintained in a normal physiological state for a few weeks or months. On the other hand, it may be in the interests of the fetus for development to proceed normally and for the fetus to be born healthy, that is, if a fetus can be said to have interests. On the other hand, it may also be in the interests of the father. However, the cadaver is merely serving the interests of another, and this may bring distress to those close to the deceased. Consequently, if the fetus does benefit, it is at the expense of others whose interests are possibly being overridden. The extent of the good is unclear, even though the intention is to save a life by allowing a yet-to-be-born human being to experience personal life.

It is this intention that predominates in the majority of postmortem pregnancies, where doctors' actions are driven by a duty to rescue the fetus. This position is illustrated by the case report from a San Francisco medical team who maintained a 27-year-old woman in a brain-dead state for nine weeks, when they wrote: '… this case seems to present a straightforward instance of the medical rescue of the fetus from death' (Field et al. 1988). More significant than this, however, they argue that even if the mother had made a specific objection prior to her death against such action, the placement of her body on life support in an attempt to bring the fetus to viability is still justified:

> Although legal and ethical tradition does respect the previously expressed
> wishes of the decedent with regard to inheritance, disposition of remains and
> transplantation, this tradition would not seem to override in importance the
> obligation to save an endangered fetal life ... the mother is not harmed; no right
> of hers is violated, and great good can be done for another. (Field et al. 1988,
> 821)

This contention is based on the principle of beneficence, according to which
any action must offer clear gain to the recipient, while at the same time posing
only moderate risk to the benefactor. But does this principle oblige medical
professionals to intervene on the fetus's behalf? Although the benefit to the fetus
may initially appear substantial (its life may be saved, when without intervention
it would die) the fact that it will most probably be born prematurely (with the
attendant risk of health impairment and disability) and may subsequently require
repeated and prolonged medical treatment leads one to question whether there is in
fact a clear benefit to the fetus and subsequent child (Lindemann Nelson 1994). For
the woman-now-dead, the suggestion that she cannot be harmed and, therefore, no
longer has interests requiring consideration is, as the quote above acknowledges,
incompatible with respecting a deceased person's wishes. A person-now-dead has
interests that outlast his or her lifetime (see Chapter 2). A cadaver has both intrinsic
(that is, it is an end in and of itself) and instrumental (that is, it can be used as a
means to an end) value, and any separation of these sources of value is artificial.
By suggesting that the woman's wishes prior to death are of no consequence when
deciding on continuation of life support, Field and co-workers (1988) fail to take
account of the cadaver's intrinsic value, and as a result show disrespect for the
person-now-dead. Moreover, the benefit purportedly justifying the deviation from
a 'tradition' of respecting the prior wishes of the recently deceased is, as we have
shown, not as unequivocal as the authors claim.

The presumption is sometimes made that a pregnant woman would wish
her pregnancy to be carried to term after her death, obviating the need to seek
further justification of the procedure. However, such a presumption is not justified
(Lindemann Nelson 1994; Purdy 1990). She may not have wished to produce a
motherless child, and burden her grieving partner with sole care of a small infant.
Neither may she have desired to extend the grieving process for her family and
friends, as they watch her dead body being artificially sustained for a period of
weeks or even months (Lindemann Nelson 1994). According to Purdy (1990), in
the absence of a woman's informed consent, the decision to use her cadaver as a
'human incubator' is a violation of her autonomy, leading to the view that pregnant
women are 'mere fetal containers rather than ... first class citizens with their own
pressing interests' (Purdy 1990).

These considerations appear to outweigh the sometimes heart-rending
circumstances, including the pleas of would-be grandparents that a grandchild will
partially compensate for the loss of a child. But what about the argument that good
can come out of tragedy? The potential for good is present in some of these cases,

but this has to be weighed against the disadvantages. A difficulty in this situation is that it is frequently unclear whether a live child will constitute a 'good' for those intimately involved in the tragedy – the child may compound the tragedy. Of course, those who believe a new human life is always an immense good, will argue that the fetus/child should be rescued regardless of other considerations.

Age of the Neomort: An Unrealistic By-Way?

Over 30 years ago Willard Gaylin took a science fiction look at ways in which society could utilize cadavers (Gaylin 1974). In this, Gaylin imagined institutions of the future where brain dead bodies, now euphemistically called 'neomorts', are maintained and put to various important medical uses. Gaylin imagines bioemporiums resembling a cross between a pharmaceutical laboratory and a hospital ward. He envisages hospital beds lined up in neat rows, each with a freshly scrubbed neomort under the clean white sheets. The neomorts would have the same recognizably human faces they had before they died, the same features, even the same complexions. Each would be a perfect natural symbol, not only of humanity in general, but of the particular person who once animated the body and had his or her life in it.

Using such 'preparations', medical students could be taught the techniques of rectal or vaginal examination without fear of disturbing or embarrassing real patients. Experiments could be performed to test the toxicity of drugs by judging their effects on real human bodies without endangering anyone's health or life. Other neomorts could be used as experimental subjects, thereby eliminating use of live animals such as dogs and mice. The advantages of neomorts would be that they feel no pain, and raise no ethical issues connected with animal welfare concerns. Other neomorts could serve as living organ banks or living storage receptacles for blood antigens and platelets that cannot survive freezing. From others could be harvested blood, bone marrow, corneas and cartilage, for transfusion or transplants into living patients. Still others could be used to manufacture hormones, antitoxins and antibodies to be marketed commercially for the prevention or cure of various medical ailments.

This may seem far-fetched, and the uses to which these neomorts would be put have been somewhat overtaken by surgical simulation laboratories. Nevertheless, it is worth delving into it as a theoretical exercise, since some of the ethical considerations relevant here may also be relevant to the plastination exhibitions (Chapter 4). In formulating a response to the neomort scenario, previous considerations are still relevant, especially those concerning the prior consent of the people concerned and their relatives. Consent may also be required of those making use of such emporiums, since it is important to the people who may benefit from them that they approve of the source of the material. If they are horrified by where it has come from, or simply have reservations about its origin, they should be in a position to refuse to participate in such a venture.

Neomorts have a close relationship to us, as they were once like us. Hence, we are accountable to neomorts and must subdue our enthusiasm to view them simply as bountiful resources, despite their potentially invaluable contribution to the advancement of medical knowledge (Arnold 1977; Jonas 1974). Dignified treatment of these brain dead individuals is paramount.

There are also other considerations. The first is the definition and character of brain death, and what society should do with those who are brain dead (see Chapter 8). How do we view those who are very much like us, but will never again show any of the recognizable responses characteristic of human persons? Second, neomorts appear to represent a dramatic extension of the kinds of efforts used to sustain gestation in brain dead mothers, efforts that, as discussed previously, are surrounded by ethical ambiguity. The ambiguity in the case of neomorts is much greater on account of the general nature of the goals: providing services for a population, rather than serving the needs of the dead woman's offspring, partner and parents.

The third consideration concerns consent. What if adequate consent has been given by appropriate people for bodies to be treated like this? What if a 'consent form to become a neomort' has been willingly and freely signed? Neomorts can then be located somewhere along the continuum from the endotracheal intubation of the newly deceased at one end, to whole body dissection at the other, probably close to trauma research. Hence, in terms of the values we have already enunciated, they would be ethically acceptable. And yet, we are left with severe doubts.

In the end, neomorts may prove nothing more than deceptive fantasies; technologically feasible, but solving none of our ethical dilemmas. Care has to be taken to ensure that they do not imperil our moral sensitivities, and that they do not downgrade our moral evaluation of those who were once like us. It is possible to make use of cadavers for limited research purposes once stringent ethical criteria have been satisfied, but this is a far cry from extensive use of them in an apparently unlimited fashion.

The Nazi Legacy

At this juncture, we are making a major conceptual leap: from dead bodies to living ones. In doing this, the moral values discussed in connection with our treatment of dead bodies will serve as a useful basis for thinking about our treatment of living bodies. Assessment of the one realm helps to inform assessment of the other.

Background

The medical profession was intimately involved in the experimentation on human subjects that characterized Nazi policies. In 1929, several physicians formed the National Socialist Physicians' League to coordinate Nazi medical policy. As early as 1933, when Hitler came to power, 2,800 doctors, or 6 per cent of the profession, had already joined the League (Proctor 1992). Doctors joined the Nazi party earlier and in larger numbers than members of any other professional group – a membership rate three times that of the general population (*Bulletin of Medical Ethics* 1990). By 1942, around half of all doctors were members of the party, with 7 per cent members of the SS, the paramilitary organization within the Nazi party (Proctor 1994). As such, doctors were voluntary participants in the theorizing, planning and executing of Nazi racial policies. Post (1991, 17) comments that '… doctors were not the victims of the Nazi ideology and party, but rather active and responsible agents committed to hygienic theories with roots in Social Darwinism'.

According to Seidelman (1989) physicians in Nazi Germany played a crucial role in the eugenic and racist programs of the Hitler state – becoming involved in eugenic and racial selection, enforced sterilization, ghettoization, inhumane experimentation and extermination. Grodin and Annas (1996, 1682) have stated that '… physicians and the German states used each other: the Nazis used physicians to perform horrific tasks that would have been much harder to accomplish without the use of physicians, and physicians were granted privileges and power in the Nazi regime'.

Wikler and Barondess (1993) report that before the war years many physicians were involved in a program aimed at sterilizing the 'hereditarily deficient'. Physicians were required to identify patients who posed a risk to the genetic purity of the German people, such as the feeble-minded, schizophrenics and manic depressives, the genetically deaf or blind, carriers of Huntington's disease, epileptics and chronic alcoholics (Müller-Hill 1994). These patients were then subjected to enforced sterilization – around 400,000 people in all (Proctor 1994). During 1940 and 1941 physicians were involved in a program referred to as 'euthanasia Aktion T4'. Fit and productive Germans of all faiths were sorted from those considered to be unproductive – the mentally ill, retarded or disabled. More than 200,000 of those classified as 'defective' were rounded up and murdered. These events, supervised at all times by physicians, but also involving nurses, psychiatrists, dentists and pharmacologists (Johnstone 1989), helped to prepare the way for the events of the Holocaust.

Medical involvement in other aspects of the euthanasia program included the processing, in 1939, of 283,000 questionnaires from mental hospitals by nine professors of psychiatry and 39 doctors. Of these questionnaires, at least 75,000 were marked by these doctors to signify that the patients were to be gassed. Professor Fritz Lenz, later to be appointed professor of human genetics at the University of Gottingen, justified this program as a purely humanitarian one, and unrelated to safeguarding 'our hereditary endowment' (*Institute of Medical Ethics Bulletin* 1989).

Nurses, too, were involved both directly and indirectly in the 'medicalized killing' program (Johnstone 1989). Steppe (1992, 749) has written that '… today, we still know too little about the role that nursing played in those crimes [against humanity], but this much is clear: nurses followed orders and were involved in all phases of the systematic annihilation of masses of people'.

Often the nurse's role was to determine the drug dosages required to bring about the deaths of selected 'patients', or ensure the individual's cooperation by explaining the importance of the injection for treatment of some condition. It was not uncommon for nurses themselves to administer lethal drug doses (Lifton 1986). Nurses working in psychiatric institutions and in the concentration camps often packed up the personal belongings of their patients and accompanied them as they were transported to the death site (Steppe 1992). Midwives were required to report the births of all defective infants to Nazi physicians, with the usual result that the newborns were marked for death, while some nurses were involved in administering lethal drugs to children deemed under the euthanasia program to be either 'subnormal' or 'excitable' (Lifton 1986).

An example of unethical practices from an anatomical perspective is that of Professor Julius Hallervorden, a section leader at the Kaiser Wilhelm Institute for Brain Research in Berlin, who exploited the euthanasia program to collect the brains of its victims. Speaking to an American interrogator in 1945, Hallervorden explained that he had requested the extermination centre in Brandenburg-Görden to send him as many brains as possible and that '... there was wonderful material among these brains, beautiful mental defectives, malformations and early infantile disease. I accepted these brains of course. Where they came from and how they came to me, was really none of my business' (quoted in Pross 1992, 37).

Hallervorden, himself, is reputed to have removed many of the brains collected from this extermination centre (*Institute of Medical Ethics Bulletin* 1989; *Bulletin of Medical Ethics* 1990). During 1942, he reported that he had been able to dissect the brains of '500 feeble-minded individuals'. By March 1944, he had received 697 brains in all. It has also been reported that some prisoners at the concentration camp, Auschwitz, were executed at the order of Professor August Hirt, director of the Anatomy Department of the University of Strassbourg, in his efforts to complete a collection of skulls of 'all' races and peoples. A total of 86 Jewish prisoners from Poland were executed, and their bodies transferred to Hirt's department (Hildebrandt 2008; Lachman 1977; Seidelman 1989).

These horrendous activities represent an extreme example of the ethical perplexities raised by the use of human material and human tissue. Despite their extreme nature, they highlight an inescapable issue for all interested in learning about the human body, and especially about its structure: the origins of human tissue cannot be ignored.

Contemporary Issues

In early 1989 claims were made that tissue samples from the cadavers of victims of the Nazi executions were being used in histology slides in undergraduate classes in German medical schools (Dickman 1989b). Skeletons were also involved. The cadavers of executed criminals had been used for teaching purposes in Germany prior to 1933, but the number of such cadavers rose very considerably between 1933 and 1945. On investigation at Tübingen, four slides prepared from two cadavers of Nazi victims executed for political reasons were found. On further investigation, it was discovered that between 1933 and 1945, the University had received 1,077 bodies from an execution site in Stuttgart (Seidelman 1989). In Heidelberg, three slides dating back to 1941 and 1943 were found, as was a skull from the early 1940s. These had probably come from cadavers received from a prison and from the mental hospital at Hadamar (known for its involvement in the euthanasia program). All these items were subsequently removed from the University's collections. Many more slides of the brains of Nazi victims were found in the collections of the Max Planck Institute for Brain Research in Frankfurt, having been received by the Kaiser Wilhelm Institute for Brain Research in Berlin from a euthanasia centre between 1940 and 1944. Of 697 brains received in this way, 30 tissue samples were demonstrated to have come from these brains, and up to 400 samples have been linked circumstantially with euthanasia centres (Dickman 1989a). Following these disclosures, the Max Planck Institute agreed to cremate all slides and samples in its possession dating from the years 1933 to 1945.

A related, longer-standing controversy is that of the citing of data from Nazi experiments (Max 1989; Seidelman 1988). For instance, Moe (1984) described the use of data from Nazi hypothermia experiments performed at Dachau (see also Weitzman 1990). Over 45 research articles written since 1945 have used Nazi data, principally relating to hypothermia (Fernandez et al. 1970; Molner 1946). During World War II the German air force was losing a large number of men to hypothermia, as pilots and crew were shot down into the cold waters of the North Sea. The purpose of the Nazi's immersion-hypothermia project conducted at Dachau was to collect information about normal human physiological responses to cold and determine the effectiveness of various rewarming strategies (Pozos 1992). Between August 1942 and May 1943 an estimated 360–400 hypothermia experiments were conducted on around 280–300 victims, of whom approximately 90 per cent died during the project (Berger 1992).

Subsequent debate has centered on the ethical acceptability, or otherwise, of making use of the resulting data on hypothermia. The specific arguments in this debate will be detailed below, but at least one author suggests that citation of this work is inappropriate on scientific grounds alone (Berger 1990). Berger's analysis shows that the Dachau experiments were carried out without any organized protocol and that the methods employed were flawed and haphazard. For example, basic variables, such as subject age and nutrition level, amount of time spent in the water, specific body and bath temperatures, the method of rewarming used, and the subjects' clinical condition, were not consistently reported. There is evidence that some observations were falsified and fabricated, there are numerous internal inconsistencies in the data, and in many instances, conclusions are drawn that are not justified by the results presented. Furthermore, Sigmund Rascher, the director of the project, was not a trained scientist, and was apparently motivated by the attractions of power and material gain (Berger 1994). He was eventually charged by the Nazis with various crimes, among them scientific fraud, and was executed. Berger (1990, 1440) has written that '... on analysis, the Dachau hypothermia study has all the ingredients of a scientific fraud, and rejection of the data on purely scientific grounds is inevitable'.

Berger (1992, 131) has also suggested:

> ... the compromised scientific base of the Dachau hypothermia experiments renders the ethical discussion about the use of the results moot, inappropriate, and even harmful. Had it been appreciated that the data from Dachau are not reliable, the entire effort would have been dismissed by scientists and the ethical debate probably never would have gotten off the ground.

Contrary to this, some writers believe that, although the results of the project as a whole are invalid, certain individual findings (for example, the rate and characteristic pattern of cooling, and fatal temperature range) are scientifically sound and still potentially useful (Katz and Pozos 1992). If this position is adopted, the debate over the *moral* acceptability of citing this data remains relevant.

A similar example that has gained widespread attention in recent times is the use of an anatomical atlas created during World War II by Eduard Pernkopf. Pernkopf was an ardent Nazi and it is suspected that many of the subjects of the illustrations in the atlas were victims of the Nazi regime (Israel and Seidelman 1996). Pernkopf was head of the Medical Faculty at the University of Vienna in 1938, and a member of the Nazi party, and it is known that the University's Anatomy Department regularly received the cadavers of those executed by the Nazis (Charatan 1997). There are two diametrically opposed views over the continued use of Pernkopf's atlas. Opposing positions have been put forward by Hildebrandt (2006) and Riggs (1998). There are those who would like to see the atlas banned on the basis of the evil implicit in its creation and because this evil will be further perpetrated, or even justified, by the continued use of the atlas. Additional arguments are that the banning of the book would prevent a profit being made from the exploitation of human life and that the atlas is easily replaced by other anatomical atlases or teaching materials. Others argue for the continued use of the atlas (with a note on its provenance) on the grounds that: good can be derived from evil; the continued use of the atlas is the most fitting tribute to those who died; and the atlas is a valuable tool for teaching not only anatomy but also ethics and history.

Reaching a decision about the acceptability, or otherwise, of using this data depends on whether one accepts or rejects the moral complicity argument. The notion of moral complicity works from the premise that if the execution of people under the Nazi regime was morally wrong, then the subsequent use of material derived from such executions is also morally wrong (see The Centrality of Moral Complicity). There is an indissoluble ethical link between the two, with the origin of the material affecting what can later be done with it. A long established position has been to argue that the unethically derived material can be used ethically on condition that the wrongs are acknowledged and recurrence is prevented (Weitzman 1990). This argument could be applied to the use of Pernkopf's atlas with the provisions that the details of its origin are acknowledged and that it is used as a tool to heighten ethical awareness and educate future generations, thus preventing any possibility of recurrence.

An additional consideration with regard to the use of the atlas is that it is widely considered to be a classic anatomical atlas, of such high quality that it would be extremely difficult to replace (Hildebrandt 2006). If this is the case, it could be argued that continued use of the book (with appropriate historical note) is warranted. However, the use of other unethically obtained anatomical specimens for teaching purposes has been rejected on the grounds that they could be replaced by other human material obtained today in an ethical fashion. This suggests that, while there may be very rare instances where the results of unethically derived material may be used for research purposes (there is no way in which that work could ever be repeated ethically), it is highly unlikely that this justification will ever apply to teaching materials.

Another issue raised more recently is the continuing use of eponyms, that is, titles of medical disorders named after the person who originally described them, who in this case were associated with Nazi medical atrocities. 'Reiter's syndrome' is a rheumatological syndrome named after Hans Reiter, who as president of the Reich health office was responsible for devising, approving and supervising numerous heinous and unethical medical experiments. There have been a number of calls for a renaming of this syndrome to strip the eponymic honour given thus far to such a man (Panush et al. 2003; Panush et al. 2007; Strous and Edelman 2007). In addition, substituting the term 'reactive arthritis' would help to clarify the outdated and clinically imprecise terminology and classification. A number of other doctors who committed medical crimes in Nazi Germany have various syndromes named after them, including Hallervorden, Scherer, Spatz and Eppinger. The latter conducted experiments on Gypsy prisoners at Dachau concentration camp to test the potability of sea water; the subjects died of extreme dehydration after six to twelve days (Strous and Edelman 2007).

Scientific research can be viewed as having two aspects. First, there is the research itself, that is, how the research is carried out. This includes the design and methodology of the experiment: the way the experiment has been set up, the hypothesis put forward, and the methodology used to test the hypothesis. Second, there is the data, that is, the results of the experiment. Research is deemed to be good science (it is scientifically valid), if it has focused on attempting to answer logical questions using the correct methods and if it has recorded the data accurately and used appropriate analytical procedures. Where these do not occur, the study is scientifically invalid: it is bad science. Most of the Nazi experiments are considered to be 'bad science and bad ethics' (Angell 1990). However, it would be too simplistic to assume that 'bad science and bad ethics' necessarily go together. Simply because research is conducted in an unethical manner does not mean that the experimental results will automatically be scientifically invalid.

Similarly, research that is scientifically valid is not necessarily based on a sound ethical foundation: we must not assume that all good science is ethical (Angell 1990).

Further Unethical Experiments

The unethical experiments conducted by Japanese physicians and scientists during World War II are by no means as well known as are the actions of the Nazis, to the extent that Powell (1981) has described them as 'a hidden chapter in history'. Between 1930 and 1945, Japanese researchers conducted trials of biological warfare, using various disease agents such as anthrax, cholera, typhoid and typhus. A network of bacteriological warfare units is known to have existed mainly in China and throughout south-eastern Asia (Rich 1995). The principal testing site was a prison camp known as Unit 731 situated on mainland China, which included an airfield and planes used for dropping bombs containing biological agents. It is reported that at least 11 Chinese cities were used as targets for biological warfare attacks, and that in one case, a bomb containing bubonic plague-infested fleas was dropped on a Chinese city causing almost 100 deaths (McNeill 1993). British, American, Australian and New Zealand prisoners of war were also said to have been used as subjects. Williams and Wallace (1989) have reported that prisoners in Unit 731 were often executed once they were no longer fit for germ tests and have described some of the experiments that were performed including dehydration, prolonged exposure to X-rays, replacing prisoners' own blood with horse blood, and freezing prisoners' limbs and subsequently thawing them by various methods. Other procedures ranged from the deliberate infection of prisoners with syphilis to investigate methods of preventing the disease, to the explosion of fragmentation bombs beside prisoners' legs and buttocks to test the effectiveness of the bombs as a means of causing gas gangrene infection. More than 3,000 people were reported to have been killed at Unit 731 (McNeill 1993).

Unlike the perpetrators of wartime experiments in Germany, Japanese researchers involved in unethical experiments were given immunity from prosecution by the United States in exchange for information on biological warfare. Many of these investigators became influential and respected figures in modern Japan (Powell 1981). Williams and Wallace (1989) have listed 15 Japanese doctors who took part in the fatal experiments during the war and who subsequently went on to become professors within university medical schools and research facilities. Other men who worked in Unit 731 were allegedly given high ranking positions in Japanese institutions and companies, and many received awards for their contribution to society (McNeill 1993).

In offering immunity from prosecution to the Japanese experimenters, the Command of the American Occupation Forces placed greater value on obtaining information relevant to the development of the United States' own biological warfare program than on bringing to justice those responsible for using highly unethical methods. In addition to secretly granting immunity to the experimenters, the US government deliberately denounced and withheld vital evidence from the International Military Tribunal for the Far East.

According to Powell (1981), the American Forces Command placed great weight on the fact that the Japanese experiments were 'the only source of scientifically controlled experiments' on the effects of biological warfare on human beings, and they feared that trials of the scientists would lead to this information becoming available to other countries. Thus the motive for the United States' differential treatment of war criminals in Germany and Japan was political expediency (McNeill 1993). Calls have been made for the current US government to issue an official apology and offer some form of compensation to the victims of Japanese medical war crimes (Nie 2006). Nie's second proposal (2006) is for international codes of medical ethics and human rights to include a clause forbidding any state or group from being an accessory to unethical medicine and other human rights violations.

Ongoing Experimentation

Medicine is always in danger of moral failure, and all too frequently individuals and even groups of practitioners succumb.

The well-known Tuskegee syphilis study ran from 1932 through to the mid 1960s. In this study, hundreds of poor African American men suffering from syphilis were denied treatment known to be effective in order to study the natural course of the disease (Jones 1981). The length of this study and its blatant disregard of clear-cut moral values stands as an indictment of US medicine. One does not need rigorously thought-out ethical principles to recognize the tragic dimensions of this study.

The Jewish Chronic Disease Hospital case in 1963 appears to have gone further than the Tuskegee study, since it involved active intervention. In this instance, 22 chronically ill people were injected with live cancer cells in an investigation to examine the rate of rejection of the cells in patients already afflicted with diseases. Patients were not told they were subjects in an experiment; on the contrary they were led to believe that the injections were part of their treatment (Katz 1972).

Then there were the government-sponsored radiation experiments carried out in the United States at the height of the Cold War on military personnel, hospital patients, institutionalized children and prisoners (Brandt and Freidenfelds 1996; Moreno and Lederer 1996). The subjects in this instance were nothing more than guinea pigs, serving as experimental subjects in studies designed to inflict injury and distress. Once again, their unethical nature was blatant.

A slightly different example is provided by the New Zealand cervical cancer case. This ran from 1966 to the mid 1970s, and in it women diagnosed with carcinoma *in situ* were left untreated to determine the natural course of the disease. As a result, a number of women developed invasive carcinoma unnecessarily and some died (Cartwright 1988). The unethical nature of this study in many ways mirrors that of the previous examples, since the women concerned were kept in ignorance of their role in this experiment and hence were unable to consent to the procedure to which they were subjected. The lack of informed consent was the determinative factor in this case.

The Centrality of Moral Complicity

The two related controversies that have previously been encountered, that of the use of Nazi-derived material, and of any data resulting from study of this material, share the same central ethical principle – that of *moral complicity* (Weitzman 1990). According to this, those who use material or data obtained unethically are themselves implicated in the original unethical practices. It is as if they themselves are acting unethically (Max 1989). The ramifications of the moral complicity stance are discussed more fully in Chapter 5. In broad terms, only two responses are possible to this dilemma: the moral complicity principle either is *accepted* and use of the material or data is banned, or the principle is *rejected* and the material or data is used as any ethically derived material or data would be. The former response will be considered first since this has provided the impetus for this debate.

Lest we imagine that moral complicity is of interest to scientists alone, it is worth broadening our vistas by reference to the arts. In Israel all live performances of the music of Richard Wagner have been banned since 1938 to the present day (Waterman 2006). This is due to the fact that Wagner was a rabid anti-Semite; his music was a favourite of Hitler's and used by the Nazis at public rallies. There was also a temporary ban on live performances of two other German composers tainted by Nazism, Carl Orff and Richard Strauss. This is a striking example of acting out the consequences of the notion of moral complicity.

A number of reasons are normally given for adopting what we shall refer to as the negative stance (the acceptance of moral complicity and its implications). These reasons are independent, although they have a common core, and most advocates of moral complicity use elements of each of them to bolster their position.

A first reason for refusing to use the material or data stems from a desire to show respect for those killed under appalling circumstances. It is argued that respect is most clearly demonstrated by cremating any remains still extant, and by refusing to use them or any Nazi-derived data for scientific or clinical purposes today (Post 1991). Such refusal is regarded as the sole way in which a nation's guilt can be absolved. It is also argued that the personhood of those experimented on without their consent should be vigorously asserted, and that this can only be done by refusing to use any material or data emanating from an unethical source.

A second reason is that its use implicates people today in Nazi crimes. The contention here is that those using the material become one with the perpetrators of the original crimes, since our motives today cannot be isolated from the manner in which the material was obtained in the first place. From this view, even to cite unethical work is to validate it, and to demonstrate the existence of a continuous thread linking apparently respectable current research with ethically abhorrent work in the Nazi era. The essence of the moral complicity argument is that this link alters the character of the apparently respectable studies today, by tainting the pedigree of the material or data on which they are based. This argument has been well expressed by Max (1989, 133): 'To use the data legitimizes the original abuse. If the violation occurs in the course of the experiment, then the findings are tainted. To use them is a kind of reward, which creates a climate that does not deter similar violations by others.'

A third reason for refusing to use the material or data was the participation of physicians in Nazi policy-making and exterminating practice (*Institute of Medical Ethics Bulletin* 1989). Regrettably, similar attitudes have been encountered in physicians in a number of much more recent situations (Jones 1989b, 1990). In other words, the unethical behaviour behind the Nazi atrocities was not an isolated aberration, but is far more deep-seated than frequently admitted. Hence, the argument goes, the conscience of today's medical profession needs to be prodded and elevated so that the possibilities of such events recurring is minimized.

Powerful as these arguments may appear, the contrary stance is also a serious one. This alternative position, a willingness to use Nazi-based material or data, is based on a perceived ability to separate the evil of the original act from the good intentions of contemporary work. A central argument here is that, regardless of current standards, the data continue to exist. If the data are valid, they cannot be invalidated no matter how objectionable the unethical behaviour used to obtain them in the first place. From this viewpoint, data obtained unethically are no different from data obtained ethically. The major proviso is that the data are scientifically valid; only when there is any question about this (Berger 1990, 1992, 1994; Weitzman 1990, see The Nazi Legacy – Contemporary Issues), should the data be ignored. In similar vein, clinical treatment devised in an unethical manner will still prove of value as a form of treatment. Its efficacy is unaffected, even if the way in which it was devised is considered unethical and is regretted.

This basis underpins the validity of citing Nazi data, such as the work of Rudin on the inheritance of schizophrenia, Von Verschuer on the genetics of twin research, and to a lesser extent Mengele on the developmental anomalies of cleft palate and harelip, as well as the cold exposure data gathered by Alexander in 1946 (Seidelman 1988). Since such data are unobtainable using today's more rigorous ethical standards, they are of especial significance in some areas of scientific work. It was this argument that proved persuasive for the Command of the American Occupation Forces in their decision regarding the appropriate treatment of Japanese doctors and researchers involved in conducting unethical experiments during World War II (see Further Unethical Experiments).

When allowed to stand alone, this principle is open to the objections cited above – that it lends credence, and even respectability, to the unethical experiments themselves. It gives the impression that one should be grateful for the Nazi experimentation, even while rejecting its moral character. Is this moral complicity in its most hypocritical form? One way around these objections is the stringent application of the principle provided by Moe (1984). She has argued that good may be derived from evil, on one condition: that the horror inherent in the data is addressed. Moe (1984, 7) has written:

> A decision to use the [unethically obtained] data should not be made without regret or without acknowledging the incomprehensible horror that produced them. We cannot imply an approval of the methods. Nor, however, should we let the inhumanity of the experiments blind us to the possibility that some good may be salvaged from the ashes.

Weitzman (1990), writing from a Jewish perspective, believes that it is our obligation to take the knowledge we possess and use it in a responsible manner. He writes: 'if we can save a life, we must, for we are commanded to do so.' However, in view of the terrible price at which the knowledge was bought in this instance, he recognizes certain stipulations governing the use of Nazi-derived knowledge. These are, firstly, that we never forget the victims, and fully acknowledge the moral flaws in procuring the material whenever it is used. Second, we must continue to learn the lessons of the Holocaust, and third, consideration should be given to limiting access to Nazi research data, to ensure that it is handled sensitively. It is at this point that the response we have encountered to the unethical experiments in Japan is to be queried. Recall that the US government offered immunity from prosecution to the researchers involved, in exchange for access to the information and results that were obtained through unethical experimentation. Not only did this response make use of available data, but it also modified the condemnation of those responsible for carrying out the unethical experiments. By doing the latter, it went beyond mere use of data; it failed to condemn (perhaps effectively condoning) the unethical actions themselves, and as a result tainted the American Command.

A second argument for the utilization of data obtained by unethical means is that the scientific and clinical studies carried out today, on the basis of clearly delineated and accepted ethical principles, have no link to studies carried out in the 1930s and 1940s on the basis of concepts such as racial hygiene. To ensure that such concepts are never again incorporated into medical thinking an understanding of ethical principles is paramount. Greene (1992) argues that, because the Holocaust has implications for everyone presently involved in biomedical research and practice, the details of Nazi experiments should be taught to students openly and regularly rather than banned. Furthermore, they should be presented, not as a separate ethics or history course, but in the context of the normal medical curriculum. In this way, he suggests, students will be forced to confront the reality of the experiments: that they were 'medical' and 'scientific' and, furthermore, that they were events of relatively recent history.

According to those who argue in this manner, society at large, and the medical profession in particular, have, over the past 50 years, learned the crucial significance of informed consent for all medical research and treatment. Even though this is a lesson that stems from the Nuremberg Code and hence from the Nazi experience, learning this lesson opens the way to the use of Nazi-derived data without compromising present standards and practice. Central to this argument is the contention that we now operate within a vastly different ethical framework from the Nazi one of the 1930s and 1940s, and that our present code is not likely to be prejudiced by reference to a limited amount of data or material emanating from objectionable Nazi practices.

While we do not wish to disagree with these sentiments, the medical profession has to be continually vigilant to ensure that its members do not depart from the highest of ethical standards. This is always a possibility, as so tragically demonstrated on so many occasions in the past. Erring on the side of providing too much protection for patients is preferable to providing too little protection.

Chapter 4

The Plastinated Body

The Transformation of Dissection

As we have seen in previous chapters the conventional picture of anatomy is that of dead bodies lying moribund in dissecting rooms or of body parts and organs in bottles on shelves in anatomy museums. This is the world of medical education, and it is a world that has cast a powerful spell over generations of medical students in particular. Dissecting cadavers has been core business for aspiring doctors, and of course it was the need to obtain bodies that moulded the history of anatomy in the eighteenth and nineteenth centuries.

Integral to dissection have been the methods of preserving bodies, with the emphasis squarely on formaldehyde mixtures. However, regardless of the precise mixtures employed, and these have varied, the dominant impression remaining with students and staff has been the smell of the fixatives, the texture of the wet tissues, and a general aura of greyness and drabness. No wonder the dissecting room has so often been regarded as an unwelcome and forbidding place, perhaps even a hostile place where learning takes place in spite of the environment. As cadavers undergo dissection, and as the once whole body becomes fragmented, the scene of dissolution intensifies.

And yet dissection and all it stands for has played a crucial role in anatomical education, as students have done their best to come to terms with the organization of the human body. And yet a query remains. Are there no better ways of presenting human material, ways that are less off putting and more welcoming? In previous chapters we have touched on some possibilities. In the present one we are confronted with a technical development that still utilizes actual human material and real human bodies. This owes its existence to a new preservation technique, plastination.

This in itself need not be a cause of controversy or general public interest. In itself, plastination simply enables human material, body parts and organs to be handled far more readily, without the smell of formalin or the wet, dripping specimens. Pre-dissected body parts subsequently plastinated are what anatomists refer to as plastinated prosections. While they are generally used to complement actual dissecting regimes, they enlarge the scope of what can be studied and introduce far more educational variety into the dissecting room and museum.

Used in this manner the technique of plastination serves as an excellent adjunct to conventional dissecting room learning. The context within which these plastinated human specimens are used is entirely educational. Their value is as an educational tool, and no one would have raised any eyebrows at the advent of this new technique. However, this educational use does not aim to plastinate any body parts larger than limbs or the torso, since an educational rationale has no place for larger pieces. This is because students have to see inside the regions, as they attempt to follow vessels and nerves, and trace intricate relationships between organs. And they have to do this for themselves. This is a learning environment, and that entails hands-on experience.

Plastination, as the general public has come to know it, utilizes numerous whole body specimens, aligned to emphasize activities with which we are familiar in our everyday lives. This is the world of large-scale exhibitions, where the educational element, however it may be described, is of an entirely different character from that encountered in the dissecting room. Alongside this, and perhaps dominating it, are powerful forces of entertainment and commercialism. And it is to these that we shall devote our attention in this chapter, since these public exhibitions take us far from the strictly educational character of the dissecting room with its carefully orchestrated ethical dimensions.

It is difficult to appreciate how the development of a new technique for preserving the dead human body can have had such far-reaching repercussions as that of plastination. In the hands of Gunther von Hagens, an expert craftsman and entrepreneur, plastination forms the basis of a dramatic series of exhibitions, *Body Worlds*. The sterile world of anatomical cadavers has been transformed into a life-like plastic world of running, skiing, baseball playing 'plastinates' (gestalt or whole body plastinated cadavers). While the modernity of some of the pieces is striking, so is the resemblance of others to poses found in Renaissance art and in some instances modeled on *motifs* of Michelangelo and Vesalius.

The controversy stems from 1995 when *Body Worlds*, with its public display of plastinated specimens, made its first appearance at the National Science Center in Tokyo. However, this particular exhibition did not produce much in the way of controversy. That occurred when the exhibition moved to Mannheim, since it was at this time that theologians and anatomists entered the fray. Never before in modern times had an exhibition of this nature been staged with such panache and forthrightness. By breaking a host of unspoken conventions, it astounded and angered one group after another, chief among which were theologians and anatomists. While the reasons for their negativity varied, they highlighted what to them was the astounding insolence of von Hagens, as one cherished boundary after another was dashed. He was accused of endangering human dignity, and of bringing a whole profession – that of anatomy – into disrepute. For anatomists cadavers were to be dissected and analyzed in private, far away from the prying eyes of the public. It is, they argued, inappropriate for body parts and dissected torsos to be exposed to public gaze, since this would reduce them to objects of morbid curiosity and effete entertainment. In doing this, their dignity as human remains would be placed in jeopardy, a concern of as great significance for anatomists as for theologians. In short, *Body Worlds* was an object of offence, challenging all that we hold dear about the remains of people who were once like us.

Responses of this nature reflect moral repugnance at what is viewed as a denigration of humans in our treatment of them. Foremost behind this response is the lifelikeness of these exhibited cadavers, a lifelikeness that appears to contradict their deathliness. In giving to dead bodies characteristics of the living, sitting, standing and even running, they are being made into something they are not. In doing this, those behind the exhibition are exploiting their memory, and defiling what it means to be human. In the face of these criticisms von Hagens and his supporters have defended the exhibition as a celebration of the wonder and fragility of the human body.

Body Worlds 1 has since transmuted into *Body Worlds 2*, *3* and *4*, and the number and variety of plastinates has proliferated. Von Hagens has exhibited his plastinates in Japan, the UK and over much of the United States, garnering media attention worldwide.

It is no exaggeration, then, to claim that *Body Worlds* is an enigma, more so to anatomists than to almost any other group. This statement may itself seem to be an enigma, because surely anatomists of all people should feel at home in an exhibition of dead human bodies. Death on display is their trade. Surely, they should not be squeamish at the sight of dissected people with 'exploded' joints and skulls, or in their cross-sectioned glory. They may not be squeamish, but neither are they convinced.

The unyielding educational rationale of the anatomy museum has little in common with the publicity-seeking, attention-grabbing bravado of any of the four *Body Worlds* exhibitions. Health science students are replaced by the general public, the educational drive to understand details is replaced by wonder at the body's muscles, nerves and organs, and the secrecy surrounding the dissected body is replaced by an explicit openness unknown in the world of anatomy.

The move from the highly uncertain and tentative world of eighteenth-century dissection into the scientifically sterile world of the modern dissecting room is one we have taken for granted. However, it has come at a cost, namely, that the world of the cadaver has been deliberately shrouded in a funereal mist, by excluding the general public from knowledge of what occurs during dissection (and postmortem examinations) and what is done with and to retained tissues. Unable or unwilling to debate the ethical and cultural issues surrounding the dissecting process, anatomists (and also pathologists) have relied upon favourable and often vague legislation. It has been generally assumed that what went on in these halls of mystery is ethical, and in many societies that has largely been the case, even though a few major ethical lapses have occurred.

The lack of serious thinking about ethical issues surrounding use of the human body and human remains has left anatomists and many other medical people peculiarly unprepared to meet the challenges of very recent years, especially those of *Body Worlds*.

These exhibitions can be used to illustrate basic anatomical and physiological functions. The organization of body systems like the digestive, respiratory and urinary systems can be demonstrated in appropriately dissected body regions.

Cross sections of the body can be used to display bones, muscles, organs and vessels in amazing detail: all precise and accurate.

The effects of disease processes can also be readily demonstrated and explained. What are the effects of smoking on lungs or alcohol on the liver? What do artificial hips or knees look like?

Anyone entering an exhibition like this could be forgiven for thinking that what they were seeing were models of the human body – very life-like plastic models. The shock is to realize that these are not models but real (dead) people, who were once living and breathing and thinking just like us. Instead of having been buried or cremated they are standing there before us, albeit in a dissected state. It is this life-likeness that both attracts and appalls onlookers.

This is a new way of depicting and demonstrating the dead human body. Although plastination is used extensively in anatomy departments for teaching and research purposes, whole bodies are not displayed in such dramatic fashion. There is no need to do so for university level teaching, where the emphasis is on the structure of organs, or the relationship between muscles, nerves and vessels. It is, therefore, to the plastinates that we need to turn our attention.

Historical Forerunners

The preservation and display of real human bodies did not originate with von Hagens. Its more direct antecedent lies in the work of Honoré Fragonard in the eighteenth century. This French anatomist excelled in preserving cadavers and used the educational merits of the technique for artistic endeavours well beyond that of von Hagens's.

Working between 1766 and 1771, Fragonard produced thousands of anatomical specimens intended for students of comparative anatomy, but his most interesting works are the 50 or so elaborately posed *écorchés*.[1] These include the dramatic *Horseman of the Apocalypse* and the aggressive *Man with a Mandible*.

Fragonard's work is now contained in the Fragonard Museum at the Veterinary School in Maisons-Alfort, which describes him as 'choos[ing] to stage Death, using the human body as artistic material according to his fantasy'.[2]

His work would today elicit general revulsion, as epitomized in the all-too-aptly titled *Human Fetuses Dancing a Jig* and various sexually moralizing and erotic specimens. Though von Hagens has deliberately modelled one of his pieces, *Rearing Horse with Rider*, on Fragonard's work, he is yet to stoop to such levels.

The social climate of eighteenth century Paris was not too dissimilar to that of today, where the public's appetite for scientific understanding encouraged the display of anatomical specimens such as Fragonard's. As is the case today, some

---

1   *Ecorché* is a French term meaning an anatomical specimen with the skin removed to display anatomical detail.

2   See the museum's website: http://musee.vet-alfort.fr/ (accessed 1 April 2008).

of Fragonard's academic contemporaries deplored his work as artistically brilliant but scientifically banal (Simon 2002).

Frederik Ruysch (1638–1731) had been making similarly unsettling anatomical preparations in the Netherlands (Luyendijk-Elshout 1970; Rifkin et al. 2006). He had access to a large amount of anatomical material that he often dissected and displayed in large embalming jars.

What causes modern disquiet, however, was the preponderance of children and fetuses dressed in pretty embroidered garments, or often just their sleeved arms presenting various organs for view. Ruysch's museum also contained dried preparations featuring fetal skeletons in various poses arranged in landscapes formed from gall- and bladder-stones with vascular trees and bronchial tubes as a bizarre kind of anatomical flora. These dioramas were reproduced in the engravings of Cornelius Huybert.[3] The fetuses hold symbols of life's transience, with one weeping into a handkerchief made of mesentery. The aim appears to have been 'to endow death with elegance and moral value' (Luyendijk-Elshout 1970).

Anatomists such as Ruysch and Fragonard transformed and presented specimens in a crudely scientific fashion, and their aims appear to have been primarily art and popular amusement, though with an educational spin off.

As such they inhabit a category of anatomist distinct from that of Vesalius, who used art as a medium with the principal aim of education. Nevertheless, even this was not education in the sense of a narrowly medical orientation and with a limited audience in mind. Vesalius' illustrations, for example, were intended to educate the general public as well as medical students and also to serve as models for painters and sculptors.

And so we have to ask into which category, popular amusement or general education, does *Body Worlds* fall? Von Hagens identifies himself with anatomists such as Vesalius and Leonardo (Institute for Plastination 2006d), although without entirely eschewing an association with Fragonard's art (Institute for Plastination 2006a).

The question itself raises another consideration, and this is the extent to which one can move from the seventeenth and eighteenth centuries directly into the twenty-first century. The cultural contexts are quite different, as are the educational and entertainment contexts. After all, people like Vesalius and Leonardo were undertaking research: they were the bench scientists of today. Von Hagens inhabits a different world: in no way can his plastinates be classed as research. They mimic what has gone before, no matter how technically brilliant they may be. The strongest sense in which they are educational is, therefore, in a teaching sense. However, he is breaking no new ground in teaching, since all the details of anatomical structure and relationships manifest in *Body Worlds* are well known.

If we conclude that *Body Worlds* has more of the characteristics of entertainment than of education, we still have to ask what it is competing against in a twenty-first

---

3   See the Dream Anatomy website: www.nlm.nih.gov/exhibition/dreamanatomy/da_ dream_part.html (accessed 1 April 2008).

century environment. In a highly visual world of graphic images, including those of horrific accidents, our attention is caught by similarly graphic images in the exhibition hall. Perhaps this explains in part why the gestalt plastinates dominate *Body Worlds*. Education does not demand them, but entertainment does.

Displaying Human Remains as Artistic Objects

Over the centuries there are numerous illustrations of cadavers having been employed for non-scientific purposes: human organs as part of artistic displays, and skulls and skeletons in plays or trade displays.

Many artistic works have revealed the human body in its nakedness. However, an artist like Kiki Smith has taken this further and portrayed solitary organs, human orifices, and bodily fluids, including dynamic situations such as semen leaking down a man's leg and milk trickling from a woman's breasts (Tallman 1992). An artist like this is attempting, not simply to describe the body, but to address its processes, failures and traumas within the context of depicting the body as a social construct. Smith is attempting to underline the relevance of our experience of the body and of the realization of the ways in which this experience is manipulated by external forces. She argues that society's attitudes towards the body have shaped and controlled the relationship of individuals to their bodies. In her art she attempts to achieve this by presenting images that may shock and disgust. She also entices viewers to address issues such as death, prevailing attitudes towards the body and gender, and the most primal of human concerns, including the difference between self and other, and between that which can and cannot be controlled. As Tallman (1992, 175) writes: 'In all these instances, it is the body that unites us – and separates us, ultimately and irretrievably.'

In 1989 the director of a London gallery and a sculptor were convicted of 'outraging public decency' because they had exhibited a sculpture incorporating human fetuses in earrings (Häyry and Häyry 1991). In 1997, the British sculptor Anthony Noel-Kelly caused a furore when he exhibited his sculptures, which involved casts of various parts of the human body, sprayed with silver and gold gilt (Sawday 1997). Kelly was sentenced to nine months' imprisonment and the laboratory assistant at the Royal College of Surgeons, who had helped Kelly obtain the body parts, was given a six-month suspended sentence.

Interesting as such criminal charges are, what grounds are there for such a reaction? No physical harm had been caused to anyone, including the dead bodies. Some people could possibly have been shocked by such exhibits, but these would be limited to those attending the gallery. There could have been moral or symbolic harm, but this itself raises further considerations, since human mummies, skeletons and fetuses are regularly exhibited in museums. Do these cause moral harm?

While Kelly's sculptures did not actually involve human tissue in the finished work, the use of body parts was essential for its completion and one assumes that, while the individuals gave their consent for their body to be used in medical teaching and/or research, they did not envisage their body being used for this artistic purpose. In the case of the fetuses, it is highly unlikely that the mothers' consent had been obtained to keep – let alone exhibit – them. However, this has been an extremely common situation. When exhibited in museums, the aim is to instruct interested members of the community in aspects of fetal development. In other words, the display focuses on the fetuses as objects of serious scientific interest. While this does not legitimize all such displays, it narrows the context within which they may be exhibited, with particular fetuses serving as representatives of the fetal community.

By contrast, when used for artistic purposes, they cease to function as representatives of the fetal community, becoming instead tools to further an artist's objectives. However, artists wishing to depict fetuses could equally well use replicas for this purpose, since the object of attention is not fetuses *per se*. But what if mothers gave their permission for fetuses to be used in this way for artistic purposes? Consent in this instance may be inadequate and misguided, since it does not have the best interests of the fetal community at heart, the interests of which should take preference over the far more restricted interests of women who decided to abort the fetuses in question.

Using fetuses in this way demeans the interests of fetuses in general, suggesting as it does that fetuses are brought into being in order to serve as artistic objects. Even if this was not the motive (as it undoubtedly was not), fetuses can only be employed as decorative objects if this is what they are for. A similar argument applies to the incorporation of skulls, skeletons or body parts in sculptures or multi-media works of art.

The Advent of Plastination

While artworks incorporating human material, such as the fetus earrings, have been the subject of general opprobrium, the plastination exhibitions pioneered by Gunther von Hagens have been welcomed by many. Some expert commentators may have decried *Body Worlds* as a grossly inappropriate use of human material, but this has been disregarded by large sections of the public who have flocked to see *Body Worlds*. To begin to understand this phenomenon we must first look to the origins of the plastination technique.

Plastination is a method of preserving human or animal tissues by replacing the tissue fluids with plastic. The specimens preserved in this manner are dry, odourless and durable, thereby making them much easier to handle, while at the same time the process retains the natural structure of the tissues. The plastination technique is a relatively recent innovation, pioneered by Dr Gunther von Hagens at Heidelberg University in 1978 (von Hagens 1979) and new techniques are constantly being developed and refined.

Specimens for plastination are firstly embalmed to halt decomposition and dissected to display the desired structures. The plastination process is composed of two exchange phases. Firstly, the specimen is placed in an acetone bath and the tissue fluids are replaced by acetone through diffusion. In the second phase, forced impregnation, the acetone is extracted under a vacuum and gradually replaced with liquid plastic. The impregnation process can take only a few days for thin body slices, but weeks for whole-body specimens. The specimen, while still pliable, is then placed in the desired position, and finally it is hardened by curing with a special gas. The types of plastic used and the precise process are modified to best preserve various types of tissue and thin slices. Ultimately, plastics have replaced the 70 per cent of the tissue that was originally composed of water and lipids. The rest of the tissue, from the cells to the natural surface relief, remains unaltered down to the microscopic level.

Plastination is now used widely for the teaching of anatomy to health science and veterinary students (Jones 2002a; Latorre et al. 2007; Reidenberg and Latiman 2002). There is significant pressure on the anatomy curriculum to reduce the amount of teaching from cadaveric dissection. However, modern teaching aids such as models and computer programs often fail to convey the true size, shape, colour and texture of the real tissue. Plastinated human specimens are far superior to anatomical models, since they illustrate real human material with its considerable anatomical variability mirroring what is found in the more traditional dissecting room cadavers, which themselves reflect the variability found in life. Plastinated specimens, however, offer the convenience of anatomical models in terms of storage, durability, safety, aesthetics and cost effectiveness (O'Sullivan and Mitchell 1995). Body part slices can be correlated with computed tomography (CT) and magnetic resonance imaging (MRI) scans for reference and radiological teaching.

Plastination proves particularly useful in producing gross specimens for examination in pathology teaching. Compared to the traditional wet pathology specimens kept in display cases, plastinated specimens better demonstrate specific features, proving more popular with students (Dawson et al. 1990). Specimens can also be coloured before plastination to highlight specific anatomical features (Steinke and Spanel-Borowski 2006). The role of plastinated human specimens in teaching is, therefore, assured.

Moreover, their place as a research tool is being increasingly appreciated since they preserve delicate structures and their interconnections, enabling them to be traced microscopically (Jones 2002a). Ultra-thin plastinated slices can be used to construct precise three-dimensional computer models of anatomical structures (Sora et al. 2007). Plastination techniques have also been used to study topic areas as variable as the female urethra (Fritsch et al. 2006), the carpal tunnel (Sora and Genser-Strobl 2005), and skin ligaments (Nash et al. 2004). It is becoming clear that they have advantages over traditional histology techniques and that they allow ready movement between macroscopic and microscopic perspectives.

Uses such as these in teaching and research are uncontroversial; their value within academic and educational contexts is unrivalled. Plastination as an educational tool, which was the original reason for its development, raises no especial ethical queries. The same cannot be said for its derivative use in the *Body Worlds* exhibitions, since this takes us into substantially different realms, anatomically, socially and ethically.

Plastination as an Art Form

These exhibitions raise perplexing questions. Are their objectives principally anatomical or artistic? Do they set out to educate or entertain? The ethical queries about issues of informed consent and the bequest of bodies for dissection extend to philosophical ones about whether plastinates have more in common with plastic anatomical models than with traditional human cadavers. Or perhaps plastinates are making philosophical statements about death and mortality. Since the life-like poses of the plastinates give the impression of being alive rather than dead, are the donors seeking immortality through plastination?

As we saw in Chapter 1, the Europe of 300–400 years ago was intrigued with the human body. Anatomists, such as Vesalius, collaborated with artists to produce illustrations of astounding anatomical accuracy, but also of aesthetic beauty. Sawday (1995, 103) writes:

> No matter to what level the dissection has reached, the body in these images is still alive. In both pre- and post-Vesalian illustration, of course, this convention was taken to extraordinary lengths, as flayed and dissected bodies ambled through pastoral landscapes or reclined in richly furnished chambers, as though oblivious to the violent reduction to which they have been subjected.

This description could equally apply to von Hagens's plastinates, and it is this tradition that he has deliberately appropriated. Von Hagens has intentionally modeled himself after the long tradition of anatomy artists. Even the black fedora he religiously wears is based on that which the anatomist Dr Nicolaes Tulp wears in Rembrandt's painting of him (Institute for Plastination 2006c). His aim to 'democratize anatomy' is allied with the ethos of the Renaissance anatomists and was upheld in the public autopsy he performed in 2002, the first for 170 years (BBC News 2002).

If a reversion to the culture of Renaissance anatomy and its public availability is von Hagens's aim, it appears that he has reached it. On personally experiencing the exhibition, Walter (2004b, 616) writes:

> It feels like we are back in the sixteenth century, before anatomy classes were restricted to medical students. The body's been closed up for two or three hundred years, and now von Hagens has opened it up for Joe Public again. He really *is* in the Renaissance tradition. I watch visitors' faces and they look like Dr Tulp's students in Rembrandt's painting.

Coming Face to Face with Plastinates

The *Body Worlds* exhibitions contain two broad categories of human specimens: body parts and the whole body or gestalt plastinates. The body parts reflect modern medical illustration from the early nineteenth century to the present day. By contrast, it is the plastinates that dominate and that represent a new development in the display of cadaveric material. However, even more striking is the manner in which many of them are displayed.

The gestalt plastinates are shocking to the modern eye, which has become accustomed to the reduction of the body to its component parts. However, this would not have been the case for audiences living between the sixteenth and eighteenth centuries when anatomy art was in vogue. As we have already seen, this was epitomized by the work of Vesalius, with his representations of the whole body, often partly dissected, and given a semblance of life by the apparently active poses of the body. His dissections and sketches that appeared in his landmark *The Fabric of the Human Body* in 1543 were revolutionary, featuring as they did accurately detailed skeletons and muscle-men (*écorchés*) posing partly dissected in a rural landscape.[4]

It is from anatomists and artists of this era that von Hagens frequently claims a historical precedent for his work. What is so striking about many of the gestalt plastinates is that they have been dissected and shaped to make them resemble artistic forms familiar from Renaissance art. For example, the *Skin Man* plastinate, with his flayed skin held aloft, is recognizable as St Bartholomew from Michelangelo's work in the Sistine Chapel (1508–1512). This motif was used by Juan Valverde de Amusco, the Spanish anatomist, in his 1560 anatomy textbook (*Anatomia del corpo humano*).[5]

Other examples abound. Von Hagens's *Praying Skeleton* is immediately recognizable as a plastinated version of the pose used in the 1733 picture by William Cheselden.[6] The *Angel* plastinate, whose back muscles have been everted to form wings, is familiar from Jacques Fabian Gautier d'Agoty's *Flayed Angel* of 1746,[7] a picture of which adorns the exhibition walls. The *Thinker* plastinate, an arterial corrosion cast that leans on a pedestal contemplating a head, almost precisely mimics the pose of one of Vesalius' skeletons, the pedestal of which bears the inscription in translation: 'Genius lives on, all else is mortal'.[8]

However, the plastinates are not limited to reflections of Renaissance art, since *Body Worlds* also contains many images familiar from modern art. For example,

---

4　See the Dream Anatomy Gallery online: www.nlm.nih.gov/exhibition/dreamanatomy/da_g_I-B-1-07.html (accessed 1 April 2008).

5　See the Dream Anatomy Gallery online: www.nlm.nih.gov/exhibition/dreamanatomy/da_g_I-B-2-01.html (accessed 1 April 2008).

6　*Osteographia, or the Anatomy of the Bones*, London, 1733.

7　*Myologie complètte en couleur et grandeur naturelle*, plate XIV, Paris, 1746.

8　Andreas Vesalius, *De humani corporis fabrica libri septem*, Basel, 1543.

the *Drawer Man* is reminiscent of Salvador Dali's *Anthropomorphic Cupboard*, while the muscles of the *Runner* flutter out as with the Italian futurist Umberto Boccioni's 'Unique Forms of Continuity in Space' (Wetz 2000).

These artistic links are reinforced by the images of Renaissance anatomy art on banners that hang throughout the exhibitions. It remains to be asked if these references to the Renaissance are meant to somehow legitimize von Hagens's work. This may be his intention as he styles himself a modern anatomy artist, a Renaissance man in the contemporary world. However, von Hagens is manifestly more than this.

Important as these artistic allusions may be, one gets the impression that von Hagens is aiming to reach a far wider audience for whom such references are largely indecipherable.

Accordingly, many of the *Body Worlds* plastinates are posed as if participating in some sporting activity, including basketball, athletics, soccer, gymnastics, ballet, hurdles, baseball, archery and skateboarding. The very breadth of the sports represented ensures that at least one of them will connect with the viewer. The plastinate who holds aloft an Olympic-type flame embodies the added dimension these sporting plastinates have of exhibiting the functional physicality of the body in all its pursuits.

Some of the newer plastinates include particularly modern themes, such as the *Caller* who stands talking on his cell phone. And then there is the *Poker Playing Trio* which features in a scene in the James Bond film *Casino Royale* (Der Spiegel 2006). Perhaps this is democratization at work, and yet one is left wondering why von Hagens departs in this way into modernity. By doing this he eschews the image of the Renaissance man. He gives the impression of being the entertainer, rather than the philosopher searching for meaning in the face of human death and dissolution.

Over the years the *Body Worlds* exhibitions have had a mixed reception from the public. Because the original exhibition in Japan was well received, the outrage elicited by the German shows came as a surprise, but was no doubt driven by the history of Nazi atrocities and subsequent sensitivity to bioethical transgressions (Working 2005). The UK shows also faced significant antagonism, which Walter concludes is due to a number of distinct factors: Britons rarely view the recently dead at funerals or even the dry dead (e.g. Catholic relics), the practice of reusing graves is considered unacceptable, whereas it is common in other European countries, and the abuse of human remains by avant-garde artists and doctors has had a high profile (Walter 2004b). In contrast, in the United States the exhibitions have proved hugely popular, with little public opposition. Von Hagens attributes this to the open mindedness, curiosity, focus on health and body consciousness of the average American (Working 2005). Schulte-Sasse (2006) contends that in the United States the exhibition has undergone significant changes in context and presentation that have enhanced the museum ethos and made the exhibition more respectable and thus more publicly appealing.

What's the Difference between a Corpse and a Plastinate?

The removal of the 'exterior face' (skin and surface features) is a crucial aspect of the *Body Worlds* exhibitions, as highlighted by the advertising slogan 'fascination beneath the surface'. The absence of skin provides anonymity to the individual plastinates, although it does reveal the individuality of their internal features, what von Hagens calls the 'interior face'. It also makes the plastinates more accessible to the viewer, since with their skin removed the plastinates look less like a corpse and make it harder for the viewer to identify the specimen as a real human person like themselves (Walter 2004a). For many this helps dispel negative associations of death.

This raises the question of the status of the plastinate and the respect subsequently due to them. Are they to be considered the equivalent of a corpse, or are they more like a plastic anatomical model? Von Hagens addresses this issue by delineating a 'system for categorizing the various forms of post-mortem corporeal existence' (von Hagens 2001, 274). Von Hagens defines a corpse as a dead body that is decomposing and is to be mourned. From this he distinguishes both wet and dry cadavers that have been preserved by various natural and artificial means; the plastinates fit into the latter category. Plastinates have undergone a major qualitative change with 70 per cent of the original tissue having been replaced with plastic.

And so we are faced with a real, if deeply perplexing, question: Is the plastinate any longer a human body? Barilan (2006) points out that while water and fat have been removed in the process of plastination, more 'significant' constituents such as proteins and nucleic acids remain. However, he also adds that the 'significance' of these constituents is culturally determined. Kuppers (2004) asks, 'Does the plastic preserve the flesh, or is the flesh gone?'. The plastinate certainly retains many human qualities and much of the cadaver's physical substance, but a considerable transformation has taken place. All the familiar characteristics of a dead body have been removed, causing the viewer to perceive the plastinate as something less (or something more) than a cadaver, though still 'retaining enough of a corpse-like identity to require some respect' (Walter 2004b, 621). The significance of this transformation varies according to the viewer's values and preconceptions. Does the process of plastination shift the body further down a continuum from dead body to unidentifiable modified tissue to even a plastic model? Or does the process of plastination create a completely new substance and a category of body not previously conceived?

At one end of the spectrum the plastinate is *more* than a visual depiction of a human body. In this, it stands in contrast to the greatest artistic works of Vesalius and Leonardo. In similar manner the plastinate is *more* than a plastic model of a human body. At the other end of the spectrum the plastinate is *less* than the corpse of a recently deceased person, as plastics have replaced biological tissue. A limited qualitative change has taken place, but it is not a total transformation. The biological 'mould' remains, and it is this that imparts both individuality and humanness to the plastinate. This mould is less definitive than that of the preserved cadaver in a dissecting room, but it has not been eradicated.

The body cannot have disappeared, neither has it disintegrated. The 30 per cent that remains is what bestows upon it ethical significance as human remains. The plastinate occupies an intermediary position between a corpse and a plastic model, but it is far closer to the former than the latter. Hence, in viewing a plastinate, we are viewing a highly modified human form, and from an ethical stance it is this that necessitates treating it with respect and ensuring that it is accorded whatever dignity we consider human cadavers should be given.

Communicating with Plastinates

As we have seen, the life-like poses of the gestalt plastinates are firmly established in the tradition of Renaissance anatomy art. The purpose for this was probably two-fold: to show the connection between anatomical form and physical function, and also to serve as a commentary on human destiny (Sawday 1995).

Von Hagens has appropriated both purposes as justification for the active postures of his plastinates. In addition, he claims that he poses the plastinates in these ways to commemorate the life, rather than the death, of the donor.

He has moved in this direction from one iteration of *Body Worlds* to the next. Consequently, while the plastinates in *Body Worlds 1* had a static and lifeless appearance, that to some viewers seemed anxious and frightening (Weiss 2006), those in *Body Worlds 3* are thought to be far more welcoming. Von Hagens justifies the active poses by saying, 'specimens that have been plastinated without such gestures often appear doll-like by comparison' (von Hagens 2000, 34). The intention has been to get away from presenting dead bodies in their 'deadness' (Skulstad 2006), and so the later exhibitions are designed to be less about dead bodies and more about the dynamic body, about life.

It is for this reason that the newer plastinates are placed in more emotionally engaging positions, with more serene facial expressions, helping the viewer to 'connect' with the plastinates. In addition, these are animated by the imagination of the viewers to suggest living, moving bodies (von Hagens 2001). The absence of a protective case also helps the viewer relate to the plastinate, imagining it as just another body standing in the crowd.

However, the further one moves from the lifeless appearance of the corpse the greater the interpretive element that is being introduced. The Vesalian illustrators introduced Italian landscapes in an attempt to legitimize dissection and the work of the anatomist. Von Hagens introduces games and sporting activities to legitimize, not anatomy, but his own version of anatomical commercial exhibitions. These poses give the impression of life and vitality, and represent activities that are highly significant culturally, and yet the cadavers are as lifeless as any conventionally preserved cadaver. Nevertheless, they have served their purpose as cultural icons.

Depersonalization and Re-personalization

There are two opposing conceptual movements occurring in the preparation and display of the plastinates in exhibitions such as those of von Hagens. First, as already stated, the cadaver is depersonalized by the removal of the skin and external identifying information, and also by the substitution of much of the tissue with plastic and the resultant sensory effect. Thus the plastinate is made physically approachable and emotionally acceptable as it (according to von Hagens at least) is no longer a decomposing body to be mourned.

This is followed by the re-personalization of the plastinate, by the addition of naturalistic poses and familiar accessories (e.g. chess set, soccer ball or cell phone). It is this second transformation that both incites disquiet from some spectators and is deemed necessary by von Hagens to engage the viewer (Walter 2004b).

These dissecting and reanimating tasks, the depersonalizing and re-personalizing processes, are purportedly required to achieve the stated aim of creating a palatable and popular exhibition that will educate the general public. This may also be the major reason for the lifelike poses – to serve as a means of attracting sufficient numbers of the public to make *Body Worlds* a highly successful commercial venture.

Each process constitutes a step in the transformation of the corpse into the plastinate-for-display. Depersonalization drives a wedge between the person who was once that body and the anonymous plastinate. For many this is a source of dissonance. But dissonance arises again as the re-personalizing process aims to provide the plastinate with the accoutrements of a living human being.

While one can criticize von Hagens for slanting the manner in which the plastinates are displayed to enhance their commercial viability, the readiness with which some of his critics (e.g. Burns 2007) condemn plastination as a violation of human dignity is unhelpful. Depersonalizing the cadaver to be used in education (or even entertainment) may actually protect the dignity of the deceased. The re-personalizing process is highly problematic on account of the impression it conveys of blurring the distinction between the living and the dead, rather than because it imperils human dignity. Perhaps it is more our pained sensibilities, perturbed by the transformation of plastination, that cause us to reach for the readily available protestation of human dignity.

Between Art and Science

The flagship *Body Worlds* exhibition induced and signalled a change in the way the general public could approach the human body and death. By observing the bodily interior without the messiness of flesh and decay, without the emotional connotations of death, and without the fear-filled clinical setting, the viewer is able to shrug off that which would have previously held him at a distance. Death has been made more palatable.

In accomplishing this feat, far more people are let into the secrets of the body's interior. However, this democratization of the body is itself a threat to a taboo that protected a host of professional secrets. No wonder then that much of the academic criticism of *Body Worlds* has come from the medical-scientific establishment that views the technique of plastination exclusively in a medical-scientific context. Sawday (1995) has commented that, while it is currently virtually impossible to think of the body outside a prevailing medical-scientific discourse, this was not always the case. Von Hagens gives the impression of wanting to break this dominance, and celebrate once again the virtues of the Renaissance anatomy artist.

The *Body Worlds* exhibition can, therefore, be seen according to a medical-scientific ethos or an artistic ethos, or a mixture of the two. Additionally, each can be approached as education or entertainment, or as a blend of both. It is this diversity that proves so problematic when assessing the nature of *Body Worlds*, as it transmutes from *Body Worlds 1* to *2*, *3* and *4*.

Von Hagens's work is often debated in the context of a distinction between art and science, but how easily can such a conceptual division be made? In former times the two were often fused in both philosophical and practical terms. In analyzing the work of Fragonard, the French eighteenth-century anatomist, Simon (2002, 76) concludes that 'the distinction between art and science in the context of anatomical preparations really became clear only in the course of the nineteenth century'. Martin Kemp describes this change as the 'draining of obvious ornamentation, stylishness, and pictorial seductions from much of institutionalised science', creating what he calls the 'non-style' of modern science (Kemp 2000, 4). The distinction is palpable when Kemp compares the work of Vesalius and others with the medical illustration of *Gray's Anatomy*, which he describes as 'the most remorselessly unexciting book ever written on an engaging subject' (Kemp 2000, 71). Von Hagens belongs to the world of Vesalius and not that of *Gray's Anatomy*, although one can question the validity of Kemp's depiction of *Gray's Anatomy* or any comparable anatomy text or atlas.

The novelty of this division between art and science causes boundaries to be blurred, clouding any discussion about work such as von Hagens's that seeks unfeasibly simplistic conclusions. Moore and Brown (2004) note that von Hagens's work can be viewed as a response to the recent calls for a reintegration of the humanities and sciences, which, however, has proved to be less palatable than it was in theory.

There is certainly a general interest in learning about the body, and the proliferation of copycat plastination exhibitions[9] has proven that there is a market to be tapped. The body has become a popular topic in many museum exhibits,

---

9   The two principal copycat exhibitions, *BODIES ... The Exhibition* and *Bodies Revealed* are promoted by Premier Exhibitions and run in the United States and England respectively. Other copycat exhibitions include *The Amazing Human Body* in Australia, *Our Body: The Universe Within* in the United States, *Mysteries of the Human Body* in South

and the dead body frequently features in TV programs such as *CSI: Crime Scene Investigation* and various spin-offs. Linke attributes this 'contemporary fascination with corpses' to 'an intense desire for realism and authenticity among a consumer public haunted by the contemporary struggles with memory, history and temporality' (Linke 2005). Von Hagens also acknowledges the 'tremendous desire for unadulterated realism' amongst a public living in a 'media-dominated world' as one of the key attractions of *Body Worlds* (Linke 2005). He capitalizes on this by advertising the exhibitions with the caption 'The Anatomical Exhibition of *Real* Human Bodies' (emphasis added).

It is interesting that these comments all relate to the medical-scientific context, and not to the artistic ones. Perhaps there is no escape from this ambivalence. One gets the impression that the artistic ethos is of far greater importance to von Hagens than to the general public. Nevertheless, it may well be that it is the potentially substantial artistic merit involved in creating the plastinates that enables them to be objects of medical-scientific interest.

Some commentators have taken issue with von Hagens's habit of attaching his signature and the date of creation to the gestalt plastinates (Burns 2007). This is certainly problematic, implying a degree of ownership and artistic manufacture that is barely appropriate for one working with human material. Although it is distasteful to compare von Hagens to a sculptor working with human flesh, there is no doubting the eminent skill displayed in his dissections, skill of a level that cannot truly be appreciated by those without dissecting experience (Jones and Whitaker 2007). Such artistic craftsmanship is regularly found within science, for example in the surgeon who performs a particularly difficult procedure with flair and efficiency. Von Hagens himself aptly uses the word '*Könnenskunst*' [skilled art] to describe this proficiency (von Hagens 2001, 273). However, it remains debatable whether his labour merits a signature. Von Hagens may be concerned with establishing the authenticity of his plastinates amongst the proliferation of copycat exhibitions, in which the poses he has used appear to have been copied. This is a legitimate concern since some of these exhibitions use unclaimed (as opposed to bequeathed) bodies, an issue to which we now turn.

The Importance of Voluntary Donation

Many objections to *Body Worlds* lose their sting when one considers that most of the donors appear to have given fully informed consent to the processing, use and display of their bodies. It could be contended that the donors did not truly appreciate what their final form would be, but again this is negated by the fact that over 7,500 individuals have signed up to donate their bodies, many after viewing the exhibitions. The institute seeks the donors' input on how they wish

---

Korea, *Jintai Plastonomic: Mysteries of the Human Body* in Japan and *Cuerpos entrañables* in Spain.

to be displayed once plastinated, although it is unclear how much say the donors ultimately have. Did the *Soccer Player* ever play soccer? Could the *Skateboarder* ever perform such a manoeuvre in life? Von Hagens has related the process of donation that led to the creation of one plastinate, the monumental *Rearing Horse and Rider* (Institute for Plastination 2006b). After viewing and reviewing the original exhibition and facing a terminal illness, the donor approached von Hagens. Von Hagens says:

> He was an imposing figure and as his health deteriorated, we began to speak of how he wished to be presented. He told me he wanted a striking pose, and I showed him Fragonard's horse and rider in the donation book. It captured his imagination and we talked about the aesthetics and ethics of the image and the pose in a very lengthy discussion one evening … I felt deeply obliged to present him as triumphant. (Institute for Plastination 2006b, 3)

Though entirely anonymized by the removal of the 'exterior face' and the absence of any identifying information, the plastinate remains reflective of the donor's personality and moulded by his personal choice. Von Hagens has made every effort to preserve at least this donor's distinctive personal dignity. However, not all the plastinates are from donated bodies; unclaimed bodies have also been used, but these were all acquired by legal means (von Hagens 2003), as is common practice for medical schools in many countries (see Chapter 2).

Informed consent is a crucial ethical determinant, according to which it is ethically preferable to use bequeathed rather than unclaimed bodies. This sets a high ethical standard that is not maintained across the anatomical world for cadavers used in dissecting rooms. Hence, it would be churlish to criticize von Hagens for using unclaimed bodies in addition to bequeathed ones.

BODIES … the Exhibition, a copycat exhibition promoted by Premier Exhibitions, has recently been investigated by the New York State attorney general's office for failing to ensure that the bodies displayed were not from Chinese prisoners who may have been tortured and executed (Wilson 2008). Premier Exhibitions had repeatedly assured the public that there was no evidence that the unclaimed bodies supplied to them by Chinese police had been subject to human rights offences. However, this lack of evidence was not considered sufficient. Premier must now provide documentation of the source of the body, cause of death, and the decedent's consent to display any new bodies or parts in New York State. To display previously obtained bodies they must clearly advertise that the bodies may be those of Chinese prisoners who may have been victims of torture and execution. This settlement signals a heightened awareness on behalf of the general public of the importance of informed consent in the display of human remains.

While informed consent is foundational, it does not automatically justify what is subsequently done to the bequeathed bodies. Plastination, and the manner in which plastinates are displayed in *Body Worlds*, has to be justified on artistic or educational grounds, or both. But if informed consent is in place, the strictures placed on plastination are that much less demanding.

Body Worlds as a Philosophical Statement

The philosophical pretensions of the *Body Worlds* exhibits are apparent in the banners decorating the exhibition and the merchandise that feature quotes from philosophers and poets such as Goethe, Nietzsche, Kant, Descartes, Shakespeare and Seneca. For example:

> Anatomical dissection gives the human mind an opportunity to compare the dead with the living, things severed with things intact, things destroyed with things evolving, and opens up the profoundness of nature to us more than any other endeavour or consideration. (Goethe, quoted in Schulte-Sasse 2006, 374)

Such references provide a tacit philosophical validation for the exhibition. They direct viewers to consider not only the wonder and horror of the plastinates but also the defining aspects of humanity as well as their own death and corporeal beauty.

Over time the exhibitions have moved from a sterile approach with a medical focus to one seeking to engender veneration and awe. Whalley says that 'the tone is intentionally spiritual' (Skulstad 2006). The *Praying Skeleton*, which kneels before a cross, holding his heart aloft, offers little in terms of educational merit. It is intended to honour Christianity as the religion that assisted the development of modern human anatomy, and to acknowledge the fact that many of the body donors are Christian (Rathgeb 2002).

However, von Hagens also imbues the exhibitions with his own philosophical statements. For him the plastinates are examples of the 'post-mortal body' (PRNewswire 2006). He considers that he, through plastination, has transformed them and in doing so has moved them beyond death. The plastinates comprise a new category of body, neither fresh corpse nor decaying remains. Von Hagens describes the plastinates as 'frozen in time between death and decay' (Schulte-Sasse 2006), for they will never decompose, and thus have achieved a form of immortality. This is immortality, not in any spiritual sense, but of physical permanence. This is very much a post-Christian, secular form of immortality (Stern 2003).

The animated poses of the plastinates may also be an attempt to escape from the reality of death by giving the impression that these cadavers are continuing to exist in much the same way as when they were alive. Of course, there are major differences: they are dissected; and yet there is a hint that we can live on as plastinates, which seem to have attained their own form of everlasting existence. And yet it is a very impoverished form of everlasting life.

Do Plastinates Challenge our Worldview?

In one of his quotes on display in the exhibition von Hagens states, 'The plastinated, post-mortal body illuminates the soul by its very absence ... Plastination transforms the body, an object of individual mourning into an object of reverence, learning, enlightenment and appreciation' (Skulstad 2006).

The goals of *Body Worlds* as expressed in this quotation highlight the problems endemic to the exhibitions. The vast range of von Hagens's thinking and aspirations crosses many disciplinary boundaries. This is as true for anatomists as it is for theologians and social scientists. While anatomists are at home with the use of plastination as a learning tool, they are less at home with the categories of reverence, enlightenment and appreciation. It may be that they have much to learn, and that *Body Worlds* has a part to play in their own education. But the philosophical overtones of *Body Worlds* are intensely problematic.

One has to ask whether running throughout all von Hagens's endeavours there is not an attempt to escape from the reality of death, by giving the impression that these cadavers are continuing to exist in much the same way as when they were alive. While there are major differences, there is a hint that we can live on as plastinates, with post-mortal bodies. This is not the ageless existence that transfixes transhumanists (see Chapter 9), but plastinates appear to have attained their own form of everlasting existence.

Even this everlasting existence brings with it demanding ethical questions. At some point decisions will have to be made about how to dispose of this imperishable material that is human and yet is not quite human. And is this the point we are searching for? In acquiring some form of everlasting existence have these plastinates ceased to be human? One observer expressed his response with these words:

> Each of ... [the] corpses is, at one level, a perfect human specimen that is a real privilege to observe at close quarters. And yet, the absence of a personality, friends, family and history leaves a gaping and eerie vacuum that forcefully calls into question what it is to be human and reminds us of what few of us like to dwell on – our mortality. They are bodies with no soul. (Nicholls 2002, 47)

Everlasting existence may, in one sense, have been achieved, but only by sacrificing the human core of the plastinates. The replacement of dead human tissue with plastic leaves nothing more than plasticized remnants of what was once a human person, fascinating and yet perplexing, uplifting and yet troublesome. We seem to have created a new form of existence. Perhaps plastinates is indeed an appropriate term, and yet we have not come to terms with what this means.

The multidimensional nature of *Body Worlds* reflects the complex thought world of its founder and director. Regardless of what we make of these exhibitions, they serve as a reminder that a technique can be used in a multitude of different ways with a range of applications. There is a spectrum from the narrowly focused teaching application of plastination within a strict medical-scientific framework to the intensely commercial use of plastination centred on exhibitions aimed at the general public. Along this continuum, the technique is being employed to serve scientific and educational ends, artistic and commercial ends, and possibly to challenge the conventional notions of the meaning of the dead human body. It is no wonder that responses to plastination, particularly in its public manifestation, are varied and contradictory.

Chapter 5
The Transplanted Body

Human Organ Transplantation

In previous chapters we have attempted to trace the broad variety of perspectives that can be found in Western societies on the cultural and religious significance of cadavers, as well as on the historical development of ideas regarding cadavers. In doing this, we have encountered societies' reactions to the dead human body, and in the light of these what procedures societies will or will not allow to be carried out on dead human bodies. Although some of the discussion has touched on clinical areas, these have been relatively peripheral to the main focus of the discussion, which has centred on the cadaver itself or on perceptions of the cadaver as a whole or skeletal or tissue remains.

With this chapter we move into a more overtly clinical domain, with our attention directed towards organ donation and transplantation. However, even these will be looked at through the eyes of those whose main interest is in the human cadaver, rather than the living recipient in need of a transplant. In doing so we are not suggesting that the cadaver has greater significance than the patient in need of a transplanted organ, only that the emphasis in this instance is on the former rather than the latter, which we hope may bring fresh insights into the social and ethical issues surrounding organ transplantation.

Scientific and Clinical Developments

In 1954 the first successful kidney transplantation was performed in the United States. Recipient and donor were identical twin brothers, thereby avoiding the problem of biological incompatibility. More kidney transplants between identical twins followed, and a recipient identical twin who had received a kidney transplant in 1956 successfully completed a pregnancy two years after the transplant. She went on to become a grandmother, and was one of the longest surviving kidney transplant recipients (Murray 1992).

Prior to this, kidney transplantation was performed sporadically during the first half of this century, but planned programmes for human organ transplantation commenced only in the late 1940s. Clinicians began kidney transplantation in non-immunosuppressed human patients, in the face of pessimistic warnings from both scientists and other clinicians (Murray 1992). Even the outstanding biologist Peter Medawar (1957) claimed that human allotransplantation (transplantation between two genetically non-identical humans) would never prove viable because the roots of individuality were so deep and impenetrable. However, major developments in the understanding of skin grafting and acquired immunological tolerance, along with surgical developments in transplantation, led to the first successful kidney allotransplantation.

In order for this to occur, major developments in the use of genetically unrelated transplants had to await the introduction of immunosuppressive drugs. This occurred in the late 1950s, and led to the first successful unrelated cadaveric allotransplant in 1962. By 1965, one-year survival rates of grafted kidneys from living related donors approached 80 per cent, with survival rates of kidneys from cadavers approaching 65 per cent. Further developments have improved these rates, and have led to a general acceptance of cadaveric kidney transplants (Pfaff et al. 1994).

The transplantation of other organs followed in the wake of the success with kidneys. The first heart transplant was performed in South Africa in 1967, and while this was followed by a bleak period in heart transplantation, when one failure followed another, heart transplantation later became a recognized form of treatment. The number of heart transplants per year peaked in 1994 and has been steadily decreasing since (Taylor et al. 2005). Worldwide a total in excess of 70,000 cardiac transplant procedures have been carried out to date (Taylor et al. 2005). Transplants of other organs, including single and double lung transplants, heart-lung transplants, and transplants of the pancreas and liver have also been successfully undertaken. In the United States in 2006 the patient survival rate one year after transplantation was 95 per cent for kidneys from a deceased donor and 98 per cent from a living donor, 95 per cent for pancreases, 88 per cent for hearts, 88 per cent for livers from a deceased donor and 91 per cent from a living donor, 85 per cent for lungs and 67 per cent for heart-lungs (Organ Procurement and Transplantation Network 2007c). Besides organs, certain tissues can be transplanted, most commonly blood and bone marrow, but also *dura mater*, one of three meningeal layers that surround the brain and spinal cord (Takahashi et al. 1994), corneas, tendons and ligaments (Prottas 1992), and most recently, whole bones (Wojtas 1994).

The first hand transplant in modern times was performed in Ecuador in 1963. However, the graft was rejected after three weeks due to insufficient immunosuppression (*Medical Tribune and Medical News* 1964; Gilbert 1964). After this setback it was not until it was discovered in the late 1990s that the same immunotherapy used for organ transplants was also effective in preventing the rejection of highly immunogenic skin, that another hand transplant was attempted. In 1998 a team at Lyons in France performed the first successful hand transplant (Dubernard et al. 1999). Since then 23 more hands have been transplanted to 17 patients with generally no major side effects or complications (Gander et al. 2006; Lanzetta et al. 2004). All recipients experienced transient acute rejection, but this was easily managed by temporarily increasing immunosuppressive treatment. By monitoring the appearance of the skin, rejection can easily be diagnosed and promptly treated, leading to lower rates of graft rejection than with internal organs (Lanzetta et al. 2004).

The recipient of the first successful hand transplant (performed by the Lyons team) has since had his transplanted hand reamputated after failure to continue immunosuppressive treatment caused rejection (Kanitakis et al. 2003). The recipient claimed the hand was not functioning well, that he was mentally detached from it, and that both he and many of those close to him found it repulsive (BBC News 2001).

Although most other hand transplant recipients have reported an increased quality of life (Gander et al. 2006), the problem with the Lyons recipient highlights the additional issues associated with transplanting a hand compared to, for example, a kidney. It takes months and years of physical rehabilitation for the transplanted hand to regain functional use and discriminative sensation. Compare this with a kidney that starts to function almost immediately. Compliance with the rehabilitation program is crucial if the hand is to function well. In addition, in due course the recipient has to accept the transplanted hand as their own, thereby incorporating it into their body image.

The first partial face transplant was performed in 2005 by the same team that performed the first successful hand transplant (Devauchelle et al. 2006). The recipient was a woman who had lost her lips, chin, distal nose, and adjacent parts of both cheeks in a dog attack. It was considered that conventional autologous tissue reconstruction (reconstruction using the patient's own tissue) would not be able to produce a satisfactory functional or aesthetic outcome. Following the transplant and physical rehabilitation, the patient can again speak and eat properly, and as the scars have healed and lip control has returned, she has progressively been able to return to a normal social life (BBC News 2006a). A similar partial face transplant was performed in China in 2006 on a man who was severely disfigured after a bear attack and who since that time had lived as a recluse (Macartney 2006). A fuller face transplant (of lips, cheek, nose and mouth) has recently been performed on a 30-year-old French man suffering from severe neurofibromatosis, a rare genetic disease in which tumours have progressively disfigured the subject's face (Watt 2008). All three transplants have been successful thus far in terms of appearance, sensitivity and acceptance by the patient (Devauchelle et al. 2006). A full face transplant has not yet been attempted, although it is being explored (Morris et al. 2007) and a UK team has been approved to begin selecting candidates (BBC News 2006c).

Face transplants pose many of the same ethical problems as hand and other transplants, although the psychosocial issues are greatly magnified. The face is closely linked to personal identity, it is 'a window to our inner selves – it represents the entire personality and is the focus of attention in every social interaction' (Coull 2003). It is these identity and interpersonal factors raised by facial disfigurement that create much of the desire for a facial transplant, but the same factors give pause when considering such intervention (Swindell 2007). Early fears, frequently expressed in science fiction narratives, of the direct transfer of facial features from donor to recipient and the attendant fear of identity theft, are misleading. The donor's soft-tissue features and the recipient's own underlying bone structure merge to create a new 'hybrid' face. However, it is important that the recipient and family are well prepared for the limitations of the transplant in terms of appearance and functionality. A strong sense of self, resilience, emotional stability and social support are essential in a candidate for facial transplantation (Furr et al. 2007). Ironically, those patients who are most psychosocially suited to a face transplant are those who will have best adjusted to living with severe facial disfigurement (Morris et al. 2007).

The candidate also needs to understand the consequences of a failed face transplant. The chances of chronic rejection are not yet known, but experience with other organ transplants suggests it is certainly a possibility. While a transplanted hand could be reamputated with relative ease, a rejected face transplant would require skin grafts to cover the exposed areas, with the possibility that the end result may be worse than the original condition (Morris et al. 2007).

Another emerging transplant procedure is uterus transplantation, which is being considered to allow women with an absent, malformed or injured uterus to carry a pregnancy (Altchek 2003). This may be an alternative to gestational surrogacy.

In 2000 a Saudi Arabian team transplanted a donated uterus into a woman whose uterus had been surgically removed due to postpartum hemorrhage (Fageeh et al. 2002). Acute rejection of the organ was managed and hormone treatment led to two menstrual cycles. However, after 99 days the uterus was removed in a necrotized state due to clotting in the uterus's vasculature thought to be caused by inadequate uterine structural support. The uterus is a particularly difficult organ to transplant due to its complicated vascular system. While some animal experiments have been conducted (Sieunarine et al. 2005; Wranning et al. 2006), occasionally producing successful pregnancies (Racho El-Akouri et al. 2003), these are not useful models for the human situation (Pearson 2007).

The requisite immunosuppression carries risks for a pregnancy, although the short-term risks are minimal for pregnancies in renal transplant recipients (Armenti et al. 1998). However, the risks to a fetus being carried in a transplanted uterus are as yet unknown. While a transplanted uterus *per se* could be removed if complications arose, the way in which the pregnant uterus ought to be managed has yet to be addressed (Caplan et al. 2007). Since the ability to bear a child may fulfill a deep emotional and social need, a uterus transplant may increase the quality of a woman's life, but minimization of the risks of harm to both woman and child-to-be is essential ethically. Caution is essential, and yet a US group has plans to proceed and has begun screening potential candidates (Stein 2007).

Any ethical analysis of face, hand and uterus transplants should take account of the fact that they are not necessary to sustain life. In this sense, they are less ethically compelling than are heart and liver transplants (Agich 2003). The aim to improve the quality of life can be compared to the justification for kidney transplantation when dialysis is still an option (Baily 2007). Conventional reconstructive surgery for those with hand and face injuries is limited and requires multiple follow-up surgeries, whereas allotransplantation may provide superior functional and aesthetic outcomes. The devastating psychological and social problems caused by severe facial disfigurement may justify significant intervention regardless of significant risk (Barker et al. 2006; Furr et al. 2007). Nevertheless, these risks must be assessed and made clear to potential transplant recipients. The lifelong immunosuppression required to prevent rejection increases the incidence of opportunistic infections, and in the long term may lead to malignancies and severe toxicity resulting from diabetes and kidney failure (Francois et al. 2000; Wiggins et al. 2004), although these have yet to be observed.

Donation of Cadaveric Organs

The need for organ donors is vast. In the United States, approximately 96,388 people were waiting for some form of organ transplantation in June 2007 (Organ Procurement and Transplantation Network 2007a). Of these, 75 per cent were waiting for a kidney transplant, 18 per cent were waiting for a liver, and 2 per cent were awaiting a heart. A recent analysis of trends in organ transplantation has shown that for the period 1989–1996 the total number of transplants increased in both Western Europe (increase of 3,756) and North America (increase of 6,936). In the United States from 1996 to 2005 the total number of transplants steadily increased from 19,752 transplants (from 9,208 donors) to 28,930 transplants (from 14,488 donors) (Organ Procurement and Transplantation Network 2007c, 2007b). In the UK the total number of people donating organs increased from 1,079 in 1996 to 1,363 in 2005 (UK Transplant 2006). However, the number of deceased donors decreased, while living donations increased. Because deceased donors on average provide three organs and living donors only one, this means that in the UK the total number of transplants actually decreased slightly (UK Transplant 2006). Kidney transplants account for around 59 per cent of all transplants (Organ Procurement and Transplantation Network 2007b).

Surveys of the general public have consistently shown that although people are aware of the need for donor organs, they are reluctant to donate their own organs or to consent to the donation of organs from relatives (Evans and Manninen 1988). In the UK 90 per cent of the population support organ donation (UK Transplant 2003), though only 25 per cent have signed up to donate their organs (UK Transplant 2008). In a study of public attitudes to organ donation and autopsy conducted in Sweden (Sanner 1994b), 62 per cent of respondents were willing to donate their organs for transplantation, compared with 84 per cent who were prepared to agree to an autopsy. In a second study, Sanner (1994a) explored reasons for refusing to consent to organ transplantation. These included:

- *the illusion of lingering life* – a feeling that the integrity of the dead body should be maintained, as if the deceased continues to be regarded as a living person;
- *the need to respect the dead* as a way of showing respect for the individual that once was;

- *distrust* of the medical establishment and biomedical development and of the criteria for brain death, and a feeling of anxiety concerning one's powerlessness;
- *the feeling that transplantation is contrary to nature*, including discomfort at the thought of one's organs surviving in another person's body, or a fear of offending God or nature.

Inevitably, attitudes such as these reduce the number of potential organ donors. There is also evidence linking life-saving measures, such as laws making the wearing of seat belts compulsory, to the lower number of available donors (Manninen and Evans 1985), while the AIDS epidemic has also had a negative impact.

In the United States the federally initiated Organ Donation Breakthrough Collaborative was introduced in 2003, leading to a jump in organ donation rates in 2004. The aim of the Collaborative is to identify the measures used in regions with the highest organ procurement rates and disseminate these best practices widely. These strategies include high-profile public and professional education campaigns, more liberal donor selection criteria, improved minority participation, improved identification of potential donors and timely referral to organ donation specialists (Marks et al. 2006).

Some European countries have witnessed actual reductions in organ donations in the 1990s. For example, donations in Germany dropped by 20 per cent in 1994 alone, the major reasons appearing to be the questioning of brain death criteria by Bishops of the Evangelical (Protestant) Church (Nicholson 1994). Currently around 70 per cent of relatives will refuse to donate the organs of a brain-dead patient (Wesslau et al. 2007). In France, the proportion of relatives refusing consent for organs to be taken from their next of kin grew from 27 per cent to 66 per cent in the space of only four years (Dorozynski 1995). The current refusal rate remains high in France, around 30–50 per cent (Houssin 2003).

Two crucial ethical requirements are apparent when using cadaveric organs for transplantation: the determination of when the potential donor has died, and the informed and voluntary consent of the donor prior to death. The first of these requirements introduces the question of brain death, a subject dealt with in detail in Chapter 8.

Consent in Cadaveric Organ Donation

Discussion about consent introduces two diametrically opposite notions: *opt-in* and *opt-out*. Opt-in systems (*informed consent*) have predominated in most Western societies until recent years, with their stipulation that consent is explicitly required from the donor when still alive – in the form of an organ donor card or data on a driver's licence. If consent has not been provided in this manner, it may be possible for the dead person's family to provide it on their behalf. This is far from ideal, given the circumstances of a tragic death (in so many cases) and the necessity of having to make a rapid decision when grieving. In New Zealand, next of kin have a right of veto over the wishes of the deceased to donate their organs. Rightly or wrongly, this emphasizes the interests of living next of kin over the posthumous interests of the deceased. Given this situation, organ donors in New Zealand are encouraged to discuss their preferences for organ donation with next of kin, so that differences of view and confusion at the time of donation can be resolved or minimized. In contrast, in the opt-out (*presumed consent*) position consent is assumed to have been given, unless people have expressly stated their opposition to this possibility during life. Inevitably there are intermediate positions between what may be regarded as these two extremes. Regardless of which position is adopted, the notion of consent ought not to be neglected, due to the fundamental ethical requirement to respect individual freedom of choice and self-determination.

Opt-In Policy (Informed Consent)

The strength of the opt-in policy is its recognition of the importance of the integrity of the dead body, which is to remain intact unless specific consent is given to do otherwise. Also, actively consenting to the donation of organs for transplantation reflects altruism on the part of the deceased, or the deceased's next of kin. Additionally, requiring informed consent signifies respect for the autonomy of the deceased (Kleinman and Lowy 1993). These arguments alone are not definitive, although they direct attention towards the moral values and cultural perspectives of the deceased, and those close to them.

A drawback of the opt-in position is its focus on the deceased's wishes to the exclusion of all others with interests in the transplantation. These include the next of kin of the deceased, as well as potential recipients and their families. Less obviously, it also excludes society in general, since society is obliged to shoulder the economic burden of those with conditions such as kidney failure and end-stage heart disease and who could potentially benefit from transplants. These sets of interrelationships and possibly competing interests may be overlooked, if our moral gaze is focused exclusively on the deceased. However, these considerations do not automatically lead to ignoring the deceased's wishes, or to an opt-out policy (more light will be shed on this when we consider some intermediate positions). Rather, they emphasize the breadth of the concerns to be addressed when advocating organ donation as an option for individuals and family members in the event of an untimely, trauma-related death.

But do people considering organ donation receive sufficient accurate information about what is involved? Are they making a free choice? Gillam (1992, 32) has written:

> Potential donors are not asked to consider that their families may be distressed at
> the prospect of organs being retrieved when their loved one still *looks* alive, even

though diagnosed dead on brain death criteria; that the families may feel guilty or be unable to grieve properly; that the organs may be removed but never used; that the organs removed may not in fact save lives, because not all transplants actually work.

Reasons such as these have some force, and yet they introduce factors beyond the control of the deceased, or of anyone contemplating being an organ donor. It is also questionable whether these are ethical considerations, as long as adequately informed consent has been provided and the health care teams involved are operating in an efficient, professional manner. Probably of greater importance is the inadequate supply of organs available for transplantation under an opt-in system, which alone has led to considerable pressures to move away from this approach in favour of an opt-out policy.

Opt-Out Policy (Presumed Consent)

The presumed consent policy operates in many countries including Belgium, Austria, Denmark, France, Israel, Singapore, Spain and Turkey (Abadie and Gay 2006). About 40 per cent of Europe requires explicit consent (opt-in), leaving 60 per cent with presumed consent (opt-out), under which an individual is presumed to consent to being an organ donor, unless he or she specifically refuses and carries a 'non-organ donor' card. Belgium, for instance, has operated under a presumed consent system for the past 20 or so years, with only 2 per cent of the population opting out. In Austria, any deceased foreigners' organs may be taken.

In Singapore, an opt-out policy was introduced in 1987 with passage of the Human Organ Transplant Act. This presumes that all mentally competent citizens or permanent residents between the ages of 21 and 60 who become victims of fatal accidents are kidney donors unless they have registered prior dissent. Organs from the mentally incapacitated and minors may be removed, but only with the consent of their families or legal representatives (Teo 1991). Until 2007 Muslims were excluded from the opt-out scheme, instead having to pledge their kidneys voluntarily (BBC News 2007a). The donation of other organs is voluntary for all citizens. What is of particular interest about this policy is that various incentives and disincentives have been included: the immediate family members of kidney donors enjoy cut-price treatment at government hospitals for five years, and should a person have need of a kidney transplant, priority of access to kidneys will be given to those who have not dissented from the policy.

In India the massive shortage of organs and illegal organ trade have prompted a proposed amendment to the Transplant of Human Organs Act 1994 implementing the presumed consent policy (*Times of India* 2008). Modeled on the Spanish system, India's policy would allow families to object only if the decedent had previously registered objection to organ donation in writing. To increase public awareness the policy would be gradually introduced, beginning with the routine removal of corneas from brain-dead patients in government hospitals. In addition, the amendment proposes incentives for family members, including free medical care in the hospital where the donation was made, subsidized health insurance, preferred status on transplant waiting lists and discounts on rail tickets.

These incentives and disincentives raise questions of coercion and discrimination (Gillon 1995), and whether medical benefits are indirect forms of payment for donated organs. There is undoubtedly an element of external influence, although it may not overshadow the motives of those who wish to donate their organs for humanitarian and altruistic motives (Teo 1991).

The obvious advantage of the presumed consent system is that far more organs become available for retrieval and subsequent transplantation (as Teo (1991) has demonstrated for Singapore; and Abadie and Gay (2006) have shown for continental Europe). This is the pragmatic argument, and it is both the strength and the rationale of this system. However, presumed consent severely limits people's right to make decisions about their priorities regarding their own dead body, thereby undermining individual self-determination. In this respect it can appear that the use of unclaimed bodies in dissection (see Chapter 2) and presumed consent fit into the same category.

Proponents of presumed consent argue that the value of self-determination must be balanced by another value, that of maximizing overall benefit by lives saved from the increased availability of organs. In view of this close relationship between the two, how important is the freedom to choose what is done to one's body after death?

But can the debate be confined to only two sets of interests: those of the deceased and those of prospective recipients? Kennedy (1988) thinks not. He recognizes a whole set of competing interests: the deceased; the spouse and relatives; the potential donor; and society at large (with the economic burden of caring for those awaiting transplants, and the unnecessary deaths of many people). Kennedy's sympathies lie with the potential organ recipient and society at large, on the ground that only in this way will the needs of those with organ failure be satisfied. His communitarian view is shared by others (Menzel 1991; Nelson 1992).

In the opt-out scenario, use of one's organs is not inevitable, since it can be avoided by simply opting out. Therefore, contrary to the appearance of similarity mentioned earlier, the situation is not the same as with the use of unclaimed bodies for dissection: in that instance, the only way out was by having relatives or money. The organ donation situation cannot be equated with this, since a previous decision to opt-out is possible, as long as this decision is communicated to the authorities in the appropriate manner. In practice, the situation may not be this straight-forward, particularly for the uninformed, or those on the periphery of society, who are unlikely to know about opting-out, let alone being in a position to do anything about it. If individuals and families are not told they can opt-out, or how they may object to organ donation, presumed consent could essentially become a means of avoiding consent altogether. Although safeguards could be established to ensure that individuals are informed of their rights, such safeguards would be difficult to maintain in the absence of active discussion of the issue (Council for Ethical and Judicial Affairs 1994). Every effort is required, therefore, to prevent compromise of the safeguards, since if this is not achieved, opt-out poses considerable problems.

Intermediate Positions

There are intermediate positions between the opt-in and opt-out schemes. One such intermediate position is the policy of *required request*. According to this, hospital administrators or physicians are legally responsible for ensuring that the next of kin or legal guardians are asked about their willingness to donate the deceased's organs and tissues after death (Caplan 1984). This is a policy that operates in many states in the United States, although the amount of information supplied to families, the degree of monitoring of individual hospitals, and the provision of penalties for failing to comply, vary considerably. Despite these measures, the policy of required request appears to have had little effect on the availability of donated organs (Bodenham et al. 1989).

Spain introduced a new centralized system of organ donation in 1989, which has dramatically increased the rate of organ donation in that country. The appointment of specially trained transplant coordinators and an efficient system of media management allowing for clear, open and positive communication with the general public have contributed to the success of the system (Boddington 1996). More generally, suggestions to remedy the poor responses to organ procurement have included: educating the public by allaying fears that potential donors may not receive sufficiently aggressive medical treatment in the event of an accident; making a public commitment that cadavers will be respectfully treated; and ensuring that there are fair policies for distributing donated organs (Teo 1992). Other strategies include improving the diagnosis of brain-dead patients to increase the cadaver donor pool, using financial incentives to encourage donations and exploring further the use of animal sources (Caplan et al. 1991, see section Xenotransplantation: Crossing Species Boundaries).

A related proposal is a policy of *mandated choice* under which individuals would be required to declare their preference either for or against becoming an organ donor at a nominated time, such as the renewal of driver's licences. According to its proponents, this approach promotes individual autonomy in organ donation decisions, and reduces stress on surviving family members and physicians, by eliminating doubt as to the deceased's wishes (Chouhan and Draper 2003; Council for Ethical and Judicial Affairs 1994; Spital 1996).

Additional possibilities are based on *payment*. In the first of these, payment is made for cadaveric organ donation. Peters (1991) has proposed that US $1,000 be paid as a death benefit to motivate families of potential organ donors. He argues that concern must focus, not on altruism, but on collective responsibility for maximizing life-saving organ recovery.

In reply, Pellegrino (1991) considers that any proposal that creates a deliberate conflict between altruism and self-interest reduces our freedom to make a gift to a stranger. He also argues that it undermines the consent process, placing a family's interests above those of the deceased's, reflecting their wishes rather than the individual's. Pellegrino (1991) also considers that the insufficient supply of organs for donation is an indictment of the level of altruism in society and that this will not be improved by eliminating altruism altogether.

An alternative strategy involves *legalizing a market approach*, so that people are provided with an incentive to consider seriously selling their organs (for example, Brams 1977; Delmonico et al. 2002). This has been the focus of much discussion in the realm of living organ donation, particularly as a way to address the black market of living-donor kidneys (Friedman and Friedman 2006; Goodwin 2006). Under this 'rewarded gifting' system, different types of inducements are possible, such as payment to the deceased's relatives, reimbursement for funeral expenses, health insurance rebates for potential donors (Gerrand 1994), or tax breaks for the estates of donors (Gorman 1991). An argument in favour of a market system is that it would allow buyers and sellers to be tissue-matched in advance, thereby increasing the success rate of transplantation. Another possible justification is that a commercial market would respect individual autonomy and freedom, while giving to individuals opportunities to exercise personal generosity (Brams 1977).

Against these arguments it has to be asked whether it is acceptable for human organs to be viewed as commodities (Teo 1992). As discussed in Chapter 2, the body is generally regarded as possessing a special moral significance and dignity (Kass 1985), making it immoral for human body parts to be treated as objects to be purchased. It is also possible that commercialization may undermine the importance societies place on communal values like altruism and goodwill (Teo 1992).

What emerges from this discussion is that problems connected with the supply of organs appear to stem not solely from a narrow ethical focus on opt-in or opt-out schemes. They have to be seen against the priority societies as a whole place on organ transplantation. Improving the efficiency of central distribution systems may help alleviate many of the perceived failings of an opt-in scheme, while maintaining altruism as the ethical bedrock of donation.

Organ Transplantation Abuses in China

What had been an open secret for some time was confirmed in 2006 when the Chinese government admitted that organs from executed prisoners were used for transplantation (Magnier and Zarembo 2006). However, the government asserted that they were trying to reform the system, improving record-keeping and establishing a code of conduct. In July 2006 China declared organ sales to be illegal. In an attempt to assist the monitoring of transplant procedures, only a small number of specific hospitals are now authorized to perform transplants. In 2007 the government imposed restrictions on organ transplants for foreigners, banning organ transplants to foreigners on tourist visas and international advertising by hospitals, and requiring any transplants to foreign patients to be specifically authorized by health authorities (Cody 2007). However, the considerable profits to be made in the organ transplantation business make this very difficult to police.

Officials claim that the organs are only taken with the prisoners' express permission, as they volunteer their organs as a 'present to society' (BBC News 2006d). But what kind of consent can prisoners on death row give? The very low rate of voluntary organ donation among Chinese citizens for cultural reasons suggests that, at the least, some form of coercion is involved when prisoners 'volunteer' their organs.

The timing and manner in which the prisoners are executed are managed in such a way as to specifically allow organs to be removed in a good state for transplantation into a matched recipient (Briggs 1996). The prisoners undergo blood tests before execution so that when a certain matched organ is required it can be supplied with minimal delay. The availability and short waiting times for organ transplants have been much vaunted on website advertising, attracting many desperate foreigners for whom waiting times at home have proved far too long (Matas and Kilgour 2007).

The number of prisoners China executes every year is not known, but conservative estimates place it at around 80 per cent of all executions reported worldwide (Magnier and Zarembo 2006). In China the death penalty is meted out for a variety of offences, including non-violent crimes such as drug trafficking, embezzlement, burglary and political crimes (Briggs 1996). There have also been claims that practitioners of Falun Gong, a Buddhist movement forbidden in China, have been particularly badly treated, frequently being executed and their organs harvested (Matas and Kilgour 2007). Because certification of brain death is not required in China before organs are removed, there is the potential that organs may be harvested from prisoners who are still neurologically alive (Diflo 2004; Parry 2006).

Cadavers as Life-Saving Devices

We appear to have arrived at the point of acknowledging that cadavers can be used to save lives. Does this mean that cadavers can be used indiscriminately in the salvaging of human lives? The previous discussion has pointed to the ambivalence of any answer, partly on account of the myriad scientific and clinical factors to be considered, and partly because of the delicate relationship between living people and cadavers. The use of cadavers for saving lives is not, therefore, a simple issue, and whatever answers are provided in different contexts have to be nuanced ones.

The approach we have adopted to organ transplantation stems from a view of the cadaver within the dissecting room context, whereby we have to view cadavers as more than simply life-saving devices. Important as is the latter, it is not the sole determinant of our view of the cadaver. Were this to happen, cadavers could be used for any life-saving purpose without recourse to consent of any description or reference to the views of next of kin. It would be strange indeed, if the centrality of altruism and the close relationship between what we are as living persons and what cadavers are, were lost sight of when the aim is to enhance the quality of living patients' lives. It is the wide range of uses to which cadavers can be put, as well as their potential to assist living people in many ways, that points to the need for a consistent approach across all relevant areas.

Organ Transplantation in Infants: The Use of Anencephalics

In June 2007 in the United States there were 248 children (under the age of 17 years) on the waiting list in need of heart transplants, and a further 20 were in need of a heart and lung transplant. 765 paediatric patients needed new kidneys and 712 were in need of a new liver (Organ Procurement and Transplantation Network 2007d). Present methods of identifying potential donors come nowhere near meeting this demand, and approximately 180–250 children on the transplant waiting list die every year (Organ Procurement and Transplantation Network 2007d).

A major difference between organ transplantation in children and adults lies in the sources of suitable organs. The majority of adult organ donations are from previously healthy people who suffer a stroke. By contrast, relatively few infants and young children become donors in this manner (McCullagh 1993). The lack of an adequate supply of appropriately sized organs suitable for donation has led to proposals that organs be taken from infants suffering from anencephaly, a condition in which major portions of the brain, skull and scalp are congenitally absent due to a disruption in the process of development. Although most anencephalic infants are stillborn, in which case the use of their organs for transplantation is not feasible, approximately 25–45 per cent are live births (Walters and Ashwal 1988). In most instances, these infants will die within a few hours or days of birth (O'Rourke and deBlois 1994), but during this brief period they retain residual brainstem function and so are not dead using a whole brain definition of death (see Chapter 8).

The most common cause of death in anencephalic infants is cardio-respiratory arrest. This is problematic for those wishing to remove organs for transplantation because the lack of oxygen irreparably damages the tissues making them unsuitable for transplantation (Harrison 1986a). As a result, some physicians have placed anencephalic infants on ventilation immediately following birth, with subsequent periodic examinations for the occurrence of brain death; when this is diagnosed the organs are harvested (Peabody et al. 1989). Because there is no possibility of higher brain activity or cognitive function in anencephalic infants, their placement on life support is solely for the benefit of someone else. In view of the dilemmas inherent in keeping infants 'alive' until their organs can be transplanted, it has been suggested that whole brain death criteria should be replaced by higher brain (cerebral) death criteria (see discussion in Chapter 8), or that a new 'brain-absent' category be created to cover anencephalics (Harrison 1986b). In this way anencephalics could be considered to be 'dead' when their organs are still suitable for transplantation.

Several reasons have been given as justification for the use of anencephalic infants as organ donors. The first is the vast demand for suitable transplants (Caplan 1987). While demand undoubtedly exists, this is not sufficient justification for the use of anencephalic infants as a means to this end. A second reason is that, by donating the organs of their anencephalic infant, parents are able to feel that their child's life has had meaning, with the donation helping to alleviate some of their anguish (Harrison 1986a). The third reason is that these infants are beyond suffering, cannot be harmed and, hence, have no interests in the way they are treated (Caplan 1987). It may be argued that anencephalic infants are in a unique position among humans in that they have no history of consciousness and no possibility of ever becoming conscious (Council for Ethical and Judicial Affairs 1995).

The viewpoint of the parents is significant in this instance, recognizing as it does the close physical relationship between the mother and anencephalic fetus/ infant, and the psychological relationships that can exist among the parents and the anencephalic fetus/infant. The wish on their part to maintain a pregnancy to term, with the prospect of donating the infant's organs, constitutes substantial justification for their use in this manner if possible. However, the strictures already discussed are considerable and will mean that only a limited number of anencephalics will become available for donation purposes.

Neural Transplantation: The Use of Fetuses

The dead bodies in this case are those of the human fetuses, from whom brain tissue is to be taken. It is immediately evident that this situation parallels that of organ transplantation, where the organs are removed from deceased adults (or infants) as previously discussed. There are differences, as we shall see, but they are minor compared with the similarities and with the central role played by cadaveric material.

Fetal neural transplantation (neural grafting) refers to the transplantation of fetal brain cells into the brain of an adult, and as a field of research it has become one of the foremost research areas within biology. It holds out the hope of providing a therapeutic approach to some of the worst neurodegenerative diseases of human beings (including Parkinson's disease, Alzheimer's disease, and Huntington's disease), as well as to damage to the brain and spinal cord caused by trauma and tumours, for which currently there is either no or very limited available therapy.

The thousands of laboratory studies conducted to date demonstrate that transplants of developing central nervous system tissue have a remarkable capacity to develop in their new environment, to integrate with host tissue, to exert functional effects, and to promote functional recovery after brain damage (Fisher and Gage 1993; Lindvall 1998). However, numerous questions still remain, and the clinical situation remains far from clear. A great deal of basic research into many aspects of neural grafting has been conducted and is currently in progress; for instance, investigations into the optimum graft location and number (Goren et al. 2005); strategies for improving graft survival (Macauley et al. 2004); the effectiveness of combining two types of tissue in one graft (Puschban et al. 2000) or grafting to multiple targets (Ramachandran et al. 2002); and the mechanism of action of the grafts (Sørensen et al. 2005). Clinical case reports are pointing to the need for further basic research into technical issues such as the reasons for cell death during graft development and the long-term efficacy of grafts (Tabbal et al. 1998). With further technical refinements, it is not unreasonable to anticipate that these approaches may eventually open up new possibilities for intervening in neurodegenerative diseases, and for stimulating regeneration and functional improvement in human beings.

Of all the neurodegenerative conditions that might eventually benefit from neural grafting, the one on which most attention has been focused is Parkinson's disease. This is because of the discreteness of the degeneration within the brain of a Parkinsonism sufferer – all the symptoms of Parkinsonism result from damage to a collection of structures in the brain known as the basal ganglia. The neurons which are destroyed are principally important in the control of movement. Since these neurons function by releasing one particular chemical neurotransmitter, dopamine, their damage in Parkinsonism leads to a loss of dopamine and a consequent inability by the basal ganglia to function effectively in motor activity. The drugs used as the most common current therapy for Parkinson's disease have many unpleasant side effects, which limit their usefulness in many patients.

Success with an animal model of the disease led investigators to consider seriously that reconstructing the dopamine pathways in the brain by neural grafting may prove an effective and permanent therapy for human Parkinsonism. Clinical trials using implants of human fetal midbrain tissue into the brains of patients with Parkinson's disease have been carried out in over 350 patients (Master et al. 2007). The first such procedure took place in China in 1985, although it was not reported until 1987 (Jiang et al. 1987). Only fleeting improvement was observed. In Mexico in September 1987, two patients with Parkinson's disease received transplants of fetal tissue, with claims of an 'evident objective improvement in the symptoms of Parkinson's disease in both cases' (Madrazo et al. 1988). In Sweden in November and December 1987, two further patients received transplants of human fetal dopamine nerve cells (Lindvall et al. 1989), and in the same year, this time in Britain, two more patients underwent this procedure (Hitchcock et al. 1988).

What has emerged is some improvement of motor symptoms, to either a minor or moderate extent following the implant, although in no case has there been a complete reversal of symptoms (Isacson and Deacon 1997; Lindvall 1997; Olanow et al. 1997). Symptomatic improvement has generally been found to commence immediately or in the first six months, with continued improvement occurring up to 30 months post-transplantation. To date, few significant adverse effects have been noted and there is evidence of the survival and integration of grafted dopaminergic neurons into the host brain (Hagell and Brundin 2001; Kordower et al. 1998; Wenning et al. 1997). In a long-term follow-up study, Lopez-Lozano et al (1997) have shown that clinical recovery persisted in 70 per cent of patients for five years following implantation. Similar positive results have been reported by others (Hauser et al. 1999).

On the negative side, functional recovery in fetal neural trials was only ever partial, indicating a need for procedures to be improved and refined. Results have been unpredictable and highly variable from the outset. Furthermore, some of the more recent, larger controlled trials have produced poor results associated with side effects and morbidity (Freed et al. 2001; Freeman et al. 2003; Olanow et al. 2003). It appears that even a functioning graft cannot protect the dopaminergic neurons in areas outside the graft from the progressive degeneration associated with Parkinson's disease (Mendez et al. 2008; Piccini et al. 2005). The controlled trials have also revealed a much greater success rate with neural grafting in younger as opposed to older patients (Clarkson 2001; Freed et al. 2001). The rate of progression of Parkinson's disease, which increases with age of onset, appears to reduce the likelihood of a successful clinical outcome (Linazasoro 2006). This is troubling because Parkinson's disease is a disease of old age; if fetal neural grafting is principally effective in younger patients, then only a small minority of those afflicted with Parkinson's disease are likely to benefit from the procedure.

Since the publication of the results of these controlled trials few further studies have been undertaken. Rather, efforts have concentrated on elucidating the underlying causes of the side effects that became evident in the double-blind trials (Piccini et al. 1999), and of 'fine-tuning' transplantation methodologies (Mendez et al. 2005). Before trials can continue a number of important additional issues must be addressed including: standardization of graft preparation and composition; development of better criteria for patient selection with regard to disease severity and patient age; optimization of graft placement; and elucidation of the role of immunosuppression on clinical outcomes (Lindvall and Bjorklund 2004; Winkler et al. 2005).

Recently three papers have reported on postmortem studies of the brains of Parkinson's patients who underwent fetal neural transplantation 9 to 16 years previously (Kordower et al. 2008; Li et al. 2008; Mendez et al. 2008). While the grafts had survived and integrated into the host brains in varying degrees, some grafts showed evidence of Lewy body pathology: the disease had propagated from the host to the graft (Kordower et al. 2008; Li et al. 2008). However, no pathology was found in another set of subjects (Mendez et al. 2008). The mechanism by which intrinsic factors in the Parkinsonian brain could affect graft cells is unclear, and these findings question the validity of the transplantation approach, particularly in light of the limited clinical improvement experienced by subjects (Braak and Del Tredici 2008). Despite this, the authors of the postmortem studies still express cautious optimism.

The Network of European CNS Transplantation and Restoration (NECTAR) has raised concerns over the study by Freed and co-workers (2001). In particular, this group objects to the use of cultured donor tissue, the lack of immunosuppression, the short one-year time-line of the study and the use of sham neurosurgical procedures (Nikkhah 2001). Sham surgery (performing much of the surgical intervention which enables provision of the experimental treatment, while crucially not providing the treatment itself) has also come in for criticism on purely ethical grounds (Macklin 1999; Polgar and Ng 2005). However, Olanow (2005) considers it the only way to exclude the possibility of placebo effects, which can be prominent in Parkinson's disease studies. Other ethical issues regarding the design of these clinical trials must be addressed, including the long-term follow-up of patients, the number of patients necessary for statistical significance, standardization of research protocols, and the undue optimism of researchers despite years of trials producing unsatisfactory results (Jones and Galvin 2006).

Neural grafting is a surgical procedure that remains highly experimental and many further detailed follow-up reports are still required. The extent of symptomatic relief observed so far in operated Parkinsonian patients is not great enough to justify using the procedure in a large number of patients (Goetz et al. 2005; Olanow et al. 2003). Neural grafting will only be helpful clinically if the transplantation of cells can be performed with minimal risk, and lead to a reliable improvement comparable to, or better than, that obtained with conventional drug treatments or the rapidly expanding number of alternative surgical approaches, particularly deep brain stimulation (Okun and Vitek 2004; Volkmann 2007).

The potential role of fetal neural transplants in treating neurological conditions other than Parkinson's continues to be investigated. Greatest interest is being shown in Huntington's disease (Bachoud-Levi et al. 2006; Keene et al. 2007); Alzheimer's disease (Isenmann et al. 1996); disorders primarily affecting the hippocampus, such as temporal lobe epilepsy and stroke (Darsalia et al. 2007; Shetty and Turner 1996); traumatic brain injury (Gao et al. 2006; Kanelos and McDeavitt 1998); intracerebral hemorrhage (Altumbabic and Del Bigio 1998); cerebral ischemia (Borlongan et al. 1998); and in cases of spinal cord injury (Asada et al. 1998; Tarasenko et al. 2007). It is of grave concern that fetal neural transplantation is being applied to other neurodegenerative disorders when trials with Parkinson's disease have all but come to a halt due to limited clinical improvement and unacceptable risks to patients.

The history of fetal neural transplantation trials is instructive for experimentation in related neural transplantation paradigms. Attention is being turned to the use of stem cells, both embryonic and endogenous adult neural stem cells, to treat Parkinson's and other neurodegenerative diseases. While these stem cells may produce functional neuronal and glial cells in culture, they must be shown to produce clinically significant quantities of the desired cell types and promote long-lasting functional improvements in established animal models before being used in clinical trials (Galvin and Jones 2006). Thorough and rigorous preclinical research is required before clinical trials can be scientifically and ethically justified.

Moral Complicity: An Exploration

The ethical debate surrounding fetal neural transplantation focuses on the use of tissue from fetuses made available by induced abortion, and particular attention needs to be paid to the ethical dimensions of this debate. The issue cannot be side-stepped by suggesting the use of other fetal material. Tissue from spontaneously aborted human fetuses, ectopic pregnancies, stillbirths, or extra-embryonic tissue would not be satisfactory due to the high levels of chromosomal abnormalities, tissue damage and contamination, and the lack of available tissue.

A central issue in considering fetal neural transplantation is the status given to the human fetus. In order to arrive at a workable policy, an assumption is made, and this is that the fetus warrants a special moral status. This is a mid-position between those that would give the fetus no special moral status, and those who would provide it with total protection. According to this mid-position, since we afford respect to an adult human cadaver, we are also to do so, albeit in a modified fashion, to the dead fetus. To ensure such respect is given, certain provisos are indicated: the fetus must be dead when the neural tissue is removed, the abortion should not be influenced in any way by the prospect of grafting fetal tissue, and the abortion and grafting procedures should be conducted completely separately (Jones 1989a).

Along with the special status bestowed upon the human fetus, this mid-position approach also concedes another point, namely, that abortion may be a moral wrong. Once again, ethical viewpoints within society vary enormously on abortion, and what is being argued here is that, even accepting the most conservative viewpoint on abortion, it is still possible to explore the dimensions of the debate regarding the ethical acceptability of the use of tissue taken from aborted fetuses.

Against this background, it is possible to identify four distinct positions on this question (Gillam 1989):

1. Fetal tissue transplants are wrong, since experimental results to date are not good enough to warrant clinical application.
2. Fetal tissue transplants are wrong, because abortion is morally wrong and the wrongness of abortion cannot be isolated from any subsequent ethical decision concerning use of the fetal tissue.
3. Fetal tissue transplants are acceptable, because there is nothing morally wrong with abortion. Any safeguards that are required are to protect the woman having the abortion.
4. Fetal tissue transplants are acceptable, even if abortion is considered morally wrong. Such a separation is feasible because the two procedures are morally separate, as long as safeguards are in place to ensure that the abortion decision is kept separate from the transplant decision.

Position one expresses the state of development of the scientific and clinical studies, and so has no direct relevance for abortion.

Position two may be characterized as an *abortion-dependent* viewpoint, which considers the moral abhorrence of abortion to be so great that it taints beyond acceptability any possible beneficial uses of the resulting fetal material. This is, in essence, the moral complicity argument. Generally associated with this position are fears that clinical uses of aborted material will lead to an increase in the rate of induced abortion in the community (Nolan 1988).

Position three, the clinical benefit (*abortion irrelevant*) stance, regards induced abortion as morally acceptable or, at least, of limited moral concern when placed alongside the potential benefits offered by fetal tissue transplantation. Implicit within this viewpoint is a lower moral status for the fetus than for the adult, whether mother or patient. Restrictions are called for, but these reflect the mother's interests rather than those of the fetus.

Position four is an *abortion-independent* position, and can be espoused even by those who view the fetus as deserving of profound respect. The thrust of this position depends entirely on the ability to view as morally acceptable a procedure (fetal tissue transplantation) that would not be possible apart from what many regard as a morally unacceptable procedure (induced abortion). Basic to this viewpoint is a complete separation in practice of the two procedures, a separation made possible by a rejection of the moral complicity argument (Gillam 1998; Jones 1991).

Positions two, three and four revolve around a moral judgment regarding the abortion. Position three states that there is nothing morally wrong in abortion, having bestowed limited moral value on the fetus. Positions two and four consider the moral complicity principle, and respond to it in opposite ways. If the debate is confined to these terms, it revolves around the validity or otherwise of the moral complicity argument. Either the moral complicity principle is accepted, and the use of any fetal tissue from induced abortions implicates all those using the tissue in the morally evil act of the abortion (position two); or moral complicity is rejected and the two actions are seen as separate, both morally and procedurally (position four).

In our view, there are a number of problems with the moral complicity argument. The first is that it is used selectively. As we saw in Chapter 3, moral complicity appears frequently in arguments over the use or otherwise of data and material emanating from the Nazi era, but appears to be ignored in discussions of other areas dependent upon the use of human material. Whenever human tissue is used, there is almost inevitably the possibility of complicity in some moral evil. This may be complicity in the road toll when organs are used from the victims of car crashes, in homicide when organs are used from murder victims, in suicide when organs are used from those who have committed suicide, or in poverty when the cadavers of the destitute are used for dissection. To suggest that the surgeon or anatomist is in a supportive alliance with intoxicated car drivers, murderers, those who commit suicide, or an inequitable social system, bears little relationship to moral reality. They are not accomplices in the prior evil by seeking to achieve some good from a contingent event over which they had no control (Robertson 1988). There *is* a moral distance between the evil and the intended good, a moral distance that emerges repeatedly in society's use of human material. We are obliged to be consistent in our use of ethical principles. The acceptance of the moral complicity argument in other spheres should lead to its acceptance in this sphere; similarly, its rejection here should lead to its rejection elsewhere (Jones 1991).

In the second place, we routinely act on the assumption that good can come from evil. As a general principle, we are prepared to benefit from tragedies, and this is regarded as an ethically valid stance as long as we are in no way responsible for the tragedies and would have prevented them had we been in a position to do so. Examples of this are not difficult to find. Many studies of malnourished children have thrown a great deal of light on the effects of malnutrition on the developing brain, while studies of the after-effects of the atom bomb explosions at Hiroshima and Nagasaki have been enormously valuable in understanding the long-term effects of radiation on human populations. More recently, studies have been made of the brains of suicide victims, in an attempt to throw light on the causes of depression (Cui et al. 2007). As societies, we are prepared to benefit from tragedies, with the one proviso that the tragedies are not intentionally caused in order to yield scientific data.

Consequently, it appears that, in most published reports, the use of fetal material for transplantation purposes is in accordance with our use of human material in many other situations. The Human Fetal Tissue Transplantation Research Panel (1988) in their report, for instance, concluded that 'the use of fetal tissue in research is acceptable public policy because abortion is legal and … the research in question is intended to achieve significant medical goals' (quoted in Annas 1993, 182). The Panel concluded that abortion and fetal tissue use are entirely separable issues and that transplanting fetal tissue, therefore, can be ethically isolated from any immorality associated with the source of the tissue.

In the case of fetal tissue transplants, it is essential to ensure that there is no procedural connection between the abortion and the transplantation, and that the manner of fetal death is not modified in any way in order to facilitate subsequent use of the tissue (Max 1989). Under these conditions it is possible to affirm that fetal tissue transplantation is acceptable, even if abortion is considered morally wrong, on the ground that respect for the dead fetus is not demonstrated solely by its immediate disposal. Respect may also emanate from its subsequent use to provide the gift of life to another in the human community, in accordance with the reasoning commonly used for organ transplantation from adult cadavers.

However, such arguments do not justify *all* uses to which neural grafting is put. Basic to these remarks is a proviso, namely, that there must be clinical and scientific justification for the grafting. If this is lacking, ethical justification for the procedure disappears. For example, the transplantation of brain tissue from three- to five-month-old fetuses is scientifically dubious since at this developmental stage the brain tissue is not optimally effective for graft growth. In addition, to attempt to improve the intelligence quotients of patients with senile dementia via fetal tissue grafts (Lin et al. 1994) is completely unwarranted, scientifically. In this context scientific and moral reasoning both argue against the use of such grafts.

Xenotransplantation: Crossing Species Boundaries

The inadequacy of the supply of cadaveric organs for transplantation has led research workers to explore the possibility of using animals as a source of transplantable organs and tissues: xenografting or xenotransplantation. In addition, fetal grafting has failed to break free of the ethical difficulties that accompany the use of human fetal tissue and its intimate association with induced abortion, a difficulty that the transplantation of animal tissues would circumvent.

The term 'xenotransplantation' covers all procedures involving the transfer of tissues between different species. As such, it includes therapies, such as the transplantation of pig heart valves into humans, as well as more recent controversial experiments, such as implanting human fetal neural cells into rats to investigate neuronal growth patterns.

At first glance, this topic may appear peripheral to the subject of this book, that is, human cadavers, since attention is directed more towards the use of organs or tissue from *animal* cadavers than from human cadavers. This is true, and yet the notion of crossing species boundaries includes utilizing tissue from humans in animals and *vice versa*. While complete human cadavers are not usually involved, the modification of humans using tissue from non-humans takes us into a realm a small distance removed from that of conventional same-species transplantation (allotransplantation).

Choosing an Animal Model

Early attempts at xenotransplantation using tissue from dogs, calves, lambs, goats, rabbits and apes were comparatively numerous, but wholly unsuccessful (Deschamps et al. 2005). There was a burst of research into xenografting in the early 1960s, with a number of attempts to transplant kidneys from either chimpanzees (Reemtsma et al. 1964) or baboons (Starzl et al. 1964) into human patients. However, a lack of long-term success with this procedure (the longest functioning graft from these trials lasted nine months; Reemtsma et al. 1964) led to the abandonment of this approach (Calne 1993). Its reappearance more recently is due to the introduction of immunosuppressive drugs, particularly *cyclosporin A*, in the early 1980s. These drugs have revolutionized organ transplantation.

In 1984 xenografting made international headlines with the case of Baby Fae, an infant born with a fatal form of congenital heart disease who, at the age of 15 days, became the recipient of a baboon's heart. The infant survived for only 20 days, but the surgical team responsible for the operation believed the outcome was sufficiently favourable to warrant further investigation of the procedure (Bailey et al. 1985). They reported that the regime of immunosuppressive drugs they had used had almost totally prevented cell-mediated rejection, and that graft failure had instead resulted from a progressive, potentially avoidable response to the incompatible blood group. Since the Baby Fae case, there have been two further instances of baboon-to-human transplantation. In both, adult sufferers of hepatitis received baboon livers but both operations proved unsuccessful (Nelson 1992).

Many researchers now argue that non-human primates are an inappropriate source of organs and propose, as an alternative, the use of organs from the pig (Dunning et al. 1994). Many primate species are endangered and are officially protected (for example, chimpanzees). Those primates that are more plentiful, such as the baboon, are more distantly removed from human beings, requiring recipients to undergo large amounts of immunosuppressive treatment following the transplant (Calne 1993). The US Food and Drug Administration has effectively banned xenotransplants from nonhuman primates since 1999 because the similarities between nonhuman primates and humans may promote the transmission of diseases between the two species (d'Apice 2005).

The advantages of the pig are several-fold. Pigs are domesticated, have large litters, are suitable for genetic modification, and can be bred in a pathogen-free environment. Furthermore, the pig has a similar physiology to human beings in terms of the heart, liver and pancreatic islets (which have been successfully transplanted into a number of diabetic patients; Groth et al. 1998; Valdes-Gonzalez et al. 2005; Valdes-Gonzalez et al. 2007), and pig organs grow rapidly to the size of human ones (White and Wallwork 1993). A report by the Nuffield Council on Bioethics (1996) favours the use of pig rather than primate organs for transplantation into humans.

Experiments to date indicate that xenotransplantation is worth pursuing as a therapeutic option. Animal organs could be used as replacement or 'bridging' organs, while patients wait for human organs to become available. Some patients have already been connected to extracorporeal animal kidneys prior to cadaveric kidney transplantation (Bengtsson et al. 1998; Breimer et al. 1996). Patients waiting for a liver transplant have been treated with a variety of extracorporeal liver support systems. Artificial systems can cleanse toxins from the blood, but only hepatocyte-containing systems can provide other missing liver-specific functions, for which porcine hepatocytes have proved effective (Rozga 2006; Santoro et al. 2007). The transplantation of fetal neural xenogenic (originating from a species different from the recipient) cells has resulted in alleviation of symptoms for Parkinson's disease patients (Deacon et al. 1997; Fink et al. 2000), while xenogenic neuroblasts are able to reconstitute damaged circuitry and establish axonal connections within the host brain (Isacson et al. 1998). Diabetic patients respond to pig insulin, with evidence that porcine pancreatic islet cells survive following transplantation to human patients (Reinholt et al. 1998; Valdes-Gonzalez et al. 2005). A potential advantage of xenotransplantation is that cells such as neuroblasts can be prepared sterile in large amounts from special pathogen-free donors at defined embryonic ages.

The biggest problem associated with xenotransplantation is host immune rejection of the transplanted tissue, a problem also encountered in allotransplants. However, in xenotransplantation there are more 'discordant signals' (resulting from the donor and host cell-surface markers differing from one another), thereby increasing the activation and intensity of the host's immune response. There are three main types of rejection; hyperacute, delayed graft, and T-cell mediated rejection (Weiss 1998a). Genetic modification techniques have been developed to overcome some forms of rejection (Cooper et al. 2007; Weiss 1998a) and it is possible that T-cell mediated rejection may be ameliorated by immunosuppressive therapy. There is every reason to believe that rejection problems will be substantially overcome in the future.

Xenozoonotic Infections

Xenotransplantation creates a ready passage for viruses, since both physical barriers and natural host immunity are compromised in transplant recipients. The usual physical barriers, like skin and mucosal surfaces, offer no protection against viruses within cells transplanted into the body (Weiss 1998b). Since transplant recipients are routinely given immunosuppresive drugs to prevent rejection of the transplant, these patients make ideal hosts for viruses and other microorganisms. Unfortunately, all strategies implemented to prevent rejection of xenografts – genetic modification of the donor animals, immunosuppression therapy, treatment of the recipient by the induction of immune tolerance, and antibody removal – may only serve to increase the host's susceptibility to pathogens (Butler 1998; Weiss 1998a).

The risk from xenozoonosis or xenosis (the transfer of infection via xenotransplantation) is difficult to assess. There have been several occurrences where viruses, amongst them HIV, ebola, severe acute respiratory syndrome (SARS), and avian H5N1 influenza virus, have crossed species barriers to infect humans (Formenty et al. 1999; Peiris 2003; Shortridge et al. 1998). These instances demonstrate that retroviruses or other pathogens from animals have the potential to infect human cells. Whether these agents will replicate in human cells *in vivo* remains debatable. If replication were to occur, it is not known whether this infection would cause disease, and if it did, it is not clear whether the disease would be capable of being transmitted to other humans (Tackaberry and Ganz 1998). More recent reports have suggested that the risk of xenozoonosis is less than first thought, although it should not be discounted (Fishman 2005; Yang et al. 2004).

A major uncertainty is the nature of any infecting microorganism or virus (Brown et al. 1998). Pathogens that may be latent or inconsequentially pathogenic in the donor animal (e.g. endogenous retroviruses) may cause significant disease in a human recipient. Furthermore, novel organisms may have unconventional clinical symptoms, making infectious agents difficult to identify and treat (Bach et al. 1998; Weiss 1998a).

There are at least three known porcine endogenous retroviruses (PERVs) in the pig genome, two of which have been shown to infect human cells in culture (Günzburg and Salmons 2000). This may or may not occur *in vivo*. The few patients who have received xenotransplants of porcine islet cells or fetal neuronal cells, or who have been extracorporeally attached to pig kidneys or bioreactors containing porcine hepatocytes, have so far shown no evidence of PERV infection (Dinsmore et al. 2000; Sauer et al. 2003; Valdes-Gonzalez et al. 2005).

As the occurrence of xenoses resulting from xenotransplantation could have a serious impact on the general population, it has been recommended that the most appropriate ethical response is for the public to have an opportunity to discuss and consent to (or decline) any xenotransplantation proposal relating to an individual (Bach et al. 1998). This underlines a crucial consideration, namely, that if treatment of individuals has implications for others, the wider community may well have an interest in that treatment. It has been suggested that xenotransplant recipients be monitored by initial quarantine isolation, followed by extensive long-term testing (including microbiological screening and blood, serological and viral genome detection tests) (Collignon 1998). Restricting the international travel of xenotransplant recipients would limit xenotourism, whereby patients travel overseas to receive xenotransplants banned in their own county (Sykes et al. 2003). It has also been proposed that recipients should be past childbearing age and ought not to donate their blood or organs, and that strategies to contain potential xenozoonotic outbreaks within the community should be in place (Collignon 1998; Isacson and Breakefield 1997).

It is at this juncture that clinical and ethical considerations meet head on, since a balance will have to be found between patients' autonomy and right to confidentiality and the right of the wider public to be protected from risks of xenoses (Hughes 2007). In other words, the interests of the individual may be inseparable from more general interests (Weiss 1998a).

Ethical Considerations

The central query is whether it is morally wrong for human beings to make use of animals for our own health related purposes. Xenotransplantation has been justified on the grounds that human beings possess the capacity for complex cognition (including rationalization, self-awareness, social interaction and the possession of consciousness), whereas non-human animals do not (Caplan 1992). If xenotransplantation is to be justified on this basis, critics argue that the principle could also be extended to include, for arguments sake, a severely retarded child. If we are to treat human and non-human animals of equivalent cognitive ability in different ways, some argue we are guilty of 'speciesism'; allowing unequal treatment of beings equal in morally relevant characteristics based solely on the species to which each belongs (Kushner and Belliotti 1985; Singer 1975). Other objections to xenotransplantation are based on concerns about the quality of informed consent obtained from (or on behalf of) recipients, given that this procedure is still in many ways experimental (Nelson 1992). Critics have also suggested that it is inequitable to commit vast resources to xenografting, with its uncertain results, compared with the pressing need for primary and preventive health care measures (see Caplan 1992).

The speciesist argument, if accepted, is an argument against most, if not all, experimental uses of animals, since all the requirements controlling research on humans would have to be applied equally to the use of animals – there would be no reason for distinguishing between experiments on rats or mice, and the use of pigs' organs in a human subject. Some have suggested that the speciesist argument is not founded on a rational basis (Campbell et al. 2005), since non-human animals do not have rights and are not considered moral agents. For instance, an animal predator is not morally reprehensible in the sense that a violently aggressive human being is. It is true that neither infants nor the severely intellectually handicapped are morally responsible for their actions. However, we have an overriding obligation to nurture infants so that they may become full members of the community of moral agents. Similarly, we have a special obligation to offer the severely intellectually handicapped every opportunity to become active and cared-for members of the human community, an obligation that far exceeds any obligations not to harm non-human animals. Campbell et al. (2005, 235) summarize this position as follows:

> The differences between humans and other animals are both real and relevant to treating them as being of unequal moral status. Humans alone are capable of that moral agency which commands absolute respect. Humans alone carry the responsibility for determining how the welfare of their own species is to be balanced against the welfare of other living creatures. Only humans must decide when it is right to experiment or to desist from experiments: rats, pigs, dogs and other mammals depend on the morality of those decisions.

This does not give humans the right to do whatever they like to non-human animals, since we are to act as moral agents. We are to take seriously the welfare of other animals. By the same token, it does not automatically proscribe the use of animals in ways that will benefit humans (or even other animals). This leaves xenotransplantation as a possibility to be considered, although it places a moral burden on those employing it to oversee the welfare of donor animals as they would the welfare of human donors in other circumstances.

The objection to xenotransplantation based on consent and a possibly inadequate experimental procedure is precisely the same as in any other equivalent situation. No experimental surgery on human patients can be justified until there are reliable grounds for believing that it will enhance patients' quality of life. This requirement is not confined to xenotransplantation, but neither is the requirement any less stringent in xenotransplantation than in other therapeutic areas. In similar vein, the resource issue is a general one, to be assessed on its own merits. It is not an argument *per se* against xenotransplantation, any more than it is against the use of artificial reproductive technologies, intensive care of very premature babies, or the performance of expensive surgical operations on the elderly.

Many of the ethical concerns that have been raised in relation to xenotransplantation are not unique to this field, but are commonly raised to a variety of new developments in biomedicine. The unnaturalness of xenotransplantation (Mepham et al. 1997) is as great or as little an issue here as in any other area, since anything humans do to alter the natural order is, by definition, unnatural. Without interfering with nature, it would not be possible to 'free human lives from the destructive effects of such natural phenomena as infectious agents, droughts and hurricanes' (Hughes 1998, 19). The ethical issue is not with the unnaturalness *per se*, but its consequences for the wellbeing of patients. In these terms, xenotransplantation may be no more unnatural than the use of antibiotics in the treatment of infection, or of dialysis procedures. Each stands or falls on its merits and is considered appropriate as long as the intended good of the procedure or intervention outweigh its disadvantages. Society's views on what is natural or unnatural often change as new technologies become familiar. Consequently, arguments based on unnaturalness alone are not sufficient to condemn xenotransplantation.

'Playing God' concerns are often espoused as a reason for opposing xenotransplantation, the implication being that scientists have been given great power over things which should not be tampered with. However, humans already have the ability to exercise vast control over the natural order, and, by and large, these abilities are wisely used. Any tampering with fundamental biological processes should be carried out with caution and humility; what is called for are intelligence and compassion. This is not an argument against xenotransplantation, unless it can be demonstrated that the objectives are doomed to failure. Since xenotransplantation is aimed at alleviating illness and rectifying pathology, such therapeutic objectives should, in principle, be lauded rather than condemned.

Breaching Species Boundaries

A more precise concern is that xenotransplantation disrespects the sanctity of both human and animal life by blurring species boundaries (Mepham et al. 1997). In current debate these boundaries are not clearly enunciated and one has to start by asking what they are (Robert and Baylis 2003). The concept may be used to distinguish one group of animals from others, which by definition, are incapable of interbreeding. Does this mean that eradication of a species boundary would signify that the genetically altered animal or the human transplant recipient would be incapable of interbreeding with other members of their respective species? Since this far-reaching prospect is probably not what is envisaged by a blurring or breaching of the species boundary, we have to ask what is in view. We propose that the debate be conducted on two initial levels: the biological (ranging from the macroscopic to the microscopic and genetic) and the psychological. What is required is an assessment of the nature and consequences of such a breach in each case. In attempting to do this, we will consider non-neural and neural xenotransplantation respectively.

At a general biological level, xenotransplantation has direct links with allotransplantation, when the tissue to be transplanted is an organ like a kidney, heart or lung. Organs such as these serve purely mechanical functions. Consequently, in clinical terms, the transplantation of a kidney can be compared ethically to the use of dialysis equipment, since the therapeutic goals are comparable. Hence, in principle, xenotransplantation appears no less ethical than the use of any other mechanical aid to either improve or restore bodily functions, or cope with physical impairment.

Consider, for example, the transplantation of a pig kidney into a human. If the transplanted kidney functioned to keep the person alive and increase their quality of life, the ethical issues accompanying xenotransplantation are comparable to those of allotransplantation. This suggests that species boundaries are of limited importance compared to the potential benefits of xenotransplantation.

Even if the pig was genetically altered to express human cell surface proteins and therefore prevent hyperacute rejection, species boundaries would not become blurred. Only a few out of several thousand human genes would be inserted into the pig, which would continue to look, behave and be regarded as a pig. This is because any particular gene only contributes to the specification of the characteristics of a species when it acts in combination with the other genes of that genome. Hence, the insertion of certain human genes into a pig would destroy the integrity of neither the pig donor nor the human host (Nuffield Council on Bioethics 1996).

Is the transplantation of neural cells from one species to another different from the transplantation of an organ such as a kidney? Does the involvement of neural tissues, with psychological overtones, move us away from the 'mechanical' argument? The increased ethical concerns with the xenotransplantation of nervous tissue are understandable, since procedures that potentially affect personality and personhood are directed at the very nature of our humanity. The question, therefore, is whether an individual's humanity will be affected by xenotransplants. In order to address this question, consider first standard neurosurgery and psychosurgery. These procedures may cause considerable damage, either deliberately or inadvertently, in order to help the patient (by removing a tumour, repairing an aneurysm, or altering behavioural features). Procedures such as these are generally regarded as ethical, as long as they are carried out with a therapeutic intent. Surely a procedure such as xenotransplantation, which attempts to heal or reduce the effects of lesions, cannot be less ethical than a surgical procedure which destroys brain tissue, if both the xenotransplantation and the surgery are administered in the best interests of the patient. Engels (1999), arguing against xenotransplantation, claims one objection to be that it will be necessary for patients and their relatives to be closely monitored on a long-term basis, and that 'this could seriously affect their quality of life'. While this is always a possibility, surely a successful outcome of a xenograft procedure would have major implications (for the better) for a patient's life.

It is difficult to see how the ethical issues associated with xenotransplantation would be different from any allotransplantation undertaken in the neural area. Just as there are similarities with the non-neural situation above (where the significance of a kidney stems from its functional attributes regardless of its species origin), likewise a neuron's significance is in its functional capabilities and in the connections and circuits of which it is a part.

While it is tempting to highlight the species origin of transplanted neurons, it may be far more important scientifically to concentrate on the brain region being studied, and the character and extent of the neurons, growth factors and transmitters being transplanted. It is likely that the human, porcine or rodent origin of the cells will prove significantly less important, in functional terms, than the connections these neurons make, and the networks into which they are incorporated. Hence, as with other tissues, the ethical considerations associated with the allotransplantation and xenotransplantation of neural tissues are closely tied in with scientific ones.

What is it that makes one brain different from another? Neurons and their synapses come under the influence of a whole host of internal and external factors. It may be that there is not a significant difference between neurons from different species (apart possibly from the speed of development), since it is the environment and context within which they develop and function that are determinative of an individual's ultimate personality. All the neurons of a brain are subject to the same environmental influences, and so transplanted neural cells will have much the same influence on personality as host neurons.

Experience with neural allotransplants to date (to alleviate conditions such as Parkinson's and Huntington's diseases) do not suggest that the presence of another human's neural cells inside our brains makes us different people. It may be that crossing personal and even species boundaries is irrelevant.

Many of the ethical issues associated with xenotransplantation are vague fears, usually not clearly articulated, about the blurring of species boundaries and the resultant consequences for an individual's personality and self-image. Were such consequences to occur, the case against xenotransplantation would be persuasive, since they would override the therapeutic goals of alleviating the symptoms of conditions like Parkinson's disease. However, it would be unwise to allow such fears to threaten potential therapeutic regimes that may hold out hope for patients with serious neurodegenerative conditions.

The central question should be whether the individual will be enhanced or diminished as a person by xenotransplantation. This should always be our principal concern, no matter what medical intervention is being considered, whether it be neurosurgery, psychosurgery, allotransplantation or xenotransplantation. All related issues should be analyzed in light of the neural and psychological integrity of the individual, in terms of their self-awareness and self-identity. Xenotransplantation remains a question of balance; between what is best for the patient and a host of ill-defined and as yet unanswered scientific and ethical questions. These issues are complex and challenging and will not be satisfactorily resolved in the short term.

Xenotransplantation appears to represent an intermediate approach within the array of organ replacement procedures. Whether or not it assumes a significant role will depend on its scientific and clinical usefulness, rather than on general ethical considerations. As long as xenografting operates within the framework of appropriate consent and careful scientific parameters, it should be pursued as a serious contribution to organ transplantation.

Chapter 6
The Indigenous Body

Background

In this chapter the focus of attention moves from cadavers as a whole, and tissues in general, to skeletal remains. This is a move from the realm of anatomy to that of physical anthropology, and also from human beings who have died recently to those who may have died many years ago. In spite of these shifts in emphases, we have not left the sphere of the human body, nor of the many ethical dilemmas that are inherent in the treatment of human remains.

In recent years it has become relatively commonplace to hear of skeletal remains that had been held by an anatomy department, medical school or museum for many years having been returned to tribes for subsequent reburial. As we consider the repatriation of human skeletal remains, two opposing forces soon become evident. On one side are the Western scientific values of archaeology; on the other, there is the global cultural renaissance among indigenous peoples. For some writers these two perspectives are implacable opponents, the former representing sensitivity and the latter militancy and obduracy (Gough 1996). For others, there is concern that the burial of skeletal remains represents the destruction of ancient evidence by indigenous communities and is little better than European cultural imperialism (Mulvaney 1989, 1991). Within anthropology there is the additional concern that physical anthropology as a field of academic study is under threat, as the freedom of scholarly and scientific disciplines to define their own goals and chart their own course are gradually replaced by a repatriation agenda (Maslen 1995; Meighan 1992, 1993).

Views of this nature have emerged against the background of the many cases of repatriation since the early 1990s. For instance, in 1991 the University of Edinburgh returned nine Tasmanian Aboriginal skulls, housed for more than a century in its anatomy department, to Australian government representatives. Also returned was a collection of over 300 Aboriginal bones, including skulls or cranial fragments and four skeletons (Aldhous 1991). Remains of Aboriginal skeletal material have also been returned from other European universities and museums, including Bradford University, the Pitt-Rivers Museum at Oxford, the Peterborough City Museum and Dublin University. Australian universities and museums have also returned skeletal material for reburial, including the particularly contentious return of human remains from Kow Swamp by the Museum of Victoria. These bones were estimated to have been between 9,000 and 15,000 years old (Mulvaney 1990), and raise the issue of where the responsibility lies for bones hundreds of generations removed from living Aboriginal Australians (Mulvaney 1991). Similarly, 14,000-

year-old bones from Coobool Creek in the Murray Black collection (1,800 skeletons) were returned some years ago to Aboriginal communities (Ewing 1990; Mulvaney 1989).

Following a change to UK law in 2004 allowing repatriation of human remains from British museums, a claim was made for the return of the remains of 17 Tasmanian individuals from London's Natural History Museum. The Museum's trustees agreed to the repatriation, recognizing the priority of indigenous claims to the remains over potential scientific value, although they planned to first carry out further testing (Giles 2006). The Tasmanian claimants opposed the proposed testing as further desecration of the remains and took the dispute to the British High Court. In May 2007 the remains were returned to Tasmania without further testing, although the Tasmanian Aboriginal Centre agreed to share responsibility for previously extracted DNA with the Natural History Museum, allowing the possibility of further study (May 2007).

The British climate of increasing sensitivity to indigenous claims for the return of human remains is being tested by the recent activities of modern British Pagans and Druids (Kohn 2006; Randerson 2007). Drawing on the success of similar claims of indigenous groups such as the Australian Aboriginals, Pagan organizations such as 'Honouring the Ancient Dead' (www.honour.org.uk) seek to promote what they term 'respectful treatment' of ancient human remains. They claim that, in the case of 'those human remains without modern genealogical and cultural descendants ... human remains found or stored in a particular area should be regarded as the collective responsibility of that area's modern residents' (Restall Orr and Bienkowski 2006). In the case of Lindow Man (a well-preserved Iron Age man discovered in 1983 in a peat bog), they have argued for the relocation of his remains from London to Manchester, where the peat bog was located. It is doubtful whether modern Pagans can demonstrate ancestry or continuity of beliefs, customs and language (as required by UK Government guidelines), yet some museums are taking their claims seriously.

In the United States, remains of Native American people have been returned for reburial by universities such as Stanford, Minnesota, South Dakota and Nebraska, and by the Smithsonian Institute, which had a collection of 18,000 mostly prehistoric bones (Bahn 1989; Lindley 1989). A bitterly divisive case of repatriation involved the 1991 return by the Smithsonian of 756 sets of skeletal remains, comprising an estimated 1,000 individuals and a large collection of associated funerary objects to the people of Larsen Bay, Kodiak Island, on the southwest coast of Alaska. The bones dated back 2,000 years and had been collected in the 1930s from around 800 unmarked graves. The scale of this repatriation was unprecedented in the history of the museum and negotiations between the two parties were protracted and sometimes hostile (Bray and Killion 1994). Other contentious repatriations include those of remains from the 2,000-year-old Adena mound in West Virginia, and a 10,000-year-old skeleton in Idaho (Meighan 1993). It has been estimated that between the Mississippi River and the Continental Divide and the Canadian and Mexican borders, 5,124 excavated mortuary sites have so far produced the remains of 52,540 individuals (Rose et al. 1996).

In 1996, bones estimated to be 9,200 years old were uncovered on the shore of the Columbia River near the town of Kennewick, in Washington state. Since the bones made up one of the oldest and most complete skeletons ever found in the Pacific Northwest many scientists were excited by the potential of the bones to yield important information about the lives and ethnic background of the first people to colonize America. This was especially so since the so-called 'Kennewick Man' had Caucasoid features, suggesting he may not be an ancestor of any of the local Native American tribes (Lemonick 1996). Under the National American Graves Protection and Repatriation Act (NAGPRA), which we will explore in greater detail in the next section, the indigenous people of the area, the Umatillas, claimed all scientific investigations should cease and that the remains should be returned to them for reburial. The US Army Corps of Engineers, who controlled the land on which the remains were found, agreed with this course of action and reburial was only prevented by a group of eight scientists who instituted legal proceedings in an attempt to gain permission to study Kennewick Man. Extensive litigation between the scientists and a coalition of tribes claiming reburial rights followed and in 2004 the US Ninth Circuit Court of Appeals ruled in the scientists' favour, a decision which the tribes chose not to appeal. The Circuit Court ruled that the cultural link between the present-day tribes and the ancient remains was not sufficiently demonstrable and thus NAGPRA did not apply (Weimer 2005). This ruling allowed scientific study, which to date has been of limited extent as scientists negotiate with government agencies on a study protocol (Dalton 2005).

The time-scale of these skeletal remains is crucial, ranging from those a few generations removed to others emanating from as many as 400–1,200 generations before the present (Mulvaney 1989). This time-span reflects, at its recent end, spiritual and cultural values similar to those of contemporary societies, and at its remote end values with particular significance for global history.

These examples are not isolated instances. They constitute a major trend, from which practically no country, museum or anatomy department can escape. The problematic and contentious nature of this trend is implicit within the contemporary study of human skeletal remains, and therefore within our understanding of how the dead human body is to be treated.

Policy Developments

Up until the late 1960s there was very little discussion of the ethics of anthropology and the professional responsibilities of anthropologists. It was not until a number of crises within anthropology stimulated ethical discourse that various groups started voluntarily to establish codes of ethics (Fluehr-Lobban 2003; Pels 1999).

In 1989, the World Archaeological Congress issued the Vermillion Accord, with its stress on mutual respect and cooperation between archaeologists and indigenous peoples (Bulmer 1991). Included in this Accord was respect for the mortal remains of the dead and respect for the wishes of the dead concerning disposition, on the one hand, and respect for the scientific research value of skeletal remains on the other. This was followed in 1991 by a more specific outline of ethical principles for archaeologists working with indigenous populations. These include:

- to acknowledge the importance of indigenous cultural heritage, including sites, places, objects, artefacts, human remains, to the survival of indigenous cultures;
- to acknowledge the importance of protecting cultural heritage to the well-being of indigenous peoples;
- to acknowledge that the important relationship between indigenous peoples and their cultural heritage exists irrespective of legal ownership;
- to acknowledge that indigenous cultural heritage rightfully belongs to the indigenous descendants of that heritage;
- to seek, whenever possible, representation of indigenous peoples in agencies funding or authorizing research to be certain their view is considered as critically important in setting research standards, questions, priorities and goals (quoted in Powell et al. 1993, 6–7).

A number of professional bodies in the United States, including the American Anthropological Association, the Society for American Archaeology, the American Association of Physical Anthropologists and the Society of American Archaeology have all issued professional ethical guidelines (Alfonso and Powell 2007).

The Australian Archaeological Association has issued a policy supporting the transfer of post-1788 remains to communities (Meehan 1984). The Association endorsed the return of Aboriginal skeletal remains of known individuals according to the wishes of the deceased, or to an appropriate Aboriginal community. Particular emphasis was placed on fostering collaboration between the Aboriginal community and archaeological profession, with the aim of protecting and preserving prehistoric sites. The Association also advocated the establishment of Aboriginal Keeping Places and the training of Aboriginal people to maintain these Places. The policy stressed that all other Aboriginal skeletal remains are of scientific importance and should not be destroyed through reburial or cremation. The Association's more recent code of ethics, last amended in 2004,[1] emphasizes acknowledging the importance of cultural heritage to indigenous communities and managing archaeological material with agreement with concerned communities. This is balanced against the impetus to advocate for the conservation, curation and preservation of archaeological material.

In a number of jurisdictions, legislation has been passed to regulate the storage, study and repatriation of human skeletal material. In 1990, the US Congress passed NAGPRA, which was the culmination of more than two decades of lobbying

---

1   www.australianarchaeologicalassociation.com.au/ethics (accessed 8 April 2008).

by Native American groups for the return of human remains (for an historical overview, see Ferguson 1996).

NAGPRA asserts that human remains do not belong to individuals, or to institutional or governmental organizations, although descendants have the right to determine what happens to human remains. The law grants Native Americans and Hawaiians the right to repatriate human remains from federal and Indian land. To make this feasible, institutions are required to prepare inventories of their collections of human skeletal remains, while criteria are provided to assist in assessing which tribal group is the appropriate custodian of given remains. In spite of this, there have been difficulties in determining which tribe or tribes are most closely affiliated with the skeletal remains and associated artefacts (Morenon 2003). NAGPRA does not ban excavation of, or research on, Native American skeletons, although this may only occur with a permit and after consultation with Native Americans concerning what is done with the skeletal material. The law also requires adherence to professional standards, stipulates how inadvertent discoveries are to be handled, and imposes strong penalties for illegal trade (Weimer 2005). The Kennewick Man dispute has prompted judicial review of NAGPRA, particularly the definition of 'Native American', and has highlighted the fact that remains of great age and unclear identity, such as Kennewick Man, were not a primary focus of NAGPRA's drafters (Bruning 2006).

In other jurisdictions, Australian federal law states that all remains pre-1770 are by definition Aboriginal and must be controlled by Aboriginal authorities. In Israel, a revised interpretation by the government of the Antiquities Act led to the reburial of all human remains younger than 5,000 years (Koch and Sillen 1996).

The UK Human Tissue Act 2004, which applies in England, Wales and Northern Ireland, made consent the fundamental requirement for the use of human remains, including for public display in museums. However, the Act contains a number of exceptions that allow historical human remains to be displayed without consent. Exempt remains include those that have been imported, or have been derived prior to the Act coming into force (in 2006) and when more than 100 years has passed since the individuals' death. Material held in existing collections before the Act came into force is also exempt from the requirements for consent and for licensing by the Human Tissue Authority. From September 2006 any new human material collected from an individual who died less than 100 years ago can only be publicly displayed after full consent from the decedent and under licence from the Human Tissue Authority (Department for Culture Media and Sport 2005).

The Act has also given nine specified national museums the power to de-accession human remains in their collections from a person reasonably believed to have died less than 1,000 years before the Act came into force. Prior to the 2004 Act these nine museums were barred from doing so by the Museums Act 1964. This new legislation developed out of a joint declaration between the Prime Ministers of the United Kingdom and Australia in an effort to encourage repatriation of human remains to Australian indigenous communities. The time limit of 1,000 years was included to prevent deaccession of ancient material such as Egyptian mummies (Department for Culture Media and Sport 2005).

Contemporary Case Study

Archaeologists and anthropologists in New Zealand are facing the same ethical issues as have arisen in Australia, the United Kingdom and the United States. The indigenous population of New Zealand, the Māori, are becoming increasingly active in determining the disposition of the skeletal remains of their ancestors as well as items of cultural significance (taonga Māori). In contrast to most other countries the repatriation of Māori remains in New Zealand generally occurs in a co-operative, respectful and low-profile manner, because Māori are in a much stronger position in their own country than are most other indigenous populations (Hole 2007). In current legislation, excavated material belongs to the Crown and archaeologists must apply to the government for permission to excavate. The granting of such a permit is conditional upon approval of the local Māori people and, where excavation is approved, researchers hold the material for the museum which will ultimately store it.

This is an uneasy compromise, and there are prospects that the situation will change, allowing tribes (iwi) to own and control the material from all prehistoric sites within their tribal area (rohe). However, the situation is volatile and even if iwi ownership becomes law for artefacts, inter-tribal disputes are likely to follow significant discoveries in disputed areas, with the possibility that such conflicts may become the subject of protracted legal battles.

The Resource Management Act (1991) provides a clear mandate for consideration of Māori cultural values, and for Māori guardianship through the transfer of powers from local governmental authorities to iwi authorities. There is also strong provision in the Historic Places Act (1993) for consideration of Māori cultural values and for the delegation of functions and powers to Māori.

Museums in New Zealand have been governed by a series of Antiquities Acts (1901, 1908, 1962, 1975), renamed the Protected Objects Act in 2006, and together these represent an interesting development of perceptions of the respective differences between the Māori and Pakeha (non-Māori) concepts of property. According to the current Protected Objects Act (1975), the Māori Land Court may grant custody of taonga tūturu (cultural artefacts) to the people having the best claim on it, but the artefact remains the property of the Crown, even when removed from the burial of an identified party. The definition of taonga tūturu does not include human remains as it was considered culturally inappropriate to categorize these as objects. The Act imposes significant restrictions on archaeological activity, including a requirement for Māori concurrence to archaeological investigations. However, awareness and recognition of indigenous rights issues are gradually increasing, largely through increasing Māori representation on boards and committees.

Government policy adopted in 2003 supports the repatriation of Māori kōiwi tangata (ancestral remains) to New Zealand and to the communities of origin. The government funds the Museum of New Zealand, Te Papa Tongarewa, to undertake this work on its behalf. Te Papa's formal repatriation program works closely with iwi to request the repatriation of remains from overseas institutions. These kōiwi tangata are then stored in their ancestral remains vault (wahi tapu) while research is conducted to confirm the iwi of origin, to whom the remains are then returned. Repatriation of kōiwi tangata from national museums is also encouraged, such as the agreement to return the remains of 53 individuals from Canterbury Museum to the Rangitane iwi in 2006 (New Zealand Press Association 2006).

One viewpoint within the New Zealand museum community is that museums serve as the physical caretaker for the taonga that live there, but that the wairua (spiritual aspect) of the taonga is solely the province of the appropriate Māori group, even if they cannot under the law be its physical custodian. Calls have been made for museums to function less as the final resting places for artefacts, and to acknowledge formally the continuing relevance of taonga to a dynamic Māori culture, as well as to New Zealand culture in general (Hogan 1995).

Some argue that museums should consider becoming sacred repositories for human remains, when the latter are relatively recent, identifiable and claimed by living descendants or appropriate cultural representatives. One of the driving forces behind this idea is the offence experienced by Māori people at the display of mokomokai (smoked tattooed heads), the head being considered particularly sacred (Hole 2007). A sacred repository is seen as a culturally appropriate place for the care of human remains, and allows for *bona fide* research under strictly controlled conditions. Going along with this is an ethic of non-ownership, in that museums should care for and act as custodians of human remains, but not determine ownership. Repatriation emerges as a natural consequence of such an approach, leading to the view that museums have an obligation to return the remains when requested to do so by the appropriate representatives of the deceased. A number of mokomokai have recently been returned to New Zealand from overseas institutions. In 2007 nine mokomokai were repatriated from the University of Aberdeen and 14 from the Field Museum of Natural History in Chicago. It is believed that more than 200 mokomokai remain in overseas institutions (Okeroa 2007).

Each individual iwi has responsibility for establishing its own guidelines on the appropriate treatment of human remains. Ngāi Tahu, the largest tribal group of New Zealand's South Island, has been the first iwi to produce a definitive policy on the manner in which any human remains (kōiwi tangata) found in its rohe are to be managed (Gillies and O'Regan 1994). As a general principle, the policy specifies that authority and control over ancestral bones should be re-vested with iwi. The tribe regards the collection and possession of tribal kōiwi tangata by anyone other than the tribe itself as abhorrent and culturally insensitive. Their clear preference is that, wherever possible, kōiwi tangata *in situ* should not be disturbed and that the integrity of burial sites should remain intact. Where the kōiwi tangata have already been removed from the site, the policy calls for the repatriation to the iwi of those remains under its jurisdiction. The iwi has negotiated the establishment of secure keeping places (wahi tapu) within existing museums to where the kōiwi tangata may be removed, pending scientific investigation and a final decision regarding their proper place (Gillies and O'Regan 1994).

It is interesting that this policy applies to all kōiwi tangata in the Ngāi Tahu rohe, and that it applies equally to remains of any Polynesian people for which no locality or origin is known. Ngāi Tahu claims jurisdiction until such time as it can be demonstrated that the bones are not kōiwi tangata of Ngāi Tahu ancestry. The aim of this policy is to get the Crown to waive its claim to the ownership of artefacts under the Antiquities Act (1975). This is because the policy endeavours to allow grave artefacts to be reburied with the relevant kōiwi tangata.

Far from advocating wholesale reburial of all material, Ngāi Tahu's policy recognizes that scholarly investigation can play a role in furthering an understanding of tribal ancestry, and acknowledges that appropriate research in this area is a legitimate scientific interest. However, the policy reserves the right of iwi to consider and edit for reasons of cultural sensitivity any material proposed for publication. For remains unearthed now, the options suggested are immediate reburial, or removal to a safe keeping place pending scientific investigation. The policy does not specify the basis on which decisions of this nature are to be made, but it sets out that researchers' proposals for the study of kōiwi tangata are to be assessed by an advisory committee made up of local iwi leaders.

In relation to human genetic information, one Māori perspective is that tissue and other bodily material taken from Māori always belongs to Māori, who must always be in a position to make informed decisions on how such material is to be used. Any scientific intrusion that precludes acknowledgement of the Māori worldview is said to alienate Māori through further colonization (Baird et al. 1995).

A dominant theme is the central place of Māori cultural values and a Māori worldview when considering any aspect of Māori cultural or skeletal remains. It follows that decision-making on anything Māori should rest with Māori authorities rather than with governmental authorities or archaeologists. Accepting this, museums and universities, with their collections of Māori artefacts and skeletal remains appear to occupy an uneasy middle ground, representing on the one hand the official/government position as the keepers of remains, but on the other beginning to appreciate the cultural perspectives of the Māori people. It is in this context that it is appropriate for museums to act as responsible caretakers or keepers, or even sacred repositories, of artefacts and remains, but not as owners.

The Māori situation also highlights the inappropriateness of seeking homogeneous solutions, since it is the cultural values of individual iwi that are seen to be important; there is no one Māori viewpoint. This may throw light on the problematic nature of claims – that tribes have spiritual jurisdiction over 'their' geographical region, even though the remains may pre-date that tribe's arrival in the region. This is because claims from an indigenous perspective may interact vigorously with those of another indigenous perspective, let alone a Western one.

The same can be said of ethical perspectives that do not take as their starting point particular indigenous perspectives.

Scientific Interest and Indigenous Concerns

A possible conclusion to draw from these developments is that there is considerable tension between scientific interest and the provision of valuable clues to humanity's past, and the sacred feelings and beliefs of indigenous peoples. At one extreme, this may lead to antipathy between scientists and indigenous peoples, although as some of the policies make clear, antagonism is not inevitable if an awareness of both positions is taken into account (Goldstein and Kintigh 1990; Murray 1996; Ortner 1994). Issues of sovereignty, and frustration at the lack of recognition of unique cultural values and worldview, underpin many of the claims by indigenous peoples for the return of ancestral remains. One suggestion is that of custodianship, whereby the indigenous groups act as custodians of the material rather than as all-inclusive owners of it (Mulvaney 1991). For some, this is more in harmony with the ethos of traditional culture, and is a reflection that science and archaeology are not white racial monopolies but are increasingly open to the participation of indigenous peoples. In South Africa, this custodianship principle underlies the proposal to establish a community-run museum on the site of excavations, from which base the local people can grant scientists permission to study skeletal remains (Koch and Sillen 1996). In New Zealand terms, it is precisely this type of leadership shown by some Māori groups that has led to the insights and valuable possibilities of a policy such as that described above.

Science, too, can be viewed as a culture, with its own system of ethics. Goldstein and Kintigh (1990, 586) have written that 'although anthropologists are concerned about the cultural beliefs of the people they study, they also want to pursue the "truth"'. Human skeletal material provides essential information on topics ranging from the organization of tribal societies to the origin of diseases, such as rheumatoid arthritis. Data of potential interest include blood groups and other genetic features, which are of considerable importance for tracing interconnections between individuals from different regions. Significant information on dietary and nutritional changes, life expectancy patterns and population density, health and diseases, surgical knowledge and ritual practices also become available (Mulvaney 1989, 1990). Within a scientific framework, skeletal remains are part of the world's heritage, since the information they yield is relevant to, and may even be said to belong to, all human communities. In this sense the remains are of such general interest that they should not be restricted to direct, let alone indirect, descendants.

When viewed alongside these arguments, the position of some indigenous peoples is strikingly different, since it emphasizes respect for the remains of tribal ancestors, and the religious and cultural importance of such respect. In many instances, this notion of respect is accompanied by a right to determine precisely how the remains are treated, a right that contradicts any general interest others may express in the material. The focus on respect may itself be closely linked with a desire for restitution in the face of past mistreatment (past disrespect), and therefore be part of an ongoing struggle for rights and recognition. Cantwell concludes that 'many of the participants at the reburials ... were not only reburying their dead ancestors and addressing religious concerns, but were also redeeming past social injustice, renegotiating the status quo and affirming their modern social and religious identity' (Cantwell 2000, 79).

At a different level there is the perception that much of the scientific work fails to use the skeletal remains available to investigators, or that when it does, the information obtained in these studies is not passed on to, or shared with, indigenous communities themselves (Elson 1989). In view of this, the communities feel they are little more than bystanders, the remains of their forebears being used as a form of colonialism. With these considerations in mind, Australian archaeologist and physical anthropologist Colin Pardoe has devised a model for research which attempts to acknowledge Aboriginal interest and control without sacrificing scientific rigour. An important part of this model is the production of 'community reports' which are circulated to the Aboriginal people in the areas in which Pardoe has been working (Pardoe 1990, 1991). The community reports contain information that has been discovered concerning a particular excavation and an outline of what further work could be undertaken and its value, were permission for further study to be granted. Pardoe (1990) writes: '... community reports are a way of placing the assessment of scientific value firmly in the hands of Aboriginal people'. Approaches of this nature, based on cooperation and collaboration with indigenous communities, would appear to be the most promising way forward for the discipline of archaeology.

As already indicated, the scientific and indigenous positions are not inevitably poles apart. They represent two extremes that constitute the substratum from which confrontation can flourish. Additional complexities are introduced by the uniqueness of each case, the unwillingness of governments to support science when seeking reconciliation with indigenous peoples, and the increasing pressure to support the politics of indigenous heritage (Murray 1996).

Pullar (1994) believes that the core difference between the scientific community and indigenous peoples is their fundamentally different worldviews. According to him, it is because the two groups do not share the same concepts concerning time, death and self-identity, and either do not recognize the differences or are unable to comprehend the other group's position, that repatriation negotiations can become so highly emotionally charged. Sadongei and Cash (2007) contend that differing value orientations around the body are central to this conflict. While a Western value orientation narrowly views human remains as a set of bodily objects, indigenous orientations tend to view them as a set of symbols, the associations of which extend the body to the natural and social environments. The differences in the concept of time is also an excellent illustration of how these worldviews collide. Pullar (1994, 19) writes:

> Western scientists see time as linear ... a sequence of events containing generations of people. In the western world people are usually concerned with only a very few generations into the past, rarely further back than their grandparents ... to indigenous people, time is circular. Those ancestors who may have died hundreds of years ago are ... still members of the group of people living today.

The Māori understanding of time also differs significantly from the traditional Western perspective. According to the latter, the past lies behind the individual and the future stretches out in front of him/her. In Māori culture, the reverse is true – the past stretches out in front of the individual, because events of the past are well known, while the future is seen as standing behind them, because it cannot be seen, and is unknowable. Consequently, the Māori regard the past as intertwined with the present, and feel a spiritual link to their ancestors, who are accorded much higher value than in those cultures where they merely signify part of an historical record. Hence, demonstration of respect for indigenous peoples' cultural beliefs must also incorporate respect for the remains of their ancestors.

The significance of this perception becomes even more relevant when it is recognized that scientific data are not empirically given, but are constructed in relation to a specific worldview. According to Bray and Grant (1994, 157):

> Science should ... be understood as embedded within a particular socioeconomic configuration and associated with a specific world-view. As the ideological and political motivations of scientific inquiry and so-called facts become more transparent, it is possible to see how indigenous interpretations of culture history can be admitted as alternative ways of understanding the past.

From this, it is a short step to questioning the nature of science: from the perspective of archaeologists and anthropologists, to that of indigenous groups. While discussion is usually based on the premise that this debate centres on science versus non-science (or even anti-science), it may on occasion centre on a clash between alternative approaches to science.

Assessing the Claims

An assessment of indigenous claims of ownership of skeletal remains has to take account of three variables (Jones and Harris 1998). The first is the age of the skeletal material, which extends from the very recent past to as much as 400 to 1,200 generations ago. The second variable is the time the material was unearthed, which varies from the present day back to the eighteenth and nineteenth centuries. The third variable is the manner of the individuals' death – at its extremes either natural death or murder. These three variables can be thought of as three independently operating sliding scales. Any example of unearthed skeletal material will fit anywhere along the continuum of each variable, resulting in a variety of permutations.

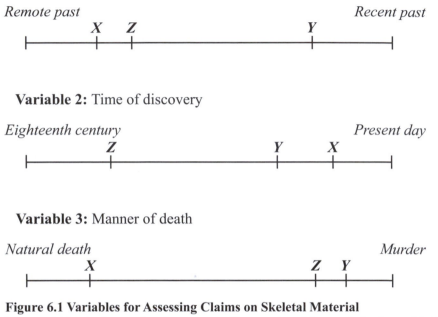

Variable 1: Age of material

Remote past   *Recent past*

         X   Z   Y

Variable 2: Time of discovery

Eighteenth century   *Present day*

          Z   Y   X

Variable 3: Manner of death

Natural death   *Murder*

        X   Z Y

Figure 6.1 Variables for Assessing Claims on Skeletal Material
Three variables that have to be taken account of in assessing claims on skeletal material. *X*, *Y* and *Z* denote specimens of human remains.
Source: Adapted from Jones and Harris (1998).

Specimen *X* (Figure 6.1) is prehistoric material, unearthed recently, where death of the individual appears to have been due to natural causes. The predominant issue in this instance is its prehistoric dating, and whether any indigenous groups should be able to lay claim to it. Specimen *Y* is from the recent past, was uncovered 100 years ago, and probably resulted from murder. Indigenous groups in the past have laid claim to have material in this category returned to them for reburial, on account of its provenance and association with an atrocity committed against the group. Specimen *Z* is again prehistoric, has been in a museum for many years, and there appears to have been some form of ritual murder. No serious research has ever been carried out on this material. In this instance, no indigenous group is requesting the return of the material, which has never been viewed as of scientific interest.

Each of these cases raises ethical issues, based on who has sovereignty over the material, the relevance of the age of the material for claims of sovereignty, whether any group (including museums and universities) can possess human material, and the significance or otherwise of the manner of death of these individuals. The way in which human remains are kept and what is done with these remains during this period are also of ethical interest.

Our fundamental premise is that respect for the beliefs and feelings of indigenous peoples is implicit within the respect we show them as human persons and that the human dignity of entire groups of peoples is inextricably bound up with a study of the past (see also Bray 1996). Consequently, the most appropriate application of the basic ethical principles of autonomy, beneficence, non-maleficence and justice, requires re-thinking. These principles have to be applied to groups of people rather than simply individuals, and welfare of the groups involves taking account of the past.

Acknowledgement of the autonomy of indigenous peoples invests in them responsibility for deciding what is done to skeletal material. In similar vein, beneficence and non-maleficence suggest that the scientific community takes serious note of the cultural mores of indigenous peoples, and acknowledges the importance of skeletal remains to such groups. The application of justice suggests that account is taken of any injustices in the past.

This interpretation may have negative implications for the scientific community, which is claiming to act on behalf of the interests of human beings in general. A balance has to be attained between these two sets of interests, with preference being given to indigenous groups, on the ground that the harm done to indigenous peoples by ignoring their interests is greater than any harm that may result from ignoring the interests of the scientific community. But this conclusion does not hold when the skeletal remains are prehistoric, and are not directly linked to indigenous peoples today. In this circumstance, general human interests should take precedence given the lack of significant interests on the part of indigenous groups.

The three specimens depicted in Figure 6.1 highlight the unusual pressures brought to bear on these principles. Consider the autonomy of indigenous peoples who might have an interest in specimen X. Their interest is dependent on their ability to demonstrate links between this prehistoric material and themselves, even though there may be debate about what constitutes such links. In the absence of such links, their autonomy is not jeopardized by the specimen being studied by others. With regard to specimen Y, the indigenous group has good grounds, on the basis of all four ethical principles, for sovereignty over the material. By reburying it, this group is not laying claim to possess the material, but to honour the remains of those now dead. In the case of specimen Z, the ethical principles are not placed at risk as far as any indigenous group is concerned. What is important here is the way in which human remains in general are treated, since maintaining human remains in the absence of any good reasons is itself an indignity.

Human Skeletal Material and Consent

We have seen thus far that a close association exists between the dead body and a known human person (Campbell et al. 2005). This association is based on movement from the living to the dead, from knowledge of them as living persons to respect for those features most intimately associated with them when alive and functioning as people. Even though this argument is based on a knowledge of *individual* persons and their respective bodies, it can be extended to groups of persons and their bodies. However, can it be extended the far greater distance to the skeletal remains of people long since deceased?

It probably can be, but there appear to be limits, since most people do not have misgivings about looking at the remains of prehistoric individuals, or Egyptian mummies. The anonymity of these remains protects both us and them, in that we do not expect too much of them but at the same time they are sufficiently similar to more familiar human bodies to demand something of us. They usher forth awe and reverence. Even in circumstances where no link can be established with a particular living person or group of people, the material is still of human origin; it retains moral value, since it retains human connotations even in the absence of links with the present.

Consider the ethical framework of a parallel area – that of handling genetic information. In this case a distinction is made between the storage of personal genetic information about a specific person, and the storage of anonymous genomic information in data banks. Information about identifiable individuals directly relates to specific people, and is relevant to their welfare and wellbeing. As such, it is generally accepted that it should only be obtained after the person has given his/her informed consent, the results should be kept confidential by those who gather it, and should be shared only with those to whom it refers. For anonymous genomic information, however, such ethical constraints do not apply because the information is impersonal data widely applicable to humanity in general, just as information on the structure and function of the liver is impersonal information of general applicability (Campbell et al. 2005; Maddox 1992).

As with impersonal genetic information, ancient skeletal remains, where no links can be established with either a direct descendant or group of descendants, should be available for reputable scientific investigation, since the findings will, in the broadest terms, be applicable to all humanity. Using this approach, prehistoric bones from the Murray Black collection, the Larsen Bay collection and Kennewick Man, for instance, would not be reburied.

It is generally accepted that the study of human material is important for an understanding of human culture and, in principle, there are no ethical problems as long as consent has been obtained (Goldstein and Kintigh 1990). Along the same lines, there is a legitimate place for the scientific study of archaeological human remains. But does this apply in the absence of adequate consent? Until a few years ago, consent was rarely sought for the study of archaeological remains from anyone, even in cases where there were people with a direct interest in them. This either makes study of these ethically questionable, or renders consent less relevant than when dealing with other human remains.

In our view consent should be obtained whenever possible, since the remains in question are human ones. Where this was not done for material collected 50–150 years ago, a compromise position is that discussions should now be held with living descendants. The goal of such discussion is agreement between archaeologists and indigenous communities regarding the fate of the material, the options being open for continuing study, the establishment of keeping places with agreed access arrangements, or reburial. If the latter eventuates, one possibility is a defined time for scientific study of the remains prior to reburial. Ideally, such cooperative solutions should be made earlier rather than later, and in a context of communion with, and sensitivity to, the concerns of any descendants (see also Goldstein and Kintigh 1990).

But what about those remains lacking identifiable descendants, in particular prehistoric remains? What becomes of consent? The distance of many of the remains from the present, and the inevitable lack of clear associations with the living, suggests that whatever consent may be required is far less demanding than that required when dealing with identifiable and identifiably related remains. Consent becomes of secondary importance, since what is now of preeminent significance is the contribution the material can make to an understanding of human development and culture. An allied conclusion is that this general significance cannot, in this instance, be overridden by the demands of special interest groups calling for reburial.

Newly Discovered Remains

What about skeletal remains discovered today? Should these automatically be handed over to living descendants for immediate reburial?

The descendants could benefit from study of the remains, by for instance, being provided with assistance in definitively identifying the material. Beyond this, scientific examination of the material in the field may be able to provide basic identification of the person, indicating their height and weight, and an estimate of how long ago the burial took place. This would give an impression of the person/people represented by the skeletal material. A more extensive possibility, dependent upon a few days access to the material in a laboratory, might include the provision of data on age, sex and health status. Measurements could be taken and information (including photographs and radiographs) recorded in a permanent database. Retention of skeleton fragments opens the possibility for future analyses including DNA, isotope or trace element analysis (Ross 1992). Inevitably, these benefits reflect a Western science perspective, and have to be seen alongside the perceptions of the indigenous groups about how data like these might benefit them.

In South Africa the scientific study of human skeletal remains is able to offer practical benefits for living indigenous people. A little time ago, the South African government set the target of returning 30 per cent of the country's arable land to its original owners over a five-year period. The commission established to assess the land claims recognizes graves as legitimate evidence of occupation before the introduction of the segregation and apartheid laws, and exhumed bones can be used as evidence in support of the land claim if DNA tests link the remains to living people (Koch and Sillen 1996).

There is a hierarchy of possibilities here, each step along the way depending upon a close working relationship between indigenous groups and scientists (and all dependent on the granting of appropriate permission). Even if such possibilities are rarely acted upon, they are meant to stimulate discussion about the reasoning behind reburial when information of interest to indigenous groups can be elicited.

What about recently uncovered material from the prehistoric past? Since there are no known descendants, scientists involved in uncovering the material should have a major say in its short-term fate, because its availability is entirely dependent on their efforts. There are no convincing differences between this material and any that has lingered in museums for many years.

Human Remains of Prehistoric Origin

Various archaeologists and anthropologists have questioned the wisdom of handing back remains to indigenous groups, when the age of the material gives it a significance beyond these groups. This is in line with our conclusions. Strongly held views have been expressed by some Australian archaeologists in connection with Aboriginal skeletal remains. Examples are Mulvaney (1989) and Meighan (1992). Mulvaney (1991, 16) has written:

> Kow Swamp bones ... are rare survivals from the millions of burials which have occurred and vanished across the past 15,000 years. Their kin cannot be presumed to have shared the same cultural values or religious concepts of this generation ... this vast time factor, combined with their distinctive physical differences, ensure that any line of descent is to the Aboriginal race everywhere, not to Echuca people alone.

Later in the same article, he likened the reburial of prehistoric human remains with the destruction of the Egyptian pyramids, or the razing of the Taj Mahal. He argues that were these events to occur 'people of all races, creeds and cultures would appeal to those same universal human values which govern UNESCO principles ... why should Australia's Aboriginal past, or its present indigenes, be exempt from applying considerations of cross-cultural values?' (Mulvaney 1991, 18). Along the same lines, Gough (1996, 133–134) has written:

> The humans whose remains have been excavated in the past 70 years were the predecessors of modern Aborigines, but not necessarily the direct ancestors of any particular Aboriginal group. Hardly a single one of the famous archaeological

sites in Australia was known to modern Aborigines, much less venerated ... the sites had been forgotten and deserted for as much as ten or twenty thousand years ... it is absurd that one generation of activists ... should claim the right to hide or destroy material that would be of immense value to future generations of Australians of all racial backgrounds.

Ancient human remains have the potential to throw a great deal of light on the prehistory of humankind, including information on the nutrition, health, stature, life expectancy and population density of various peoples. Greater understandings of the ways in which communities were organized, what technologies were available and the cultural practices of societal groups are also possible from scientific examination of such materials (Bonnichsen and Schneider 1995; Gough 1996; Mulvaney 1991). In some instances, the resulting information has been used by certain groups for specific aims, such as indigenous Australians of Tasmania using research findings to support political and land claim aspirations (Mulvaney 1991). More generally, however, the data is of worldwide interest since it relates to people who form part of the ancestry of modern day humankind.

The conclusion we have arrived at, that prehistoric remains 'belong' to humanity in general rather than to any local interests, has a number of provisos. The baseline is that all studies must have a legitimate scientific rationale. Since the research work is of general interest to humankind, any findings must be made available to the community at large so that all may benefit. The scientific community does not have the right to claim ownership of human remains. On the contrary, the scientist's role is akin to that of a custodian, who, through well-considered and methodologically sound research, has the potential to enrich the common heritage of all peoples.

Within a North American context, Bray (1996) identifies those she sees as stake-holders in the past: 'physical anthropologists and Native American rights advocates, museum curators and antiquities dealers, tribal government officials and traditional religious leaders, archaeological experts and would-be researchers, government agents and non-Federally recognized tribes, pan-Indian organizations and tribal historians'. We agree: all peoples, regardless of their ethnic background or cultural affiliation, are stake-holders in the past. Hence, a resolution of the issue of the future of human remains dating from prehistoric times, is as much a matter for the community at large as it is for any specific cultural groups.

Some have suggested that the view that scientific endeavour benefits all humanity is used to rationalize the scientific community's preemption of power over information and information sources (Grose 1996). In many contemporary societies, indigenous communities are reappropriating the power to author their own histories, which often means disputing the scientific version – not necessarily because this is wrong, but because it does not contribute to the version of history which the indigenous communities wish to affirm (Weiner, personal communication, 25 March 1997). It is possible to dismiss these varying worldviews as 'mysticism', lacking solid evidence (Meighan 1992), but such an approach is unhelpful.

Bray (1996) suggests that rather than focusing on establishing an authentic or authorized version of the past, different interpretations should be presented for discussion to ensure that the past not only remains a source of inspiration, but also serves democratic goals. Scientists must accept that knowledge need not always be universal and that their own truth will not necessarily be accepted by others. For their part, indigenous cultures must accept that scientists have a legitimate interest in exploring the past. Respect and sensitivity must be shown by those on both sides of the equation (Meighan 1992). The world consists of a collection of different knowledge systems, some big and encompassing, others small and focused. Recognizing where the limits of one's own knowledge system are is a step towards tolerance of others (Weiner, personal communication, 25 March 1997).

Past Mistreatment and Moral Complicity

The intellectual environment in which so much of today's human skeletal material was obtained was characterized by enthusiasm for craniology, phrenology and by evolutionary ideas concerned with the relative advancement of different races. In Britain the collecting of human bones was 'a kind of mid-Victorian mania, shared by amateurs and professionals alike', who 'all felt that they were contributing to the study of British antiquity' (MacDonald 2005, 96). Quite apart from this motivation, the plundering was generally not in accordance with established archaeological practice or ethical behaviour. Take for instance the Murray Black Collection in Australia, where skeletal remains were acquired through grave robbing (Mulvaney 1989).

The obsession with fitting people into racial categories led to a fascination with collecting skulls, especially those of the Australian Aborigines who were thought to represent a 'primitive' race. The Aborigines' perceived status as a possible evolutionary link between human kind and the ape became a central concern of anatomists in the latter part of the nineteenth century, and led inexorably to the dissection of Aboriginal cadavers and a huge demand for Aboriginal skulls (Markus 1990; Monaghan 1991). Studies of the cranial capacities of Aboriginal people were used as evidence of their racial inferiority (Fry and Pulleine 1931). In the United States, a similar research agenda led to the establishment of collections of the remains of Native Americans (Ferguson 1996; Powell et al. 1993).

Delamothe (1991) has written that 'the world's colonizers were using evolutionary theory to buttress their claims to racial superiority over the people they were colonizing'. Conclusions drawn from the scientific study of Aboriginal bones were used to sanction and institutionalize twentieth century racism (Monaghan 1991). While the predominant views of indigenous groups' racial inferiority had a direct impact on the lives of native peoples across the world, the effect was particularly profound in early twentieth-century Australia. There, the dominant European culture used Aborigines' supposed racial inferiority as a justification for denying them adult suffrage and for laws that not only forcibly segregated them from the white population, but allowed for the removal of half-caste Aboriginal children from their parents (Monaghan 1991). The legal status of the Aborigine at this time was analogous to that of children or the insane (Markus 1990). As a point of interest, citizenship became unconditionally available to Aborigines only in 1967 (Pardoe 1991).

But was this sequence of events merely a historical curiosity? Such erroneous concepts are undeniably tragic errors, but since they are no longer held within anthropological circles, one could argue that they amount to little more than an unsavoury historical episode in the unfolding of what is now a respectable academic discipline. This response might be satisfactory but for one factor – the continuing existence in university departments and museums of the human material on which these ideas were seemingly based. It is this material that constitutes an indissoluble link between past and present. This has been recognized by Riding In (1992), who insists that researchers should not use any data obtained from 'immoral' forms of archaeological research. Furthermore, he believes that universities and libraries should remove from their collections all works that contain references to such studies. Should the uses to which this material was put a hundred or so years ago have repercussions for our view of this material in the present?

Let us suppose that this material had been collected, and simply displayed in museums (or left in drawers) without any thought being given to its purported evolutionary significance? If that had been the case, would the material in question differ in any respect from the material we are considering with its previous use in wayward evolutionary studies? The material itself would be unchanged, but in all probability it would not have been collected in the first place since it would have held no relevance to supposedly scholarly theories. Hence, the context provided by the material's original collection is significant.

The building of such collections involved grave robbing, contract killing, massacres and murder (Monaghan 1991). It has been estimated that the graves of 5,000–10,000 Australian Aborigines were opened, the bodies dismembered and parts stolen for scientific studies. Additionally, bodies were decapitated, so that the heads could be added to collections (Monaghan 1991). Aboriginal deaths were often the result of massacres connected with the dispersal of indigenous settlements. As a result, study of the skulls was closely linked to racial inferiority concepts, either because Aborigines were killed on this pretext, or because, once they had been killed, their remains were acquired to demonstrate this same point scientifically.

MacDonald (2005) has examined the collecting of Tasmanian Aboriginal skeletons in some detail. The Tasmanian Aboriginal people were thought to be distinctly different from those on the Australian mainland, and were considered 'savages', the lowest form of human existence at the opposite end on a linear racial scale from Europeans. By the mid-nineteenth century Tasmanian Aboriginals were on the brink of extinction; their bodies were rare collectables and Tasmanian bones became culturally laden gifts between the colonial men and English scientists. The first whole Tasmanian skeleton was sent to Europe in 1871 by Morton Allport.

The recipient, the Anthropological Institute of Great Britain and Ireland, was very pleased to receive such a rare example thought to provide important evidence about the history of humankind.

The circumstances surrounding these collections have much in common with the collecting of cadavers in Britain in the eighteenth and early nineteenth centuries (Chapter 2), and even with Nazi experimentation during World War II (Chapter 3; Jones and Fennell 1991; Proctor 1992; Richardson 1988). In all these instances, unethical practices were employed in order to obtain human material required for research and teaching endeavours. Nevertheless, the guiding principles behind these activities varied considerably, from principles with which we have considerable sympathy today (obtaining an accurate picture of the dead human body, as in early anatomy), to those with which we have no sympathy (experiments using living humans without their consent, such as the Nazi experiments).

Where do these anthropological collections fit in? Their original intention was research rather than teaching, and hence some appear to fit more closely with the Nazi work (although comparisons of this nature can be misleading). Now that the collections exist, the only justification for keeping them in laboratories and museums stems from their research potential. Educational reasons are not relevant, since casts of the material are sufficient for this purpose.

This leaves any new research reasons, those that could not have been contemplated 50–100 years ago. Such reasons do exist, namely, DNA polymerase chain reaction testing, particularly of teeth and bone fragments, as part of research into the genetics and demography of our ancestors (Hagelberg 1998; Keyser-Tracqui and Ludes 2005). The application of this technique remains limited due to DNA damage and contamination (Mulligan 2005). However, this and other biomolecular techniques may help answer the major archaeological questions of human evolution, migration, domestication and disease (Hunter 2007). In addition, since many current anthropological concepts are vastly different from those of years ago, the study of archaeological material (or casts) is essential if current concepts are to be tested and elaborated. All scientific studies are theory driven, and since ideas and interpretations are constantly changing, new generations of anthropologists need access to relevant human material if their academic discipline is to remain scientifically vibrant.

It is at this point that the notion of moral complicity becomes a relevant consideration (see Chapters 3 and 5). As we have seen, according to this argument, those who use material or data obtained unethically are themselves implicated in the unethical practices – as if they themselves are acting unethically. As in other areas, two responses predominate, and these are usually polarized ones. For some writers, such as Hagelberg (1990, 14), moral complicity must be rejected. As she writes:

> [T]he study of skeletal remains can truly enhance our understanding and appreciation of past cultures and make us mourn their destruction. Naturally, scientists have a vested interest in wishing to preserve the integrity of skeletal collections, but the return of these collections to their presumed descendants will

not make any oppressed people less oppressed and may only serve to alienate
cultural and ethnic minorities even more from the mainstream of modern life.

In similar vein, Neiburger (1990, 297) claims that far from rectifying the
wrongs committed against indigenous peoples, the return of remains will 'destroy
the heritage of many prehistoric peoples, retard land claim litigation and narrow
rights and freedoms ... [and] will harm the very people it is meant to help'.

On the other hand, acceptance of moral complicity and its consequences,
leads to an emphasis on past atrocities, with serious ethical implications for the
professions implicated in atrocities, especially anthropologists. Delamothe (1991,
1564) writes: 'Our medical forebears, particularly anatomists and pathologists,
were deeply implicated in this whole gruesome business – from body snatching
to racial theorizing that ended in genocide. Restitution of the human remains will
hardly atone for their deeds, but it seems the least bad option at our disposal.'

Acceptance of the moral complicity argument leads inevitably to reburial
of this material, not so much because this accords with the wishes of living
descendants but because of the inherent evil of the actions that led to its existence.
Alternatively, rejection of the argument leaves the way open for serious discussion
of how this material may be used within contemporary society.

As argued elsewhere, moral complicity is problematic (Jones 1991). In this
instance, its acceptance does not automatically lead to protection of the rights or
wishes of living descendants, since it is too blunt an instrument to accomplish
this. The moral complicity argument leads to reburial of much anthropological
material, even when there is no suggestion that gross atrocities were committed. It
errs in this direction because the material was probably obtained under conditions
unacceptable by present-day ethical standards. Those wishing to work on the
material today were not responsible for any atrocities committed 80–120 years
ago (neither were some anthropologists of the time), and in no way could they
have stopped them. They were not, therefore, implicated in the unethical activities
of those times. Even though they are now in a position to benefit from them, we
find no moral connection between the killing and grave robbing of 100 years ago
and work undertaken today. What is important is the rationale for the proposed
contemporary scientific work, the quality of this work, and its potential value to
the human community (including the descendants of those whose bones are to be
studied), as well as the scientific community.

A case can be made for studying archaeological remains in spite of past
atrocities and wayward scientific theories, as long as the myriad factors relevant
to this material are taken into account (see following section). The opposing
argument, as expressed by Delamothe, is essentially a pragmatic one. It stands
or falls on the influence of reburial on race relations. While this may accomplish
limited political goals, it lacks a consistent ethical base.

Guidelines for Study of Human Skeletal Remains

When considering what is to be done with the extensive collections of human remains worldwide, it is helpful to compare the possibilities with those outlined for archival human tissue which was, in all probability, taken without consent (Chapter 2). There are four different approaches to dealing with this material: disposal, use in teaching, use in research or continued storage (Jones et al. 2003).

Disposal of the tissue through burial may satisfy indigenous claims for traditional methods of respectful treatment. However, this must be weighed against research and/or teaching purposes which may ultimately benefit the community. The use of the tissue in teaching and research is a legitimate cause. Nevertheless, this prospect does not justify the retention of remains in the vague hope that it may serve some ill-defined teaching or research purpose at some indefinite time in the future.

The final option is that the remains stay in storage. This allows for the use of the tissue in future research projects, ones with likely benefits for science or medicine. However, the mere stockpiling of human remains in the absence of a convincing research paradigm, is ethically unacceptable. This is akin to the misuse of tissue in the previously discussed organ retention scandals (Chapter 2). Cassman and co-workers (2007, 23) contend that museum acquisitions of newly discovered human remains should be limited to building planned collections rather than haphazardly opportunistic collections exhibiting a 'packrat collecting strategy'.

Since we are opposed to wholesale reburial, it is imperative to decide how best to deal with stored human skeletal remains. We cannot justify a situation whereby thousands of skeletal remains from the recent past linger unstudied in universities and museums for years on end. If they are in storage for scientific purposes, ongoing (even if sporadic) scientific work is essential to justify their maintenance. However, considerable care is required before imposing arbitrary time limits for study prior to reburial. Ames and co-workers (1988) contend that the argument in favour of keeping objects in case of future developments in scientific techniques, must be weighed against other scientific considerations, such as the relative uniqueness of the object and its theoretical relevance, as well as more practical considerations such as physical limitations of museum storage. The expectation that one day someone may want to work on them is not a sufficient reason for keeping them. This argument is similar to that opposing the use of 100 rats in a scientific study, when the research project requires the use of ten. The excess 90 rats serve no scientific purpose, and cannot be justified ethically. Human material can only be kept ethically if the purposes for which it is being kept have ethical justification. Storage *per se* (except when equated with burial) fails to satisfy this criterion. Neither can educational purposes be used as justification for unlimited storage, since casts of the material are sufficient for teaching.

These are arguments against the indefinite keeping of material obtained in the recent past. The problem is that any studies that could be undertaken within the next five to ten years will be limited by the techniques available and also by current concepts. We have little idea what might be done with the material in another 50 years. There appear to be two options: reburial, or the use of safe keeping places. The reburial of human material will definitely have detrimental repercussions for prospective scientific investigations, militating as it does against the Western scientific ethos. The reproducibility of scientific results is crucial to the nature of scientific investigations, while the availability of raw data and raw material for a number of years is important if checking for fraud is required.

In those cases where an individual or group of individuals can be identified as descendants of the human material, there should be agreement between national authorities and descendants of the material in question over issues relating to its storage in accessible sites, and scientific study. Accessibility is a two-way phenomenon, serving the interests of both the scientific and indigenous communities, although preeminence should be given to indigenous communities since this is their material to 'give'. From this, it follows that the rights and wishes of the people being studied supersede the research needs of the scientific communities (Zimmerman 1989). Put negatively, archaeologists and anthropologists do not have preeminent rights to human remains and objects considered sacred by living communities (Klesert and Powell 1993; Ucko 1991). Scientific imperialism does not rest on an ethical foundation. The use of human material, especially when it is from the recent past, can only be ethically justified when carried out within the context of human obligations, fears, expectations, and hopes. To ignore this context, as expressed by those having a direct interest in the material itself, does untold damage to the cause of investigating human material.

Where material is to be held in safe keeping places, its use for scientific purposes will depend entirely on the granting of permission by those indigenous people with responsibility for it. Close cooperation and mutual trust between its custodians and scientists (who themselves could belong to the indigenous groups in question) will be essential. It is also vital that the material be treated in a manner which recognizes its cultural, spiritual, scientific and educational importance, and it should be regarded with the same degree of respect that would be given to any grave or burial place.

If scientific investigation is permitted, the results of the studies must be openly shared with those with a direct cultural and/or religious interest in the material. Failure to do this is a reflection of cultural arrogance on the part of the scientific community, and is an implicit rejection of the potential significance of the remains to living cultures. It is in this context that we begin to appreciate the need for indigenous anthropologists. This may also play a role in breaking down the dichotomy between anthropologists and scientists on the one hand, and indigenous peoples on the other. Against an American background, Trigger (1995, 837) argues: 'Only attracting an ever larger number of Native Americans to become anthropologists and museologists will terminate Americanist anthropology's role as a colonizing discipline and help to rescue it from its untenable position on the "racial" firing line.'

When we turn to the case of very ancient remains where no direct descendants can be established, there exists no presumption in favour of returning the material to indigenous groups. Material in this category is not left in a vacuum, but neither is its degree of protection as great as when the material is of known provenance. Where direct descendants are not identifiable, the interests of humanity in general should take precedence over the lack of significant interests on the part of any specific group, and the remains should be made available for reputable scientific investigation. The lack of clear associations with the living also suggests that consent to undertake scientific study is of secondary importance, since what becomes preeminent is enhancing the material's ability to contribute to our understanding of human development and culture. These guidelines should apply equally to recently uncovered material from the prehistoric past – scientists involved in uncovering the material should have a major say in its short-term fate, since its availability is entirely dependent on their efforts.

The Iroame

These proposals can be illustrated by a set of scenarios concerning a fictitious group, the Iroame, who are known to have inhabited a region for 500 years. In each instance, human skeletal remains are uncovered, but the circumstances surrounding the discoveries vary.

In scenario one, the unearthed remains are found to be approximately 100 years old. Because they are of relatively recent origin, direct descendants are able to be identified. The descendants are informed of the discovery, take responsibility for deciding what should happen to the remains, and rebury them.

In scenario two, the bones discovered are shown to be around 300 years old. As in the first scenario, a group of direct descendants is identified. The remains are returned to these people, who decide to maintain them in a safe keeping place pending further discussions with local anthropologists.

According to scenario three, bones dating back 1,000 years are found. Scientific analysis of the age of the remains and data on the length of occupation of the Iroame means that the bones belong to a group of people predating the colonization of the region by the Iroame people. The Iroame accept that the remains do not have ancestral links with their people, since they lay no claim to having inhabited the region for more than 500 years, but nevertheless they claim sovereignty over the remains since the material is of indigenous origin. In this case, the remains are of significance to all people, not to one particular group alone. The government grants the Iroame sovereignty over the remains, a decision based on purely political grounds.

In a fourth scenario, the circumstances of this scenario are similar to those outlined in scenario three, except that the Iroame people deny the scientific view that they have resided in the region for only 500 years. They claim to have been living in the area from the beginning of time, and thus deny that the bones could possibly predate their occupation of the area. The government grants the Iroame possession of the remains.

These scenarios suggest that three variables determine the nature of the debate in any given situation: (a) scientific data (in particular, the age of the bones and the evidence regarding the length of occupancy by the group involved); (b) the cultural values of the group and (c) the governmental response to both (a) and (b). Any decision will depend on the balance attained between each of these factors. As a result, two equivalent situations in different countries may result in different solutions. The response of politicians to the claims of indigenous cultures is by far the most fickle of all the factors. Priority must, therefore, be given to attempting to find a balance between the scientific data and the group's cultural values.

We have emphasized the scientific data, since it is this which provides insight into the remains themselves. Without the scientific input, the existence of the material would frequently remain unknown. In these four scenarios the scientific data are a contributing factor in scenarios one and two, and a major factor in scenarios three and four. Cultural values are a major factor in one and two, and a contributing factor in four. These observations point to the critical importance of a cooperative relationship between scientists and indigenous people. A recognition of the perspective of each party is a precondition for viable discussions, let alone any agreements.

In scenarios one, two and four, the scientific data and cultural values have essential contributions to make to any resolution of the issue involved. However, in scenario four, there appears to be irreconcilable conflict, since the worldviews of the two parties are incapable of emerging with a meeting point that will respect the integrity of both. A governmental response is required, although this will not be an ethical resolution to the conflict. In this situation, we would hope that the political response is a temporary one, although if human remains are reburied they will have been lost to scientific investigation forever. Scenario four is the only instance in which irreconcilable discord occurs.

Scenario three presents a cautionary lesson, in that a political response is imposed when the scientific issues do not demand this, and the cultural issues may be resolved after full discussion. An ethically sound way forward may prove possible in this instance and every effort should be expended to ensure that this occurs.

Ethical perspectives provide a basis for mutually beneficial discussions, and should be developed further before the debates on repatriation issues have all been resolved politically. In the final analysis, many indigenous cultures have uses for archaeological and anthropological study, whether these be learning more about their past, or gaining knowledge to assist in the management of their heritage resources. For their part, scientists have an opportunity to add a fresh humanistic dimension to their research, by incorporating an appreciation of the power their work has in constructing a knowledge of the past (Ferguson 1996). In reviewing the wider implications of the repatriation debate for the discipline of archaeology as a whole Murray (1996, 219) has written:

... archaeology [has] to leave the safety of 'scientific objectivity' and travel to a disciplinary space where archaeological knowledge is de-colonized and the distinction between producers and consumers of that knowledge is broken down ... the act of seeking reconciliation between archaeologists and indigenous peoples sets up a process of consultation and interaction which tells us that this unknown post-colonial landscape will be created by us all, in a form as yet unknown. Equally important, it seems clear enough that this process, now that it is begun, has no end-point.

Chapter 7
The Developing Body

Introduction

This chapter may be regarded as an aberration as we move from the world of the dead into the world of the living, by turning our attention to the human embryo. This is no longer the world of cadavers; it is the twilight zone between the world of non-existence and that of the hardly alive, between uncoordinated tissues and the ongoing life of a coherent organism. Just as we have sought to determine the ethical significance of cadavers, we must now consider the ethical significance of the earliest stages of human life. Where should the human embryo sit within a continuum of values, which extends from the limited value of tissues and cells to the full moral status accorded to human persons?

The degree to which we can interact with the embryo has radically increased in recent times. It is only over the past 30–40 years, with the advent of *in vitro* fertilization (IVF) that the viable human embryo has become available for study in a laboratory setting. Previously the living human embryo was largely unknown territory, confined as it was within a pregnant woman. Knowledge of the human embryo was limited to observations of embryos obtained following abortions or maternal death, and from what could be inferred from studies of non-human embryos. Now human embryos are the subject of rigorous and often destructive scientific scrutiny. Embryology has moved out of the descriptive realm of these early studies into the interactive domain of experimentation and analysis. This introduces a vast array of new ethical considerations.

Embryonic Development

To begin to understand the issues involved, a brief overview of embryonic development is required (Jones and Whitaker 2008). Embryonic development begins when an egg is successfully fertilized by a single sperm, a process that takes between 26 and 30 hours to complete. The resultant single cell, the zygote, is totipotent, that is, it has the potential to differentiate into the specialized cells that form every tissue in the fetus, together with associated non-fetal tissue, principally the placenta. In other words it has the potential to give rise to a complete new individual.

On the second day of development, this single cell divides to produce two, then four, then eight, smaller, identical cells. These are the blastomeres, which at the eight-cell stage are only loosely associated with one another, each retaining the totipotency which was present in the zygote. By the 32-cell stage, they have become increasingly adherent and closely packed, and have almost definitely lost this equal developmental potential.

By day five the embryo consists of well over 100 cells and is termed a blastocyst. The outer cells of the blastocyst (trophectoderm) differentiate to form a surface layer that will eventually form the placenta. By contrast, the inner cells of the blastocyst (inner cell mass) are still undifferentiated (unspecialized), retaining the potential to form every type of tissue involved in the construction of the fetus. Since these cells cannot differentiate into non-fetal tissue, they are no longer totipotent, but are instead pluripotent. Around day seven the blastocyst embeds in the wall of the uterus, marking the beginning of implantation, which is usually completed by day 14.

At 15 to 16 days' gestation the primitive streak, a transitory developmental structure, becomes evident in the midline of the embryo. After this stage the presence of a single primitive streak signifies the existence of a single individual (two primitive streaks are necessary for twins). The cells of the embryo are now committed to forming specialized tissues and organs, meaning they are multipotent. The primitive streak instigates the appearance of the neural plate, from which arises the first rudiment of the nervous system a week or so later.

These different embryological stages are of considerable significance for ethical discussions of the procedures that societies consider can be undertaken on embryos. For instance, the appearance of the primitive streak has been widely regarded as marking a point of transition, with many arguing that (for a range of reasons that will be discussed) no coherent entity exists prior to this time. Hence, it is argued that it is misleading to refer to any earlier stage as a human individual (e.g. Shannon and Walter 2003). The designation of the embryo as a human individual only becomes tenable with the occurrence of the embryo's definitive orientation after 14 days' gestation, following primitive streak formation. Although it can seem like rather esoteric scientific knowledge, these embryological factors are deemed by many to have great ethical and regulatory significance, so that in those societies where research on human embryos is permitted a 14-day upper limit to research dominates.

This 14-day limit on embryo experimentation is based on the notion that, prior to this time, the nature of the embryo is such that it warrants diminished moral status compared to embryos that have developed past the 14-day stage. In order to understand this ethical distinction it is necessary to delve further into the nature of the embryo prior to implantation. The descriptive term for these earliest stages of embryonic development is preimplantation embryo, a term that carries with it no ethical or regulatory baggage. It needs to be distinguished from the closely related term pre-embryo, which is far more than an abbreviation of preimplantation embryo. Pre-embryo is a relatively recent concept, with its basis in biology, although the drive to define its status is largely due to its potential ethical significance.

The push to delineate this first two weeks of development as a separate unit, namely the pre-embryo, stems in part from the assertion that much of the early embryo does not give rise to the later fetus and hence the ongoing individual. Rather, it is largely concerned with the production of support tissues, such as the trophectoderm (which later becomes the placenta). The termination of this period (around 14–16 days' gestation) is recognized as a watershed in early development. For instance, McLaren (1986b) considers that at about 16 days after fertilization, all the cells derived from the fertilized egg are committed, either to being part of the ongoing individual (embryo), or to the supporting tissues outside it. Looked at in a different way, it can be said that the embryo proper does not exist for the first two weeks following fertilization, but is formed entirely from a tiny subset of all the cells generated during this early period by the fertilized egg (McLaren 1986a). Austin (1989) favours confining the term 'embryo' to that which will become the fetus, arguing that use of the same term to denote all products of conception for the first two weeks is confusing.

In other words, the term 'pre-embryo' is being used to describe the products of conception up to the appearance of the primitive streak at 14–16 days after fertilization, and therefore to the major developmental events concerned with formation of extra-embryonic structures. This leaves the term 'embryo' to cover the developing structure from 14–16 days onwards for the next few weeks. However, as Austin (1989) points out, even use of the term 'pre-embryo' indicates that an embryo originates as a very small part of a pre-embryo, and co-exists with the pre-embryo as the latter differentiates into the placenta, prior to the embryo becoming a fetus. Ford (1988) would like to see the term 'pre-embryo' replaced with 'proembryo' to indicate that the developing embryonic cells have not yet become an embryonic human individual but are committed to that path. Either way, the primitive streak at around 14–16 days' gestation is seen by various writers as marking the end of the pre-embryonic period, and the beginning of the embryonic period.

Adoption of the term 'pre-embryo' fails to resolve ethical issues surrounding the first 14 days of development, since if two or more primitive streaks form, multiple embryos are produced. Indeed, with appropriate scientific manipulation, a pre-embryo can be cloned to produce a great number of identical embryos. Taken together, these considerations make it very difficult to relate the embryo to its progenitor in a straightforward manner. Hence it may be more judicious to retain the concept of preimplantation embryo.

This biological knowledge of early human life raises, in an even more poignant fashion than previously, the question of when the early human individual acquires moral significance. This question should not be taken to presuppose an answer, since it might still be argued that a biological answer is an inappropriate one. Nevertheless, this biological approach raises important considerations at the intersection between biology and ethics, which brings us into the realm of bioethics.

The Natural Wastage of Embryos

'Pregnancy wastage' is defined as the loss of an embryo or fetus during the period of gestation. In other words, it is the failure of a fertilized egg to result in the birth of a living newborn (Jones 2007a); it encompasses spontaneous abortion, fetal death, trophoblastic disease, ectopic pregnancy and prematurity (Simpson 2007). Of these, spontaneous abortion stands out, with 90 per cent of pregnancy wastage occurring during the first trimester of gestation. Research into the frequency of pregnancy wastage estimates this to be around 60–70 per cent (Macklon et al. 2002). The significance of these figures emerges by considering that, for a 50 per cent mortality, two pregnancies are required for one live birth, while for a 75 per cent mortality four pregnancies are required. These figures are not intended to give rough estimates such as these a facade of accuracy they do not possess.

A major reason for this astronomically high rate of pregnancy wastage is to be found in chromosomal abnormalities. The frequency of these in spontaneous abortions varies from 8 to 83 per cent (Strom et al. 1992), with the most frequently quoted overall figures being in the vicinity of 40 to 50 per cent (Wolf and Horger 1995). This very large variation stems principally from the ages of the abortuses (aborted fetuses) examined. Additionally, the rate of spontaneous abortions and the frequency of chromosomal anomalies among abortuses increase with maternal age.

The mechanisms for eliminating chromosomal anomalies during pregnancy appear to be extremely efficient. A long-held figure is that over 99 per cent of chromosomal abnormalities are eliminated through spontaneous abortion or fetal death (Schlesselman 1979). Of these, trisomy (the presence of one extra chromosome) accounts for 50 per cent of chromosomally abnormal specimens in humans, the most common occurrence being trisomy 16 (Hassold and Hunt 2001). The absence of a sex chromosome (45,X anomaly, also known as Turner Syndrome) is found in 10 per cent of spontaneous abortions, and this has a prenatal mortality of 98 per cent (Hassold and Hunt 2001). Triploidy, in which there is a complete extra set of chromosomes, occurs in 10–20 per cent of chromosomally abnormal abortuses (Macklon et al. 2002). Only about 1 per cent of triploid conceptuses reach term (Jones 1987).

In our view, pregnancy wastage poses a major challenge to those holding the view that the embryo has full moral status (Jones 1987, 2007a). Some dismiss this problem by comparing the prenatal loss of human life to the high infant mortality rates in the Middle Ages or in developing countries today. However, there is a difference. To attempt to save every fetus about to be spontaneously aborted would mean allowing into life an astronomically large number (perhaps 2.5 million per year in the United States) of abnormal children. While this is not even feasible at present (even if anyone wished to do it), the question facing us is whether, theoretically and ethically, this would be justifiable. In this instance, to save life is to produce handicapped life. The 'protective mechanism' of spontaneous abortion would be overridden, thereby uncovering vast sources of developmental abnormalities. It is this element in the pregnancy wastage debate that makes it so different from efforts to decrease perinatal mortality rates, where to save life is (in most instances) to save healthy, normal life. This is the crux of the ethical dilemma of pregnancy wastage. By its very nature it raises imponderable issues for the status of the embryo.

Ethical Positions Regarding Embryos (and Fetuses)

Embryos Have Full Moral Status

Many people believe that even the earliest embryos, from fertilization onwards, have the same moral status as a typical adult human – in other words, embryos have the value of moral persons, and are capable of being harmed and benefited in a similar way to us (e.g. George 2001; Hui 2002; President's Council on Bioethics 2002). Those who hold the view that embryos have full moral status consider that destroying embryos counts as murder, and is ethically commensurate with killing a person (Song 2003).

Personhood is given different definitions by ethicists, and continues to be the subject of a great deal of debate (Fleischer 1999; Macklin 1983). Nevertheless, the definitions agree that they must, at least, capture the incontestable full moral status of self-aware, rational, autonomous human beings. Such moral persons have plans, goals and preferences (or 'interests'), and satisfaction or frustration of these interests can cause them benefit or harm, respectively. Moral persons are capable of reasoning about their actions, and governing them in a moral sense, making them full participants in the moral community. The focus of much of the debate over moral personhood centres on who, or what, qualifies as a person, and it is on this point that the moral status of embryos often hinges.

According to the view that embryos have full moral status, the process of embryonic development is simply the development of a person. If things go well, the embryo *in utero* will develop into an adult human, and therefore be a moral person (President's Council on Bioethics 2002, 152–3). Since this process begins at fertilization, it follows that embryos at all stages of development are to be treated as persons with absolute value (George 2001, 64). Underlying these conclusions is the idea of potentiality: whatever we are now, was present in potential form in the embryos from which we developed. But do we do this in any other area of life? Is a caterpillar the same as a butterfly, and is a 3-day-old human embryo the same as a 30-year-old adult? In each case numerous processes both internal and external are required before the one becomes the other, and we do not generally treat both as if they are identical. To use an example of Peter Singer's (1993, 153), boiling an egg is simply not the same as boiling a live chicken.

The intentions of those who hold the 'embryo has full moral status' position are to enhance the value and moral standing of embryonic and fetal life. Some employ a 'benefit of the doubt' approach. According to this, if there is any question about the value to be ascribed to an embryo, it is to be given the benefit of the doubt by ascribing greater rather than lesser value. Although it is impossible to prove that personhood begins at fertilization (a position agreed to by most writers), the argument adopted by this approach is to err on the protectionist side and conclude that fertilization has to be its starting point (Ford 2002, 64; Song 2003). The aim of this approach is to protect the vulnerable and disadvantaged, and to ensure that we never commit murder by destroying what may be embryonic persons.

The promises held out for human embryonic stem cell research by way of developing new therapies are irrelevant. If research on human embryos is morally equivalent to murdering human persons, this is the gravest of harms, that can never be offset by any potential benefits, no matter how great. Moreover, the routine destruction of embryos to provide a source of embryonic stem cells would constitute a further step towards the instrumentalization of human life. It would be little more than exploiting our fellow human beings as a resource for our own ends, and hence would be unconscionable (Cohen 2007, 64; President's Council on Bioethics 2002, 167–9).

Embryos Have No Moral Status

Others view the embryo at its blastocyst stage as a mere collection of cells that is in no way a moral person, and thus has none of the rights of other humans (Cohen 2007, 78–80). This, they claim, is borne out by the evidence that the pre-embryo is capable of dividing to eventually form multiple persons, indicating that personhood does not exist at this time (Cohen 2007, 79; Singer 1993, 157). On such a view, it is ridiculous to claim that embryos are capable of being harmed or benefited like moral persons. They are insensate and have no awareness or capacity to think and value – they have no interests that matter to them in the way our interests matter to us (President's Council on Bioethics 2002, 148). Their use for any purpose whatsoever is ethically defensible, providing they are obtained in an ethical manner. On this view of the moral status of embryos, it might actually be unethical *not* to use surplus IVF embryos for research that aims to alleviate human suffering.

This position draws on the generally held view that it is not wrong to destroy egg and sperm *before* they have united, and asks why it should be wrong to destroy them immediately *after* they have united (Singer 1993, 160). On this basis, some conclude that we are not morally obliged to preserve the life of the embryo or early fetus, and that there may be grounds to justify ending this life. Both embryo and fetus can be regarded as a thing, and not a person, until that point in development when brain function or sentience can be established (which itself is highly debatable and has been put at anything from six to 36 weeks' gestation (Jones 1998)). Once sentience has been acquired, an embryo or fetus has an interest in avoiding suffering and therefore gains sufficient moral status to make it wrong to inflict unnecessary pain upon it. A variation of this argument is to place emphasis upon when a nervous system can first be recognized.

A central problem with this approach is that it lacks plausibility in the face of an almost universally held intuitive judgement that we have a moral obligation as people to nurture the very young within our midst (President's Council on Bioethics 2002, 159). It fails to take account of the commitments we have to the welfare and survival of infants and also, to varying extents, of fetuses (Sommers 1985). The human family has obligations to the prenatal and neonatal, and in more general terms to those unable to look after themselves, since all these are completely dependent on the actions of responsible moral agents committed to their care. Apart from such actions, neither fetuses nor the newborn would survive. What this approach emphasizes is the importance of relationships within the human community, including relationships with those who, using neurological and behavioural criteria, are barely members of that community. In other words, neurological and behavioural criteria alone are not sufficient to tell us how we should act towards fetuses and infants, since they fail to take account of the commitments so crucial to our life together within the human community (Jones 1987, 2007a).

As will have become evident from the wording of this objection, it applies far more to fetuses than to embryos. Nevertheless, it reminds us of the moral significance of relationships within the human community. In the case of *in vitro* embryos the participants are clinicians/scientists as well as the parents-to-be, fetus and embryo.

Gradualist Position

Given the problems evident in both of these extreme positions, many adopt a position somewhere between them, hoping to capture the advantages, and avoid the pitfalls, of each. This position typically considers that embryos have rights and are owed protections, perhaps due to their potential to become moral persons or due to shared genetic heritage, but that these rights and protections are to some degree weaker than those of full moral persons (Gillett 2004; Holm 2003; Scott 2006). On this view, an embryo's rights and protections must be weighed against the potential benefits of using the embryo for research. The ethical defensibility of each research project will, therefore, depend to a large extent on the potential benefits of the research.

This position takes seriously the continuum of biological development. There is no point in development, no matter how early on, when the embryo or fetus does not display *some* elements of personhood – no matter how rudimentary, or possess the potential to display these elements. The potential for full personhood is there, and because of this both the embryo and fetus have a variable claim to life and respect. This claim becomes stronger as development proceeds, so that by some time later on in development (probably during the third trimester for practical purposes), the claim is so strong that the consequences of killing a fetus are the same as those of killing an actual person – whether child or adult. An analogy with a painting can illustrate this idea, as shown by Gillett (2004). When a painting is begun, consisting of merely a few brush strokes, it has less value, however this value (and therefore the care and protection we might afford it) increases as the painting gains complexity and nears completion (Gillett 2004, 243). This mirrors most people's responses in ordinary life, where we recognize a difference between the accidental loss of an embryo and the birth of a stillborn child. Both entail the death of a human being, and yet under most circumstances the loss of a life-which-almost-made-it is felt much more acutely than that of a life-which-had-hardly-begun-to-develop.

Inevitably, a gradualist approach satisfies neither extreme. Advocates of the 'embryo has full moral status' viewpoint regard it as too permissive, whereas the 'embryo is not a person' school view it as too restrictive. To make the debate more complex, advocates of the 'potential person' stance vary in their interpretations (see Engelhardt 1986, 122; Feinberg 1984; Tooley 1983). Nevertheless, its gradualist emphasis strikes a chord with many on biological, philosophical, intuitive and pragmatic grounds. It helps many through the maze of problems in the difficult prenatal and neonatal areas, and constitutes a helpful ethical basis for tackling specific ethical issues in the reproductive arena. We are at ease within the broad dimensions of this approach.

Within a gradualist perspective the distinction is made by some writers between the first 14 days of development and everything subsequent to that point. There are numerous reasons for placing the emphasis here, but they focus on the thought that, no matter what criteria are employed, nothing resembling an individual can be detected prior to 14 days (Shannon and Walter 2003). This leads to the conclusion that what is present is more akin to human tissue with premoral value than to anything recognizable as a 'me'. Useful as this interpretation has proved, it is at odds with a pure gradualist notion that recognizes an increase in moral status *within* the preimplantation stage, that is, from days 1–14. While our scientific abilities to make distinctions within this stage are currently limited, it would be unwise to accept too readily that it will never prove possible to distinguish between the pre-blastocyst and blastocyst prior to the appearance of the primitive streak.

Embryos in a Human Context

When people ask: 'when does human life begin?', what sort of answer do they expect? Are they looking for an answer that is scientific, philosophical, theological, social or a mixture of all four? As we think about this question, we should also ask ourselves why we are interested in it and in the answer that may emerge. What issues will an answer help us resolve? How might an answer to this basic question affect the way in which we value, and therefore treat, embryonic and fetal humans? Might it have ramifications for the manner in which we treat children and adults? In particular, might it influence the way in which we respond to those living in numerous African countries today where even the most basic public health measures and medical therapies are largely unavailable? The humanness of these people is not in any doubt, and yet the way in which they live and die is light years removed from where those in developed societies are at. What is the comparative value of a young mother in a village in Ethiopia, and of an embryo in a fertility clinic in Cambridge or London or Sydney?

Abortion has been the traditional reason behind asking the question of when human life begins, and ethical discussions on the reproductive technologies continue to be dominated by abortion. But there is a snag here, since the emphasis in abortion is on the late embryo and fetus (from 7–8 weeks onwards), whereas bioethical discussions on reproductive issues focus on the early embryo, in particular on the pre-implantation embryo. These differences in timing may be of profound ethical significance, a significance that is completely missed if the discussion commences with the parameters set by abortion. What has become paramount is the status of the very early human embryo, especially the blastocyst at 5–7 days post-fertilization. The status of blastocysts is central to ethical debate, since they are capable of serving as a source of stem cells.

When we ask the question 'when does human life begin?' what are we asking? Are we talking about a new human existence, in the sense in which a new *biological* unit has come into play? In other words, is it the same as asking when does a new dog life begin for a dog or a new rat life for a rat? At the purely biological level, it is self-evident that a new human life begins once the process of fertilization has been completed, simply because that is the start of a whole host of processes that, given a supportive environment and minimal abnormalities, will end in an adult organism, whether this be human, dog or rat.

But is a biological answer the one most people are interested in? To this question there is a wide variety of answers, because what people are generally concerned with is how much *value* or *protection* should be bestowed upon an embryo.

This is the reason why a distinction between human life and personhood is frequently introduced, a distinction between '*being human*' (as with the biological definition) and '*being a person*' (when the biological entity should be valued as a human person). What this distinction signifies is that, with the recognition of personhood, an individual must be valued and protected exactly as all human persons should be valued and protected. By implication, there may be those who are human, but who are not persons in the fullest sense, and therefore do not have the protection we normally expect to give to persons. Possibly early embryos fit into this category, especially early embryos in the laboratory.

On the surface, considerations of this nature give the appearance of being worthlessly erudite and far removed from everyday reality. And yet, when confronted by decisions about undertaking IVF, carrying out PGD, or conducting research on human embryos, they assume major significance. This is a daily issue for those working in fertility clinics, where decisions are being made about which embryos to implant in a woman undergoing IVF, those considered to be viable or those considered non-viable.

However, there is an additional ethical issue that has not featured prominently in ethical debate, and this is whether there is any difference in status between the blastocysts in a woman's uterus and the blastocysts in a laboratory, that is, between *in vivo* (*in utero*) and *in vitro* blastocysts respectively? Blastocysts are found naturally, as well as artificially, in a range of environments, some of which enhance their ontogenetic development, whereas others hinder it. In other words, some blastocysts possess the inherent, as well as environmental, potential to become flourishing individuals; others lack this potential on one or other score. Is it conceivable that there may be a differential value between these two groups of blastocysts, on the ground that the prospects of developing into a new individual are present in the first group but absent in the second? And how are they to be valued in comparison with children and adults? The way in which one answers these questions will determine the lengths to which one is prepared to go to protect blastocysts.

Human embryos never exist in isolation of others, even in the laboratory, and it can be argued that they should always be viewed within the context of the human community. Their existence is dependent upon others within this community and on the relationships they have with others. This observation elicits two responses. *One* is to argue that, since they are the weakest of all human forms, they should be protected under all circumstances. Their dependence upon other human beings is the crucial ethical and theological driver, leading to opposition to their use in any research or therapeutic projects. An *alternative* response is to assess the worth of very early embryos alongside that of other human beings. It is a comparative worth. But once the claim of comparative worth, as opposed to absolute worth, is made, the whole tenor of ethical discussion changes. This is because the relationships within the human community are brought to the fore, and the spotlight is directed onto human decision-making, human responsibility and human control.

Considerations of this nature have not entered into traditional moral discourse. For example, Pope John Paul II in *Gospel of Life* (1995) stated:

> The human being is to be respected and treated as a person from the moment of conception; and therefore from that same moment his rights as a person must be recognized, among which in the first place is the inviolable right of every innocent human being to life.

In line with this, Norman Ford, the Roman Catholic ethicist, argues that a spiritual soul is required to render human nature rational, and that because the fetus is a living being with a rational human nature, a spiritual soul is created within the embryo at the very beginning of each human existence (Ford 2007). For Ford, an immaterial soul cannot be derived from matter, and hence must be created at the inception of an individual's life (Ford 1988). Consequently, once an individual with a rational human nature is formed, it is at that point that human personhood begins. Embryos are as much persons as are children and the severely retarded. Considerations such as the development of the brain and nervous system as the basis of self-consciousness are irrelevant.

The foundation for this stance is to be found in the writings of Aristotle and Aquinas, with their claim that intellectual acts require an immaterial soul or life-principle. For Ford (Ford 2007) the moral significance of the human embryo is based on the existence and meaningfulness of a non-material reality. In his words, '[t]he traditional concept is based on the ontological constitution of a person, who is a subject of moral inviolability' (Ford 2007). It follows that there is no place for a consideration of scientific perspectives, with their developmental insights.

Over against this approach Ford places what he describes as the *contemporary secular concept*, with its focus on the ability of human beings to have rationally self-conscious acts and interests (Ford 2007). This secular concept is summed up in the work of philosophers such as Michael Tooley, Peter Singer, and Michael Lockwood, for whom identity as a human being depends upon a capacity for consciousness that in turn requires a sufficient level of functioning of the brain. While this may be correct, Ford appears to allow for no intermediary position between this extreme and the traditional one he enunciates. The contrast is stark. On the one hand we must grant absolute moral value to the earliest of embryos, even when there is no hint of any function, since they represent the substance of a continuing person with a soul. The alternative position is to grant moral value only in the very latest stages of gestation (if then) when a minimal degree of rationally self-conscious activity capable of expressing interests or desires becomes evident. There is no intermediate position.

Perhaps surprisingly, similar conclusions have been reached using quite a different approach by Robert George and Christopher Tollefsen in their recent book, *Embryo: A Defense of Human Life* (George and Tollefsen 2008). For them the middle ground is nothing but quicksand. More importantly, though, they claim to base their position entirely on science, by locating humanity in a biological program rather than in a soul. This program, with its DNA and epigenetic factors, is oriented toward developing a brain, and commences at conception; as a result, personhood must also commence at conception. They oppose the production of spare IVF embryos and any research that would pose a risk to an embryo's health (Saletan 2008).

For these writers (neither of whom is a scientist) modern embryology and human developmental biology establish categorically that human embryos are wholes and not simply parts. Embryos are, therefore, 'determinate individuals' (George and Tollefsen 2008) that endure throughout the developmental process, before and after birth. The individuals we are as adults are the same organisms as when we were embryos. Hence if we claim that adults are to be protected, so must embryos be protected, since there is a continuum between the two. George and Tollefsen reject critiques of their position based on the phenomenon of twinning, or that many of the early cells will become the placenta and not the future individual, or on the occurrence of parthenogenesis. For them the developmental program trumps all.

While these authors claim to be relying entirely on physical scientific data, there is a metaphysical element to their claims. What is the relationship between a developmental program and the moral value we place upon that program? And is the developmental program of the embryo as neatly separated from the maternal aspect of that program as they assume? Not only this, the developmental substratum of the program manifests itself through gradual unfolding and numerous transitional features, as the embryo makes its way towards greater individuality and increasing separation from the mother, with the placenta eventually being dispensed with. Underlying the position espoused by George and Tollefsen (2008) is an assumption that there is no relationship between biological development and increasing moral clarity, an assumption that has been injected into their interpretation of the embryology. Ultimately, their absoluteness is far removed from the tentativeness of scientific understanding.

Assured as are some of these stances, we simply do not know at the blastocyst stage whether a meaningful new human life has come into existence. Human tissue is present, but is a blastocyst more than this, especially when *in vitro* blastocysts still have to be placed in a woman's uterus to mature into human individuals?

These queries point in the same direction as those who regard 14 days' gestation or even more as a biologically and theologically significant transition into a discernible new human life (Ford 1988). For instance, Shannon and Walter (Shannon and Walter 2003) are adamant that one cannot speak of the existence of an individual until about three weeks into development, when individualization has occurred. Before that time, they claim, the pre-implantation embryo represents what is common to humanity. They consider that pre-implantation embryos have a pre-moral value in that they are living, bear the human genome, and have a teleology directed to the moral category of personhood (Shannon and Walter 2003, 130).

From this we do not conclude that we can do anything we like with early embryos, since it is the nature of the decision-making that is crucial. The choices are serious clinical choices, between blastocysts capable of developing further and those incapable of doing so, between blastocysts that will likely develop into healthy individuals and those that will not. Even the use of blastocysts in research should be governed by a serious therapeutic rationale and the well-grounded hope that it will lead to an improvement in the welfare of individuals and the community.

An additional criterion is that any use of human embryos should be a last resort, and should not be used as long as there remain viable alternatives. Any research endeavours should also be assessed within the broader framework of the legitimacy of the science itself. Are we, as societies, becoming too dependent upon technological inroads into reproduction? Are we becoming obsessed with biological normality? Questions of this nature do not presuppose particular answers, but serve to make us cautious of technological imperialism.

All elements of this discussion have been at the borders of what might be described as *certainties* and *uncertainties*. These refer, respectively, to areas where we definitely know how we should act, and those where there is considerable doubt. Unsatisfactory as this may sound, it is a familiar position for those writing on biomedical issues. The challenge is to achieve a balanced perspective of all border issues, especially as they relate to core certainties. For instance, there is much about embryonic life that we do not know, but we do know that embryos are more important than easily replaceable human tissues like skin and mucosa, since they have a potential to become like one of us. On the other hand, embryos are neither theologically nor ethically more important than children and adults. As a result, human embryos should not dominate our thinking to the exclusion of everyone else. There is a balance to be attained between maleficence and beneficence (Peters 2007). Wisdom lies in determining this balance, wisdom that should inform everything from ethical reflection through to a society's policies.

Embryos and Stem Cells

Much interest in embryos at the present time centres on their potential for research and therapy, with the thrust of the ethical debate revolving around their use as a source of embryonic stem cells, the potential of which may be revolutionary. If this potential is only partially realized, regenerative medicine could transcend barriers in ways only barely imagined at present. These positive vistas have been counter-balanced by a welter of concerns, ranging from the ever-present ethical dilemmas precipitated by the moral status of the human embryo, to a confusing array of conflicting claims regarding the scientific superiority of adult stem cell sources. What comes to the fore here is the balance between beneficence and maleficence: beneficence towards those with serious illnesses (who could possibly benefit from stem cell therapies) and maleficence towards embryos (which would be destroyed in the act of extracting stem cells from them). Reaching a consensus has proved elusive and regulations on embryonic stem cell research vary widely between countries.

What are Embryonic Stem Cells?

Human embryonic stem cells burst into the limelight in 1998, when they were first successfully derived (Thomson et al. 1998). Besides reproducing themselves sustainably and indefinitely in culture (self-renewal), these cells also maintain the developmental potential to form derivatives of all three embryonic germ cell layers. Such pluripotency enables them to become almost any kind of tissue in the body, as long as appropriate conditions prevail. It is this latter property that is the distinguishing mark of embryonic (as opposed to adult) stem cells (Towns and Jones 2004). The potential of this discovery to allow for the standardized production of large, purified populations of cells and neurons is vast, particularly with regard to diseases that result from the death or dysfunction of just one or a few cell types, such as Parkinson's disease or juvenile-onset diabetes mellitus.

Embryonic stem cells are derived from the inner cell mass of early embryos at the blastocyst stage, which, as already discussed, occurs at about five to seven days after fertilization. By this time the blastocyst has differentiated into just two cell types – the inner cell mass and the surrounding trophectoderm cells (which will later form the placenta). Embryonic stem cells, when extracted from the inner cell mass, possess an ability to create all the cell lines of the individual (embryo, fetus) but not the individual itself.

A fundamental ethical consideration is that in order to obtain embryonic cells the blastocyst (early embryo) has to be destroyed, since the inner cell mass is disrupted. At present, there is no way of obtaining embryonic cells and maintaining the embryo as a living entity. In the future it may prove possible to eliminate the blastocyst stage altogether (see *Alternatives to Embryonic Stem Cells*).

Embryonic Versus Adult Stem Cells

In contrast to embryonic stem cells, the process of obtaining stem cells from adult tissues is minimally invasive. For the sake of simplicity, stem cells from all sources other than embryos are termed 'adult stem cells', although this categorization is deceptive. This is because they are derived from a number of sources:

- the germ cells or organs of aborted fetuses;
- the blood cells of umbilical cords at the time of birth;
- some adult tissues (such as bone marrow) or
- mature adult tissue cells reprogrammed to behave like stem cells.

Each of these sources presents a different picture, since each has a different potential with different abilities. While these do not concern us here, they are very important scientifically and clinically.

The major category difference between embryonic and adult stem cells, especially in ethical debate, highlights their respective sources: blastocysts in the embryonic variety as against skin cells or mucosa in the adult variety. While this gives the appearance of being cut and dried, the actual identification of stem cells depends to a large extent upon the environment. Indeed, there is a dynamic interplay between all types of stem cells and their immediate microenvironment, the components of which have an impact on stem cells in that they affect the precise directions in which stem cells subsequently develop. What this means is that both adult and embryonic stem cells demonstrate considerable plasticity.

Although this plasticity of adult stem cells could be used to conclude that the use of embryonic stem cells is unnecessary, this would be unwarranted. While several experiments indicate that adult stem cells have some plasticity (Ferrari et al. 1998; Johnson et al. 2005; Zhao et al. 2002), care should be taken in interpreting these results. Claims of adult stem cell pluripotency are undermined by questions surrounding the accurate identification of product cells, the frequency at which such events occur and whether the observed effects are due to hybrid formation rather than transdifferentiation. Overall, there are few confirmed reports of pluripotent adult human stem cells, and even these may not stand up to serious critical assessment (Committee on the Biological and Biomedical Applications of Stem Cell Research 2002; Holden 2007). Additionally, the self-renewal capacity of adult stem cells is yet to be fully substantiated. Hence, although research on adult stem cells is undoubtedly warranted, the current literature indicates that the potential of embryonic stem cells outweighs that of adult stem cells. The scientific literature points towards the importance of ongoing research with both adult and embryonic sources, since the adult variety is probably more limited in the range of cell types and tissues into which it can differentiate compared with any embryonic counterparts.

The Fascination of Stem Cells

The interest attached to stem cells is as intense as it is contentious; its ability to divide opinion is legendary. Why is this? One answer dominates public debate, although it constitutes half a satisfactory answer. The answer that is constantly touted in the popular press is that stem cells hold out the prospect of curing numerous diseases. In the long term there could be considerable potential for the use of tissues derived from stem cells in the treatment of a wide range of disorders by replacing cells that have become damaged or diseased. Examples commonly provided include the use of insulin-secreting cells for diabetes, nerve cells in stroke or Parkinson's disease, or liver cells to repair a damaged organ. Beyond these examples, major attention is focused on the use of stem cells that are genetically compatible with the person being treated. Further advances in understanding how organs regenerate would in turn increase the range of possible treatments that could be envisaged in future.

The other reason, of which one hears remarkably little in the public arena, is that stem cells are of enormous scientific interest (Jones 2007a). Their fascination for the scientific community lies in their research potential, since they provide a tool for investigating fundamental questions about the way in which developing cells differentiate and how it might prove feasible to change the direction of differentiation. Control of such fundamental processes opens the way into a fascinating new universe in developmental biology. Research of this nature may have spin offs in therapy, but the driving force is the research itself.

For as long as this research driver is overlooked, the ethical debate will remain ephemeral, since a fundamental constituent has been omitted. To make matters even worse, moral and scientific sides of the debate have been unhelpfully stirred together with almost unbridled passion by too many participants. And the fault lies on both sides. On the scientific and clinical side are voices determined to be heard by exaggerating the potential of embryonic stem cells – cures galore lie just around the corner, patients with Parkinson's disease will once more be able to live a full life, patients with spinal cord damage will walk normally again, and even those with Alzheimer's disease will be able to throw off the shackles of memory loss and confusion (Jones 2007a). Whether any of these will one day be achieved is an unknown. One thing is certain: most of these outcomes do not lie around the corner. To suggest otherwise is tragically misleading; one might even say fraudulent.

The dichotomy demonstrated by this debate is disquieting, since both sides of the debate are being driven by simplistic agendas. The effect is to throw doubt on the legitimacy of the public debate. Scientific and clinical research prospers in an environment far removed from political pressure, where successes and failures are treated as integral to the research process. Unfortunately this is not the case where embryos and stem cells are concerned, since every success and every failure has scientifico-political overtones, all of which are anathema to the best interests of human beings, both pre- and postnatal.

The Source of Embryos

There are a number of sources of embryos from which embryonic stem cells can be obtained. The first of these is non-viable embryos created via IVF. These have no potential to develop into a living individual and may be regarded by some as clusters of human cells. They represent human tissue, and should be treated with respect but have no potential to implant.

Second, and far more important in practice, are surplus embryos created via IVF. These were created for potential implantation into a woman but are no longer required for reproductive purposes, and hence are destroyed. They are distinct from non-viable embryos in the fact that, were they placed in an appropriate uterine environment they would have the potential to form a living individual. Allowing the creation of surplus embryos inevitably means that some of the embryos created will be destroyed. Legislation in many countries prohibits the indefinite frozen storage of surplus embryos, and thus many embryos are destroyed by thawing.

Allowing the use of surplus embryos is generally considered to be the least contentious path, as they were created for reproductive purposes, as part of an IVF program, and not purely for research ends. It is also possible to procedurally separate the decision to destroy surplus embryos from the decision to use them for research. The initial decision not to retain them in storage, since they are no longer required for reproductive purposes, can be fulfilled by a separate decision – to allow them to be used for research purposes. Procedural separation is important in seeking to prevent exploitation and coercion in this sensitive area. While most commentators argue along these lines, there are some who adopt the opposite stance. For them the initial reproductive context means that embryo use in research is more problematic, since it thwarts the goal of reproduction. We are not convinced by this stance since it gives the impression that the production of embryos for research purposes represents a higher end than their use in reproduction.

The third source of embryos are those created via IVF specifically for research purposes. The ethical difference between the creation of embryos specifically for research purposes and the use of surplus embryos lies in the fact that with those created for research the destruction of the embryos is premeditated, and there can be no separation of the decision to destroy the embryo and the decision to use it for research.

The arguments for allowing one and not the other are not concerned with the harm to the embryo itself. They focus primarily on the intended use of the embryo rather than the outcome, which is the same in both cases. Surplus IVF embryos were created for potential implantation into a woman but are no longer required for reproductive purposes. In contrast, where embryos are created for research there is no intention that they will ever develop into human beings, thus they are a means to an end, not an end in themselves. A significant number of people consider the creation of embryos for research as inconsistent with a principle of respect for human dignity, representing a further step in the instrumentalization of human life. Creating embryos for research is viewed as treating them as a commodity, rather than bestowing dignity and respect on viable embryos as potential members of the human race.

However, arguments over dignity and respect must be tempered by the realities of what is considered an appropriate use of the embryo within our societies. In very many societies, procedures such as IVF, prenatal diagnosis, pre-implantation genetic diagnosis (PGD), and the creation, storage and destruction of surplus embryos are allowed, so that only limited respect is given to the early embryo. Is there inconsistency in allowing the production of surplus embryos in IVF but rejecting research possibilities? The result of both is the creation and destruction of embryos. Does the creation of embryos via IVF for research purposes diminish the respect bestowed upon embryos, and is there a significant difference between creating surplus embryos in IVF and creating embryos for research?

A fourth source of embryos is their creation using somatic cell nuclear transfer (SCNT), or therapeutic cloning, for research purposes. Arguments for and against the creation of embryos via SCNT are similar to those for the creation of embryos via IVF. The difference between this source and the creation of embryos specifically for research purposes using IVF lies merely in the way in which the embryos are created.

An argument against allowing therapeutic cloning is based on the view that it is the beginning of a 'slippery slope' toward reproductive cloning. This states that, while SCNT research may be considered acceptable, it will inevitably lead to reproductive cloning and a devaluation of human life in general. Justification of this position depends on the demonstration that there is a necessary connection between therapeutic and reproductive cloning. For some, it is entirely possible to legislate in favour of the creation of embryos for research via SCNT but draw the line at reproductive cloning. A somewhat different area of concern is that SCNT could result in an improper use of women's bodies by creating a demand for human eggs, since the technology inevitably creates a market for them. The supply of eggs, it is argued, could only be established and maintained by purchasing them, a procedure that would almost inevitably lead to the exploitation of poorer women, who would be the most likely to sell their eggs.

A fifth source is that provided by human admixed (interspecies) embryos created for research purposes. While the idea of hybrid embryos evokes images of man-beast creations, this is light years away from where researchers are at. Realizing the fanciful nature of such images is important to determining the correct ethical context for such a proposal. In an effort to combat the shortage of human eggs, SCNT could be performed using animal eggs instead, to create a 'cytoplasmic hybrid' (for further discussion, see *Human Admixed Embryos*). Hybrid embryos would only be used for research, not reproductive, purposes. Once the creation of embryos for research is permitted, the differences between embryos created via IVF or SCNT on the one hand, and by the admixing of species on the other appear to be minor.

Yet a further theoretical source is provided by altered nuclear transfer (ANT). This has been proposed as a way around the moral concerns associated with standard human embryo research (Hurlbut 2004). ANT is similar to SCNT, except that the somatic cell nucleus is altered so that a gene or genes essential for embryogenesis are absent. The resulting entity would, so it is argued, lack the potential to develop into a normal embryo and a future individual. Stem cells could be extracted from the resulting biological entity, and the missing gene(s) reinserted to produce normal pluripotent stem cells. Proponents of ANT suggest that creating embryo-like entities avoids the usual ethical controversy because their lack of potentiality disqualifies them as embryos in the true sense (Hurlbut et al. 2006). However, questions have been raised as to the value of this claim. It has been suggested that in reality ANT would simply be creating disabled embryos programmed for an early death (Holden and Vogel 2004). Few people appear to be satisfied by this proposal. Those who deem the early embryo to have full moral status are likely to object, arguing that the creation of non-functioning embryos is offensive. Conversely, advocates of embryo research are unlikely to be satisfied by a proposal that is likely to significantly limit research possibilities.

The potentiality of the embryo has generally been discussed in isolation of the environment in which the embryo is located. This, however, may be misleading. Prior to the 1970s, there was only one possible environment: the uterus. This is no longer the case. Blastocysts now exist in the laboratory (*in vitro* blastocysts). These are the blastocysts brought into existence by technical means, generally in IVF programs, but sometimes for research purposes. Thus, two categories of blastocysts can now be distinguished: *in vitro* blastocysts and *in utero* blastocysts. These can also be referred to as 'blastocysts within an environment hostile to further development' and 'blastocysts within an environment congenial to further development', respectively (Jones 2005b). With these two categories we have entered new territory, both scientifically and ethically.

Embryos only have the potential to become new individuals if they exist in an environment conducive to this development. For instance, embryos in a laboratory setting lack such potential, which can only be realized when placed in a woman's uterus. It would seem, therefore, that the moral status bestowed upon embryos is actually bestowed upon embryos within a supportive environment, although until recent times this has been taken for granted.

In utero blastocysts are totipotent since they have the potential of producing a human individual. *In vitro* blastocysts have no such potential for as long as they remain in the laboratory. Those on which research is conducted never acquire this potential since research on human embryos beyond 14 days is currently forbidden. Nevertheless, *in vitro* blastocysts can be described as *potentially* totipotent

(Towns and Jones 2004), a description that applies to all blastocysts surplus to the requirements of a clinical IVF program. Such surplus embryos could become totipotent if donated to another couple for reproductive purposes, since they would then become *in utero* blastocysts.

Blastocysts created by SCNT would be *artificially produced blastocysts* growing in an *artificial environment* (Jones 2005a). These SCNT blastocysts represent the extreme end of a natural-artificial continuum. The artificial element in their production is more pronounced than for IVF embryos, where fertilization has occurred, albeit artificially. Both types of blastocyst are maintained in an artificial laboratory environment that precludes further development. They are not totipotent unless placed in a woman's uterus. Together, they stand in contrast to naturally fertilized blastocysts at the opposite end of this continuum, and that exist in a uterine environment favourable to further development (Jones 2007b).

Ways of Obtaining Embryos – Ethical and Regulatory Issues

Two groups of issues are immediately apparent. First, there are the ethical issues of consent and ethical justification of embryo use for research purposes. Second, there are issues of compliance with regulations extant in the country of origin.

All research using human tissue raises consent issues. In general, the requirement to obtain informed consent recognizes the need for researchers to show respect for persons, the persons in this instance being those who have brought the embryos into existence. This also applies where embryos are to be used for the extraction of human embryonic stem cell lines. In this instance, additional requirements may be made for obtaining consent from the embryo donor. This is because human embryonic stem cell lines may be cultured for long periods of time and used in a number of different research projects, some of which will not be able to be envisaged when consent is sought. The consent obtained from the embryo donors should indicate an understanding and acceptance of this fact. They should also be made aware that once a cell line is created using their embryo, they will have no control over the research uses to which the cell line is put. Neither will they be able to withdraw their consent for the use of any cell lines derived from the embryo. Donors should also understand that products with a commercial value may be created using cell lines derived from their embryo and should accept that they will receive no compensation for profits made from these products.

There are two questions relevant to deciding whether a research project using human embryonic stem cells is justified. First: can the research objective be met by using other approaches that do not involve human embryonic stem cells? Possible alternative approaches include using animal embryonic stem cells or adult stem cells.

If the research objective cannot be met using other approaches, a second question follows: Are the benefits of this research likely to justify the use of human embryonic stem cells? It is inappropriate to allow research that was likely to provide trivial or insignificant benefits.

In spite of this safeguard against unnecessary use of embryonic stem cells for research, it is important to recognize that a welter of basic research will be necessary in order to obtain sufficient knowledge of human developmental pathways to allow therapies to be designed. This basic research will need to involve as many different types of stem cells as possible, including human embryonic stem cells. The necessity of ensuring that human embryonic stem cells are used appropriately is to be balanced against the need to ensure that this basic research can go ahead. Herein lies the ethical tension inherent within any research protocols utilizing embryonic tissue.

Stem Cell Regulations

As one scans the regulations on embryonic stem cells worldwide, four dominant positions emerge (Jones and Towns 2006). These vary from position A, the prohibition of all embryo research (found in Austria, Cyprus, Costa Rica, Italy, Ireland, Lithuania, Norway and Poland (International Stem Cell Forum Ethics Working Party 2006; Jones and Towns 2006)); to position D, which allows the creation of human embryos specifically for research via both fertilization and SCNT (found in Belgium, Japan, Singapore, South Korea, Sweden, Israel and the United Kingdom (International Stem Cell Forum Ethics Working Party 2006; Jones and Towns 2006)). In addition, there are two intermediate positions. Of these, position B (found in Germany and the United States (Jones and Towns 2006)) confines the use of embryonic stem cells to those currently in existence, in that they were extracted prior to some specified date, thereby prohibiting the extraction of embryonic stem cells and the utilization of embryonic stem cells derived in the future. Position C (found in Canada, Greece, Finland, Hungary, the Netherlands, Taiwan and Australia (Jones and Towns 2006)) allows for the use and ongoing isolation of embryonic stem cells from surplus IVF embryos.

Position A is compatible with the stance that human life commences at fertilization, allowing nothing to be done to the embryo that is not in its best interests. Such a stance would also be expected to disapprove of IVF, on the grounds that its development and further refinement have necessitated research on embryos. Further, IVF programs that incorporate the production of surplus embryos would also be unacceptable since these programs inevitably result in the production of numerous embryos that have to be discarded. By the same token, this position fails to contribute to any research or subsequent therapy dependent upon the use of embryonic stem cells, and it must be asked if adherents of position A should condone access to such potential therapies. Consequently, its emphasis is entirely on the harm done to embryos, ignoring the good that might accrue to others in the human community through the therapeutic potential of embryonic stem cells.

It is in this latter context that position B comes into its own, with its allowance of some research on human embryos, alongside the intention of protecting human embryos. This is achieved by allowing research only on stem cell lines already in existence. In other words, the embryos from which these lines were extracted have already been destroyed. That is a *fait accompli*, and so it may seem reasonable to utilize those stem cells in scientific research. On the other hand, the destruction of any further embryos is forbidden. The social and political compromise is masterly, giving as it does the impression that both sides of this tantalizing argument have been placated. Research can continue in a limited way, and some health benefits might emerge from it. Hence, it is not deaf to the plight of people with severe degenerating conditions who could, possibly, benefit from scientific advances (Jones and Towns 2006). At the same time, those advocating protection of human embryos can legitimately feel that their case has been supported, by preventing the destruction of any more embryos for research (and possibly therapeutic) purposes. Position B represents a compromise, an uneasy one in our opinion, made possible by accepting the use of material that, in the eyes of those wishing to protect every embryo, is 'ethically tainted or unethically derived'.

There is also a problem with the consistency of policy. Position B proves problematic in societies that permit IVF programs that produce surplus embryos, since most of these will be discarded. From this it follows that restrictive embryonic stem cell guidelines do nothing to protect the large numbers of embryos that are being destroyed daily by IVF procedures in fertility clinics. They do little more than prevent research on embryos destined to be destroyed. Hence position B appears to introduce an unnecessary compromise that has no substantial ethical base.

These considerations suggest that, for those whose stance emphasizes full moral status from fertilization onwards, position A is the more consistent of the two positions. However, position A suffers from neglect of any interests beyond those of the very early embryo. This fails to do justice to the obligations of living in community, loving our neighbours as ourselves, and seeking to bring healing and wholeness to those in need. It raises the question of whether the whole of our focus should be on the very earliest stages of embryonic development to the exclusion of all other stages, let alone postnatal life whether in sickness or in health.

Position C provides a protective view of the human embryo, within the framework of what we consider is a more consistent ethical stance. This is because embryonic stem cell research is limited to surplus embryos from IVF programs, with a procedural separation between the initial decision to discard embryos and the subsequent decision to donate them for research. This allows both the utilization and extraction of new embryonic stem cells, and eliminates arbitrary time limits on extraction.

Of course, this position accepts the destruction of embryos. But, as outlined previously, the destruction is of *in vitro* blastocysts that will in all probability have no future as human individuals. Although produced in IVF programs, with the intention of producing new individuals, these early embryos are no longer required. There are some similarities between this situation and that found in normal fertilization where 60 to 70 per cent of embryos are incapable of developing further through abnormalities (see *The Natural Wastage of Embryos*). In our view position C fulfils a broader range of imperatives, seeking to improve the health status of numerous individuals suffering from common debilitating conditions, as well as treating early embryos with the care and respect due to human tissue.

But what about the creation of embryos for research purposes, either by fertilization or SCNT, and the move to position D? This gives the impression of representing a dramatic moral shift since embryos are being created solely for research purposes. We accept this and have reservations about this position. Nevertheless, the differences between positions C and D may be less dramatic than frequently depicted.

A dominant concern with the move to the production of embryos for research, whether or not for embryonic stem cells, is that it represents a major ethical and cultural shift in perspective. Human material is being brought into existence solely for the benefit of researchers and/or commercial interests. Regardless of these benefits and interests, they are achieved at the expense of embryos. In no sense can they be said to benefit embryos or take account of their interests. What has become important is the freedom of scientists to explore human material brought into existence for scientific exploration alone, although hopefully with a therapeutic rationale.

Many see position D as part of this much wider debate centring on the role of scientific enterprise in intruding into the human condition. This, in turn, is a matter of trust – trust in scientists as a whole to work for human welfare. Unfortunately, in many quarters there is little trust that scientists will work in this manner. The vituperative debate over embryonic stem cells has seen too many scientific groups arguing relentlessly for the freedom to explore as they wish on the ground that startling new therapies lie around the corner. The lack of realism in these claims is matched only by their self-serving nature, their goals being to garner financial and political support. It is no wonder that position D is regarded by many with suspicion and as an illustration of scientists intruding into quasi-sacred human domains. Unjustified as such a conclusion may be, it behoves scientists to look far more closely at what they are seeking to do, and to justify their research protocols in broad cultural terms as well as in narrow scientific ones.

Human Admixed Embryos

As mentioned previously, stem cell research is pushing moral boundaries by venturing into activities that involve the mixing of tissue or genes from different species. This has already occurred in xenotransplantation (see Chapter 5), and many of the same ethical issues arise in both areas. However, the fact that human admixed (interspecies) embryos involve the intermingling of species within an *embryo* may introduce different ethical concerns, or make similar concerns more acute.

Hybrid embryos are created by the fusion of gametes from human and non-human animals to produce an embryo which is a genetic mix of the contributing species. Cytoplasmic hybrids (cybrids) are created by performing SCNT to introduce a somatic cell from one species (e.g. human) into an enucleated egg from another. Cybrids allow the creation of stem cells from adult somatic cells without the use of human eggs, which may be particularly useful in deriving stem cell lines from individuals with diseases that may then be studied in the resulting stem cells. Chimeric embryos are created by inserting stem cells from one species into an existing embryo of another (e.g. rabbit or cow). The aim is to produce particular types of stem cell lines, or to examine how stem cells develop in the embryo. For obvious ethical reasons it is difficult to monitor stem cell development in human embryos, so the creation of chimeras is seen as a useful way to undertake some of this work without harming human subjects.

The 2008 UK debate on the Human Fertilization and Embryology Bill brought the opposing arguments into the open. Scientists in favour of allowing the production of human admixed embryos argued that it will assist in the study of normal embryonic development and genetic disease, including a range of conditions such as motor neuron disease, Alzheimer's, Parkinson's and some cancers. For supporters of the bill, such work is an inherently moral endeavour, since its aim is to harness the potential of stem cell research for the benefit of human health. Its practice should be controlled by law and subject to parlimentary scrutiny. Opponents tend to see such developments as a threat to human nature. It is thought to promote a mechanical view of the world devoid of moral boundaries, allowing human tissue to be manipulated and reformulated according to the whims of idealogically driven scientists. Some of the extreme statements on both sides are unhelpful, whether these procedures are to give scientists the power to save lives, or alternately the freedom to indulge in Frankenstein-like activities. The reality will be far less grandiose.

Leaving aside the uses of human admixed embryos and stem cells, many find their creation morally unconscionable at worst, and problematic at best. Cohen (2007) identifies four main objections: it is unnatural; it crosses species boundaries; it is morally repugnant; it violates human dignity. Conceptually, these objections have a great deal in common. They all appeal to a value or rule that is offended by the creation of admixed embryos, which means that the practice is intrinsically wrong.

The argument based on the crossing of species boundaries runs something like this:

1. species boundaries must be preserved;
2. creation of interspecies embryos destroys species boundaries;
3. therefore creation of interspecies embryos is wrong.

But exactly why must species boundaries be preserved? Proponents of this view must demonstrate the moral significance of species boundaries (however species may be defined). This often leads to the difficult position of attempting to find moral significance in a certain configuration or number of chromosomes and attempting to succesfully navigate moral obligations to beings in so-called 'marginal cases' – e.g. non-human animals who are more reasonable and sentient than some humans (e.g. anencephalic infants). Nevertheless there have been some sophisticated attempts to do this, although ultimately many fall prey to logical fallacies and inconsistencies (see Thompson 1997).

The objection based on moral repugnance takes this form:

1. moral repugnance is sufficient justification for negative moral judgements;
2. creation of interspecies embryos is morally repugnant;
3. therefore creation of interspecies embryos is morally wrong.

It is possible to attempt to defend this as a fundamental value, as Mary Midgely has for moral repugnance (Midgely 2000), along with Leon Kass (1997). However, we are not persuaded by the view that repugnance *per se* is sufficient justification for a moral judgement, recalling historical examples of repugnance at homogenized and pasteurized milk, racial mixing, and homosexuality. Interestingly, a case for repugnance can be made in the case of foods like milk, where feelings of disgust are sufficient to justify our choice not to eat a particular food, however this is not a *moral* choice, merely a choice based on taste (Agar 2004). In the absence of a rational justification for our moral judgements, repugnance is too variable, fallible and unpredictable to be the basis for moral judgements.

However, it may be that sentiments of disgust are deeply ingrained warning signs that alert us to moral wrongs, which are then to be explained rationally (Hauskeller 2006). It could be that species integrity allows us to preserve a coherent, familiar moral terrain, with species boundaries acting as an important part of our system of social conventions which guide appropriate moral conduct. However this conduct is ultimately justified by factors other than species membership *per se* (Robert and Baylis 2003). This leaves those objecting to the creation of interspecies embryos in the difficult position of seeking alternative moral justifications for intrinsic objections to the practice, or accepting that their objection might be unsuccesful if, on balance, it were shown that the creation of interspecies embryos had the potential for great benefit, as proponents of the practice claim (Karpowicz 2003).

Objections based on unnaturalness and human dignity have the same form as the unmodified arguments for species integrity and repugnance. However they generally stand or fall on the strength of their initial claims. In the case of unnaturalness, this is that activities or entities that are unnatural are wrong; in the case of human dignity, this is that any practice that degrades human dignity is wrong. Modern arguments based on naturalness commonly draw on the natural law tradition in ethics. This use of natural law identifies the good with the natural, so that medical and scientific practices emerge as unnatural interference with the natural order of things. The species integrity objection can be seen as another example of an appeal to a natural order (the order of natural species), which is judged to be good, and should therefore be protected. Judgements based on naturalness often resemble those based on moral repugnance, in that many practices that are uncontroversially accepted now have historically been judged as contrary to the natural order. An example of this is the provided by Leon Kass's

(1971) arguments against IVF. This raises questions of how one defines what is natural, and the justification for grounding moral goodness in the natural order.

Violation of human dignity is a further objection, and yet is a notoriously difficult concept to characterize and defend morally (see Ashcroft 2005; Macklin 2003). According to Cohen (2007), Kant's conception of human dignity is based in the fact that humans are moral agents, able to set ends for themselves and pursue them rationally. She claims that this moral capacity will be impaired in human admixed embryos, stating: 'it would be wrong to encase within an animal's body those physical components of humans that are necessary for exercising the cluster of capacities associated with human dignity because this would eliminate or diminish those very capactities' (Cohen 2007, 126). However, Cohen's objection only has moral force as an objection to the creation of post-natal interspecies life, not admixed embryos. Moreover, it is conceivable that hybrid and chimeric technologies could be used to enhance the capacities of interspecies individuals beyond that typical of humans (Savulescu 2003) – Cohen's position seems compatible with, or even to promote, this possibility, although it is unlikely that this is her intention.

Despite these issues, claims that there is something special about human life that is disrupted or diminshed by the creation of interspecies embryos have a special resonance for many. Becuase of this, concepts of dignity are likely to be reformulated and refined in a continual attempt to articulate and defend this deeply held moral intuition.

This debate situates the creation of hybrid and chimeric embryos in the same heated domain of ethical contention as other embryonic stem cell research, with neither side likely to be persuaded by the arguments of the other. We therefore turn now to discussing some of the ways stem cell researchers have responded to this controversial environment by seeking to mitigate or avoid objections to their practices, while still continuing their work.

Alternatives to Embryonic Stem Cells

The approach taken by scientists working with stem cells mirrors that of scientists working in another ethically contentious area of research, *viz.* animal experimentation. 'The Three Rs' is a concept proposed in 1959 by Russel and Burch, which has become fundamental to the improvement of the ethical defensibility of animal research. Briefly, the three Rs are: *reduction* of the number of animals used in any experiment to the minimum considered necessary to show any statistically significant differences between treatment groups; *refinement* of experimental techniques in order to minimise potential harm to experimental subjects; and *replacement* of sentient animals with non-sentient alternatives, such as tissue culture or computer-based models. Although this concept does not appear to have been applied in an explicit way in the area of stem cell research, the same goals appear to underly the development of research programs in this area. The essential difference, of course, is the focus of the three Rs, which is animals in the case of animal experimentation, and the embryo in stem cell research.

Reduction of embryo use in stem cell research is exemplified by the limiting of research to existing stem cell lines (position B). This stance is based on the idea that embryo destruction is wrong, so that we ought not to destroy any embryos in order to produce further stem cell lines. However, the creation of existing stem cell lines through the destruction of embryos cannot be undone, and benefit (a moral good) ought to be gained from them if possible, through continued research on existing lines (President's Council on Bioethics 2005, 28).

A great deal of work in stem cell research has focussed on refining the methods used to produce viable embryonic stem cell lines so that the harm incurred by embryos in the course of research is minimised or removed altogether. An example of this is the attempt to develop a technique allowing a stem cell line to be derived from a single blastomere extracted from the blastocyst without destroying it (President's Council on Bioethics 2005, 24–36). Blastomere extraction without embryo destruction is rountinely practised in preimplantation genetic diagnosis (PGD), resulting in no ill effects for the embryo and subsequent child (Kuliev and Verlinsky 2005). However, deriving a viable stem cell line from the extracted balstomere is very difficult, although there is some evidence of success in animals (Chung et al. 2006) and deriving human stem cell lines using this method (Lanza 2005, cited in Cohen 2007; Klimanskaya et al. 2006). It is doubtful that this technique will resolve the ethical issues surrounding stem cell research. From a technical standpoint, the efficiency of the process is poor, with a low success rate of deriving established stem cell lines from extracted blastomeres (Klimanskaya et al. 2006), and the quality of the stem cells produced is unknown (Mertes et al. 2006). Ethically, it is unlikely that those who consider the embryo to have full moral status will consider this a justifiable manipulation (although they may be small, there are nevertheless attendant risks associated with the procedure) of an embryo that is to be implanted and carried to term, especially since the procedure is unlikely to be undertaken for the benefit of the future child. Also of concern is the fact that the extracted blastomere may be totipotent, meaning that it has the capacity to form an entire individual – for some, this endows it with full moral status, and the procedure is in the same ethical territory as destructive embryonic stem cell research.

Another approach has been to replace the use of embryos in stem cell research by pursuing techniques which allow the 'de-differentiation' of adult somatic cells back into pluripotent stem cells. If successful, this would remove the need for stem cells to be extracted from embryos, and side-step the ethical problems attendant on embryo manipulation and destruction. Until very recently, technical problems made this an attractive but elusive goal. However, in late 2007, two research groups published evidence that they had successfully achieved the creation of human 'induced pluripotent stem cells' from adult somatic cells (Takahashi et al. 2007; Yu et al. 2007). Both groups acknowledge that more work is needed to fully characterize the stem cells they produced and compare them to embryonic stem cell lines, in order to determine whether the de-differentiated stem cells can replace embryonic stem cells in medical and scientific applications. Ethically, this technique appears to remove many of the most pressing ethical problems associated with the derivation of stem cells from embryonic sources. However, the technical context is that of work in embryonic stem cells, and so that ethical separation may not be as great as sometimes claimed. It is also possible that, as the technique advances, it may be possible to regress adult somatic cells beyond pluripotency to totipotency, resulting (as in the case of live blastomere extraction) in a stem cell that is capable of forming an entire individual (President's Council on Bioethics 2005, 51). This stem cell would be viewed by some as functionally and morally equivalent to a human embryo, and thus posessing full moral status, putting the scientific project once again into the domain of ethical contention.

Fascinating as is this possibility, it may well be misleading. The potential of an embryo or stem cell is dependent on many factors, including its own inherent properties and the environment in which it is situated. The totipotency of a stem cell does not make it functionally equivalent to an embryo *in utero*.

The pursuit of alternatives to embryonic stem cells is not a vain one. Like all human endeavours, and scientific ones in particular, ethical issues arise as a matter of course. These issues can be objections to scientific practices, or obligations that demand the vigorous pursuit of scientific activity. Both of these require detailed scrutiny to determine whether or not they are well founded.

Chapter 8

The Thinking Body

Introduction

For most people the brain is a fascinating yet perplexing organ. It is an organ unlike any other in the body, since it is 'me' in a way in which my liver, kidneys or pancreas is not me (Jones 2005b). Our brains appear to make us the sort of people we are, both in the case of outstanding individuals and those with severe brain abnormalities. When brains go wrong in some fundamental way, the individuals may be dramatically changed, since certain forms of damage can have major repercussions for our personalities. The person whom we knew and instantly recognized as Peter or Miriam may no longer be that same person; while remnants of the person remain, the interactions that were cherished may have vanished completely.

The title of this chapter, The Thinking Body, is more than a semantic nicety tying it in with the other body-based chapters. It is a forceful reminder that the brain is as much a part of the human body as is any other organ or tissue. The physicality of the brain is its glory as well as its frailty. When the brain ceases to function, the individual person dies. What this amounts to will be explored in the following sections, as will the tragic situations of the gradual deterioration of the brain in dementia. Not surprisingly, ethical dilemmas permeate these scenarios. Consideration of these situations fits neatly into a book on the cadaver, even if they bring us face to face with the nearly dead and the ethical queries associated with knowing how to deal with these.

But what about the living and perhaps flourishing brain, where there may not be overt pathology but where the challenge is to know how far we should intrude into the functioning of these brains and therefore individuals? This is the realm of neuroimaging that we will take up in the latter part of this chapter. While this section does not introduce us to dead or even dying brains, it reveals something of the techniques that emphasize the physical nature of our thought processes. This is important in the context of this book since it shows the importance of the structural integrity of the brain.

In one sense, the brain is nothing more than any other organ we like to name, in that it can be described, dissected and understood in anatomical and physiological terms just like any of the other organs. But it also eludes us, simply because our view and knowledge of the world and ourselves are products of our brains. It is because of the organization of our brains that we are able to love and create, to enjoy beautiful things, and even to respond and wonder. The development of the cerebral hemispheres means we can think in abstract terms, plan ahead and ponder the significance of the past; we have values and goals, and are aware of our responsibility for ourselves and other people; we know we are transient, and we establish relationships with others.

But have we over-emphasized a mere physical structure? Surely, some will argue, there is something grander about human beings than a mere physical object that, after death, can be preserved and kept in a box. We agree. We are conscious beings who have goals, desires and responsibilities. Our brains are foundational for all we are, but it is *we* who are significant; it is *we* who are interested in understanding ourselves (and our brains). Damage to our brains may have devastating consequences for all we are and hope to be, pointing to the indispensable role played by our brains in making us what we are. But it is *we* who have meaning, not our brains. Consequently, personhood, that which makes us the people we are with all the potential we have, is more than brain activity *per se*. Nevertheless, there is an indissoluble link between the two (Jones 2005b).

A scientific study of the nervous system by itself will not tell us all we want to know about people and their functioning. And yet when confronted by a barely functioning brain, on account of immaturity at the beginning of life or degeneration at the end of life, neural activity cannot be ignored. The lack of any functioning of the central nervous system, no matter what state one's body is in, must have implications for our assessment of the meaningfulness of that human life.

Having addressed the ethical significance of the emerging individual in the last chapter, we now move into a similarly vague zone at the end of life, exploring when a human being can be considered dead, and therefore suitable for organ donation, dissection or burial.

Brain Death

Before the advent of sophisticated rescue and intensive care technology patients were declared dead when breathing and cardiac activity had stopped, because the failure of this single vital organ system led to death of the entire organism. However, once the technology was available to maintain these functions artificially, a clear boundary between life and death was no longer apparent.

The technological capability to keep the human body functioning despite the failure of vital organs or organ systems then raised the question of when a person should be allowed to die, in other words, when it would be ethical to halt life-sustaining treatment. Among other things, this debate involves an evaluation of burdens and benefits for the individual patient – including organ donors and recipients – through to the caregivers, families and even to society at large.

The contemporary debate about brain death began in 1959, when Mollaret and Goulon introduced the term *coma dépassé*, to describe a state of irreversible unconsciousness, as verified with isoelectric electroencephalogram findings and the absence of mesencephalic reflexes in 23 patients (Mollaret and Goulon 1959). Following this original study, two reasons emerged for elaborating 'brain death' criteria (Annas 1988). The first concerned provision of appropriate care to patients whose brains were damaged irreversibly but who did not die because of improved methods of resuscitation. Decisions had to be made about when artificial life support should be halted and the patient declared dead – a matter of relevance for the suffering and grieving relatives, and for those involved in managing the just distribution of scarce and expensive intensive care resources (President's Commission for the Study of Ethical Problems in Medicine and Biomedical and Behavioral Research 1981). The second reason was grounded in the developments surrounding organ transplantation and the need for viable, intact organs from cadavers, where brain-based criteria of death were seen to mitigate concerns that organ removal was 'killing' the donor.

The Developing Debate

Since the onset of the brain death formulation, intense debate followed in many countries about the relationship between 'brain death' and 'death'. A major area of concern was whether a brain dead patient was dead, especially if cardiac arrest had not occurred.

In 1979 the Conference of Medical Royal Colleges concluded 'that the identification of brain death means that the patient is dead, whether or not the function of some organs, such as a heart beat, is still maintained by artificial means' (Conference of Medical Royal Colleges and their Faculties in the UK 1979). This expresses the viewpoint that brain dead individuals are no longer living persons; that is, brain death is being equated with human death (Skegg 1988).

The only model statute that suggested a relation between the two standards for determining death – irreversible cessation of cardiac and respiratory functions and irreversible cessation of all brain functions, including the brain stem – was the Capron-Kass proposal in 1972, the model that was the most widely adopted in the United States before the drafting of the US Uniform Determination of Death Act (Capron 2001).

The Uniform Determination of Death Act was proposed by President's Commission study *Defining Death* (1981). It reaffirmed the application of a whole brain definition for brain death while not abandoning cardiopulmonary criteria of death. According to this: 'An individual who has sustained either (1) irreversible cessation of the circulatory and respiratory functions, or (2) irreversible cessation of all functions of the entire brain, including the brain stem, is dead. A determination of death must be made in accordance with accepted medical standards' (President's Commission for the Study of Ethical Problems in Medicine and Biomedical and Behavioral Research 1981, 2).

The Act has since been adopted by most US states and is intended 'to provide a comprehensive and medically sound basis for determining death in all situations' (Uniform Law Commissioners 2002).

Since the first mention of brain death, three competing concepts of brain death have originated from the continuous debate: the concept of whole brain death, brain stem death and the higher brain formulation.

Whole Brain Definition of Death

Publication in 1968 of the Harvard criteria for a permanently non-functioning brain, a condition referred to at that time as 'irreversible coma' (Ad Hoc Committee of the Harvard Medical School to Examine the Definition of Brain Death 1968), marked a seminal piece of work in the debate on brain death. The Committee's primary purpose was to define irreversible coma 'as a new criterion for death', this new criterion being total and irreversible loss of functioning of the whole brain, encompassing the cerebral hemispheres and the brainstem.

In this vein, Veith has written:

> Almost all segments of society will agree that some capacity to think, to perceive, to respond, and to regulate and integrate bodily functions is essential to human nature. Thus, if none of these brain functions are present and will ever return, it is no longer appropriate to consider a person as a whole as being alive. (Veith et al. 1977, 1653)

Put simply, the brainstem is responsible for maintaining most of the homeostatic functions essential for life, whilst the cerebral hemispheres are the loci of consciousness and higher cognitive functions.

The termination of brain stem functions is rapidly followed by cessation of function of the higher parts of the brain. Irreversible loss of the brain stem's essential integrative functions occurs at a point in the dying process beyond the loss of the criteria indicative of personhood, and thus brain stem death is an indicator of whole brain death (Lamb 1985). In other words, death of the brain stem is a necessary and sufficient condition for death of the brain as a whole. This emphasis on a brain stem definition means that death does not occur until both the brain as a whole and the body as a whole are irreversibly dysfunctional.

The whole brain definition of death is a biological concept of death, in the sense that there is no material difference between the deaths of a dog, cat or human being (Lamb 1985). In each case, what is last lost of the brain is brain stem function, that is, the ability to integrate functions within a biological system. This occurs regardless of the animal's capacity for self-consciousness.

Walton (1980) supports the whole brain definition, and bases his argument on tutiorism, that is, where there is vagueness or doubt, it is best to err on the side of caution. According to Walton, basing death on the irreversible destruction of the whole brain is the only safe option, since it is impossible to rule out the possibility that brain-stem reflexes could indicate some form of sensation or feeling, even if higher mental activity is not present (Walton 1980, 69). Walton's advocacy of a whole brain definition also follows from his desire for clear, well established, and widely corroborated criteria, with a clinical picture of pathological destruction leading to death in a short time. This, he asserts, protects it from slippery slope arguments.

While early accounts appear to have assumed complete loss of all brain functions, and destruction of all structures in the brain stem and cerebral hemispheres, this is an over-simplification. It has, for instance, been shown that cellular function in the hypothalamus and pituitary gland can persist even after whole brain death has been declared (Halevy and Brody 1993). However, this may not be all that significant (Bernat 2002), particularly as these structures are perfused by extracranial vessels (Wijdicks 2000, cited in Baron et al. 2006). Small nests of cells may hence continue functioning, although these no longer contribute to the functioning of the organism as an autonomous whole. If this is the case, their continued functioning becomes irrelevant to the dead person (Bernat 1992; Doyle and Robichaud 2004).

Some critiques of the whole brain definition maintain that, while the criterion of a completely destroyed brain may be satisfied, the human organism can continue to function as an integrated whole with the aid of artificial devices (Tomlinson 1984). Consequently, death of the brain will not mark the irreversible loss of the integrated functioning of the various subsystems and, given this, cannot be used as the criterion of death of the organism as a whole (Potts 2001; Shewmon 2001). Tomlinson's concern is that the present consensus will break down as new technologies emerge, capable of keeping brain dead subjects functioning indefinitely without subsystem failures (see also Wikler 1993).

Interesting as this critique is, it relies on a flawed definition of life (and, by corollary, death). If a brain region has been destroyed it has been destroyed, regardless of whether this loss can be bypassed using technology. It is difficult to see why an individual is said to be alive, simply because that individual is 'breathing' with the aid of a respirator, any more than an individual with no legs can be said to be 'walking' with the assistance of a wheel chair. Similarly, Veatch (2005) contests the equation of death with somatic integration of the body, proposing instead that it is 'embodied consciousness', rather than bodily function, that is crucial.

McMahan rejects the whole brain definition on the grounds that it does not do justice to either the intuition that death should involve the loss of integrated biological function, or the intuition that it should involve permanent loss of consciousness (McMahan 1995, 2002). He argues that, while whole brain death is certainly sufficient for permanent loss of consciousness, it is not necessary, as shown by humans in persistent vegetative states (McMahan 2002, 427).

Despite these critical voices, the whole brain formulation, as the original concept of brain death, serves as the foundation of the brain death concept in the United States and the majority of European countries (Haupt and Rudolf 1999).

The Higher Brain Definition of Death

As explorations have continued into a brain-based definition of death, increasing reliance has been placed on the irreversible loss of functions concerned with central aspects of personhood. These aspects have been promoted by several classical and contemporary writers and have been summarized by Beauchamp (1999) as self-consciousness, the capacity for rationality and for acting freely, and the ability to communicate with others by command of a language. It is these brain functions that Veatch (1993) sees as characteristic of our human existence and of our meaning as human persons. He believes that it is the loss of these higher functions, that are served by the cortex and not the brain stem, that should define death (Veatch 1973), hence the term cerebral (or neocortical) death. He argues that persons with dead brains are 'individuals who are dead', rather than persons who are 'brain dead'.

Today the term cerebral (neocortical) death has been widely replaced by the 'higher brain definition of death', which places far greater emphasis on functional losses than the structural concept of cerebral death. The movement to the newer term also reflects an awareness of an inability to locate with precision functional damage to anatomical sites of the brain.

The major contrast between the whole brain definition and the higher brain definition of death is an emphasis on the loss of bodily integration in the former case, and a loss of consciousness in the latter. Debate centres on whether the most fitting emphasis is the irreversible loss of bodily capacities in general, or the irreversible loss of specified capacities characteristic of the personal life of human beings. The choice between the whole brain formulation of death and the higher brain definition of death is, therefore, the choice between two definitions of death, entailing radically divergent concepts akin to the biological and personalist positions, respectively. The question is: are the respective positions dealing equally with 'death'? Is death a binary quality or can an individual with whole brain death be 'more dead' than one with higher brain death? And if individuals with intact integrative functions (signifying an intact brain stem), but without the marks of personhood (damage to the cerebral hemispheres) are said to be alive, are they alive in any meaningful sense?

Objections to the higher brain definition revolve around biological and personalist concepts of death. Those in favour of a biological concept will not accept a personalist concept, and hence will deny a higher brain definition. This appears to be an insurmountable difference, which is well presented by Lamb (1985), when he writes that: 'life without conscious experience may be meaningless, possibly futile, but it does not amount to death ... the concept of "death" can only be applied to organisms, not persons' (Lamb 1985, 92–94). A similar sentiment has also been expressed by James Bernat:

> the concept of death is applicable only to an organism because death fundamentally is a biological phenomenon. By contrast, personhood is a

psychological or spiritual concept. Personhood may be lost, such as, according to some, in a patient in a permanent state of unconsciousness, but personhood cannot die except metaphorically … I recognize only one type of death, that of the organism. (Bernat 1998, 16)

At a more practical level, Lamb (1985) argues against a higher brain definition of death. His critique revolves mainly around uncertainties: in particular, whether cessation of higher brain functions entails a total loss of consciousness and awareness, whether there is total absence of sentience when the brain stem is still functioning, uncertainty concerning the meaning of loss of cognitive faculties, and problems with determination of the precise time of death. He finds that common sense intuitions about death run counter to higher brain formulations and accepting the latter would require the advocacy of benign neglect and, at best, euthanasia.

To date the advocacy of the higher brain definition is limited to academic scholars; it has not been approved by any medical society and has not been adopted into law in any country or jurisdiction (Bernat 2005a). Nevertheless, elements of its rationale cannot be summarily dismissed. It raises penetrating questions about the cessation of personhood, focusing attention on the qualities that make us persons and on to the responsibilities lying at the core of human communities.

The Ongoing Debate

Since the beginning of the brain death debate in the 1960s, the concept of brain death has become widely accepted and is entrenched in legislation and practice guidelines throughout the developed and developing world (Wijdicks 2002). Nevertheless, as discussed previously, there remain areas of persistent controversy, that it is anticipated will continue as the prevailing perceptions and paradigms alter against a background of ongoing diagnostic advances.

The discussions continue to revolve around the significance of the brain (and in particular the cerebral hemispheres) for our lives as human beings. We are more than our brains, but equally we are more than our bodies. Hence, personalist and biological definitions in their purest versions fail to do justice to the issues at stake. Is it helpful, then, to limit ourselves to the diametrically opposed options that death equates either with ceasing to be living persons or living bodies?

A whole brain definition, with its emphasis on death of the body, fails to satisfy when confronted with a patient who is little more than a ventilated corpse. When spontaneous respiration and circulation have ceased, any suggestion that a ventilated body is not dead fails to satisfy our intuitions about what it means to be alive. The person we knew is equally remote when the higher brain alone has been destroyed. We are reminded of the person that once was, but we find it difficult to go further than this. A higher brain definition acknowledges this loss even in the presence of lingering biological life. We view the ventilated body as still of considerable significance, and the mere fact that 'life' (in the form of spontaneous respiration and circulation) is still present reminds us that we have to be even more cautious in our decision-making than when all biological life has been destroyed.

These persistent disagreements notwithstanding, efforts have to be made to standardize definitions and guidelines within and between countries (Baron et al. 2006; Haupt and Rudolf 1999) as ongoing lack of clarity only serves to confuse the public, giving rise to a suspicion that death is a malleable concept that can be adjusted for dubious purposes (Arnold and Younger 1993).

Persistent Vegetative State

It may seem odd to devote a separate section to the persistent vegetative state (PVS) when the higher brain definition of death, of which PVS is the clinical manifestation, has already been discussed. It may also seem curious because the vegetative state is the rarest form of disability in patients rescued from life threatening brain damage today. And yet it provokes great interest because of the paradoxical situation of a person who is wakeful and yet not aware (Royal College of Physicians 2003). PVS is not only a clinical issue but, as Veatch (1993) has cogently argued, a moral issue, in that it entails making decisions about whether a *person* is dead and not simply whether a *body* is dead.

The scene may be set by introducing three cases, the first of which is that of Karen Ann Quinlan – it was the dilemma surrounding her illness in 1975 that catapulted the PVS into the moral and legal spotlight.

At the age of 21 Karen Ann Quinlan had a cardiopulmonary arrest following an accidental ingestion of a combination of prescription sedatives and alcohol. It was soon clear that she was in a PVS and eventually her parents requested that 'extraordinary' treatment – in particular, mechanical ventilation – be discontinued, since in their eyes her condition was hopeless. The doctors refused this request and her parents took the case to the US Supreme Court. The Quinlans eventually won the case, and the ventilator was removed. However, Karen began breathing for herself and was transferred to a nursing home where she remained in a PVS for another nine years, before dying of an overwhelming infection. Over the ten year period, Karen never regained consciousness, but the episode led to a debate about the appropriateness of life-sustaining treatment in patients who are in a PVS, and the question when it can be right to allow a patient to die. This in turn led to the development of medico-legal guidelines for the care of such patients (Armstrong and Colen 1988; Executive Board of the American Academy of Neurology 1988).

A second illustration is provided by the case of Tony Bland. In 1989, 17-year-old Tony Bland attended a soccer match at Hillsborough Stadium in Sheffield, England. During the match the crowd surged against a locked gate, killing 95 people and injuring 200. Tony was among those crushed and after some minutes of oxygen deprivation, he was left in a PVS. For three-and-a-half years he was fed through a nasogastric tube until the British High Court, the Court of Appeal and five Law Lords ruled that it would not be unlawful to withdraw artificial feeding and hydration. In March 1993, doctors stopped the hydration, nutrition and drug treatment and Tony Bland died nine days later.

A more recent American case, and one that received intensive media attention, was that of 27-year-old Terri Schiavo who, after a cardiac arrest in 1990, was in a coma for two months only to proceed into a PVS. A protracted and emotionally charged battle between her parents and her husband ensued, on whether or not to remove her feeding tube. The central divide was differing views on whether or not she was 'alive' and still herself though in a PVS. Her parents argued that she had been misdiagnosed and that she was not in a PVS but rather in a minimally conscious state. After numerous petitions, appeals and court hearings the tubes were ultimately removed in 2005 and Terri died 13 days later. The postmortem revealed that she had been in a PVS.

The cases of Karen Ann Quinlan, Tony Bland and Terri Schiavo raise fundamental questions about the definition of being a person and the goals of medicine. While the lives of these patients are stable, they appear not to be worth living, and as a result these patients present themselves as candidates for non-treatment. They are not necessarily suffering from a terminal condition, but nevertheless find themselves dependent on medical measures for survival. Inevitably, these patients focus attention on the dilemma presented by the definition of death. Are PVS patients alive or dead? If they are alive, they demonstrate few, if any, of the characteristic features of human personhood: if they are dead, they continue to display some of the features of bodily life. Alternatively, they may be dying, although the stability of their condition throws this designation into doubt. In view of these seeming contradictions, the PVS has been described either as the lowest-functioning phase of life or the highest functioning phase of death (Wikler 1988). Does keeping people biologically alive in these circumstances make sense? Whose interests are served by sustaining a life so limited in scope?

These cases, furthermore, direct attention towards the role of families and next of kin. Their obligations become unclear if PVS patients were to be categorized as being dead. In what senses can and should a family 'care' for someone who is dead? Even if this is not the case, caring in this instance is likely to take on significantly different dimensions compared to that of a living, responding patient.

PVS patients are vulnerable, but in what sense, given that they appear to be unable to suffer? It may be that our focus is wrong, and that the ones who are most vulnerable are the living – the families and caregivers, who often wrestle with continuing responsibilities and ongoing concern for the PVS patient.

Description

Patients in a vegetative state are distinguished by an irregular, cyclic, state of circadian sleeping and waking, unaccompanied by any self-awareness or recognition of external stimuli. They may move their trunk or limbs in meaningless ways, and may occasionally smile, or shed tears. They may even utter grunts or scream. There are motor activities, but no evidence of psychological awareness or any apparent capacity to engage in learned behaviour. Most vegetative patients retain good to normal reflexive regulation of vision and eye movement, but ability to track moving objects with their eyes is lacking. In most patients the gag, cough, suck and swallow reflexes are preserved, and gastrointestinal functions remain nearly normal. It is the latter that enable the maintenance of long-term internal regulation for prolonged periods in some patients, as long as external needs are attended to (Multi-Society Task Force on the Persistent Vegetative State 1994b).

The pathological features of PVS vary from individual to individual, depending on the causative factor as well as the interval between brain injury and death. Commonly, following oxygen deprivation to the brain and raised intracranial pressure there is extensive multifocal or diffuse death within the layers of the cerebral cortex, plus the loss of neurons in other specific areas of the brain (namely, the hippocampus and thalamus; Graham et al. 2005b; Graham et al. 2005a). Diffuse damage to white matter tracts is the principal structural injury caused by acute trauma (such as in road accidents) (Graham et al. 2005a), a major cause of the vegetative stage. Non-traumatic injuries (for example, strokes, infection and tumours) are another frequent cause of PVS. Apart from these acute insults, the endstage of chronically dementing conditions in adults, such as Alzheimer's disease (which will be discussed later) can terminate in a vegetative state (Jaul and Calderon-Margalit 2007; Jennett 2001).

Although the clinical criteria for recognizing the PVS are now well developed, this has only been the case over the past few years. Considerable difficulties remain in distinguishing PVS from coma, and from similar medical conditions such as the locked-in syndrome. In coma, the eyes are closed and there are no sleep-wake cycles, while in the locked-in syndrome patients are aware of themselves and their environment, but communication is exceedingly limited due to the loss of much motor function and speech (Zeman 1997). A study by Andrews et al. (1996) is testament to the difficulty of making an accurate diagnosis of PVS. Of the 40 patient records they examined, close to half (17 cases) were considered to have been misdiagnosed. A similar, more recent, study by Wilson and colleagues (2002) found that four out of 35 PVS and minimally conscious patients had been misdiagnosed, highlighting the need for intensive and frequent assessment.

Since clarification of the definition of clinical criteria for both the vegetative state and for the minimally conscious state, mistaken diagnosis has become less likely. There are a number of published criteria for diagnosis, mostly from the United States, but the latest and most authoritative are those from the Royal College of Physicians (2003) – an update of their 1996 document. The 2003 document refined the necessary conditions that must be present before diagnosis of the vegetative state can be made. This is to exclude misdiagnosis due to continuous effects of drugs, metabolic disturbance, or a treatable structural cause.

The following *necessary criteria* have been delineated for the diagnosis of the vegetative state (Royal College of Physicians 2003):

- no evidence of awareness of self or environment at any time;
- no response to visual, auditory, tactile or noxious stimuli suggesting volition or conscious purpose;
- no evidence of language comprehension or meaningful facial expression.

Non-obligatory criteria include:

- intermittent periods of eye closure and eye opening giving the appearance of a sleep-wake cycle;
- sufficiently preserved hypothalamic and brainstem function to ensure the maintenance of respiration and circulation.

Completing the diagnostic picture are further compatible clinical features (spontaneous, purposeless movements including facial expression; variably preserved cranial-nerve and spinal reflexes; shedding of tears; grunting or groaning sounds), atypical features (fixation and following of a moving object; reaction to visual menace; utterance of a single incongruous word), and incompatible features (purposeful actions; communicative acts and discriminative perception). Patients who remain in a state of reduced consciousness but do not meet the above criteria are considered to be 'minimally conscious' (Shiel et al. 2004).

The length of time over which this condition may be sustained has been a cause of confusion. It usually develops after a period of coma, and while the coma may be partially or totally reversible, it may progress to a PVS. It has been suggested that persistence of the vegetative state could be declared after four weeks (Shiel et al. 2004). In cases due to traumatic brain injury, permanence of the vegetative state could be defined after a year, and in non-traumatic cases after either three (Multi-Society Task Force on the Persistent Vegetative State 1994a) or six months (Royal College of Physicians 2003; Shiel et al. 2004). Expert observation of the patient's behaviour over a sufficient period of time is necessary to ensure correct diagnosis. Although these criteria may seem clear, problems with the accuracy of assessment persist (Shiel et al. 2004).

Four levels of treatment are recognized for PVS patients. The Multi-Society Task Force (1994a, 1577) described these in the following way:

> ... high-technology "rescue" treatments, such as mechanical ventilation, dialysis, and cardiopulmonary resuscitation; medications and other commonly ordered treatments, including antibiotics and supplemental oxygen; hydration and nutrition; and nursing or home care to maintain personal dignity and hygiene.

The highly dependent condition of the PVS patient necessitates a high standard of nursing care, including passive joint exercises, skin care, suction to prevent aspiration, incontinence management and attention to oral hygiene, to prevent avoidable complications (Royal College of Physicians 2003). Therapeutic options that may enhance recovery have been suggested, including deep-brain electrical stimulation (Glannon 2008; Yamamoto and Katayama 2005), music therapy (Magee 2005), sensory stimulation, hyperbaric oxygen therapy and drug treatment (Giacino and Whyte 2005). There have been a number of case reports of Zolpidem, a psychoactive drug usually used to treat insomnia, transiently raising consciousness in patients in a minimally conscious state and PVS (Clauss and Nel 2006; Shames and Ring 2008). However, this effect does not consistently occur (Singh et al. 2008). To date, there is still no proven intervention that can enhance recovery from the vegetative state (Whyte 2007).

The termination of all forms of life-sustaining medical treatment, including hydration and nutrition, in adult patients is accepted by a variety of medical societies and interdisciplinary bodies when advance directives are available or when relatives or a senior doctor make a competent decision on behalf of the incompetent patient (American Academy of Neurology 2007; British Medical Association 2007b; Royal College of Physicians 2003). When artificial nutrition and hydration are withdrawn, PVS patients usually die peacefully within 10 to 14 days (Andrews 2004). The immediate cause of death is dehydration and electrolyte imbalance (not malnutrition). Brain imaging studies have shown that because of the extent of brain damage painful stimuli are processed only at a very basic level, and PVS patients are not thought to consciously experience pain or suffering (Schnakers and Zasler 2007). However, as this cannot be determined with full certainty it is recommended that sedation be administered when artificial nutrition and hydration are withdrawn (Royal College of Physicians 2003).

Neuroimaging Examination of PVS

Few reports have examined patterns of brain activity following severe brain injury, to monitor and record the recovery of consciousness in vegetative and minimally conscious states (Laureys et al. 1999; Laureys et al. 2000). Neuroimaging techniques could help assess the cortical function and recovery potential of each patient by revealing the status of residual systems specialized for essential cognitive and volitional tasks (Giacino et al. 2006; Hirsch 2005).

Beckinschtein et al. (2005) describe a patient who, after two months in a vegetative state, progressed to a minimally conscious state (MCS) and then, over the next 18 months, to partial independence. A fMRI (functional Magnetic Resonance Imaging) scan was performed involving passive listening blocks of real words, white noise or silence. During the vegetative state, the word versus silence comparison revealed small clusters of activity in temporal-lobe regions, although activity was increased significantly in speech and auditory areas following recovery.

In order to gauge the degree of preserved cognitive function in vegetative patients, simple forms of processing are assessed before moving on to more complex functions (Owen et al. 2005). In one elegant paradigm vegetative patients are asked to perform mental imagery tasks during scanning. One exceptional patient, who was characterized as being in a vegetative state five months after a traumatic brain injury, showed activation patterns indistinguishable from healthy volunteers when asked to imagine various activities (Owen et al. 2006). When asked to imagine playing tennis, activation was observed in the supplementary motor area, and when asked to imagine walking through the rooms of her house, activation was observed in the premotor cortex, parahippocampal gyrus and posterior parietal cortex. The altered activation patterns occurred in direct response to a command, perhaps showing that the patient was able to perform intentional acts, evidence for awareness even when voluntary motor responsiveness was lacking (Laureys et al. 2006). However this assertion has been contested (Greenberg 2007; Nachev and Husain 2007). It should also be noted that in this specific case the patient had not been classified as being in a PVS, and when examined six months later showed clinical signs of recovery from the vegetative state (Laureys et al. 2006). This case does, however, make a convincing argument for the development of fMRI and other tools to assess cognition in vegetative patients (see also Laureys et al. 2004).

Possibilities for Recovery

There is a high rate of mortality during the first year after entering a vegetative state. However, patients that survive the first year can be kept alive for many more years. The immobility of PVS patients predisposes them to cardiovascular disease and pneumonia (Shavelle et al. 2001). If given good basic care patients in a PVS commonly survive for 5, 10 or even 20 years (Cranford 1988; Rousseau et al. 2008; Sazbon and Groswasser 1991), with the longest reported survival without recovery being 40 years (Colburn 1991).

It has been observed that the longer an individual has remained unconscious, the lower the chance of ever regaining consciousness, and that there is a greater chance of severe functional deficits if such recovery were to occur (Whyte 2007). This is probably due to the fact that over time patients with a more positive prognosis will have regained consciousness leaving the remainder of the group with a more consistently negative prognosis (Giacino and Whyte 2005). Cases due to an acute insult have relatively higher recovery rates during the first six months compared to non-traumatic cases (Multi-Society Task Force on the Persistent Vegetative State 1994a). Some of those who recover remain in a minimally conscious state.

Higashi and colleagues (1981) reported that of 110 individuals with established PVS, five patients recovered, two of them well enough to care for themselves in most aspects of daily living. Andrews (1993) in a retrospective review of 43 individuals in a PVS noted that 11 recovered, ten to the extent that they regained the capacity to communicate their needs to others. Such high proportions of recoveries could perhaps be attributed to initial misdiagnosis of PVS. However, meaningful recoveries after several months or years in PVS have been reported in very rare cases (Arts et al. 1985; Faran et al. 2006; Matsuda et al. 2003; Sara et al. 2007).

In view of the recovery data, Borthwick (1995a, 1995b) noted that PVS could not be viewed as a permanent or irreversible condition; a statement that returns us to the source of the ethical dilemma posed by the PVS condition. How are we to treat human beings who can be classified neither as dead, nor as living in a meaningful way but who may have a remote chance of regaining some elements of a meaningful life?

Ethical Categories

Even if we assume that the criteria put forward for the diagnosis of PVS are reasonably accurate, the ethical issues arising from it remain complex. According to the higher brain (personalist) definition of death, a person, and hence a meaningful life, has come to an end once consciousness and cognition have been irreversibly lost. Thus, patients in a PVS would be declared dead by this definition. Despite this, all societies and laws worldwide consider PVS patients to be alive (Bernat 2005a). But are they alive in any meaningful sense?

There is no single answer to this question, as evidenced by the cases above, where family members have in some instances asserted a right to discontinue life support and artificial feeding for the PVS patient. On other occasions, as we have seen, some family members have held the opposite perspective, their concern being to 'keep the patient alive' for as long as possible.

Requests to continue treatment when a PVS has been sustained for at least 12 months bring into focus issues of medical judgement and futility (Bernat 2005b; Schneiderman et al. 1990), and the autonomy of the family, quite apart from issues of cost and resource allocation. In some instances, the end of the patient's life may be the best outcome, but as McLean (1999) points out, a major challenge that remains is finding an ethically acceptable method for achieving this.

A number of ways of resolving this issue have been suggested. These include: redefining death, establishing criteria for treatment based on the extent of neurological damage and duration of the condition, and shifting the burden from those who want to discontinue treatment to those who want to continue it (Angell 1994).

Of these three approaches, the first is the most radical. Moving from whole brain towards a higher brain definition of death, and therefore allowing cessation of treatment (including artificial nutrition and hydration) in PVS patients after an appropriate length of time, is based on personalist criteria of death. The major objection to this, as we have already seen, is that these patients, in contrast to those with whole brain death, do not look dead. Lamb (1985) argues that no society would treat PVS patients as dead as they are not deemed fit for burial, organ removal or experimentation. At our current point of understanding of the higher brain definition of death and its ethical implications, the first approach is unlikely to constitute a way ahead in the PVS debate.

The second approach (establishing criteria for treatment based on the extent of neurological damage and duration of the condition) would retain the whole brain definition of death but would permit the discontinuation of treatment after a specific time, with the time limit depending on the severity of brain damage. While this approach may be useful in a practical sense, it fails to address the core concern of whether the PVS patient is truly alive; why discontinue treatment if the patient is still 'alive' and could remain 'alive' for a prolonged period?

The third approach would shift the burden from those who want to discontinue treatment to those who want to continue it. Currently, the presumption is that if no advance directive is available, patients in a PVS should be (or are assumed to have a prior desire for being) kept alive, and the families of those who wish to discontinue treatment must, in some countries, still argue their case before the courts. In the United States it was decided in the 1980s that these cases no longer need to come to court unless there is an irresolvable dispute between the involved parties. Similar decisions have been reached by Scottish, Dutch and many northern European courts, allowing withdrawal of artificial nutrition and hydration without court approval after six months in a PVS due to non-traumatic cause or 12 months after a traumatic cause (Bates 2005). In England and Wales, however, where the decision officially remains one to be made by medical staff, in consultation with the family, legal approval is still a requirement (Royal College of Physicians 2003). Similar laws and recommendations are found in much of southern Europe (Bates 2005). The controversy surrounding the Terri Schiavo case in the United States has prompted a reexamination of legislation regarding the role of surrogates in deciding on the withdrawal of artificial nutrition and hydration. This has revealed varying legislation at the state level and highlighted the importance of advance directives (Larriviere and Bonnie 2006).

Angell (1994) believes that it would be more appropriate to assume that PVS patients would *not* wish to be kept alive indefinitely and leave it for families who particularly objected to the discontinuation of treatment to justify their position. Surveys of doctors, nurses, outpatients and the public support this view, showing that 80–90 per cent would not want such continuing treatment (Kadish 1992). More recent media polls suggest around 80 per cent of Americans would not want to be kept alive if they were in a PVS (Blendon et al. 2005).

If patients are to prepare realistic advance directives or if families are to make a competent choice in place of a patient, it must be ensured that they are sufficiently well informed. This entails considerable public reflection on the burdens and benefits of life-sustaining treatment, including artificial nutrition and hydration, at all stages of PVS.

Consideration of burdens and benefits from the point of view of the PVS patient is problematic precisely because the condition is predicated, at least in part, on them not having a point of view at all – they are in a vegetative state. Will the patient benefit by being relieved of the burden of the PVS? Is it correct to consider this condition burdensome, given that the patient is wholly unaware of his or her predicament? Not only this, but is non-existence preferable to unconscious existence in the PVS?

What, then, are the anticipated benefits? What advantage does the PVS patient derive from continued existence? Nutritional support can preserve multiple organ systems in the PVS patient, but it cannot restore the person to a conscious, rational life (Mitchell et al. 1993). Treatment (including artificial nutrition and hydration) may be considered futile since it will, in all probability, fail to achieve the ultimate goal of any medical intervention, which is improvement of the patient's prognosis, comfort, wellbeing and general state of health (Bernat 2005b; Schneiderman et al. 1990).

Consequently, even those who are reluctant to withdraw artificial nutrition and hydration from the PVS patient due to these patients' ambivalent status, may not have a *positive* duty or obligation to continue with this treatment, especially since there is only a remote chance that the condition is not permanent (Zimmerman 1991). In similar vein, Harvey (2006) considers that sufficient moral reasons exist to render optional the treatment and feeding of permanently unconscious, terminally ill patients. For him, such a condition is so removed from normal human existence, that ending the significant burdens and suffering borne by the family and health care team, and to a lesser extent, by society at large, is the compassionate and preferable option (see also Mitchell et al. 1993; Schneiderman et al. 1990; Zimmerman 1991).

There is now a wide consensus that death after treatment withdrawal does not constitute euthanasia or suicide. In October 2000, the English High Court ruled on two cases that such withdrawal did not infringe the Human Rights Act, and was consistent with the European Convention on Human Rights (Jennett 2005). One ground on which courts have sought to distinguish killing from letting die is that the former requires affirmative life-taking actions while the latter simply allows nature to take its course (Hand and Chapman 1980). The distinction between killing and letting die (i.e. between doing and allowing harm) has been, and continues to be debated by moral philosophers, with no consensus emerging (Asscher 2008; Foot 1984; Glover 1977; Steinbock and Norcross 1994).

The above arguments show that, unlike the whole brain definition of death, the diagnostic situation of PVS is not sufficiently clear to provide clear answers as to how to deal with patients in that condition. We have, however, tried to suggest how a sensible end-of-life decision can be reached by taking into consideration the welfare of the patient as a whole, as well as the respective consequences for the family, the integrity of the health professionals, and distributive justice.

Alzheimer's Disease

Having addressed end-of-life questions in individuals who are brain dead or in a PVS, and as such exist on the margins of conscious life and death, we now move on to deal with similar issues in patients afflicted with Alzheimer's disease (AD). This is a much more common condition, but the social and ethical implications have only begun to receive the attention they deserve in recent years. Despite some significant differences in the earlier stages of the disease, it is our view that ethical thinking about Alzheimer's disease ethics can gain important insights from the established reasoning about PVS and brain death.

Alzheimer's, famously labelled 'the Disease of the Century', by Lewis Thomas is, aside from cancer, the illness most people fear as they age (Campbell 2004). About two-thirds of all people with dementia are suffering from Alzheimer's disease (Small et al. 1997) – a terminal neurodegenerative condition that slowly and progressively destroys neurons and causes a general deterioration in health. Alois Alzheimer, a German neurologist, first described the symptoms as well as the neuropathology of the disease that bears his name in 1907. Neuronal cell loss, neurofibrillary tangles and amyloid plaques are the predominant neuropathological characteristics. Neuronal cell loss is most pronounced in the cerebral cortex, hippocampus and amygdala (Wenk 2003), although selected nuclei in the brain stem are also affected (Giess and Schlote 1995).

In the early stage, the disease affects memory and mental functioning, but confusion, lability of emotions and disorientation are equally common. In the middle stage, hallucinations may set in and sufferers become increasingly dependent and apathic, requiring help with simple everyday tasks, such as dressing and toileting, in time becoming totally dependent. The late stage is marked by incontinence and the inability to walk independently. Death is often caused by other illnesses that result from a greater susceptibility to illness but can also be due to Alzheimer-related complications such as difficulty in chewing, swallowing or breathing (Kalia 2003). Despite considerable research, available treatments are primarily aimed at slowing the advance of the disease rather than arresting it entirely or reversing its symptoms (Hardy 2004; Wolf-Klein et al. 2007).

Currently, around 30 million people worldwide are believed to be affected (Hughes 2004) with the length of stay in nursing homes for Alzheimer's patients estimated to be ten times the national average for all diagnoses (Welch et al. 1992). In the absence of a cure or preventive treatment, by 2050 this number will triple as the global population ages (Hebert et al. 2003; Sloane et al. 2002). The tremendous financial toll of this disease for both individuals and society would continue to rise, leading possibly to a public health crisis, and placing a significant financial and emotional burden on the whole of the working-age population (Sloane et al. 2002; Wancata et al. 2003).

To ameliorate this potentially catastrophic effect, more effective presymptomatic identification of a predisposition to the disease, preventive intervention and therapies directed at the biological basis of the disease's pathogenesis are urgently needed. Advances in knowledge of the molecular and genetic aspects of AD are providing therapeutic targets for attacking more directly the molecular processes of the disease (Rosenberg 2001; Tsuji 2001). An effective treatment for the prevention of AD would have an enormous public health benefit (Markesbery et al. 2006). Even a prevention therapy that delayed the onset of AD by as little as five years has the potential to reduce the number of afflicted persons by perhaps a half, significantly lowering the mortality rate, though leaving a larger number of patients mildly affected (Khachaturian 1992; Sloane et al. 2002).

A number of questions similar to those addressed in the context of brain death and PVS arise when considering the condition of the Alzheimer's patient. The fact that the higher brain (cerebral cortex and hippocampus) is severely affected by the neuronal loss in AD raises the question of whether we are justified in describing victims in the late stages as truly living. Some clinicians consider the PVS to be part of the natural history of dementia (Jaul and Calderon-Margalit 2007), while others question whether severe dementia routinely ends in a PVS (Boller et al. 2002; Volicer et al. 1997). It can be argued that we ought to treat patients with very late stage Alzheimer's in a similar way to the treatment of PVS patients. This only holds, however, if these AD patients are characterized by irreversible mental incapacitation. Once again, it is also imperative to consider the needs of the patient, family and society (Mitrani et al. 2006). There can be little question that measures for prolonging life are appropriate in the early stage of dementia, although there is considerable uncertainty in the very late stages of the illness.

Personhood and Selfhood

Many authors who have contributed to the debate on Alzheimer's and personhood promote the view that a person affected with AD experiences a continuous erosion of selfhood (Dekkers and Rikkert 2007; Kitwood and Benson 1995). This is a process in which the self is thought to be increasingly devoid of content, also described as 'unbecoming' a self (Fontana and Smith 1989), ultimately culminating in the complete loss of self – the loss of the person before the body has stopped functioning (Cohen and Eisendorfer 1986, 22). Singer argues that patients in the later stages of AD who are not self-conscious, rational or autonomous do not have a legitimate claim to a right to life. For him, it is 'difficult to see the point of keeping such human beings alive if their life is, on the whole, miserable' (Singer 1993, 191–2). In similar vein, Parfit writes: 'We can plausibly claim that, if the person has ceased to exist, we have no moral reason to help his heart to go on beating, or to refrain from preventing this.' (Parfit 1984, 323)

These judgements draw, in part, on the notion that once the biographical personality of a human being has ceased to exist, the person should be judged as dead. PVS and late-stage Alzheimer's patients would therefore be defined as dead by the higher brain definition of death, providing a reason for withholding medication in the case of disease complications, avoidance of resuscitation and withdrawal of ventilation, artificial hydration and nutrition (Roth 1996). The advantages and drawbacks of shifting our definition of death towards a higher brain definition have been discussed in earlier sections. In practical clinical terms, declaring many late stage Alzheimer's patients dead by the higher brain definition could contribute to what has been described as 'malignant social psychology' (Kitwood 1990). The thrust of this designation is that practices like this may well promote stigmatization and objectification, ultimately leading to loss of self-esteem and loss of selfhood, thereby accentuating problems caused by the neuropathology itself.

A counterbalance to a stridently grounded neuropathological approach is provided by recent voices from patients, families and carers focusing on the possibility that personhood does not cease with the vanishing of the mind. Even until the very terminal stage of Alzheimer's, the affected person can sporadically articulate memories of meaningful events, and relate to others through emotions and non-verbal communication (Hubbard et al. 2002; Post 2000). Social scientist Pia Kontos (2005) summarizes these arguments in her theory of 'embodied selfhood', arguing that dementia sufferers often experience their selfhood in the same way they communicate their thoughts and feelings – in and through their bodies. Examples of how dementia sufferers retain aspects of their personality through their body include trivial aspects, such as expressive gestures, spontaneous actions and attentiveness to cleanliness and poise (Kontos 2005). More spectacular are examples of a pianist who continued to play until a year before death, although with declining skill (Roth 1996) and the distinguished painter, Willem de Kooning, who, despite his dementia, produced much-admired works of art (Kontos 2003). These examples support the view, put forward by Post that:

> The place to begin an ethics of dementia is not in moral abstractions but in listening attentively to caregivers and affected persons. The philosopher Hegel remarked that there are two kinds of knowledge: knowledge in the abstract and knowledge in the concrete. He added that only the latter is real. (Post 1995, 13)

If we want to be socially prepared for the increasing incidence of dementia in our ageing society, we have to broaden our perception of human worth. A patient suffering from late-stage Alzheimer's continues to possess dignity that ought to be respected, as his or her personality is still upheld by emotional, relational and creative criteria. At no point during the greater part of the disease should these patients be treated as PVS patients.

Nevertheless, in the final phases of Alzheimer's, where patients have reached a PVS-like or comatose stage, the only form of humane and ethical management may be to allow them to die. Attempts to resuscitate these patients, and to keep them alive with the latest medical technology, in the light of the irreversibility of the neurological damage and the imminent terminal condition, would only mean further erosion of the patient's dignity. Instead of futile life-sustaining interventions, these patients should receive hospice care (Modi et al. 2005; Murphy and Buchanon 1998). At this extreme end-point embodied selfhood breaks down and the prominence of neuropathological reality takes over.

Neuroimaging

The move from brain death and dementia to the description of a technique may elicit some surprise, and yet it marks the move from one set of ethical challenges to another set. True, it marks the transition from a consideration of pathology to one of health, but this may change. The use of neuroimaging, which is currently in its infancy, may extend to the diagnosis of PVS states and of dementia, including early manifestations of dementia. However, it is the potential power of these techniques to delve into the brain and thought processes of the living that excites alarm from commentators. This is the domain of neuroethics.

Our understanding of human behaviour and disease has been greatly enhanced by the advent of neuroimaging technologies. From humble, but significant, beginnings with the invention of electroencephalography (EEG) in 1929, decades of work by scientists and engineers has produced an array of neuroimaging tools that can visualize the brain's activity in real time. The technology is continuously being refined and EEG has now been joined by magnetoencephalography (MEG), positron emission tomography (PET), single photon emission computed tomography (SPECT) and functional Magnetic Resonance Imaging (fMRI). These imaging modalities utilize various brain signals such as electromagnetic activity (MEG), metabolic activity and blood flow (PET and SPECT), and regional blood oxygenation (fMRI). These technologies have informed the diagnosis and treatment of a broad range of neurological and psychiatric disorders, including dementia, stroke, head injury, cancer, and epilepsy. In each case readings from two different controlled conditions are compared or subtracted, statistically processed, and reconstructed via computerized data manipulation to create multicolored maps of the brain. The different techniques each have relative advantages and disadvantages, which are concisely summarized by Illes and Racine (2005).

The popularity of brain imaging necessitates a cautious evaluation of the limits of these new technologies to reveal brain structure and function. fMRI and similar methodologies do not directly measure brain activity, they measure physiological correlates of brain activity. In the case of fMRI metabolic activity, as evidenced by blood flow, is gauged. This detachment introduces a degree of uncertainty that only allows inferences to be made about activity rather than definitively recording it. Blood flow is influenced by many other variables in addition to neural activity, including the condition of red blood cells, vessels and heart muscle, and the age and general health of the individual (Illes et al. 2006). This diversity of factors must be taken into account when fMRI data are assessed and compared. While this appears to be of biological relevance alone, it also has important ethical overtones, since misinterpretation or overinterpretation can be grossly misleading.

Functional MRI will most likely prove to have the greatest lasting impact of all the brain imaging technologies, both in clinical medicine, research and on society as a whole (Illes and Racine 2005). Magnetic resonance scanners are widely available, the technology is non invasive and possesses excellent spatial and temporal resolution, and is adaptable to a variety of experimental paradigms. Indeed it is the fMRI images that are most familiar to the public as its use has spread from purely clinical realms to cognitive science, behaviour research and the law. This popularity and proliferation of uses has posed urgent problems for the rapidly developing school of neuroethics.

Neuroimaging for Disease Prediction

Newly developed neuroimaging techniques have opened up new prospects for the diagnosis and prediction of diseases such as AD. Neuroimaging is recommended at least once during the diagnostic work-up to exclude alternative causes of cognitive dysfunction (van der Flier et al. 2007). MRI can also look for the build-up of amyloid plaques on neurons, perhaps predicting future Alzheimer's disease, or even its likely age of onset (Greely 2006; Reiman 2007).

However, while new technologies such as these may greatly enhance our diagnostic skills, they may not necessarily increase our ability to prevent or cure disease in parallel. This therapeutic gap has been encountered with new genetic technologies and can be foreseen with neuroimaging (Green 2006). Scanning technologies will improve our ability to detect and predict brain pathologies, but the tools for ameliorating or curing these conditions will probably advance more slowly. It may not be appropriate to regularly use neuroimaging as a diagnostic tool for AD, for example, as it may have unintended ethical, social and economic consequences (Illes et al. 2007). As with predictive genetics, there is concern that neuroimaging which identifies an anomaly, whether manifested in symptoms or not, will also lead to social stigma, emotional distress and difficulties securing employment, health care or insurance (Illes and Racine 2005; Illes et al. 2007). For instance, insurers do not need certainty to economically justify excluding from coverage people with structural brain anomalies associated with neurological disease.

Non-Medical Applications

There is a long history of attempts to correlate neuroanatomy with behaviour, phrenology being the best known, and neuroimaging has added more technologically advanced tools to the armamentarium of such pursuits (Baskin et al. 2007). To what extent is it possible to decode mental states from brain activity in humans? In a review of human neuroimaging in 2006 John-Dylan Haynes and Geraint Rees ask the question: 'Is it possible to tell what someone is currently thinking based only on measurements of their brain activity?' (Haynes and Rees 2006). They conclude by stating: 'Decoding-based approaches show great promise in providing new empirical methods for predicting cognitive or perceptual states from brain activity'. In other words, it might be possible in future to predict behaviour from neuroimaging data. Should this turn out to be the case, it will raise a plethora of ethical concerns.

It is already possible to detect the neural correlates of an increasingly wide array of conditions and traits. These include conscious and unconscious racial attitudes (Phelps et al. 2000), emotions (Phan et al. 2002), various personality traits (Canli et al. 2001), let alone personality disorders and psychopathic conditions (Barkataki et al. 2008), and even serious criminal tendencies (Deeley et al. 2006). But the list does not end here, since there appear to be neural correlates for drug abuse such as cocaine craving (Garavan and Hester 2007), preferences for various commercial products such as well-known soft drinks (McClure et al. 2004), and for the decision-making process itself (Sanfey et al. 2006). Brain imaging has extended far beyond its original use in the purely medical realm. As Pustilnik says:

> This explosion of interest in neuroscience to illuminate the (presumably universal) workings of the human mind has spawned a veritable neuro-everything craze – from neuroethics, neuroeconomics, and neurohistory, to neurolaw and neurojurisprudence. (Pustilnik 2008, 3)

Consider the following. We are all disgusted by certain sights or actions or behaviours, some of which seem to be very basic to everyday living whereas others are far more abstract. Is there any connection between the disgust that prevents us from eating contaminated food (visceral disgust) and the disgust that some feel concerning socio-moral issues, like embryo research or homosexuality (moral repugnance)? One fMRI study showed that when subjects experience either visceral or moral disgust overlapping brain areas are activated, implying that the emotions are related (Moll et al. 2005). Even assuming that this finding is reliable, its interpretation is far from self-evident.

In another paper (Moll et al. 2006), the same authors asserted that charitable donation activates the reward system in the brain in the same way as do food, drugs and sex. By using fMRI they found that altruistic acts, such as giving away money, lit up the primitive mesolimbic reward system in the brain, explaining why it feels good to do good. The authors suggested that performing charitable acts may be hard-wired into the brain rather than being a product of culture. Once again, this conclusion represents a vast interpretive leap, but even the existence of such a tentative conclusion illustrates the power of neural information to slant and possibly undermine moral thinking.

A further study (Harbaugh et al. 2007) with a similar thrust used fMRI to examine the brains of subjects as they chose whether to voluntarily give money directly to a food bank, over against recognizing that their money was going to the food bank through mandatory taxation. The 'reward-centre' in their brains lit up in both cases even when the subjects did not have a free choice. The authors interpreted this as demonstrating the existence of pure altruism, since activation of this brain region was greater when the money was voluntarily given. While one can probably draw philosophical and theological conclusions from this result, it is noteworthy that the study was undertaken by economists, whose aim was to draw conclusions of direct relevance to the determination of taxation policy. Should neuroeconomics of this ilk concern us, since neuroscience is being used to uncover basic ingredients of human behaviour? Before going too far in this direction, it is far from clear whether fMRI used in this manner is providing information unobtainable by other means.

More fundamentally, are acts of kindness and altruism little more than a primitive urge for the good feeling produced by neurotransmitters? If so, altruism is reduced to a drive for food and sex, a conclusion that far outstrips the explanatory powers of changing patterns in blood supply or neurotransmitter levels.

These potential non-medical applications of neuroimaging raise a number of questions and concerns. Some are common to all biomedical information, such as confidentiality and privacy (Farah and Wolpe 2004). However, some questions are specific to the realm of neuroimaging, since they refer to the seat of our behaviour and attitudes.

Lie Detection

DNA analysis has revolutionized forensic studies, adding a powerful tool to criminal investigations, but raising important questions about privacy and civil liberty. In comparison, the possibilities of forensic neuroscience are yet to be realized, although these are being vigorously pursued (Green 2006). The use of neuroimaging for lie detection, monitoring and legal defence is both promising and perilous. In all cases the rights of the individual need to be balanced against the rights of society (Canli and Amin 2002).

Conventional polygraphy attempts to detect deception by monitoring physiological phenomena such as respiration, pulse, blood pressure and skin conductivity. Recent research is aimed at directly measuring brain signals corresponding to lying using fMRI, EEG, infrared light and other neuroimaging modalities (Chance and Kang 2002; Farwell and Smith 2001; Langleben et al. 2005). Attempts to deceive are correlated with increased activation of the prefrontal and anterior cingulate cortices, whereas truth-telling appears to be a baseline for human communication (Spence et al. 2004). The theory is that deception requires greater effort than truth-telling, hence the activation of higher brain regions. US defence agencies have devoted considerable funds to this research and a number of private companies are pursuing practical applications. 'Brain fingerprinting', as vigorously promoted by Lawrence Farwell, has garnered significant media attention. This technique employs EEG to measure particular brain signals (event related potentials) that are picked up a short time after a stimulus, in this case 300ms for the P300 signal. Farwell proposes that the P300 signal can be used to assess whether the stimulus is familiar to the subject (Farwell and Smith 2001). In the case of a forensic investigation, familiarity with the crime scene or other exclusive information would imply guilt, an assumption that one imagines is open to challenge. Brain fingerprinting has already been introduced in one criminal case, and further technology may prove attractive to both the prosecution and defence (Stoller and Wolpe 2007).

Neuroimaging for lie detection raises many of the legal and ethical issues common to conventional polygraphy, including privacy and civil liberty. However, the increased intrusiveness of brain imaging causes us to question a person's right to 'cognitive liberty' (Wolpe et al. 2005). Where once the state's interference was limited by an inability to read a person's thoughts, technological incursions may remove even this defence. A person may then be unable to refuse to give evidence against himself, a right currently protected by US constitutional law (Stoller and Wolpe 2007).

Alongside these ethical issues are considerable technical limitations (Wolpe et al. 2005). The validity and accuracy of the measurements taken are questionable as are the paradigms of deception used. Collaborative research has been flawed by a lack of standardized protocols, which would be essential to any practical application. There is also the question of how vulnerable the technique would be to countermeasures – subjects in research protocols are not trying to be deceptive, a situation that would probably not apply in a criminal investigation.

These technical limitations, in addition to the substantial ethical and legal problems, suggest that it would be premature to move beyond research at present, no matter how great governmental or commercial demand may be.

Neuroimaging and the Law

Neuroimaging has extended its reach into courts of law, being increasingly presented as evidence in civil and criminal cases. In a number of high-profile cases the defence has sought to admit brain images as evidence of mitigated responsibility for criminal actions (see Khoshbin (2007) and Baskin (2007) for examples). Take this partly hypothetical example (Tancredi and Brodie 2007): the defendant in a drug-dealing case is given an MRI which reveals a large pituitary tumour pressing on the frontal lobe which, his lawyer argues, impairs the defendant's judgement and grasp of consequences. Or perhaps a man is accused of a racially-motivated attack, and as evidence of the defendant's racist tendencies the prosecution submits an fMRI showing 'excessive' activation in the amygdala when the defendant is exposed to images of African Americans (Rosen 2007).

There are numerous difficulties with such examples, not least of which is defining what is 'normal' brain activation or structure across a population (Tancredi and Brodie 2007). There is no precise linear correlation between structural abnormalities or activation patterns and aberrant behaviour. Violence, aggression, racism and anti-social behaviour have not been exclusively located in specific brain regions. Since fMRI can only exhibit changes in regional blood flow, brain activity and its significance are only inferred from these patterns. There is no escape from the layers of interpretation between the original reading and behavioural conclusion, and these additional layers foster imprecision.

Brain images have also been used in courts of law to challenge the assumption that minors accused of violent crimes can be prosecuted as adults (Stepp 2008). Defence lawyers have called developmental neuroscientists to testify that the adolescent brain is not fully mature, particularly in the prefrontal cortex, which governs reasoning. The limbic system, governing emotion, is comparatively more developed and so wins over the prefrontal region, and, put simply, decisions are made more on emotion than reason (Casey et al. 2008). Adolescents are thus more likely to act impulsively and succumb to peer pressure and less likely to consider consequences than adults, arguably diminishing culpability. However, the science underpinning such conclusions is still largely speculative (Steinberg 2008), and it is perhaps premature to introduce it to the courtroom.

Brain images are visually arresting, and may prove dangerously persuasive to judges, jurors and the public (Mobbs et al. 2007). They give the impression of greater certainty than is reasonably possible. If such images are admitted as evidence those to whom the MRI is presented may not understand the substantial limitations of fMRI in this context (Tancredi and Brodie 2007).

Brain images should only be used in a court of law to establish an association between a structural abnormality or injury and a specific deficit, not to demonstrate responsibility, motivation or propensity for a particular behaviour (Khoshbin and Khoshbin 2007). Conclusions any bolder than this are premature considering the enormous complexity of the brain and our relatively poor understanding of the interactions of its many parts.

The use of brain images in courts of law is but a symptom of an increasing push to identify a neurobiology of crime. However, this notion is nothing new. Neuroscience has been used in an attempt to explain criminal behaviour and identify criminal personalities for more than 200 years as the chequered history of phrenology, lobotomy and Lombrosian biological criminology shows (Pustilnik 2008). According to the latter theory, propounded by Cesare Lombroso in the late nineteenth to early twentieth centuries, atavistic physical features, particularly of the head, indicated primitive brain defects that caused criminal behaviour. Such attempts are fundamentally flawed by their overly simplistic reductionism – violence cannot be defined as a single entity and cannot be localized in a specific brain region on a one-to-one basis. There may be some comfort to be found in classifying those who commit violent crimes as biologically atypical, and thus as distinct from 'us', but it is false comfort (Pustilnik 2008).

Predictive Neuroimaging

If neuroimaging can ascertain neurological patterns associated with certain behaviours, the technology could perhaps be used to identify people before they acted out the behaviour in question on the basis of their brain architecture. On this basis political terrorists, serial killers or pedophiles could be identified and apprehended before any crime is committed (Mobbs et al. 2007; Pustilnik 2008). Neuroimaging could perhaps be combined with genetic information to predict certain undesirable behaviours with greater certainty (Tancredi and Brodie 2007). This technology may be more at home in science fiction fantasies, but it is apparently proving attractive to some government agencies and the military (Farahany 2008; Marks 2007; Wild 2005). It is predicted by some that brain imaging could be used to identify potential terrorists, although the reality behind such predictions is probably tenuous.

Predictive neuroimaging points to employers using brain imaging to gather supposedly more accurate information on potential employees. Neuroimaging could be seen as a more reliable method than interviews and personality questionnaires. Preliminary research suggests that personality traits of interest to potential employers, such as extroversion, cooperation and persistence, could be gauged by fMRI (Canli 2004; Decety et al. 2004; Gusnard et al. 2003). Whether this technology would ever be applied to applicant screening is questionable, but it has already featured in the popular media (Dobbs 2005).

Functional MRI has been used to characterize the neural responses of self-described pedophiles when exposed to erotic material. The fMRIs of pedophiles showed 'reduced activation' of the hypothalamus and prefrontal cortex 'as compared to healthy individuals when they were viewing sexually arousing pictures of adults' (Walter et al. 2007). Such results could be taken to indicate a biological basis for pedophilia, suggesting ways of identifying pedophiles before they commit any crime. However, this possibility raises the well-known issue of presymptomatic testing, with its corollary that action can be taken against an individual before any crime has been committed. This would challenge traditional conceptions of civil liberty and justice, quite apart from which its scientific foundation needs to be established. This is not the case at present.

Equating simple biological phenomena with complicated social behaviours is overly deterministic and ultimately flawed. The simple act of finding neural correlates for certain behaviours or attitudes may not tell us anything about *causative factors*. Simply because brain region R is active when behaviour B is undertaken does not mean that changes in R cause B to take place. The opposite could be the case, in that when an individual displays behaviour B brain region R is modified, and if this occurs sufficiently often, there are significant changes to R. Yet again, the interplay between R and B may be so close that the only tenable conclusion is to state that there is no definitive causative factor.

Neuroscientists need to guard against prematurely deterministic assumptions which fail to take into account the complexity of the human brain. Such caution is necessary if neuroimaging is to avoid becoming a modern-day phrenology. The intersection of ethics, society and law with neuroscience is a murky one, but one that must be thoroughly explored.

In the area of neuroimaging, and even neuroscience more broadly, 'hyperbole has outstripped scientific reality' (Fins 2008). Futuristic propositions and clinical fantasies have dominated ethical discussion, to the neglect of the real quandaries of physicians and the needs of patients. Neuroethics must maintain a clinical base, allowing physicians to make fundamental contributions to determining acceptable and unacceptable ways forward (Jones 2008). Otherwise neuroethical discussions will remain highly speculative and increasingly irrelevant to the ethical environment of the neurology clinic.

Chapter 9

The Modified Body

Introduction

It is perhaps fitting that, in this final chapter, we discuss what can be seen as the most forward-looking of the uses of the body: its modification. As we shall see, some proponents of extreme modification embrace a vision of the future in which our bodies will be capable of feats impossible for unmodified humans. There are a few commentators who are even prepared to argue that we have a moral obligation to enhance human beings (Harris 2007; Savulescu 2005, 2006). However, many consider such enhancement of human capacities morally problematic at best, and disastrous at worst. A difficulty for those with this view is how to distinguish enhancement from the many life-enhancing practices and procedures performed daily by medical professionals and individuals, such as improved nutrition, hormonal and other pharmacological treatments, and surgery.

Conventional thought appears to be far removed from these possibilities with its simplistic distinction between therapy and enhancement. According to this approach *therapeutic* procedures aimed at restoring individuals to normality are typically applauded, whereas *enhancement* procedures aimed at improving individuals beyond what is normal are decried. In this chapter we will challenge this often held view. While this distinction may appear to be cut and dried and console many, it is based on questionable premises, that is, that the boundaries of normality are obvious and unchanging. It also presumes that all forms of enhancement are categorically unacceptable. Instead, we will propose an alternative means of categorizing modifications of the body that may help to clarify what is an often murky debate.

First, it will be useful to survey some of the instances of modifications that have occurred, or can occur, in reality, and those that are more accurately described as fantastic proposals belonging more appropriately to science fiction.

Modifications in Fantasy

It is not unusual to encounter stories in serious newspapers and magazines with headings such as 'Anyone for tennis, at the age of 150?' (Bailey 2006) and 'Do you want to live to be 800?' (McCall 2006). Aubrey de Grey, a biogerontologist at Cambridge University is the foremost proponent of visions such as these. For him and his acolytes a future world, at least 1,000 years hence, could be populated with people who are alive today and are already in their 60s. This scenario is based on the premise that ageing will have become obsolete, leading to a world populated by people enjoying a state of eternal youth. In order for this to occur, the major diseases of the twenty-first century will need to have been consigned to history (McCall 2006).

Similarly, Ronald Bailey (2006) envisages a typical family reunion at the end of this century. At this reunion there are five generations playing together, with the oldest member at 150 playing tennis with her 30-year-old great-great-granddaughter. On the eve of the twenty-second century, diabetes, Parkinson's disease and AIDS will be no more; tissues and organs will be readily regenerated, and human immortality will beckon. Technologies utilizing stem cells, constructing artificial chromosomes and creating perfect transplants will together have transformed the very essence of human nature.

Such visions are being worked out in some detail by one author after another. For instance, Joel Garreau, author of *Radical Evolution: The Promise and Peril of Enhancing our Minds, our Bodies – and What it Means to be Human* (Garreau 2005, 15) writes:

> We are at a turning point in history. For milleniums our technologies ... have been aimed at modifying our environment. Now, for the first time, our technologies are increasingly aimed inward – at altering our minds, memories, metabolisms, personalities, and progeny. This is not some science fiction future. Inexorable increases in ingenuity are opening vistas, especially in what we may call GRIN – genetic, robotic, information and nano-technologies.

This radical vision is embraced by a movement known as transhumanism (posthumanism). According to one definition: 'Transhumanism is an emerging social movement that promotes the technological enhancement of human capacities toward the end of creating a utopian era in which "post humans" will enjoy absolute morphological freedom and live for thousands of years' (Smith 2006).

Transhuman individuals will have been radically transformed – at least that is the grandiose vision. The possibilities sketched by the proponents of this philosophy are endless. The task of medicine has been reformulated, away from repair of the human body to its deconstruction and reconstruction. These postulated new individuals will have indefinite health-spans, infinite intellectual faculties, and the capability of controlling everything they are, or could become (Bostrom 2005).

Discussions of this type often make reference to H. G. Wells' 1859 novella *The Time Machine* (e.g. Stock 2002). Wells envisioned a distant future where humanity has split into two distinct species: the light and graceful Eloi and the bestial cannibalistic Morlocks. Could genetic enhancement technologies facilitate diversification to such a degree that humanity is fragmented into two or more persistent independent groups? Some commentators speculate that this indeed is what the future holds. According to one speculation the radically transformed or 'GenRich' may ultimately be so different to the untransformed 'Naturals' that they are unable to interbreed or do not desire to do so (Agar 2007).

It is tempting to dismiss these lines of thinking as little more than scientistic hyperbole, in which science fiction has dominated ethical discourse. However, they cannot be dismissed quite this readily since they inform the thinking of many serious scholars, and have captured the imagination of the popular media. Moreover, we should not lose sight of the many modifications of the body that are possible today, and have been practised at various times in history. There may well be a continuum from generally accepted modifications to which we all have become accustomed to modifications that are generally assigned to the imaginative realms of fantastic science fiction.

Modifications in Reality

Surgical Modifications

Physical modification of the body has a long history. People groups from almost every geographical area of the world have moulded the heads of infants using manual manipulation, constricting bandages, boards and stones in order to achieve a distinctive head shape (Gerszten and Gerszten 1995; Tubbs et al. 2006). The earliest archaeological evidence of intentional cranial deformation dates from 45,000 B.C. and mild forms are practised even today (FitzSimmons et al. 1998). Intentional cranial deformation has been used to indicate class and ethnicity, and to alter the aesthetics, ferocity, health and intelligence of the subject. Ancient Egyptians began moulding their heads, and those of infants, during the reign of King Akhenaton in order to emulate his distinctive head shape, which was possibly produced by hydrocephaly (Gerszten and Gerszten 1995). Queen Nefertiti is the classic example of the elongated skull and pointed chin characteristic of Egyptian nobility. A similar practice occurred in Nazi Germany where parents used cranial massage to achieve an 'Aryan' skull-type in their children, avoiding the racially despised round head (Favazza 1996, 86; Tubbs et al. 2006).

The well-known Chinese practice of foot-binding is another example of physical modification, and one which persisted for a thousand years. Starting in childhood, feet were bound using a long bandage which constricted and distorted the shape of the foot in an attempt to achieve the tiny feet of court dancers. Many of the bones in the feet were broken, the aim being to bend the toes into the sole of the foot, and bring the heel and sole as closely together as possible (Favazza 1996, 137–40). The result was debilitating for those subject to it, and revered as beautiful, prestigious and sexually alluring by Chinese men.

Tattooing is a culturally ubiquitous form of self-mutilation. Reaching its zenith in Polynesia, tattooing has been used to denote tribal distinctions, adorn bodies and mark significant life transitions (Favazza 1996). Because darker skin does not tattoo well, scarification is more popular in Africa. This technique involves making a number of superficial incisions in the skin to produce a raised scar.

Tattooing today has been embraced by the Western world. At first it was the domain of fringe groups who adorned themselves for shock value, but an increasingly broader adoption has led to the practice becoming relatively mainstream. Body piercing has followed a similar process of normalization, and as a result 'those seeking a body symbol of resistance capable of generating strong public revulsion experimented with more extreme forms of self-stigmatization, such as scalp implants and scarification, to proclaim their marginalized status' (Sullivan 2001, 4). Nonconformist body modification today includes such extreme practices as branding, extraocular implants (eyeball jewellery), transdermal implants, tongue splitting, and the shaping of ears to an elfin point.

Limb removal also has a long history, including the amputation of fingers in many aboriginal populations, which was usually a response to sickness, marriage, or death of a loved one (Favazza 1996, 132–5). More recently, individuals seeking healthy limb amputation have been described (Elliott 2003, 208–36; Favazza 1996). What is variously referred to as apotemnophilia (literally translated 'love of amputation'), body dysmorphic disorder, body integrity identity disorder or amputee identity disorder, manifests itself as an overwhelming need to modify the body in order to achieve the appearance or physicality that the individual believes to be authentic. A first-person account from a female sufferer expresses it best:

> To the general public, people like me are sick and strange, and that's where it ends. I think it is a question of fearing the unknown. I have something called body identity integrity disorder (BIID), where sufferers want to remove one or more healthy limbs. ... It is not a sexual thing, it is certainly not a fetish, and it is nothing to do with appearances. I simply cannot relate to myself with two legs: it isn't the "me" I want to be. I have long known that if I want to get on with my life I need to remove both legs. I have been trapped in the wrong body all this time and over the years I came to hate my physical self. (Smith 2007)

The sentiment of feeling 'trapped in the wrong body' has resonances with the phenomenon known as gender identity disorder, another instance of body modification in order to achieve what the individual feels to be their authentic physical self (Lawrence 2006). Is the amputation of a healthy leg from the woman quoted above a consensual mutilation of her body? Or is she in a harmed state prior to amputation, and the surgery is best regarded as therapy? Perhaps her situation is best described as extreme dissatisfaction with her body, which she wishes to enhance through amputation in order to achieve an abnormal ideal? To these questions there are no easy answers, and this is not the place to attempt to provide them. Nevertheless, they cast doubt on facile assessments of the terms 'therapy', 'enhancement' and 'mutilation', and cast doubt on clear distinctions between them.

Body modification by surgery does not fit readily into the one neat category. Think of plastic surgery procedures. While these tend to be divided into two categories, either reconstructive or cosmetic plastic surgery, this too is simplistic.

Accounts of reconstructive surgery can be dated as far back in history as 600BC, when reconstruction of the nose and ear lobe was performed in India (Brown 1986, cited in Sullivan 2001). The 'Indian method' involved cutting a nose-shaped flap of skin from the forehead and twisting it down to cover the nose. Though it left significant facial scarring, this method was effective and was again used in 1814 by the British surgeon Joseph Carpue (Patterson 1977, cited in Sullivan 2001). During World War I, New Zealand otolaryngologist Harold Gillies led a medical research unit in England which performed reconstructive surgery on injured soldiers, developing many of the techniques that would constitute modern plastic surgery (Sullivan 2001). In World War II medical developments meant that airmen were more likely to survive the horrific burns they suffered if their plane was hit. However, they were often left severely disfigured and functionally limited, requiring new reconstructive techniques and prompting bold innovation by men such as British surgeon Archibald McIndoe (Mayhew 2004).

From purely clinical beginnings at the edge of experimental surgery, cosmetic surgery has flourished into a billion-dollar industry embraced globally. The obsession with a flawless youthful appearance is characteristic of developed nations. Americans alone spend US$20 billion annually on products to enhance their appearance (Sullivan 2001). However, there is a qualitative difference between the application of creams and lotions and surrendering oneself to the surgeon's knife in the absence of any clinical need. In many ways, '[b]eauty has become a medical business' (Sullivan 2001, ix). The increasing commercialization of cosmetic surgery is evidenced by the US$4.6 to $4.9 million estimated to be spent on cosmetic surgery in the United States each year (Sullivan 2001).

Popular cosmetic surgery procedures today include eyelid tightening (blepharoplasty), nose jobs (rhinoplasty), face-lifts, breast augmentation and reduction, hair transplantation, liposuction, foreskin reconstitution, calf implants and chin augmentation. Some patients seek to eliminate obvious signs of their racial background. 'Jewish' noses, 'Asian' eyelids and 'African' lips and noses are homogenized in an effort to appear more 'American'. Cosmetic surgical interventions extend even to podiatry, where malformed feet are reshaped to suit strappy stilettos (Frank 2006).

However, cosmetic surgery is not an entirely modern phenomenon. From as early as the sixteenth century numerous attempts were made to reshape noses in particular. The too-small nose was particularly stigmatizing due to its association with syphilis. Sexually transmitted and congenital syphilis produced a characteristic physiognomy of sunken eyes and a collapsed or missing nose. The fear of contagion and the shameful immorality of syphilis made the missing nose something to be abhorred by on-lookers and concealed by the bearer (Gilman 1998, 1999). Fake noses proved an insufficient disguise, and so implants of gold, ivory and copper were used in the 1800s to replace the collapsed bridge of the nose. A sixteenth-century physician, Gaspare Tagliacozzi, had developed the use of pedicle grafts to rebuild noses, whereby a flap of skin from the cheek or upper arm was partially detached and transferred over subsequent weeks to the nose (Gilman 1999, 66).

However, this 'Italian method' was lost to Western surgery, and it was the 'Indian method' that prevailed when modern cosmetic surgery surfaced in the mid- to late-nineteenth century. Pioneers such as Johann Dieffenbach, Jacques Joseph, Frederick Kolle and Suzanne Noël, working in Europe, especially Germany and France, the UK and the United States, developed many of the surgical techniques that are used today (Rogers 1976).

The history of reconstructive rhinoplasty is closely allied with the development of corrective rhinoplasty for aesthetic reasons (Rogers 1976). The stigma of the syphilitic nose was transferred to the too-small 'pug' nose of the Irish, and Irish immigrants to the United States were known to undergo surgery in order to appear more 'American' (Sullivan 2001). 'African' and 'Jewish' noses were considered signs of a primitive nature and facial features were taken to indicate character (Gilman 1999). A red bulbous nose denoted heavy drinking and self-indulgence, and the too-long Jewish 'hawk' nose signified shrewdness. In addition to removing offending humps and bumps, paraffin injections were used to build up the bridge of the nose. However, over time the paraffin diffused with painful and disfiguring results. In addition, the scars that surgery left were barely acceptable, indicating a person vain enough, or desperate enough, to need cosmetic surgery. In 1887 the otolarygonologst John Orlando Roe revolutionized the field by using the intranasal approach to correct 'Irish' and 'Jewish' noses, leaving no external scars (Rogers 1976). These interventions are particularly brave, or perhaps foolhardy, considering that the surgery was conducted at a time before the development of anaesthesia, asepsis or antibiotics.

Finding a clear line that separates reconstructive from cosmetic plastic surgery has been, and continues to be, difficult. This quote from Gillies and Millard (1957) demonstrates how inseparable the two practices are:

> A great percentage of private practice is beauty surgery. It is here that perfection is a necessity. Reconstructive surgery is an attempt to return to normal; cosmetic surgery is an attempt to surpass the normal. No man is a plastic surgeon unless he becomes adept at both. Many never do and are a menace. It is easier to reduce than produce, but in plastic surgery it is nearly always necessary to remould after reduction. Thus anyone can cut off a bit of a nose or breast, but not so many can turn out a satisfying result.

In this quote cosmetic and reconstructive surgery are roughly equated with therapeutic and enhancing interventions. As we have seen in the case of healthy limb amputation these concepts are difficult to distinguish with regard to particular instances of body modification, however Gillies and Millard show how this is a problem for the practice of plastic surgery *per se*. The distinction centres around the elective nature of cosmetic surgery. Are cosmetic surgery patients sick? It is perhaps inaccurate to even call them 'patients', and instead the term 'clients' is often used.

Some contend that cosmetic surgery fits within the healing paradigm by virtue of its therapeutic benefits to the self esteem and confidence of the patient. Cosmetic surgeons 'operate on the body to heal the psyche' (Gilman 1998, 25). Possessing a 'good' body makes one happy, but with a 'bad' body one is doomed to unhappiness (Gilman 1998). Indeed attractiveness does have real social, psychological and economic value, in the United States at least (Sullivan 2001). This mental health rationale was first claimed in 1907 by Charles Miller and presupposes that a patient's psychological problem is attributable to a particular body part, which, when corrected, will improve the patient's mental wellbeing. However, one in five cosmetic patients are repeat clients and 37 per cent have multiple procedures performed simultaneously (Sullivan 2001).

The twentieth century was characterized by disagreement within the medical fraternity regarding whether cosmetic surgery is a legitimate branch of medicine and how it would best be regulated. Cosmetic surgeons have been ostracized by conventional plastic surgeons, although the lucrative nature of cosmetic surgery has proved far too alluring to many clinicians. And so, where once cosmetic surgery was a 'back alley' specialty aiming to fashion an inauthentic body, it has become integral to our cultural understanding of the body and meets with far greater acceptance (Gilman 1998).

Sport

In addition to surgery there are a number of other ways of modifying the body using hormones and gene therapy. While originally developed to treat clinically recognized diseases, the various remedies are continually being applied outside the medical paradigm, and no more so than to the competitive realm of sporting endeavour.

Anabolic steroids were originally developed to stimulate bone marrow in cases of hypoplastic anaemia, to induce male puberty, and treat chronic wasting conditions such as cancer and AIDS (Bhasin et al. 2003). However, the increased muscle mass and physical strength that anabolic steroids provide has made them popular with athletes in a variety of disciplines, without any therapeutic rationale. All major sports regulatory bodies have banned anabolic steroids amidst concerns about the negative health effects of long-term use (Hartgens and Kuipers 2004) and violating the spirit of sporting competition.

A number of other drugs were originally developed as therapeutic interventions for recognized medical conditions but are now used to enhance the performance of healthy athletes. Erythropoietin is widely used to treat anaemia associated with pathologies such as chronic renal failure, HIV, chemotherapy and premature birth. The resultant increase in red blood cells also raises maximum oxygen consumption capacity, boosting performance in endurance sports such as cycling and triathlons (Diamanti-Kandarakis et al. 2005). Erythropoietin doping was banned by the International Olympic Committee in 1990.

Efforts to treat muscle wasting due to diseases such as muscular dystrophy and age-associated deterioration have uncovered ways to increase muscle mass in animal models. Gene therapy to overexpress the hormone insulin-like growth factor 1 produces 'Schwarzenegger mice' whose skeletal muscles are 20–50 per cent larger than controls (Lee et al. 2004; Musaro et al. 2001). Myostatin, a protein which limits muscle growth, is another target for intervention. A mutation in Belgian blue cattle produces a truncated, ineffective form of myostatin, leading to the inflated musculature of this and other 'double-muscled' phenotypes. A similar naturally occurring loss-of-function mutation in the myostatin gene has been reported in a unusually strong child with muscle hypertrophy (Schuelke et al. 2004).

Genetically engineering mice to overexpress a gene for an enzyme involved in energy metabolism has produced unexpected and dramatic results in terms of exercise capacity and longevity (Hakimi et al. 2007). The mice overexpress PEPCK-C, a gene shared with humans, in skeletal muscle and can run for up to 6km at 20m/min, whereas control mice run at the same speed for only 0.2km before exhaustion. The transgenic mice live and breed much longer than normal mice, eat up to 60 per cent more food while remaining significantly leaner, and are markedly more aggressive. The mice have been dubbed 'mighty mice' and compared to famous ultra-endurance athletes. It is not clear how the over-expression of a single gene could have such a dramatic effect, and research into PEPCK-C will continue in an effort to understand the repatterning of energy metabolism in order to develop drugs to treat muscle-wasting disorders. However, gene therapy that produces such remarkable results could also prove very attractive to athletes looking for an advantage.

Another gene of interest among athletes is the angiotensin I-converting enzyme, a certain polymorphism of which confers improved endurance performance on those who possess it (Montgomery et al. 1998; Myerson et al. 1999). Other genes associated with endurance, muscle strength and health-related fitness phenotypes have been reported (Rankinen et al. 2006).

The advent of gene therapy has led to fears of gene doping, which both the International Olympic Committee and World Anti-Doping Agency banned in 2003. The possibility of increasing muscle size, strength and resilience through insulin-like growth factor-1 or myostatin gene therapy (Rodino-Klapac et al. 2007) has attracted athletes and worried doping testers, particularly because gene therapy would not be detectable in traditional blood or urine tests (Sweeney 2004). At present gene therapy is risky and highly experimental, but the lure of increased performance and rewards is sure to tempt athletes (Filipp 2007; Sweeney 2004).

Savulescu and co-workers (2004) argue that because it is impossible to eliminate performance enhancing drugs from sport, particularly as technology advances, they should instead be allowed if proven to be harmless. Much of an athlete's potential is due to the genetic lottery or other unequally available aids such as hypoxic air machines. Because of this, Savulescu et al. contend that 'by allowing everyone to take performance enhancing drugs, we level the playing field' (2004,

668); instead of testing for drugs, we should focus on monitoring an athlete's health and fitness to compete. While there are risks involved in pharmacological intervention and gene therapy, it could be argued that athletes should be allowed to choose for themselves. As the general public embraces enhancement technologies for body and mind it is perhaps unreasonable to expect athletes to eschew them. Some commentators suggest that changing the rules in this way would not be without precedent; we once banned women and remuneration (*Nature* 2007) and frowned upon running coaches (Sandel 2007).

Whatever the merits of the competing paradigms – prohibition of performance-enhancing drugs or their acceptance – the issue of the meaning of bodily enhancement will not go away. Is there any credible difference between a drug-enhanced physique and a nutrition-enhanced one? For some the former is a legitimate example of enhancement whereas the latter is nothing more than good nutrition. But on what grounds does nutrition escape the opprobrium of enhancement this readily? Surely all nutritional modifications cannot be justified as therapy.

Short Stature

Growth hormone (GH) derived from cadaveric pituitary glands has been used since the 1960s to treat short children with GH deficiency. DNA recombinant technology has since provided a safer source of GH, creating a great demand for GH treatment beyond the original bounds of therapy. Height brings with it psychosocial advantages, influencing employment opportunities, salaries, partner choice and apparently bestowing political advantages. For example, in the American presidential elections between 1904 and 1984, the taller candidate won 80 per cent of the time (Grumbach 1988). Even our language reflects a height bias, we 'look up' to some people, but 'look down' on others (Diekema 1990). However, the increase in ultimate adult height from GH treatment is likely to be modest, and it is uncertain if this would provide the psychological benefits desired.

It is debated whether short children without GH deficiency or another identifiable disorder should receive GH treatment, though the US Food and Drug Administration has approved such treatment in recent years (Freemark 2004). In the face of no defined disease is such treatment justifiable? The social disadvantages of extremely short stature are well accepted, but does this necessitate medical intervention? Let us consider two children with the same predicted adult height, one whose short stature is attributable to GH deficiency due to a pituitary tumour, and one with no identifiable GH deficiency but who has very short parents (Allen and Fost 1990; Daniels 2000). The first child's short stature has a recognizable medical basis, whereas the second child's does not. Consequently, treating the first child with GH would conventionally be considered therapy but for the second child it would be enhancement. However, if both prove responsive to GH treatment, achieving the same adult height and same social advantages, it seems difficult to justify increasing the height of one and not the other.

While it is socially desirable for men to be tall, it is much less so for women. As a result girls who were predicted to be particularly tall were once routinely prescribed oestrogens as growth-suppressants to avoid the purely psychological and social burdens associated with 'excessive' height. Though this practice is less common today, it still occurs (Barnard et al. 2002). One assumes this was considered an 'enhancement', and yet in this instance the enhancement was less rather than more. Moreover, it is an enhancement no longer desired. This suggests that a procedure may be ambiguously and temporarily considered enhancing. It may also be a matter of taste.

Psychopharmaceuticals

Much of the debate about modification of the body concerns modifications of the brain through the use of psychoactive drugs. This is, in many respects, the same battleground as already discussed, with debate surrounding when the use of psychoactive drugs may be thought to be therapeutic and when it is, in the words of the President's Council on Bioethics (2003) 'beyond therapy'. Psychopharmaceuticals are used to treat everything from forgetfulness and shyness to sleepiness and depression. Are any of these diseases? While clinical depression is a recognized clinical entity, what are we to make of the low-grade depression with which many people live their whole lives? If we refuse to clinically acknowledge such conditions as illnesses, does it follow that treatment is a form of enhancement? The definition of normality is central, not simply as a theoretical postulate, but as a matter of practical policy since if some forms of depression are normal we should refrain from treating them in any way. But is there any virtue in living with sub-clinical depression if it can be ameliorated?

There is a fine line between the normal and the pathological. Another illustration is provided by hyperactive children who appear to stretch the limits of normal behaviour. What was once considered normal, even if disruptive, may now fall under the rubric of pathological. The advent of drugs like Ritalin may have converted taxing behaviour into a syndrome in need of treatment. Is this genuine or has it become a means of social manipulation? The dividing line between normality and abnormality, between therapy and enhancement, has an unnervingly tenuous feel to it.

Consider next the slight deterioration of memory that often accompanies ageing. Minor forgetfulness in everyday activities could be classed as normal or abnormal, as an interesting but common phenomenon, or a mild disease state. An answer is important since mild memory losses may be a prelude to mild cognitive impairment and ultimately the dementia of Alzheimer's disease. If this is the case early treatment is the course of choice. There is no questioning the pathology of Alzheimer's disease, nor its therapeutic rationale. However, at present, the early stages are almost inevitably shrouded in a therapy-enhancement mist (Jones 2006). A resolution has considerable clinical and social consequences.

Drugs influencing memory could also prove useful in younger age groups, where improvement in test scores at school and university would be the driving force. This brings us face to face with the fears of the affluent worried well, aided and abetted by commercial pressures within the pharmaceutical industry (Arnst 2003). It also highlights the way in which society's values and desires can shape the direction and interpretation of scientific endeavour.

The drugs that treat attention deficit hyperactivity disorder (ADHD) can also be used to improve normal mental functioning, for example, problem-solving abilities. These drugs are neurocognitive enhancers that prompt us to question what it means to be a person, to be healthy and whole, to do meaningful work, and to value human life in all its imperfection. They increase the medicalization of human life, although in no way do they represent the first forays into this domain. Indeed, is medicalization *per se* to be condemned, and if so why? Does it inevitably militate against human dignity? Probably not.

These are pressing considerations since neurocognitive enhancers are widely employed for non-medical reasons. In the United States particularly, drugs such as Ritalin (methylphenidate) or Adderall (dextroamphetamine), originally aimed at people with attention-deficit disorder, and Provigil (modafinil), developed to treat narcolepsy, are used by healthy individuals to aid concentration, alertness, focus, short-term memory and wakefulness. Most studies testing the use of methylphenidate and modafinil in healthy volunteers have shown significant improvements in various aspects of cognitive function (Elliott et al. 1997; Mehta et al. 2000; Turner et al. 2003). Donepezil (Aricept) was developed as a treatment for Alzheimer's disease, but has also been shown to improve recall of training when taken by healthy, but older, pilots in a flight simulator (Yesavage et al. 2002).

Ethically one asks what, if any, are the side effects? Provigil has recently been linked to an increased risk of serious skin rash, hypersensitivity reactions and psychiatric symptoms including anxiety, hallucinations, mania and suicidal ideation (Waknine 2007). Chronic use of psychopharmaceuticals could permanently alter the brain by inhibiting the role of normal sleep to maintain neural plasticity and consolidate new memories. Considering the uncertainty of any long-term side effects, caution is advised. However, this does not prevent competent individuals who are aware of the risks from choosing to take cognition-enhancing drugs (Glannon 2006).

Psychopharmaceuticals could also be used to block the formation of traumatic memories, or even to erase them once established (Glannon 2006). Such non-conscious pathological memories can arise from trauma such as combat, rape and natural disasters, and can lead to post-traumatic stress disorder (PTSD), a debilitating mental illness caused by a heightened fear response. Trauma stimulates the release of the stress hormone epinephrine which acts on the amygdala to strengthen memory consolidation. Consequently, traumatic memories are recalled with greater emotional intensity. Normally this mechanism is beneficial, allowing an individual to appreciate the significance of the event in terms of survival. In the case of PTSD, however, the emotional intensity of the memory is debilitating.

The effects of PTSD can include anxiety, nightmares, avoidance, detachment and suicide. Conventional treatments focus on psychotherapy and anti-depressants, and often take some time to work, if they work at all. Beta-blockers such as propranolol could be administered shortly before or after the trauma to prevent the embedding of pathological memories of fearful events (Pitman et al. 2002; Vaiva et al. 2003), or during flashbacks some time after the event to erase the pathological memories (Brunet et al. 2007). Propranolol could potentially be given to individuals in the military or emergency services before a traumatic event, such as encountering a large plane crash site to perform a rescue operation. A more likely use is to treat those individuals who present to emergency departments seeking medical attention after being attacked, abused or involved in a traumatic accident. Possible side effects include concurrent erasure of beneficial emotional memories, blunting of the normal, desirable fear response and alteration of moral judgement (Levy 2007). However, it is worth noting that tens of millions of people have taken propranolol for heart conditions and hypertension without experiencing serious memory problems. Perhaps more pertinently, propranolol could be rebranded by pharmaceutical companies, whereby traumatic memories would be pathologized, in an effort to increase drug sales (Henry et al. 2007). However, amelioration of a devastating mental illness like PTSD could provide sufficient justification for its use (Henry et al. 2007).

Again, the use of psychopharmaceuticals to influence memory could theoretically be taken beyond the bounds of accepted therapeutic regimes to erase the unpleasant memories generally considered an integral part of human life. It may even be speculated that drugs could be developed to remove all traces of guilt, shame or grief. Whether such far-reaching effects will ever eventuate remains to be seen, but it seems likely that any ability that could modulate an individual's memories in this manner would have profound effects for what it means to be human.

It is the fear of this widespread use of memory-blunting drugs and associated philosophical concerns that caused the President's Council on Bioethics (2003) to condemn pharmacological manipulation of memory. The Council cited concerns about the erosion of moral responsibility, altered identity, reduced empathy and a resultant numbness to life's joys as well as its sorrows. They conclude that by employing memory-blunting drugs we may 'ease today's pain, but only by foreclosing … the possibility of being the kind of person who can live well with the whole truth – both chosen and unchosen – and the kind of person who can live well as himself' (2003, 230). The relevance of these arguments for individuals suffering from PTSD is questionable.

The move from modifying the brain to correct a perceived defect to modifying it as an enhancement is a defining feature of the neurotechnology landscape. An online poll conducted by the journal *Nature* found that one in five of the scientists and researchers who responded had used methylphenidate, modafinil or beta blockers for non-medical purposes to stimulate concentration, focus or memory (Maher 2008). Around half of those using the drugs experienced unpleasant side effects, including headaches, anxiety and sleeplessness, but these are often tolerated without altering the frequency of drug use (Maher 2008). The benefits of cognition-enhancing drugs may prove even more necessary in a competitive environment where some people are already taking them, coercing others into doing so (Sahakian and Morein-Zamir 2007). Chatterjee (2007) proposes that the history of cosmetic surgery suggests that the widespread adoption and acceptance of cosmetic neurology is inevitable.

Savulescu and Sandberg (2008) have taken the neuroenhancement debate further by proposing the use of psychopharmaceuticals to enhance romantic love and marriage. They suggest that artifically manipulating levels of testosterone, oxytocin and other hormones may help decrease the rate of divorce by enhancing pair-bonding and attachment. They claim that there is no morally relevant difference between 'marriage therapy, a massage, a glass of wine, a fancy pink, steamy potion and a pill' (Savulescu and Sandberg 2008, 37). One has to wonder whether there are morally relevant differences between anything if this conclusion is accepted at face value. It appears to reduce human beings to psychological machines, controlled by hormonal and neurotransmitter levels and nothing more. It is the 'nothing more' that is the lynch pin in this deterministic world of psychological impulses and responses.

Objections to Modifications and Enhancements

We have long attempted to modify and improve human functioning and ability through a variety of interventions, though few of these have been considered to be objectionable enhancements. Consider a simple cup of coffee to increase alertness, the holistic benefits of good nutrition, herbal supplements, or even the expanded ability provided by study and training. However, as the newer interventions more directly alter our bodies and begin to prove more effective, questions have been raised about what should and should not be permitted (British Medical Association 2007a). A number of objections have been raised against those direct manipulations of the body that are commonly classed as enhancement rather than therapy.

A commonly encountered objection is that enhancement constitutes cheating and that the promulgation of such interventions will produce, or worsen, unfair inequalities. Enhancement instinctively feels like cheating because of a profoundly held belief in modern Western society that opportunities and rewards ought to be distributed according to merit (Levy 2007). However, there is an inconsistency here, since we tend to class the use of steroids or erythropoietin in sport as cheating, but allow other performance-enhancing interventions such as the use of sophisticated equipment, nutritional supplements and expert advice in spite of the fact that these are not equally available to athletes from various nations. This is the grey area between high-tech and low-tech interventions, and it is in this area that confusion lies (Sandel 2007). Unfortunately, the confusion is rarely faced up to; instead some commentators pour scorn on selected enhancements while ignoring the profound inequalities with which we all live. For example, Francis Fukuyama (2002) contends that society will become profoundly upset if genetic enhancement interventions are used only by certain elite social groups to acquire additional social advantages. He fulminates and speculates that this distress could lead to outright violence, saying, 'the spectre of rising genetic inequality may well get people off their couches and into the streets' (Fukuyama 2002, 158). This is all very well, but it hardly enhances our thinking about how best to distinguish enhancement from routine social behaviour, let alone explicit therapy.

The fear of eugenics lies at the heart of another common objection. In this case, it is the fear that the broad application of enhancement technologies may lead to a less favourable view of disabilities and the people who have them. The concern is that they lead to increasing homogenization of society and to even greater discrimination (Levy 2007). However this fails to distinguish the 'old' state-mandated eugenics from the 'new' eugenics based on autonomy and free choice. The diversity of concepts of what constitutes a good life will ensure, to some degree, a continuing variety of interventions and outcomes. Buchanan (2008) has gone as far as to argue that if enhancements are found to increase productivity, producing widespread social benefits, the state is certain to play a role in advancing their adoption. If this eventuates, the state will be compelled to sponsor the availability of enhancements to the disadvantaged, as is generally the case with education and health care. It is deeply unfortunate that eugenics and enhancement both connote negative responses, leading to automatic rejection of whatever is associated with them.

Yet another objection to enhancement technologies stems from the concern that they may thwart the ideal of authenticity, knowing and being one's 'true self' (Taylor 1991). Some fear that direct manipulation in the human body and mind could artificially separate the individual from his or her authentic self (Elliott 1998). Whether enhancement interventions would hinder or aid self-realization is, of course, debatable. Elliott acknowledges 'the paradoxical way in which a person can see an enhancement technology as a way to achieve a more authentic self, even as the technology dramatically alters his or her identity' (Elliott 2003, xxi). This is particularly the case when one considers the transforming effect of cosmetic psychopharmacology upon those fairly healthy people who, under medication such as Prozac, become more outgoing, balanced and vivacious (Kramer 1993).

In discussing patients he has treated with Prozac who underwent such a transformation, Kramer (1993) describes the discomfiting way that Prozac redefined the patients' understanding of their authentic self. A patient might say 'I never really felt like myself until now', and upon reducing the dose and experiencing a return to their previous nature, a patient would complain 'I'm not myself' (Kramer 1993, 10). This reshaping of a person's identity concerns Elliott, since he views them as, 'not just instruments for self-improvement, or even self-transformation', but as 'tools for working on the soul' (Elliott 2003, 53). However, enhancement does not necessarily pose a threat to authenticity. Our pre-existing selves are not necessarily more authentic than that which we seek to transform ourselves into; change does not always entail faking it (Levy 2007).

A more radical philosophical objection concerns the fear that enhancement technologies will violate the integrity of the human body and mind, irreversibly changing what it means to be human (President's Council on Bioethics 2003, 289). On one reading of this argument, there are certain 'core' traits that are fundamental to human life, and are therefore inviolable. However, it is unclear what the core characteristics alluded to are (DeGrazia 2005). Do they include personality, normal ageing, gender, intelligence and memory? The assertion that altering the core characteristics is wrong, or estranges us from our humanness is far from self-evident, especially in light of the many means we currently use to enhance ourselves, and which are considered morally unproblematic, from hair dye to caffeine (DeGrazia 2005).

The President's Council also adopts a virtues-based critique of enhancement that attacks the motivations of the medical professionals who would support or further the enhancement project. The Council contrasts the noble aim of the physician intervening therapeutically with the hubristic intentions of the enhancement bioengineer:

> When a physician intervenes therapeutically to correct some deficiency or deviation from a patient's natural wholeness, he acts as a servant to the goal of health and as an assistant to nature's own powers of self-healing, themselves wondrous products of evolutionary selection. But when a bioengineer intervenes for nontherapeutic ends, he stands not as nature's servant but as her aspiring master, guided by nothing but his own will and serving ends of his own devising. (President's Council on Bioethics 2003, 287)

Allied with this are concerns regarding the drive to mastery, what Sandel calls 'a kind of hyper-agency, a Promethean aspiration to remake nature, including human nature, to serve our purposes' (Sandel 2007, 26). He contrasts this with an openness to the unbidden, by which we accept the giftedness of being human without needing to interfere – an attitude which does not limit human endeavour, but instead truly empowers it. He goes on to say:

> It is … possible to view genetic engineering as the ultimate expresssion of our resolve to see ourselves astride the world, the masters of our nature. But that vision of freedom is flawed. It threatens to banish our appreciation of life as a gift, and to leave us with nothing to affirm or behold outside our own will. (Sandel 2007, 99–100)

Others would say that the desire to enhance our lives and our selves through the development of new technology is an integral part of human nature witnessed throughout history (Ter Meulen et al. 2007). Although we might clearly find some instances of enhancement wrong – say, when it is performed without the consent of the individual undergoing it, or when it involves a radical and irreversible change and is undertaken on a whim – these are not objections to enhancement or other modifications of the body *per se*. Any serious objection to enhancement technologies *per se* must find some non-arbitrary moral distinction between the plethora of accepted practices that have been, and are currently, used to enhance our functioning, and those enhancements that are sought to be proscribed. This is a challenge that has not been met thus far. The second challenge is to provide an account of therapy and enhancement that withstands analytical scrutiny, allowing acceptable (i.e. therapeutic) medical practice to be separated from the unacceptable and frequently extreme (i.e. enhancement) practices that those objecting to enhancement wish to condemn. It is to this distinction that we now turn.

The Blurred Distinction Between Therapy and Enhancement

While therapy is directed towards restoring an ill person to health, enhancement generally has the connotation of improving 'human form or functioning beyond what is necessary to sustain or restore good health' (Juengst 1998). Any definition like this is far from precise. The possibilities are immense – from augmenting memory at one extreme through to attempts at endless extension of the human lifespan at the other. The criteria for deciding the boundaries of normality and human nature are unclear and, therefore, so are the dimensions of therapy. How can we know when we have moved from therapy into enhancement?

The therapy–enhancement distinction is usually defended by the differentiation between normality and abnormality, health and disease. This distinction is closely tied with the therapeutic rationale of medicine, which Fukuyama defines as 'to heal the sick, not to turn healthy people into gods' (Fukuyama 2002, 208). However, even the definition of disease is malleable, and largely culturally defined. Homosexuality and masturbation were once officially considered diseases, but few today would class them as such. There is a time-dependent element within all our definitions, so that today's expectations of what constitutes healthy living and a normal lifespan bear little resemblance to the expectations of 150 years ago, even within the same country or city.

Boorse (1977) proposed a biostatistical theory of the biological functioning of individuals to define health and disease. This concept of species-typical functioning as a standard of 'normal' was taken up by Daniels (1985) as the basis for defining justice in health care. Daniels's theory is as follows: disease (including deformity and disability) impedes normal functioning, restricting an individual's normal range of opportunity. In view of this, society is morally obliged to assist the individual to restore normal functioning. Conversely, society is not obliged to provide enhancement interventions that would propel an individual beyond the normal standard of functioning. Consequently, the therapy-enhancement distinction has important implications for policy-making on health care funding. Yet even this seemingly robust biostatistical theory faces problems in defining what constitutes a 'natural' baseline for any individual's functioning. After all, individuals within the same social milieu at the same point in time are highly variable biologically, due to a welter of environmental influences, both physical and social, and genetic endowments (Levy 2007). The result is that normal expectations for one individual may be far from normal for another. Hence, an intrusion that classes as therapy for one may have distinct enhancement overtones for another.

The Disease–Normality–Enhancement Continuum

The blurred nature of the normal/abnormal and therapy/enhancement boundaries becomes, as we have seen, even more indistinct when time and place elements are introduced. Present-day expectations of what constitutes good health and normal life expectancy have changed out of all recognition since the early years of the twentieth century. Moreover, our expectations bear no resemblance to those of many people today living in the majority world. Are our expectations normal, or are theirs?

In Europe in the 1840s no one was in a position to enhance cognition, or treat mental illness with psychopharmaceuticals. Their thinking, let alone their technological capabilities, was so different from ours as to be unrecognizable.

In the mid-nineteenth century in England life expectancy at birth was around 41 years, and only rose to 46 by the end of the century. Throughout this period, all the largest cities recorded life expectancies well below the national average. The northern industrial towns, particularly Manchester and Liverpool, consistently exhibited the lowest life expectancies; in the 1850s and 1860s it was around 30 or 31 years. However, the inner parts of these cities generally had an even lower life expectancy. For example, in the 1860s the life expectancy in inner Liverpool was 25 years, ranging from 15 years for the unemployed or poor to 35 years for the well-to-do. Infant mortality in inner city wards was more than 50 per cent (Szreter and Mooney 1998). By comparison, life expectancy at birth in the United Kingdom today is 78.7 years. Yet the equivalent figure for Swaziland is a mere 32.23 years (Central Intelligence Agency 2007).

The decline in mortality in the second half of the nineteenth century was due to a reduction in deaths from infectious diseases, with a reduction in water- and food-borne diseases being a major contributing factor. This reduction was due to rising standards of living, including better diet, and improvements in hygiene, such as purification of water, improved disposal of sewage, removal of refuse, sterilization and pasteurization of milk, and supervision of food handling (McKeown et al. 1975).

Improvements in the external environment, such as improvements to sanitation and water supply, proved seminal. New technologies led to the introduction of efficient sewers, and to the provision of clean drinking water. Such interventions in the external environment laid the basis for controlling the spread of diseases like cholera and dysentery, and operate at a population level.

Alongside these alterations to the environment went innovations aimed at modifying the individuals themselves. The goal of these was to equip individuals to respond to infectious agents using the newly developed procedure of vaccination. With the introduction of vaccination, intervention moved to combating disease by altering healthy people, both children and adults, and represented a major step into the unknown. The emergence of variolation in the earlier part of the eighteenth century entailed infecting non-immune patients with fluid from a smallpox pustule, and led to considerable opposition. One relatively modern commentator has written:

> The medical faculty foretold the most disastrous consequences were such barbarous treatment ... to be put into practice in England. The clergy were equally shocked and spoke of the impiety of seeking to wrest out of the Deity's hands such rights as the bestowal of smallpox and pointed out how much worse everything would be if such matters were put into the sinful hands of men. (Walker 1959, 227)

Vaccination against smallpox, using cowpox and stemming from the work of Edward Jenner in the late eighteenth century, was also considered immoral. It was seen as being contrary to God's will because the inoculation consisted of material from the 'brute animal', the implication being that it would impart bovine characteristics to human recipients (Baxby 1981).

After initial scepticism Jenner's innovation spread rapidly around the world, although his approach could not be emulated with other conditions. It was Pasteur in the late nineteenth century with his introduction of a rabies vaccine who revolutionized the treatment of what had been untreatable diseases. His innovation consisted of the laboratory modification of micro-organisms by attenuation, to render them less pathogenic but still immunogenic. The result has been the saving of hundreds of millions of lives and the transformation of the quality of life of whole generations and whole populations. Killer diseases ranging from diphtheria and tetanus to cholera, typhoid fever and the plague were brought under control, with new vaccines appearing on the horizon today for conditions such as malaria, HIV and some cancers.

The rationale of vaccination lies in modifying individuals so that they are able to combat organisms that would otherwise overwhelm them. With this medicine moved from the external realm of public health and the environment, into the inner workings of the human body. When these two operate together the quality and possibilities of human living are transformed.

To these examples of past medical enhancements, Buchanan (2008) would add cultural and technological developments such as literacy, numeracy, agriculture, computers and the establishment of institutions beyond kinship groups. He says that 'to call the great historical enhancements merely external of environmental changes is tantamount to denying that culture plays a significant role in our individual and collective identities' (Buchanan 2008, 5).

These historical episodes demonstrate that the use of science and technology to overcome ill health and premature death is now an integral part of our thinking. We have committed ourselves to a trajectory with profound implications for decision-making today. These historical episodes have been prompted by concerns with the suffering and premature demise of large numbers of individuals that in some cases have decimated whole populations. In large measure the approaches we have encountered have been successful.

Looking at lifespan, it becomes imperative to ask what our expectations should be. For contemporary Western societies a life expectancy of 40–50 years for a whole population, let alone 20–30, is very short when compared with 70–80, but what do comparisons like this mean? In 100 years' time 70–80 years may appear extremely short.

The notion of premature death is relative. For us, death at 20 years is definitely premature, although if death at this age occurs after a prolonged battle with cancer, it may be regarded as a good age compared with death in the early teens. Underlying most people's perceptions is the belief that death is an enemy to be fought and resented. Premature death is a double enemy. Perhaps this is why so much energy and expertise is expended on very premature babies, born at around 23 weeks' gestation. The underlying thrust is that death of such new life is to be fought even when there is profound clinical and ethical ambiguity.

It is unlikely, therefore, that the desire to increase life expectancy is a simple matter of therapy. The process of striving for longer life expectancy is closely associated with the desire to enhance the quality of human life. In other words, were efforts to improve the environment, alleviate living conditions and combat infectious diseases illustrations of enhancement rather than therapy? While concepts like these were completely foreign to previous generations, this is not true of us. Their aim was to extend life and transform human expectations; we would call that enhancement. What then separates it from enhancement? Our view is that to refrain to use this description is little more than semantics.

The inner Liverpool of the 2000s cannot be compared with the inner Liverpool of the 1840s, either in its physical features or in the people who live there. The twenty-first-century humans are substantially enhanced compared with their nineteenth-century counterparts, at least in biomedical terms. There is a biomedical gulf between the two.

In drawing together these considerations, the following principles emerge. First, there is a continuum from that barely technological world to our far more sophisticated technologically driven societies. There is a conceptual strand linking the two, namely, that health care seeks to bring wholeness to people and populations racked by disease and pain.

Second, human grandeur and magnificence are destroyed by illnesses of many descriptions and causes. While these are sometimes due to the self-centredness and folly of humans themselves, they are not to be ignored. The drive is to exercise at least limited control over evil in the form of disease that would ravish and destroy all that is beautiful and worthy in our world.

Third, humans have demonstrated beyond a shadow of a doubt that they are not prepared to sit back and leave everything to God or Nature. We combat diseases by modifying both the external environment and ourselves. If we approve of the measures taken to alleviate the suffering and premature death of many in these historical communities, we have already accepted the validity of improving the health of human beings by the use of artificial intrusions. Implicit within these responses is a willingness to make use of human intelligence and creativity, and an unwillingness to accept the inevitability of suffering and untimely/premature death.

This leads to our fourth conclusion. The concept of enhancement is not confined to twenty-first-century thinkers. It has been implicit within medical approaches throughout the whole of the modern medical era.

The dimensions of normality, health and therapy are never static, and their borders will always be blurred. Definitions are inevitably time and place dependent. It is a pity that discussions of enhancement are generally envisaged as lying in the future, the assumption appearing to be that we ourselves are unenhanced. This is fallacious. Technological interventions into the human condition did not commence in the latter years of the twentieth century. Compared with hunter-gatherers we must seem like posthumans (Bostrom 2005); at the very least we have been dramatically enhanced. The ethical challenges facing us are totally foreign to earlier generations, let alone the hunter-gatherers, but this is not sufficient reason to regret the technological developments wrought by previous generations.

Dissecting Enhancement

It is becoming clear that there is no definite line distinguishing therapy from enhancement. Resnik (2000, 374) came to a similar conclusion, when he wrote: 'Genetic enhancement is not inherently immoral nor is genetic therapy inherently moral. Some forms of enhancement are immoral, others are not; likewise, some types of therapy are immoral, others are not.'

All interventions that seek to modify the body (either genetically, neurologically, psychologically or physically) should be evaluated ethically on their merits. Simple therapy or enhancement labels will never provide the answer, and should be set aside in order to clarify the debate. Similarly, the widespread assumption that all forms of enhancement are equally problematic is misleading. The various modifications that constitute enhancement are not of a kind and in attempting to tease them out, we shall distinguish three categories.

Consider the plight of John, who is now 60 years of age and has poor memory. However, he has always had problems in remembering straightforward things, and as a result he has never performed well in exams. But his memory is getting worse, and it is now becoming embarrassing. He and his family also worry that he may be in the early stages of Alzheimer's disease, although the doctor is far from sure that this is the case. Everyone would be much happier if he could at least remember where he put his glasses, let alone his keys. He sometimes forgets where he is, and he now finds it impossible to remember faces. They just want him to be restored to what he was like a year or so ago, when he had a poor memory but better than what it is today. They want him to be restored to his old self; the John of old, with a fairly poor memory but something that everyone could live with. This is the world of therapy. What might enhancement mean in this case? Consider these three scenarios.

In the first scenario John is treated with a drug regime that restores his memory to what the doctor considers is normal for age. The remarkable thing for John and his family is that he can now remember far better than ever before. He does not have a super-memory; indeed, it is no better than that of many of his friends, but it is way beyond his past experience. We might describe this as enhancement, since it has gone beyond mere therapy. John is better than he has ever been before. In a very limited sense, he is a new John. This is John, mark 1.

Moving to the second scenario we find that John has received a different form of treatment, since in this instance his memory transcends that of all his acquaintances. He now has a super-memory. He thinks far more rapidly than ever in his life, he can remember dates and come to terms with ideas in an unimaginable way, and he regrets being as old as he is. If only he was 40 years younger, he could have gone to university and mapped out an exciting career. There is no doubt that this is super-John, so much so that his family is worried since they do not know how to cope with him. John has been enhanced in a spectacular manner. This is John, mark 2.

In a third scenario John's treatment has gone even further, since his treatment has not only provided him with vast intellectual powers but with some form of rejuvenation. He seems far younger than his 60 years, and his family is told that he will probably outlive them by many years. He is a younger-John, not just John with an improved memory. There are others around who received this treatment some time ago and claims are being made that they will live for hundreds of years. John's family is mystified and very unnerved by all that appears to be happening. What we have here is a radical form of enhancement, quite unlike those in the first two scenarios. This is John, mark 3.

What we have provided in these speculative stories are three categories of enhancement (Jones 2005b, 2006).

Category one refers to the enhancement of a healthy person so that they become even healthier. What if we were able to protect against early onset Alzheimer's disease or heart disease by some form of genetic manipulation? Would such individuals be super-healthy? They may be healthier than they would otherwise have been, but they are far from being illness free or perfectly healthy. They are still vulnerable to the whole range of usual diseases, excepting only early onset Alzheimer's disease or heart disease. They do not constitute some new kind of human being. Category one enhancements are simply variations of therapy, albeit highly technological variants by today's standards. But note that 'today's standards' are bound to change. Individuals whom we would consider today to be enhanced may be regarded as normal healthy individuals in the future. Changes like this are all around us. The use of vaccines as prophylactics, or the widespread adoption of public health measures such as the provision of clean water supplies as previously discussed are category one enhancements.

Category two refers to enhancement that may have nothing to do with health, such as an extension of abilities. In this instance, enhancement encompasses those with super-abilities, as opposed to those with the normal range of abilities. The enhanced may have been made more intelligent than they would have been; they may be able to think quicker or remember more; or they may be much stronger. Instead of correcting defects, normal functions have been extended.

Super-abilities may enable individuals to perform better than they would otherwise have performed, worrying education authorities and sports bodies. Such enhancement may be regarded as unfair on those not in a position to benefit from them. Nevertheless, the enhanced individuals may still perform less well than other highly talented individuals who have not been enhanced. The bar has been raised but is this substantially different from the way in which the bar is raised by good nutrition and hygiene, and by superior educational opportunities? For instance, higher socio-economic status is associated with higher intelligence (Hunt 1995).

Some view this category in more spectacular terms, envisaging future societies in which subpopulations of 'the enhanced' outstrip the 'naturals' in every imaginable way (Annas et al. 2002). This second enhancement category is more hypothetical and futuristic than category one, and is more obviously pushing the 'natural' barriers than in category one. It has also moved some distance from any health imperative. The motive for modifying people is to improve sporting or educational achievements, or simply for narcissistic reasons.

It is worth considering where cosmetic surgery fits in (see Surgical Modifications). It does not appear to fit category one, since it is rarely related to health or illness. The desire to look different, to appear much younger, or to have lighter (or darker) skin or the features of another racial group are all characteristics of category two.

Category three refers to radical transformation, the type of transformation being advocated by transhumanists, which was described earlier in this chapter. The aim of transhumanism is to use technological means to radically enhance humans with the aim of creating so-called posthumans, whose capacities extend far beyond those of current humans. Humans in the transitional stage (not yet sufficiently enhanced to qualify as posthumans) are termed 'transitional humans', or transhumans. This should be distinguished from transhumanists, who are simply individuals who accept transhumanism.

While the realm of transhumanism, and radical transformation more generally, has many manifestations, it is undergirded by the idea that features such as finitude and mortality are not mandatory. Quite apart from such features, posthumans are described as having superior intellectual faculties and the ability to mould their own emotions (Bostrom 2005). Such visions are unfailingly future-oriented, and refer to a state of existence and wellbeing far beyond anything likely to be encountered in anyone's daily experiences. For the cynic and 'unbeliever' they reside in the domain of scientific fantasy.

For this reason it is tempting to leave posthumanism to visionaries and futurologists. However, aspects of posthumanist and transhumanist thinking may be more than mere conjecture, and may actually be influencing the ethos of present biomedical research and medical practice (Waters 2006). Why is this?

Regenerative medicine is seen by some proponents of posthuman medicine as the means to radical life extension, where humans not only live to incredible ages but also retain their full mental and physical capacities without declining. The natural corollary of this is to view ageing as a disease, a phenomenon that can and should be treated and even eradicated. Does the aim of medicine then become to wage war against death, and is medical practice to concentrate less on relieving the human condition than vanquishing mortality (Immortality Institute 2004)? These ideas may appear radical and vacuous, but in some quarters they have infiltrated social, ethical and even theological debate (Kass 2001; Waters 2006).

We could easily move from a denunciation of such extreme scenarios to a rejection of any interventions in the body. This is the approach adopted by bioconservatives (Bostrom 2005), who view any use of technology to improve mental or physical functioning as broadly part of the same endeavour that attempts to indefinitely expand the lifespan or radically alter human functioning. Category one measures are now seen only in terms of the far more extreme and idealistic goals of category three, and hence are rejected in company with them. The underlying assumption is that the aims of medical research and practice have already been amended from care to absolute cure, with grave repercussions for human dignity.

The implications for ethical debate are that the possibilities of regenerative medicine, the pros and cons of gene therapy and the role of psychopharmaceuticals in a range of psychiatric conditions, are frequently evaluated against a backdrop of these radical paradigms. They are often equated with a posthumanist agenda, and are thus rejected by those who find this agenda worrying. As a result, serious discussions of enhancement have been coloured by this much wider debate and the relevant science has become submerged beneath a welter of fanciful ambitions. Regrettably this has also hampered support for the clinical aspirations of current and imminently foreseeable technologies (Junker-Kenny 2006). The intentions of most trans- and posthumanists are so far removed from scientific reality as to pose sizeable hurdles to serious ethical debate.

References

Abadie, A. and Gay, S. (2006), 'The Impact of Presumed Consent Legislation on Cadaveric Organ Donation: A Cross-Country Study', *Journal of Health Economics*, 25, 599–620.

Abse, D. (1974), *A Poet in the Family* (London: Hutchinson).

Ad Hoc Committee of the Harvard Medical School to Examine the Definition of Brain Death (1968), 'A Definition of Irreversible Coma', *Journal of the American Medical Association*, 205, 337–40.

Agar, N. (2004), *Liberal Eugenics: In Defence of Human Enhancement* (Oxford: Wiley-Blackwell).

— (2007), 'Whereto Transhumanism? The Literature Reaches a Critical Mass', *Hastings Center Report*, 37, 12–17.

Agich, G. J. (2003), 'Extension of Organ Transplantation: Some Ethical Considerations', *Mount Sinai Journal of Medicine*, 70, 141–7.

Aldhous, P. (1991), 'Bones Go Home', *Nature*, 351, 178.

Alfonso, M. P. and Powell, J. (2007), 'Ethics of Flesh and Bone, or Ethics in the Practice of Paleopathology, Osteology, and Bioarchaeology', in V. Cassman, N. Odegaard and J. Powell (eds), *Human Remains: Guide for Museums and Academic Institutions* (Lanham, MD: AltaMira Press), 5–20.

Allen, D. B. and Fost, N. C. (1990), 'Growth Hormone Therapy for Short Stature: Panacea or Pandora's Box?', *Journal of Pediatrics*, 117, 16–21.

Alta Charo, R. (2004), 'Legal Characterizations of Human Tissue', in S. Youngner, M. Anderson and R. Schapiro (eds), *Transplanting Human Tissue: Ethics, Policy, and Practice* (New York: Oxford University Press), 101–19.

Altchek, A. (2003), 'Uterus Transplantation', *Mount Sinai Journal of Medicine*, 70, 154–62.

Altumbabic, M. and Del Bigio, M. R. (1998), 'Transplantation of Fetal Brain Tissue into the Site of Intracerebral Hemorrhage in Rats', *Neuroscience Letters*, 257, 61–4.

American Academy of Neurology (2007), 'Position Statement on Laws and Regulations Concerning Life-Sustaining Treatment, Including Artificial Nutrition and Hydration, for Patients Lacking Decision-Making Capacity', *Neurology*, 68, 1097–100.

Ames, M. M., Harrison, J. D. and Nicks, T. (1988), 'Proposed Museum Policies for Ethnological Collections and the People They Represent', *Muse*, Autumn, 243–8.

Anderson, C. (1991), 'Beating the Tissue Shortage', *Nature*, 351, 595.

Andrews, K. (1993), 'Recovery of Patients after Four Months or More in the Persistent Vegetative State', *British Medical Journal*, 306, 1597–603.

— (2004), 'Medical Decision Making in the Vegetative State: Withdrawal of Nutrition and Hydration', *NeuroRehabilitation*, 19, 299–304.

Andrews, K., Murphy, L., Munday, R. and Littlewood, C. (1996), 'Misdiagnosis of the Vegetative State: Retrospective Study in a Rehabilitation Unit', *British Medical Journal*, 313, 13–16.

Angell, M. (1990), 'The Nazi Hypothermia Experiments and Unethical Research Today', *New England Journal of Medicine*, 322, 1462–4.

— (1994), 'After Quinlan: The Dilemma of the Persistent Vegetative State', *New England Journal of Medicine*, 330, 1525–6.

Angrist, A. A. (1971), 'Plea for Realistic Support of the Autopsy', *Bulletin of the New York Academy of Medicine*, 47, 758–65.

Annas, G. J. (1988), *Judging Medicine* (New Jersey: Humana Press).

— (1993), *Standard of Care: The Law of American Bioethics* (New York: Oxford University Press).

Annas, G. J., Andrews, L. and Isasi, R. (2002), 'Protecting the Endangered Human: Toward an International Treaty Prohibiting Cloning and Inheritable Alterations', *American Journal of Law & Medicine*, 28, 151–78.

Anstötz, C. (1993), 'Should a Brain-Dead Pregnant Woman Carry Her Child to Full Term? The Case of the "Erlanger Baby"', *Bioethics*, 7, 340–50.

Arap, W., Kolonin, M. G., Trepel, M., Lahdenranta, J., Cardo-Vila, M., Giordano, R. J., Mintz, P. J., Ardelt, P. U., Yao, V. J., Vidal, C. I., Chen, L., Flamm, A., Valtanen, H., Weavind, L. M., Hicks, M. E., Pollock, R. E., Botz, G. H., Bucana, C. D., Koivunen, E., Cahill, D., Troncoso, P., Baggerly, K. A., Pentz, R. D., Do, K. A., Logothetis, C. J. and Pasqualini, R. (2002), 'Steps toward Mapping the Human Vasculature by Phage Display', *Nature Medicine*, 8, 121–7.

Armenti, V. T., Moritz, M. J. and Davison, J. M. (1998), 'Drug Safety Issues in Pregnancy Following Transplantation and Immunosuppression: Effects and Outcomes', *Drug Safety*, 19, 219–32.

Armstrong, P. W. and Colen, B. D. (1988), 'From Quinlan to Jobes: The Courts and the PVS Patient', *Hastings Center Report*, 18, 37–40.

Arnold, D. (1977), 'Neomorts', *University of Toronto Medical Journal*, 54, 35–7.

Arnold, R. M. and Younger, S. (1993), 'Ethical, Psychosocial, and Public Policy Implications of Procuring Organs from Non-Heart-Beating Cadavers', *Kennedy Institute of Ethics Journal*, 3, 263–78.

Arnst, C. (2003), 'I Can't Remember', (updated 1 Sep 2003) <http://www. businessweek.com/magazine/content/03_35/b3847001_mz001.htm>, accessed 4 Apr 2008.

Arts, W. F. M., Van Dongen, H. R., Van Hof-Van Duin, J. and Lammens, E. (1985), 'Unexpected Improvement after Prolonged Post-Traumatic Vegetative State', *Journal of Neurology, Neurosurgery, and Psychiatry*, 48, 1300–03.

Asada, Y., Nakamura, T. and Kawaguchi, S. (1998), 'Peripheral Nerve Grafts for Neural Repair of Spinal Cord Injury in Neonatal Rat: Aiming at Functional Regeneration', *Transplantation Proceedings*, 30, 147–8.

Ashcroft, R. (2000), 'The Ethics of Reusing Archived Tissue for Research', *Neuropathology and Applied Neurobiology*, 26, 408–11.

— (2005), 'Making Sense of Dignity', *Journal of Medical Ethics*, 31, 679–82.

Asscher, J. (2008), 'The Moral Distinction between Killing and Letting Die in Medical Cases', *Bioethics*, 22, 278–85.

Associated Press (2006), 'How a Rogue Body Broker Got Away with It', (updated 28 Aug) <http://www.msnbc.msn.com/id/14518343/>, accessed 4 Jul 2008.

Austin, C. R. (1989), *Human Embryos* (Oxford: Oxford University Press).

Australian Health Ministers' Advisory Council Subcommittee on Ethical Autopsy Practice (2002), 'The National Code of Ethical Autopsy Practice' (Adelaide: South Australian Department of Human Services).

Bach, F. H., Fishman, J. A., Daniels, N., Proimos, J., Anderson, B., Carpenter, C. B., Forrow, L., Robson, S. C. and Fineberg, H. V. (1998), 'Uncertainty in Xenotransplantation: Individual Benefit Versus Collective Risk', *Nature Medicine*, 4, 141–4.

Bachoud-Levi, A. C., Gaura, V., Brugieres, P., Lefaucheur, J. P., Boisse, M. F., Maison, P., Baudic, S., Ribeiro, M. J., Bourdet, C., Remy, P., Cesaro, P., Hantraye, P. and Peschanski, M. (2006), 'Effect of Fetal Neural Transplants in Patients with Huntington's Disease 6 Years after Surgery: A Long-Term Follow-up Study', *Lancet Neurology*, 5, 303–9.

Bahn, P. G. (1989), 'Burying the Hatchet', *Nature*, 342, 123–4.

Bailey, L. L., Nehlsen-Cannarella, S. L., Concepcion, W. and Jolley, W. B. (1985), 'Baboon-to-Human Cardiac Xenotransplantation in a Neonate', *Journal of the American Medical Association*, 254, 3321–9.

Bailey, R. (2006), 'Anyone for Tennis, at the Age of 150?' *The Times*, 8 Apr.

Baily, M. A. (2007), 'A Donor Kidney: The Gift of Life?' *Bioethics Forum* (updated 27 Jul 2007) <http://www.bioethicsforum.org/kidney-transplantation-gift-of-life.asp>, accessed 4 Sept 2007.

Baird, D., Geering, L., Saville-Smith, K., Thompson, L. and Tuhipa, T. (1995), 'Whose Genes Are They Anyway? Report of the Health Research Council Conference on Human Genetic Information', (Auckland, New Zealand: Health Research Council of New Zealand).

Barilan, Y. M. (2006), 'Bodyworlds and the Ethics of Using Human Remains: A Preliminary Discussion', *Bioethics News*, 20, 233–47.

Barkataki, I., Kumari, V., Das, M., Sumich, A., Taylor, P. and Sharma, T. (2008), 'Neural Correlates of Deficient Response Inhibition in Mentally Disordered Violent Individuals', *Behavioral Sciences & the Law*, 26, 51–64.

Barker, J. H., Furr, A., Cunningham, M., Grossi, F., Vasilic, D., Storey, B., Wiggins, O., Majzoub, R., Vossen, M., Brouha, P., Maldonado, C., Reynolds, C. C., Francois, C., Perez-Abadia, G., Frank, J. M., Kon, M. and Banis, J. C., Jr. (2006), 'Investigation of Risk Acceptance in Facial Transplantation', *Plastic and Reconstructive Surgery*, 118, 663–70.

Barnard, N. D., Scialli, A. R. and Bobela, S. (2002), 'The Current Use of Estrogens for Growth-Suppressant Therapy in Adolescent Girls', *Journal of Pediatric and Adolescent Gynecology*, 15, 23–6.

Baron, L., Shemie, S. D., Teitelbaum, J. and Doig, C. J. (2006), 'Brief Review: History, Concept and Controversies in the Neurological Determination of Death', *Canadian Journal of Anaesthesia*, 53, 602–8.

Baskin, J. H., Edersheim, J. G. and Price, B. H. (2007), 'Is a Picture Worth a Thousand Words? Neuroimaging in the Courtroom', *American Journal of Law & Medicine*, 33, 239–69.

Bass, W. M. and Jefferson, J. (2003), *Death's Acre: Inside the Legendary Forensic Lab, the Body Farm, Where the Dead Do Tell Tales* (New York: G. P. Putnam's Sons).

Bates, D. (2005), 'The Vegetative State and the Royal College of Physicians Guidance', *Neuropsychological Rehabilitation*, 15, 175–83.

Baxby, D. (1981), *Jenner's Smallpox Vaccine: The Riddle of Vacinia Virus and Its Origin* (London: Heinemann Educational Books).

BBC News (2001), 'Surgeons Sever Transplant Hand', (updated 3 Feb 2001) <http://news.bbc.co.uk/2/hi/europe/1151553.stm>, accessed 4 Jul 2008.

— (2002), 'Controversial Autopsy Goes Ahead', (updated 20 Nov 2002) <http://news.bbc.co.uk/2/hi/health/2493291.stm>, accessed 4 Jul 2008.

— (2006a), 'Face Transplant Woman Can Smile', (updated 28 Nov 2006) <http://news.bbc.co.uk/2/hi/health/6190612.stm>, accessed 4 Jul 2008.

— (2006b), 'US Undertakers Admit Corpse Scam', (updated 19 Oct 2006) <http://news.bbc.co.uk/2/hi/americas/6064692.stm>, accessed 3 Jul 2008.

— (2006c), 'UK Gets Face Transplant Go-Ahead', (updated 25 Oct 2006) <http://news.bbc.co.uk/2/hi/health/6083392.stm>, accessed 4 Jul 2008.

— (2006d), 'Organ Sales 'Thriving' in China', (updated 27 Sept 2006) <http://news.bbc.co.uk/2/asia-pacific/5386720.stm>, accessed 4 Jul 2008.

— (2007a), 'Singapore Muslims in Donor Ruling', (updated 27 Jul 2007) <http://news.bbc.co.uk/go/pr/fr/-/2/hi/asia-pacific/6919879.stm>, accessed 3 Jul 2008.

— (2007b), 'Vultures Pick Off Human Body Farm', (updated 11 May 2007) <http://news.bbc.co.uk/go/pr/fr/-/2/hi/americas/6646177.stm>, accessed 1 Jul 2008.

Beauchamp, T. L. (1999), 'The Failure of Theories of Personhood', *Kennedy Institute of Ethics Journal*, 9, 309–24.

Becker, H. S., Geer, B., Hughes, E. C. and Strauss, A. L. (1961), *Boys in White: Student Culture in Medical School* (Chicago: University of Chicago Press).

Beckinstein, T., Tiberti, C., Niklison, J., Tamashiro, M., Ron, M., Carpintiero, S., Villarreal, M., Forcato, C., Leiguarda, R. and Manes, F. (2005), 'Assessing Level of Consciousness and Cognitive Changes from Vegetative State to Full Recovery', *Neuropsychological Rehabilitation*, 15, 307–22.

Benfield, D. G., Flaksman, R. J., Lin, T.-H., Kantak, A. D., Kokomoor, F. W. and Vollman, J. H. (1991), 'Teaching Intubation Skills Using Newly Deceased Infants', *Journal of the American Medical Association*, 265, 2360–3.

Bengtsson, A., Svalander, C. T., Molne, J., Rydberg, L. and Breimer, M. E. (1998), 'Extracorporeal ("Ex Vivo") Connection of Pig Kidneys to Humans. III. Studies of Plasma Complement Activation and Complement Deposition in the Kidney Tissue', *Xenotransplantation*, 5, 176–83.

Berger, R. L. (1990), 'Nazi Science – the Dachau Hypothermia Experiments', *New England Journal of Medicine*, 322, 1435–40.

— (1992), 'Nazi Science: Comments on the Validation of the Dachau Human Hypothermia Experiments', in A. L. Caplan (ed.), *When Medicine Went Mad: Bioethics and the Holocaust* (New Jersey: Humana Press), 109–33.

— (1994), 'Nazi Science – the Dachau Hypothermia Experiments', in J. J. Michalcyk (ed.), *Medicine, Ethics, and the Third Reich: Historical and Contemporary Issues* (Kansas City: Sheed and Ward), 87–100.

Berlioz, H. (1969), 'The Memoirs of Hector Berlioz' (London: Victor Gollancz Ltd.).

Bernat, J. L. (1992), 'How Much of the Brain Must Die in Brain Death?' *Journal of Clinical Ethics*, 3, 21–6.

— (1998), 'A Defense of the Whole-Brain Concept of Death', *Hastings Center Report*, 28, 14–23.

— (2002), *Ethical Issues in Neurology* (2nd edn; Boston: Butterworth Heinemann).

— (2005a), 'The Concept and Practice of Brain Death', in S. Laureys (ed.), *The Boundaries of Consciousness: Neurobiology and Neuropathology* (Oxford: Elsevier).

— (2005b), 'Medical Futility: Definition, Determination and Disputes in Critical Care', *Neurocritical Care*, 2, 198–205.

Bertman, S. L. and Marks, S. C. (1989), 'The Dissection Experience as a Laboratory for Self-Discovery About Death and Dying: Another Side of Clinical Anatomy', *Clinical Anatomy*, 2, 103–13.

Bhasin, S., Woodhouse, L. and Storer, T. W. (2003), 'Androgen Effects on Body Composition', *Growth Hormone & IGF Research*, 13 Suppl A, S63–71.

Bir, C. and Viano, D. C. (2004), 'Design and Injury Assessment Criteria for Blunt Ballistic Impacts', *Journal of Trauma*, 57, 1218–24.

Bir, C. A., Stewart, S. J. and Wilhelm, M. (2005), 'Skin Penetration Assessment of Less Lethal Kinetic Energy Munitions', *Journal of Forensic Sciences*, 50, 1426–9.

Blakely, R. L. (1997), 'A Clandestine Past: Discovery at the Medical College of Georgia and Theoretical Foundations', in R. L. Blakely and J. M. Harrington (eds), *Bones in the Basement: Postmortem Racism in Nineteenth-Century Medical Training* (Washington: Smithsonian Institution Press), 3–27.

Blakely, R. L. and Harrington, J. M. (eds) (1997), *Bones in the Basement: Postmortem Racism in Nineteenth-Century Medical Training* (Washington: Smithsonian Institution Press).

Blendon, R. J., Benson, J. M. and Herrmann, M. J. (2005), 'The American Public and the Terri Schiavo Case', *Archives of Internal Medicine*, 165, 2580–4.

Boddington, P. (1996), 'Organ Donation and Ethics – Could Australia Accept the Spanish Model of Organ Donation?' *Monash Bioethics Review*, 15, 33–43.

Bodenham, A., Berridge, J. C. and Park, G. R. (1989), 'Brain Stem Death and Organ Donation', *British Medical Journal*, 299, 1009–10.

Boller, F., Verny, M., Hugonot-Diener, L. and Saxton, J. (2002), 'Clinical Features and Assessment of Severe Dementia. A Review', *European Journal of Neurology*, 9, 125–36.

Bonnichsen, R. and Schneider, A. L. (1995), 'Roots', *The Sciences*, 35, 26–31.

Boorse, C. (1977), 'Health as a Theoretical Concept', *Philosophy of Science*, 44, 542–73.

Borlongan, C. V., Tajima, Y., Trojanowski, J. Q., Lee, V. M. and Sanberg, P. R. (1998), 'Cerebral Ischemia and CNS Transplantation: Differential Effects of Grafted Fetal Rat Striatal Cells and Human Neurons Derived from a Clonal Cell Line', *Neuroreport*, 9, 3703–9.

Borthwick, C. (1995a), 'Persistent Vegetative State: A Syndrome in Search of a Name, or a Judgement in Search of a Syndrome?' *Monash Bioethics Review*, 14, 20–6.

— (1995b), 'The Proof of the Vegetable: A Commentary on Medical Futility', *Journal of Medical Ethics*, 21, 205–8.

Bostrom, N. (2005), 'In Defense of Posthuman Dignity', *Bioethics*, 19, 202–14.

Botega, N. J., Metze, K., Marques, E., Cruvinel, A., Moraes, Z. V., Augusto, L. and Costa, L. A. (1997), 'Attitudes of Medical Students to Necropsy', *Journal of Clinical Pathology*, 50, 64–6.

Boyer, C. N., Holland, G. E. and Seely, J. F. (2005), 'Flash X-Ray Observations of Cavitation in Cadaver Thighs Caused by High-Velocity Bullets', *Journal of Trauma*, 59, 1463–8.

Braak, H. and Del Tredici, K. (2008), 'Assessing Fetal Nerve Cell Grafts in Parkinson's Disease', *Nature Medicine*, 14, 483–5.

Brams, M. (1977), 'Transplantable Human Organs: Should Their Sales Be Authorized by State Statutes?' *American Journal of Law & Medicine*, 3, 183–95.

Brandt, A. M. and Freidenfelds, L. (1996), 'Research Ethics after World War II: The Insular Culture of Biomedicine', *Kennedy Institute of Ethics Journal*, 6, 239–43.

Bray, T. L. (1996), 'Repatriation, Power Relations and the Politics of the Past', *Antiquity*, 70, 440–4.

Bray, T. L. and Grant, L. G. (1994), 'The Concept of Cultural Affiliation and Its Legal Significance in the Larsen Bay Repatriation', in T. L. Bray and T. W. Killion (eds), *Reckoning with the Dead: The Larsen Bay Repatriation and the Smithsonian Institute* (Washington, D.C: Smithsonian Institution Press), 153–7.

Bray, T. L. and Killion, T. W. (eds) (1994), *Reckoning with the Dead: The Larsen Bay Repatriation and the Smithsonian Institute* (Washington, DC: Smithsonian Institution Press).

Breimer, M. E., Björck, S., Svalander, C. T., Bengtsson, A., Rydberg, L., Lie-Karlsen, K., Attman, P.-O., Aurell, M. and Samuelsson, B. E. (1996), 'Extracorporeal ("Ex Vivo") Connection of Pig Kidneys to Humans. I. Clinical Data and Studies of Platelet Destruction', *Xenotransplantation*, 3, 328–39.

Briggs, J. D. (1996), 'The Use of Organs from Executed Prisoners in China', *Nephrology, Dialysis, Transplantation*, 11, 238–40.

Bristol Royal Infirmary Inquiry (2000), *Interim Report: Removal and Retention of Organs* (Bristol: Crown Copyright).

— (2001), *Learning from Bristol: The Report of the Public Inquiry into Children's Heart Surgery at the Bristol Royal Infirmary 1984–1995* (Bristol: Crown Copyright).

British Medical Association (2006), *Human Tissue Legislation: Guidance from the BMA's Medical Ethics Department* (London: British Medical Association).

— (2007a), *Boosting Your Brainpower: Ethical Aspect of Cognitive Enhancements. A Discussion Paper from the BMA* (London: British Medical Association).

— (2007b), *Withholding and Withdrawing Life-Prolonging Medical Treatment: Guidance for Decision Making* (3rd edn; London: British Medical Association).

Brown, H. G. (1984), 'Lay Perceptions of Autopsy', *Archives of Pathology and Laboratory Medicine*, 108, 446–8.

Brown, J., Matthews, A. L., Sandstrom, P. A. and Chapman, L. E. (1998), 'Xenotransplantation and the Risk of Retroviral Zoonosis', *Trends in Microbiology*, 6, 411–5.

Brunet, A., Orr, S. P., Tremblay, J., Robertson, K., Nader, K. and Pitman, R. K. (2007), 'Effect of Post-Retrieval Propranolol on Psychophysiologic Responding During Subsequent Script-Driven Traumatic Imagery in Post-Traumatic Stress Disorder', *Journal of Psychiatric Research*.

Bruning, S. B. (2006), 'Complex Legal Legacies: The Native American Graves Protection and Repatriation Act, Scientific Study and Kennewick Man', *American Antiquity*, 71, 501–21.

Buchanan, A. (2008), 'Enhancement and the Ethics of Development', *Kennedy Institute of Ethics Journal*, 18, 1–34.

Bulletin of Medical Ethics (1990), 'Bioethics Attacked in Germany', *Bulletin of Medical Ethics*, 61, 19–23.

Bulmer, S. (1991), 'Archaeology and Indigenous Rights: The World Archaeological Congress' Code of Ethics from an Archeologist's Point of View', *Archaeology in New Zealand*, 34, 55–8.

Burch, D. (2007), *Digging up the Dead: The Life and Times of Astley Cooper, an Extraordinary Surgeon* (London: Chatto & Windus).

Burdeau, C. (2004), 'Donated Bodies Used in Land Mine Tests', (updated 10 Mar 2004) <http://dir.salon.com/story/news/wire/2004/03/10/cadaver_mines/index.html>, accessed 3 Jul 2008.

Burns, J. P., Reardon, F. E. and Truog, R. D. (1994), 'Using Newly Deceased Patients to Teach Resuscitation Procedures', *New England Journal of Medicine*, 331, 1652–5.

Burns, L. (2007), 'Gunther Von Hagens' Body Worlds: Selling Beautiful Education', *American Journal of Bioethics*, 7, 12–23.

Burton, E. C., Phillips, R. S., Covinsky, K. E., Sands, L. P., Goldman, L., Dawson, N. V., Connors, A. F., Jr. and Landefeld, C. S. (2004), 'The Relation of Autopsy Rate to Physicians' Beliefs and Recommendations Regarding Autopsy', *American Journal of Medicine*, 117, 255–61.

Butler, D. (1998), 'Last Chance to Stop and Think on Risks of Xenotransplants', *Nature*, 391, 320–95.

Calne, R. (1993), 'Organs from Animals: Unlikely for a Decade', *British Medical Journal*, 307, 637–8.

Campbell, A. V., Gillett, G. and Jones, D. G. (2005), *Medical Ethics* (Melbourne: Oxford University Press).

Campbell, C. C. (2004), 'The Human Face of Alzheimer's', *New Atlantis*, 6, 3–17.

Canli, T. (2004), 'Functional Brain Mapping of Extraversion and Neuroticism: Learning from Individual Differences in Emotion Processing', *Journal of Personality*, 72, 1105–32.

Canli, T. and Amin, Z. (2002), 'Neuroimaging of Emotion and Personality: Scientific Evidence and Ethical Considerations', *Brain and Cognition*, 50, 414–31.

Canli, T., Zhao, Z., Desmond, J. E., Kang, E., Gross, J. and Gabrieli, J. D. (2001), 'An fMRI Study of Personality Influences on Brain Reactivity to Emotional Stimuli', *Behavioral Neuroscience*, 115, 33–42.

Cantwell, A.-M. (2000), 'Who Knows the Power of His Bones: Reburial Redux' in A.-M. Cantwell, E. Friedlander and M. L. Tramm (eds), *Ethics and Anthropology: Facing Future Issues in Human Biology, Globalism, and Cultural Property. Proceedings of a Meeting. 14 April 2000* (New York: Annals of the New York Academy of Sciences), 79–119.

Caplan, A. L. (1984), 'Organ Procurement: It's Not on the Cards', *Hastings Center Report*, 14, 9–12.

— (1987), 'Should Foetuses or Infants Be Utilized as Organ Donors?' *Bioethics*, 1, 119–40.

— (1992), 'Is Xenografting Morally Wrong?' *Transplantation Proceedings*, 24, 722–7.

Caplan, A. L., Perry, C., Plante, L. A., Saloma, J. and Batzer, F. R. (2007), 'Moving the Womb', *Hastings Center Report*, 37, 18–20.

Caplan, A. L., Siminoff, L., Arnold, R. and Viring, B. (1991), 'Increasing Organ and Tissue Donation: What Are the Obstacles, What Are the Options?' in

A. Novello (ed.), *The Surgeon General's Workshop on Increasing Organ Donation: Proceedings, Washington, DC, 8–10 July 1991* (Washington, DC: US Government Printing Office), 199–232.

Capron, A. M. (2001), 'Brain Death – Well Settled Yet Still Unresolved', *New England Journal of Medicine*, 344, 1244–6.

Carney, S. (2007), 'Inside India's Underground Trade in Human Remains', (updated 27 Nov 2008) <http://www.wired.com/medtech/health/magazine/15–12/ff_bones?currentPage=2>, accessed 2 Jun 2008.

Carter, A. H. (1997), *First Cut: A Season in the Human Anatomy Lab* (New York: Picador).

Cartlidge, P. H. T., Dawson, A. T., Stewart, J. H. and Vujanic, G. M. (1995), 'Value and Quality of Perinatal and Infant Postmortem Examinations: Cohort Analysis of 400 Consecutive Deaths', *British Medical Journal*, 310, 155–8.

Cartwright, S. R. (1988), *The Report of the Cervical Cancer Inquiry* (The Report of the Committee of Inquiry into Allegations Concerning the Treatment of Cervical Cancer at National Women's Hospital and into Other Related Matters; Auckland: Government Printing Office).

Casey, B. J., Getz, S. and Galvan, A. (2008), 'The Adolescent Brain', *Developmental Review*, 28, 62–77.

Cassman, V., Odegaard, N. and Powell, J. (2007), 'Policy', in V. Cassman, N. Odegaard and J. Powell (eds), *Human Remains: Guide for Museums and Academic Institutions* (Lanham, MD: AltaMira Press).

Caulfield, T. (2007), 'Biobanks and Blanket Consent: The Proper Place of the Public Good and Public Perception Rationales', *King's Law Journal*, 18, 209–26.

Central Intelligence Agency (2007), 'The World Factbook', <https://www.cia.gov/library/publications/the-world-factbook/>, accessed 17 Oct 2007.

Chance, B. and Kang, K. A. (2002), 'Vision Statement: Interacting Brain' in M. C. Roco and W. S. Bainbridge (eds), *Converging Technologies for Improving Human Performance* (Washington, DC: Technology Administration), 224–6.

Charatan, F. B. (1997), 'Investigation of Nazi Anatomy Textbook to Start', *British Medical Journal*, 314, 536.

— (2006), 'FDA Shuts Down Human Tissue Company', *British Medical Journal*, 332, 507.

Chatterjee, A. (2007), 'Cosmetic Neurology and Cosmetic Surgery: Parallels, Predictions, and Challenges', *Cambridge Quarterly of Healthcare Ethics*, 16, 129–37.

Chouhan, P. and Draper, H. (2003), 'Modified Mandated Choice for Organ Procurement', *Journal of Medical Ethics*, 29, 157–62.

Christensen, A. M. (2006), 'Moral Considerations in Body Donation for Scientific Research: A Unique Look at the University of Tennessee's Anthropological Research Facility', *Bioethics*, 20, 136–45.

Chung, Y., Klimanskaya, I., Becker, S., Marh, J., Lu, S.-J., Johnson, J., Meisner, L. and Lanza, R. (2006), 'Embryonic and Extraembryonic Stem Cell Lines Derived from Single Mouse Blastomeres', *Nature*, 439, 145–7.

Clarke, E. and Dewhurst, K. (1972), *An Illustrated History of Brain Function* (Oxford: Sanford Publications).

Clarkson, E. D. (2001), 'Fetal Tissue Transplantation for Patients with Parkinson's Disease: A Database of Published Clinical Results', *Drugs & Aging*, 18, 773–85.

Clauss, R. and Nel, W. (2006), 'Drug Induced Arousal from the Permanent Vegetative State', *NeuroRehabilitation*, 21, 23–8.

Cody, E. (2007), 'China Tightens Restrictions on Transplants', *Washington Post*, 4 Jul.

Cohen, C. B. (2007), *Renewing the Stuff of Life: Stem Cells, Ethics and Public Policy* (New York: Oxford University Press).

Cohen, D. and Eisendorfer, C. (1986), *The Loss of Self: A Family Resource for the Care of Alzheimer's Disease and Related Disorders* (London: W.W. Norton).

Colburn, D. (1991), 'The 40-Year Vigil for Rita Greene', *Washington Post*, 12 Mar.

Cole, S. and McCabe, M. (2002), 'The Green Lane Heart Library: Ethical and Cultural Implications', *New Zealand Bioethics Journal*, 3, 4–7.

Coller, B. S. (1989), 'The Newly Dead as Research Subjects', *Clinical Research*, 37, 487–94.

Coller, B. S., Scudder, L. E., Berger, H. J. and Iuliucci, J. D. (1988), 'Inhibition of Human Platelet Function *In Vivo* with a Monoclonal Antibody. With Observations on the Newly Dead as Experimental Subjects', *Annals of Internal Medicine*, 109, 635–8.

Collignon, P. J. (1998), 'Xenotransplantation: Do the Risks Outweigh the Benefits?' *Medical Journal of Australia*, 168, 516–9.

Collins English Dictionary & Thesaurus (2006), 4th edn (Glasgow: HarperCollins Publishers).

Committee on the Biological and Biomedical Applications of Stem Cell Research (2002), *Stem Cells and the Future of Regenerative Medicine* (Washington DC: National Academy Press).

Conference of Medical Royal Colleges and their Faculties in the UK (1979), 'Diagnosis of Death', *British Medical Journal*, 1, 332.

Cooper, D. K., Dorling, A., Pierson, R. N. III, Rees, M., Seebach, J., Yazer, M., Ohdan, H., Awwad, M. and Ayares, D. (2007), 'Alpha1,3-Galactosyltransferase Gene-Knockout Pigs for Xenotransplantation: Where Do We Go from Here?' *Transplantation*, 84, 1–7.

Cordner, S. M. (1992), 'The Autopsy in Decline', *Medical Journal of Australia*, 156, 448.

Cornelius, E. H. (1978), 'John Hunter as an Expert Witness', *Annals of the Royal College of Surgeons of England*, 60, 412–8.

Coull, F. (2003), 'Personal Story Offers Insight into Living with Facial Disfigurement', *Journal of Wound Care*, 12, 254–8.

Council for Ethical and Judicial Affairs (1994), 'Strategies for Cadaveric Organ Procurement: Mandated Choice and Presumed Consent', *Journal of the American Medical Association*, 272, 809–12.

— (1995), 'The Use of Anencephalic Neonates as Organ Donors', *Journal of the American Medical Association*, 273, 1614–8.

Council of Europe (2006), 'Recommendation Rec(2006)4 of the Committee of Ministers to Member States on Research on Biological Materials of Human Origin', <https://wcd.coe.int/ViewDoc.jsp?id=977859>, accessed 12 Oct 2007.

Council on Ethical and Judicial Affairs of the American Medical Association (2002), 'Performing Procedures on the Newly Deceased', *Academic Medicine*, 77, 1212–6.

Crandall, J. R., Kuhlmann, T. P. and Pilkey, W. D. (1995), 'Air and Knee Bolster Restraint System: Laboratory Sled Tests with Human Cadavers and the Hybrid III Dummy', *Journal of Trauma*, 38, 517–20.

Cranford, R. E. (1988), 'The Persistent Vegetative State: The Medical Reality (Getting the Facts Straight)', *Hastings Center Report*, 18, 27–32.

Crivellato, E. and Ribatti, D. (2007), 'A Portrait of Aristotle as an Anatomist: Historical Article', *Clinical Anatomy*, 20, 477–85.

Cui, H., Nishiguchi, N., Ivleva, E., Yanagi, M., Fukutake, M., Nushida, H., Ueno, Y., Kitamura, N., Maeda, K. and Shirakawa, O. (2007), 'Association of RGS2 Gene Polymorphisms with Suicide and Increased RGS2 Immunoreactivity in the Postmortem Brain of Suicide Victims', *Neuropsychopharmacology*, 33, 1537–44.

d'Apice, A. J. F. (2005), 'Response', *Xenotransplantation*, 12, 431–3.

Dalley, A. F., Driscoll, R. E. and Settles, H. E. (1993), 'The Uniform Anatomical Gift Act: What Every Clinical Anatomist Should Know', *Clinical Anatomy*, 6, 247–54.

Dalton, R. (2005), 'Scientists Finally Get Their Hands on Kennewick Man', *Nature*, 436, 10.

Daniels, N. (1985), *Just Health Care* (New York: Cambridge University Press).

— (2000), 'Normal Functioning and the Treatment-Enhancement Distinction', *Cambridge Quarterly of Healthcare Ethics*, 9, 309–22.

Darsalia, V., Kallur, T. and Kokaia, Z. (2007), 'Survival, Migration and Neuronal Differentiation of Human Fetal Striatal and Cortical Neural Stem Cells Grafted in Stroke-Damaged Rat Striatum', *European Journal of Neuroscience*, 26, 605–14.

Davidson, M. (1995), 'Body Trouble', *The New Physician*, 44, 30–5.

Dawson, T. P., James, R. S. and Williams, G. T. (1990), 'Silicone Plastinated Pathology Specimens and Their Teaching Potential', *Journal of Pathology*, 162, 265–72.

Deacon, T., Schumacher, J., Dinsmore, J., Thomas, C., Palmer, P., Kott, S., Edge, A., Penney, D., Kassissieh, S., Dempsey, P. and Isacson, O. (1997), 'Histological Evidence of Fetal Pig Neural Cell Survival after Transplantation into a Patient with Parkinson's Disease', *Nature Medicine*, 3, 350–3.

Decety, J., Jackson, P. L., Sommerville, J. A., Chaminade, T. and Meltzoff, A. N. (2004), 'The Neural Bases of Cooperation and Competition: An fMRI Investigation', *NeuroImage*, 23, 744–51.

Deeley, Q., Daly, E., Surguladze, S., Tunstall, N., Mezey, G., Beer, D., Ambikapathy, A., Robertson, D., Giampietro, V., Brammer, M. J., Clarke, A., Dowsett, J., Fahy, T., Phillips, M. L. and Murphy, D. G. (2006), 'Facial Emotion Processing in Criminal Psychopathy. Preliminary Functional Magnetic Resonance Imaging Study', *British Journal of Psychiatry*, 189, 533–9.

DeGrazia, D. (2005), 'Enhancement Technologies and Human Identity', *Journal of Medicine and Philosophy*, 30, 261–183.

Dekkers, W. and Rikkert, M. O. (2007), 'Memory Enhancing Drugs and Alzheimer's Disease: Enhancing the Self or Preventing the Loss of It?' *Medicine, Health Care, and Philosophy*, 10, 141–51.

Delamothe, T. (1991), 'Aboriginal Skeletons in the Closet: Time to Send Them Home', *British Medical Journal*, 303, 1564.

Delmonico, F. L., Arnold, R., Scheper-Hughes, N., Siminoff, L. A., Kahn, J. and Youngner, S. J. (2002), 'Ethical Incentives – Not Payment – for Organ Donation', *New England Journal of Medicine*, 346, 2002–5.

Department for Culture Media and Sport (2005), *Guidance for the Care of Human Remains in Museums* (London: Department for Culture Media and Sport).

Department of Health (2001a), *The Removal, Retention and Use of Human Organs and Tissue from Postmortem Examination* (London: Her Majesty's Stationery Office).

—— (2001b), *Report of a Census of Organs and Tissues Retained by Pathology Service in England* (London: Her Majesty's Stationery Office).

—— (2005), 'The Human Tissue Act 2004. New Legislation on Human Organs and Tissue', <www.dh.gov.uk/prod_consum_dh/groups/dh_digitalassets/@dh/@en/documents/digitalasset/dh_4109591.pdf>, accessed 12 Oct 2007.

Der Spiegel (2006), 'Preserved-Corpse Factory Opens in Eastern Germany', *Der Spiegel*, 16 Nov.

Deschamps, J. Y., Roux, F. A., Sai, P. and Gouin, E. (2005), 'History of Xenotransplantation', *Xenotransplantation*, 12, 91–109.

Devauchelle, B., Badet, L., Lengele, B., Morelon, E., Testelin, S., Michallet, M., D'Hauthuille, C. and Dubernard, J. M. (2006), 'First Human Face Allograft: Early Report', *Lancet*, 368, 203–9.

DeVita, M. A., Wicclair, M., Swanson, D., Valenta, C. and Schold, C. (2003), 'Research Involving the Newly Dead: An Institutional Response', *Critical Care Medicine*, 31, S385–90.

Diamanti-Kandarakis, E., Konstantinopoulos, P. A., Papailiou, J., Kandarakis, S. A., Andreopoulos, A. and Sykiotis, G. P. (2005), 'Erythropoietin Abuse and

Erythropoietin Gene Doping: Detection Strategies in the Genomic Era', *Sports Medicine*, 35, 831–40.

Dickman, S. (1989a), 'Brain Sections to Be Buried?' *Nature*, 339, 498.

— (1989b), 'Scandal over Nazi Victims' Corpses Rocks Universities', *Nature*, 337, 195.

Dickson, D. (1988), 'Human Experiment Roils French Medicine', *Science*, 239, 1370.

Diekema, D. S. (1990), 'Is Taller Really Better? Growth Hormone Therapy in Short Children', *Perspectives in Biology and Medicine*, 34, 109–23.

Diflo, T. (2004), 'Use of Organs from Executed Chinese Prisoners', *Lancet*, 364 Suppl 1, s30–1.

Dillon, W. P., Lee, R. V., Tronolone, M. J., Buckwald, S. and Foote, R. J. (1982), 'Life Support and Maternal Brain Death During Pregnancy', *Journal of the American Medical Association*, 248, 1089–91.

Dinsmore, J. H., Manhart, C., Raineri, R., Jacoby, D. B. and Moore, A. (2000), 'No Evidence for Infection of Human Cells with Porcine Endogenous Retrovirus (PERV) after Exposure to Porcine Fetal Neuronal Cells', *Transplantation*, 70, 1382–9.

Dobbs, D. (2005), 'Brain Scans for Sale: As Brain Imaging Spreads to Nonmedical Uses, Will Commerce Overtake Ethics?', *Slate*, 25 Jan.

Dorozynski, A. (1995), 'French GPs Launch Organ Donor Campaign', *British Medical Journal*, 311, 214–5.

Doyle, D. J. and Robichaud, A. (2004), 'Inconsistencies in the Ethical Declaration of Death', *Canadian Journal of Anesthesia*, 51, 280.

Dubernard, J. M., Owen, E., Herzberg, G., Lanzetta, M., Martin, X., Kapila, H., Dawahra, M. and Hakim, N. S. (1999), 'Human Hand Allograft: Report on First 6 Months', *Lancet*, 353, 1315–20.

Duma, S. M., Boggess, B. M., Crandall, J. R. and MacMahon, C. B. (2003a), 'Injury Risk Function for the Small Female Wrist in Axial Loading', *Accident; Analysis and Prevention*, 35, 869–75.

Duma, S. M., Crandall, J. R., Rudd, R. W. and Kent, R. W. (2003b), 'Small Female Head and Neck Interaction with a Deploying Side Airbag', *Accident Analysis and Prevention*, 35, 811–6.

Dunning, J. J., White, D. J. and Wallwork, J. (1994), 'The Rationale for Xenotransplantation as a Solution to the Donor Organ Shortage', *Pathologie-biologie*, 42, 231–5.

Edwards, L. F. (1952), 'Resurrection Riots During the Heroic Age of Anatomy in America', *Bulletin of the History of Medicine*, 52, 178–84.

Elliott, C. (1998), 'The Tyranny of Happiness: Ethics and Cosmetic Psychopharmacology', in E. Parens (ed.), *Enhancing Human Traits: Ethical and Social Implications* (Washingon, DC: Georgetown University Press), 177–88.

— (2003), *Better Than Well* (New York: W. W. Norton & Company).

Elliott, R., Sahakian, B. J., Matthews, K., Bannerjea, A., Rimmer, J. and Robbins, T. W. (1997), 'Effects of Methylphenidate on Spatial Working Memory and Planning in Healthy Young Adults', *Psychopharmacology*, 131, 196–206.

Elson, J. (1989), 'Returning Bones of Contention: A Bitter Debate over Spiritual Values and Scholarly Needs', *Time*, 25 Sept, 53.

Emson, H. E. (1992), 'Notes on Necropsy', *Journal of Clinical Pathology*, 45, 85–6.

Engelhardt, H. T., Jr. (1986), *The Foundations of Bioethics* (Oxford: Oxford University Press).

Engels, E.-M. (1999), 'Xenotransplantation: A Doubtful Prospect', *Biologist*, 46, 73–6.

Evans, R. W. and Manninen, D. L. (1988), 'US Public Opinion Concerning the Procurement and Distribution of Donor Organs', *Transplantation Proceedings*, 20, 781–5.

Ewing, T. (1990), 'Emphasis on "Aborigine Rights"', *Nature*, 344, 697.

Executive Board of the American Academy of Neurology (1988), 'Position of the American Academy of Neurology on Certain Aspects of the Care and Management of the Persistent Vegetative State Patient', *Neurology*, 33, 125–6.

Fageeh, W., Raffa, H., Jabbad, H. and Marzouki, A. (2002), 'Transplantation of the Human Uterus', *International Journal of Gynaecology and Obstetrics*, 76, 245–51.

Farah, M. J. and Wolpe, P. R. (2004), 'Monitoring and Manipulating Brain Function: New Neuroscience Technologies and Their Ethical Implications', *Hastings Center Report*, 34, 35–45.

Farahany, N. (2008), 'The Government Is Trying to Wrap Its Mind around Yours', *Washington Post*, 13 Apr.

Faran, S., Vatine, J. J., Lazary, A., Ohry, A., Birbaumer, N. and Kotchoubey, B. (2006), 'Late Recovery from Permanent Traumatic Vegetative State Heralded by Event-Related Potentials', *Journal of Neurology, Neurosurgery, and Psychiatry*, 77, 998–1000.

Farwell, L. A. and Smith, S. S. (2001), 'Using Brain MERMER Testing to Detect Concealed Knowledge Despite Efforts to Conceal', *Journal of Forensic Sciences*, 46, 135–43.

Favazza, A. R. (1996), *Bodies under Siege: Self-Mutilation and Body Modification in Culture and Psychiatry* (Baltimore: The Johns Hopkins University Press).

Fedarko, K. (1993), 'Bodies of Evidence', *Time*, 6 Dec, 47.

Feinberg, J. (1984), 'Potentiality, Development and Rights' in J. Feinberg (ed.), *The Problem of Abortion* (Belmont, CA: Wadsworth).

— (1985), 'The Mistreatment of Dead Bodies', *Hastings Center Report*, 15, 31–7.

Fennell, S. and Jones, D. G. (1992), 'The Bequest of Human Bodies for Dissection: A Case Study in the Otago Medical School', *New Zealand Medical Journal*, 105, 472–4.

Ferguson, T. J. (1996), 'Native Americans and the Practice of Archaeology', *Annual Review of Anthropology*, 25, 63–79.

Fernandez, J. P., O'Rourke, R. A. and Ewy, G. A. (1970), 'Rapid Active External Rewarming in Accidental Hypothermia', *Journal of the American Medical Association*, 212, 153–6.

Ferrari, G., Cusella-De Angelis, G., Coletta, M., Paolucci, E., Stornaiuolo, A., Cossu, G. and Mavilio, F. (1998), 'Muscle Regeneration by Bone Marrow-Derived Myogenic Progenitors', *Science*, 279, 1528–30.

Field, D. R., Gates, E. A., Creasy, R. K., Jonsen, A. R. and Lares, R. K. (1988), 'Maternal Brain Death During Pregnancy: Medical and Ethical Issues', *Journal of the American Medical Association*, 260, 816–22.

Filipp, F. (2007), 'Is Science Killing Sport? Gene Therapy and Its Possible Abuse in Doping', *EMBO Reports*, 8, 433–5.

Fink, J. S., Schumacher, J. M., Ellias, S. L., Palmer, E. P., Saint-Hilaire, M., Shannon, K., Penn, R., Starr, P., VanHorne, C., Kott, H. S., Dempsey, P. K., Fischman, A. J., Raineri, R., Manhart, C., Dinsmore, J. and Isacson, O. (2000), 'Porcine Xenografts in Parkinson's Disease and Huntington's Disease Patients: Preliminary Results', *Cell Transplantation*, 9, 273–8.

Fins, J. J. (2008), 'A Leg to Stand On: Sir William Osler and Wilder Penfield's "Neuroethics"', *American Journal of Bioethics*, 8, 37–46.

Fisher, L. J. and Gage, F. H. (1993), 'Grafting in the Mammalian Central Nervous System', *Physiological Reviews*, 73, 583–616.

Fishman, J. A. (2005), 'Xenosis and Xenotransplantation: Current Concepts and Challenges', *Xenotransplantation*, 12, 370.

FitzSimmons, E., Prost, J. H. and Peniston, S. (1998), 'Infant Head Molding: A Cultural Practice', *Archives of Family Medicine*, 7, 88–90.

Fleischer, T. E. (1999), 'The Personhood Wars', *Theoretical Medicine and Bioethics*, 20, 309–18.

Fluehr-Lobban, C. (2003), 'Ethics and Anthropology 1890–2000: A Review of Issues and Principles', in C. Fluehr-Lobban (ed.), *Ethics and the Profession of Anthropology* (second edn; Walnut Creek, CA: AltaMira Press), 1–28.

Fontana, A. and Smith, R. W. (1989), 'Alzheimer's Disease Victims: The 'Unbecoming' of Self and the Normalisation of Competence', *Sociological Perspectives*, 32, 35–46.

Food and Drug Administration (2006a), 'FDA Forms Task Force on Human Safety' [Press Release], (updated 30 Aug) <www.fda.gov/bbs/topics/NEWS/2006/NEW01440.html>, accessed 12 Oct 2007.

— (2006b), 'FDA Issues Guidance to Tissue Establishments' [Press Release], (updated 13 Sep) <www.fda.gov/bbs/topics/NEWS/2006/NEW01448.html>, accessed 12 Oct 2007.

— (2006c), 'Guidance for Industry: Compliance with 21 CFR Part 1271.150(C)(1) – Manufacturing Arrangements' [Webpage], <www.fda.gov/cber/gdlns/cgtpmanuf.htm>, accessed 12 Oct 2007.

Foot, P. (1984), 'Killing and Letting Die', in J. L. Garfield and P. Hennessey (eds), *Abortion: Moral and Legal Perspectives* (Amherst, MA: University of Massachusetts Press), 177–85.

Ford, N. (1988), *When Did I Begin?* (Cambridge: Cambridge University Press).

— (2002), *The Prenatal Person* (Oxford: Blackwell).

— (2007), 'The Moral Significance of the Human Foetus', in R. E. Ashcroft, A. Dawson, D. H. and M. J. R. (eds), *Principles of Health Care Ethics* (Second Edn.; Chichester: John Wiley and Sons Ltd), 387–92.

Formenty, P., Hatz, C., Le Guenno, B., Stoll, A., Rogenmoser, P. and Widmer, A. (1999), 'Human Infection Due to Ebola Virus, Subtype Cote D'ivoire: Clinical and Biologic Presentation', *Journal of Infectious Diseases*, 179, S48–53.

Fourre, M. W. (2002), 'The Performance of Procedures on the Recently Deceased', *Academic Emergency Medicine*, 9, 595–8.

Frammolino, R. (1997), 'Harvest of Corneas at Morgue Questioned', *Los Angeles Times*, 2 Nov, sec. Main News.

Francis, N. R. and Lewis, W. (2001), 'What Price Dissection? Dissection Literally Dissected', *Medical Humanities*, 27, 2–9.

Francois, C. G., Breidenbach, W. C., Maldonado, C., Kakoulidis, T. P., Hodges, A., Dubernard, J. M., Owen, E., Pei, G., Ren, X. and Barker, J. H. (2000), 'Hand Transplantation: Comparisons and Observations of the First Four Clinical Cases', *Microsurgery*, 20, 360–71.

Frank, A. W. (2006), 'Emily's Scars: Surgical Shapings, Technoluxe and Bioethics', in E. Parens (ed.), *Surgically Shaping Children* (Baltimore: Johns Hopkins University Press), 68–89.

Freed, C. R., Greene, P. E., Breeze, R. E., Tsai, W. Y., DuMouchel, W., Kao, R., Dillon, S., Winfield, H., Culver, S., Trojanowski, J. Q., Eidelberg, D. and Fahn, S. (2001), 'Transplantation of Embryonic Dopamine Neurons for Severe Parkinson's Disease', *New England Journal of Medicine*, 344, 710–19.

Freeman, T., Goetz, C., Kordower, J., Stoessl, A., Brin, M., Shannon, K., Perl, D., Godbold, J. and Olanow, C. (2003), 'Surgical Placebo Controlled Trial of Human Fetal Nigral Transplantation in Parkinson's Disease (PD)', *33rd Annual Meeting of the Society for Neuroscience* (New Orleans, LA).

Freemark, M. (2004), 'Editorial: Growth Hormone Treatment Of "Idiopathic Short Stature": Not So Fast', *Journal of Clinical Endocrinology and Metabolism*, 89, 3138–9.

Friedman, E. A. and Friedman, A. L. (2006), 'Payment for Donor Kidneys: Pros and Cons', *Kidney International*, 69, 960–2.

Fritsch, H., Pinggera, G. M., Lienemann, A., Mitterberger, M., Bartsch, G. and Strasser, H. (2006), 'What Are the Supportive Structures of the Female Urethra?', *Neurourology and Urodynamics*, 25, 128–34.

Fry, H. K. and Pulleine, R. H. (1931), 'The Mentality of the Australian Aborigine', *Australian Journal of Experimental Biology and Medical Science*, 8, 153–67.

Fukuyama, F. (2002), *Our Posthuman Future: Consequences of the Biotechnology Revolution* (New York: Picador).

Furr, L. A., Wiggins, O., Cunningham, M., Vasilic, D., Brown, C. S., Banis, J. C., Jr., Maldonado, C., Perez-Abadia, G. and Barker, J. H. (2007), 'Psychosocial Implications of Disfigurement and the Future of Human Face Transplantation', *Plastic and Reconstructive Surgery*, 120, 559–65.

Galvin, K. A. and Jones, D. G. (2006), 'Adult Human Neural Stem Cells for Autologous Cell Replacement Therapies for Neurodegenerative Disorders', *NeuroRehabilitation*, 21, 255–65.

Gander, B., Brown, C. S., Vasilic, D., Furr, A., Banis, J. C., Jr., Cunningham, M., Wiggins, O., Maldonado, C., Whitaker, I., Perez-Abadia, G., Frank, J. M. and Barker, J. H. (2006), 'Composite Tissue Allotransplantation of the Hand and Face: A New Frontier in Transplant and Reconstructive Surgery', *Transplant International*, 19, 868–80.

Gao, J., Prough, D. S., McAdoo, D. J., Grady, J. J., Parsley, M. O., Ma, L., Tarensenko, Y. I. and Wu, P. (2006), 'Transplantation of Primed Human Fetal Neural Stem Cells Improves Cognitive Function in Rats after Traumatic Brain Injury', *Experimental Neurology*, 201, 281–92.

Garavan, H. and Hester, R. (2007), 'The Role of Cognitive Control in Cocaine Dependence', *Neuropsychology Review*, 17, 337–45.

Garreau, J. (2005), *Radical Evolution: The Promise and Peril of Enhancing Our Minds, Our Bodies – and What It Means to Be Human* (New York: Doubleday).

Gaylin, W. (1974), 'Harvesting the Dead', *Harper's Magazine*, September, 23–30.

Geller, S. A. (1983), 'Autopsy', *Scientific American*, 248, 124–36.

George, R. P. (2001), *The Clash of Orthodoxies: Law, Religion and Morality in Crisis* (Wilmington, DE: ISI Books).

George, R. P. and Tollefsen, C. (2008), *A Defense of Human Life* (New York: Doubleday).

Gerrand, N. (1994), 'The Notion of Gift-Giving and Organ Donation', *Bioethics*, 8, 127–50.

Gerszten, P. C. and Gerszten, E. (1995), 'Intentional Cranial Deformation: A Disappearing Form of Self-Mutilation', *Neurosurgery*, 37, 374–81.

Giacino, J. T., Hirsch, J., Schiff, N. and Laureys, S. (2006), 'Functional Neuroimaging Applications for Assessment and Rehabilitation Planning in Patients with Disorders of Consciousness', *Archives of Physical Medicine and Rehabilitation*, 87, S67–76.

Giacino, J. T. and Whyte, J. (2005), 'The Vegetative and Minimally Conscious States: Current Knowledge and Remaining Questions', *Journal of Head Trauma Rehabilitation*, 20, 30–50.

Giess, R. and Schlote, W. (1995), 'Localisation and Association of Pathomorphological Changes at the Brainstem in Alzheimer's Disease', *Mechanisms of Ageing and Development*, 84, 209–26.

Gilbert, R. (1964), 'Transplant Is Successful with a Cadaver Forearm', *Medical Tribune and Medical News*, 5, 20.

Giles, J. (2006), 'Aboriginal Remains Head for Home', *Nature*, 444, 411.

Gillam, L. (1989), 'Fetal Tissue Transplantation: A Philosophical Approach', in L. Gillam (ed.), *Proceedings of the Conference: The Fetus as Tissue Donor: Use or Abuse?* (Melbourne: Monash University Press), 60–9.

— (1992), 'Ethical Issues in Transplantation', *Bioethics News*, 11, 28–39.

— (1998), 'The 'More-Abortions' Objection to Fetal Tissue Transplantation.' *Journal of Medicine and Philosophy*, 23, 411–27.

Gillett, G. R. (2004), *Hippocratic Reflections: Bioethics in the Clinic* (Baltimore: The Johns Hopkins University Press).

Gillies, H. D. and Millard, D. R., Jr. (1957), *The Principles and Art of Plastic Surgery* (Boston: Little, Brown & Co.).

Gillies, K. and O'Regan, G. (1994), 'Murihiku Resolution of Koiwi Tangata Management', *New Zealand Museum Journal*, 24, 30–31.

Gillon, R. (1995), 'On Giving Preference to Prior Volunteers When Allocating Organs for Transplantation', *Journal of Medical Ethics*, 21, 195–6.

Gilman, S. L. (1998), *Creating Beauty to Cure the Soul* (Durham: Duke University Press).

— (1999), *Making the Body Beautiful: A Cultural History of Aesthetic Surgery* (Princeton: Princeton University Press).

Ginifer, C. and Kelly, A. M. (1996), 'Teaching Resuscitation Skills Using the Newly Deceased', *Medical Journal of Australia*, 165, 445–7.

Glannon, W. (2006), 'Psychopharmacology and Memory', *Journal of Medical Ethics*, 32, 74–8.

— (2008), 'Neurostimulation and the Minimally Conscious State', *Bioethics*, 22, 337–45.

Glover, J. (1977), *Causing Death and Saving Lives* (London: Penguin).

Goetz, C. G., Poewe, W., Rascol, O. and Sampaio, C. (2005), 'Evidence-Based Medical Review Update: Pharmacological and Surgical Treatments of Parkinson's Disease: 2001 to 2004', *Movement Disorders*, 20, 523–39.

Goldstein, L. and Kintigh, K. (1990), 'Ethics and the Reburial Controversy', *American Antiquity*, 55, 585–91.

Goodwin, M. (2006), *Black Markets: The Supply and Demand of Body Parts* (New York: Cambridge University Press).

Goren, B., Kahveci, N., Eyigor, O., Alkan, T., Korfali, E. and Ozluk, K. (2005), 'Effects of Intranigral vs Intrastriatal Fetal Mesencephalic Neural Grafts on Motor Behavior Disorders in a Rat Parkinson Model', *Surgical Neurology*, 64 Suppl 2, S33–41.

Gorman, C. (1991), 'Matchmaker, Find Me a Match', *Time* (17 Jun), 42–3.

Gottmann Kulik, E. (2004), 'The Gift of Tissue: A Donor Mom's Perspective', in S. J. Youngner, M. W. Anserson and R. Schapiro (eds), *Transplanting Human Tissue: Ethics, Policy, and Practice* (New York: Oxford University Press), 91–8.

Gough, A. (1996), 'The New Official Religion and the Retreat of Western Science', *Archeology in New Zealand*, 39, 131–8.

Graham, D. I., Maxwell, W. L., Adams, J. H. and Jennett, B. (2005a), 'Novel Aspects of the Neuropathology of the Vegetative State after Blunt Head Injury', *Progress in Brain Research*, 150, 445–55.

Graham, D. I., Adams, J. H., Murray, L. S. and Jennett, B. (2005b), 'Neuropathology of the Vegetative State after Head Injury', *Neuropsychological Rehabilitation*, 15, 198–213.

Greely, H. T. (ed.) (2006), 'The Social Effects of Advances in Neuroscience: Legal Problems, Legal Perspectives' in J. Illes (ed.), *Neuroethics: Defining the Issues in Theory, Practice and Policy* (New York: Oxford University Press).

Green, R. M. (ed.) (2006), 'From Genome to Brainome: Charting the Lessons Learned' in J. Illes (ed.), *Neuroethics: Defining the Issues in Theory, Practice and Policy* (New York: Oxford University Press).

Greenberg, D. L. (2007), 'Comment On "Detecting Awareness in the Vegetative State"', *Science*, 315, 1221.

Greene, V. W. (1992), 'Can Scientists Use Information Derived from the Concentration Camps?' in A. L. Caplan (ed.), *When Medicine Went Mad* (New Jersey: Humana Press), 155–70.

Grodin, M. A. and Annas, G. J. (1996), 'Legacies of Nuremberg: Medical Ethics and Human Rights', *Journal of the American Medical Association*, 276, 1682–3.

Grose, T. O. (1996), 'Reading the Bones: Information Content, Value, and Ownership Issues Raised by the Native American Graves Protection and Repatriation Act', *Journal of the American Society for Information Science*, 47, 624–31.

Groth, C. G., Korsgren, O., Wennberg, L., Song, Z., Wu, G., Reinholt, F. and Tibell, A. (1998), 'Pig-to-Human Islet Transplantation', *Transplantation Proceedings*, 30.

Grumbach, M. M. (1988), 'Growth Hormone Therapy and the Short End of the Stick', *New England Journal of Medicine*, 319, 238–41.

Gundersen, H. J. (1986), 'Stereology of Arbitrary Particles. A Review of Unbiased Number and Size Estimators and the Presentation of Some New Ones, in Memory of William R. Thompson', *Journal of Microscopy*, 143, 3–45.

Günzburg, W. H. and Salmons, B. (2000), 'Xenotransplantation: Is the Risk of Viral Infection as Great as We Thought?' *Molecular Medicine Today*, 6, 199–208.

Gusnard, D. A., Ollinger, J. M., Shulman, G. L., Cloninger, C. R., Price, J. L., Van Essen, D. C. and Raichle, M. E. (2003), 'Persistence and Brain Circuitry', *Proceedings of the National Academy of Sciences of the United States of America*, 100, 3479–84.

Guterman, L. (2003), 'Crossing the Line? Medical Research on Brain-Dead People Raises Ethical Questions', *The Chronicle of Higher Education*, 49, A13–15.

Hafferty, F. W. (1991), *Into the Valley: Death and the Socialization of Medical Students* (New Haven: Yale University Press).

Hagelberg, E. (1990), 'Bones, Dry Bones', *The Times Higher Education Supplement*, 14 Dec.

— (1998), 'The DNA Detective', *The Times Higher Education Supplement*, 23 Oct, p. 17.

Hagell, P. and Brundin, P. (2001), 'Cell Survival and Clinical Outcome Following Intrastriatal Transplantation in Parkinson Disease', *Journal of Neuropathology and Experimental Neurology*, 60, 741–52.

Hakimi, P., Yang, J., Casadesus, G., Massillon, D., Tolentino-Silva, F., Nye, C. K., Cabrera, M. E., Hagen, D. R., Utter, C. B., Baghdy, Y., Johnson, D. H., Wilson, D. L., Kirwan, J. P., Kalhan, S. C. and Hanson, R. W. (2007), 'Over-Expression of the Cytosolic Form of Phosphoenolpyruvate Carboxykinase (GTP) in Skeletal Muscle Repatterns Energy Metabolism in the Mouse', *Journal of Biological Chemistry*, 282, 32844–55.

Halevy, A. and Brody, B. (1993), 'Brain Death: Reconciling Definitions, Criteria and Tests', *Annals of Internal Medicine*, 119, 519–25.

Hall, J. (2003), 'Former Crematorium Owner Pleads Guilty', *North County Times*, 19 Jul.

Halperin, E. C. (2007), 'The Poor, the Black, and the Marginalized as the Source of Cadavers in United States Anatomical Education', *Clinical Anatomy*, 20, 489–95.

Hand, M. T. and Chapman, F. B. (1980), 'Death with Dignity and the Terminally Ill: The Need for Legislative Action – Satz v. Perlmutter', *Nova Law Journal*, 4, 257–69.

Hansson, M. G., Dillner, J., Bartram, C. R., Carlson, J. A. and Helgesson, G. (2006), 'Should Donors Be Allowed to Give Broad Consent for Future Biobank Research?' *Lancet Oncology*, 7.

Harbaugh, W. T., Mayr, U. and Burghart, D. R. (2007), 'Neural Responses to Taxation and Voluntary Giving Reveal Motives for Charitable Donations', *Science*, 316, 1622–5.

Hardy, J. (2004), 'Toward Alzheimer Therapies Based on Genetic Knowledge', *Annual Review of Medicine*, 55, 15–25.

Harris, J. (2007), *Enhancing Evolution: The Ethical Case for Making Better People* (Princeton, NJ: Princeton University Press).

Harrison, M. R. (1986a), 'Organ Procurement for Children: The Anencephalic Fetus as Donor', *Lancet*, 2, 1383–6.

— (1986b), 'The Anencephalic Newborn as Organ Donor', *Hastings Center Report*, 16, 21–3.

Hartgens, F. and Kuipers, H. (2004), 'Effects of Androgenic-Anabolic Steroids in Athletes', *Sports Medicine*, 34, 513–54.

Harvey, J. C. (2006), 'The Burdens-Benefits Ratio Consideration for Medical Administration of Nutrition and Hydration to Persons in the Persistent Vegetative State', *Christian Bioethics*, 12, 99–106.

Hassold, T. and Hunt, P. (2001), 'To Err (Meiotically) Is Human: The Genesis of Human Aneuploidy', *Nature Reviews Genetics*, 2, 280–91.

Haupt, W. F. and Rudolf, J. (1999), 'European Brain Death Codes: A Comparison of National Guidelines', *Journal of Neurology*, 246, 432–7.

Hauser, R. A., Freeman, T. B., Snow, B. J., Nauert, M., Gauger, L., Kordower, J. H. and Olanow, C. W. (1999), 'Long-Term Evaluation of Bilateral Fetal Nigral Transplantation in Parkinson Disease', *Archives of Neurology*, 56, 179–87.

Hauskeller, M. (2006), 'Moral Disgust', *Ethical Perspectives* 13, 571–602.

Hayda, R., Harris, R. M. and Bass, C. D. (2004), 'Blast Injury Research: Modelling Injury Effects of Landmines, Bullets, and Bombs', *Clinical Orthopaedics and Related Research*, 422, 97–108.

Haynes, J. D. and Rees, G. (2006), 'Decoding Mental States from Brain Activity in Humans', *Nature Reviews Neuroscience*, 7, 523–34.

Häyry, H. and Häyry, M. (1991), 'The Bizarre Case of the Human Earrings', *Bioethics News*, 10, 23–4.

Hebert, L. E., Scherr, P. A., Bienias, J. L., Bennett, D. A. and Evans, D. A. (2003), 'Alzheimer Disease in the US Population: Prevalence Estimates Using the 2000 Census', *Archives of Neurology*, 60, 1119–22.

Heisel, W., Katches, M. and Kowalczyk, L. (2000), 'The Body Brokers – Part 2: Skin Merchants', *Orange County Register*, 17 Apr.

Henry, M., Fishman, J. R. and Youngner, S. J. (2007), 'Propranolol and the Prevention of Post-Traumatic Stress Disorder: Is It Wrong to Erase The "Sting" Of Bad Memories?' *American Journal of Bioethics*, 7, 12–20.

Higashi, K., Hatano, M., Abiko, S., Ihara, K., Katayama, S., Wakuta, Y., Okamura, T. and Yamashita, T. (1981), 'Five-Year Follow-up Study of Patients with Persistent Vegetative State', *Journal of Neurology, Neurosurgery, and Psychiatry*, 44, 552–4.

Hildebrandt, S. (2006), 'How the Pernkopf Controversy Facilitated a Historical and Ethical Analysis of the Anatomical Sciences in Austria and Germany: A Recommendation for the Continued Use of the Pernkopf Atlas', *Clinical Anatomy*, 19, 91–100.

— (2008), 'Capital Punishment and Anatomy: History and Ethics of an Ongoing Association', *Clinical Anatomy*, 21, 5–14.

Hirsch, J. (ed.) (2005), 'Functional Neuroimaging During Altered States of Consciousness: How and What Do We Measure?' in S. Laureys (ed.), *The Boundaries of Consciousness: Neurobiology and Neuropathology* (Amsterdam: Elsevier).

Hitchcock, E. R., Clough, C. G., Hughes, R. C. and Kenny, B. G. (1988), 'Transplantation in Parkinson's Disease: Stereotactic Implantation of Adrenal Medulla and Foetal Mesencephalon', *Acta Neurochirurgica. Supplementum*, 46, 48–50.

Hogan, A. (1995), 'Museum Acquisition and Maori Taonga', *Archaeology in New Zealand*, 38, 271–9.

Holden, C. (2007), 'Stem Cells. Stem Cell Candidates Proliferate', *Science*, 315, 761.

Holden, C. and Vogel, G. (2004), 'Cell Biology. A Technical Fix for an Ethical Bind?' *Science*, 306, 2174–6.

Hole, B. (2007), 'Playthings for the Foe: The Repatriation of Human Remains in New Zealand', *Public Archaeology*, 6, 5–27.

Holm, S. (2003), 'The Case against Stem Cell Research', *Cambridge Quarterly of Healthcare Ethics*, 12, 372–83.

Houssin, D. (2003), 'Possible Solutions to the Natural Limitations of Organ Transplantation: What Is at Stake in the Information of the Public and Education?' *Transplantation Proceedings*, 35, 1156–8.

Hubbard, G., Cook, A., Tester, S. and Downs, M. (2002), 'Beyond Words; Older People with Dementia Using and Interpreting Nonverbal Behaviour', *Journal of Aging Studies*, 16, 155–67.

Hughes, D. (2004), 'Accelerating Factors in Age-Related Atrophy', *Neurology Reviews*, 9.

Hughes, J. (1998), 'Xenografting: Ethical Issues', *Journal of Medical Ethics*, 24, 18–24.

— (2007), 'The Ethics of Xenotransplantation' in R. E. Ashcroft, A. Dawson, H. Draper and J. R. McMillan (eds), *Principles of Health Care Ethics* (2nd edn; Chichester: John Wiley and Sons).

Hui, E. C. (2002), *At the Beginning of Life: Dilemmas in Theological Ethics* (Downers Grove, IL: InterVarsity Press).

Hunt, E. (1995), 'The Role of Intelligence in Modern Society: Are Social Changes Dividing Us into Intellectual Haves and Have-Nots?' *American Scientist*, 83, 356–68.

Hunter, P. (2007), 'Dig This. Biomolecular Archaeology Provides New Insights into Past Civilizations, Cultures and Practices', *EMBO Reports*, 8, 215–7.

Hunter, R. H. (1931), *A Short History of Anatomy* (London: John Bale and Sons).

Hurlbut, W. B. (2004), 'Altered Nuclear Transfer as a Morally Acceptable Means for the Procurement of Human Embryonic Stem Cells' [Working Paper], <http://www.bioethics.gov/background/hurlbut.html>, accessed 19 Jun 2007.

Hurlbut, W. B., George, R. P. and Grompe, M. (2006), 'Seeking Consensus: A Clarification and Defense of Altered Nuclear Transfer', *Hastings Center Report*, 36, 42–50.

Illes, J. and Racine, E. (2005), 'Imaging or Imagining? A Neuroethics Challenge Informed by Genetics', *American Journal of Bioethics*, 5, 5–18.

Illes, J., Rosen, A., Greicius, M. and Racine, E. (2007), 'Prospects for Prediction: Ethics Analysis of Neuroimaging in Alzheimer's Disease', *Annals of the New York Academy of Sciences*, 1097, 278–95.

Illes, J., Racine, E. and Kirschen, M. P. (eds) (2006), 'A Picture Is Worth a 1000 Words, but Which 1000?' in J. Illes (ed.), *Neuroethics: Defining the Issues in Theory, Practice and Policy* (New York: Oxford University Press).

Immortality Institute (2004), *The Scientific Conquest of Death. Essays on Infinite Lifespans* (Buenos Aires: LibrosEnRed).

Institute for Plastination (2006a), 'Preservation and Anatomy – Traditions and the Future', <www.bodyworlds.com/en/bodydonation/preservation.html>, accessed 12 Oct 2007.

— (2006b), 'The Horse and Rider at Gunther Von Hagens' Body Worlds 3 the Anatomical Exhibition of Real Human Bodies at the Houston Museum of Natural Science', <http://www.hmns.org/files/marketing/BW3TheHorseandRider. pdf>, accessed 12 Oct 2007.

— (2006c), 'The Anatomist's Hat', <http://www.koerperwelten.de/en/gunther_ von_hagens/hat.html>, accessed 15 Dec 2006.

— (2006d), 'Anatomist, Gunther Von Hagens Named a Modern-Day Leonardo Da Vinci' [Press Release] <www.koerperwelten.de/Downloads/Modern_ Leonardo_240506.pdf>, accessed 12 Oct 2007.

Institute of Medical Ethics Bulletin (1989), 'Contemporary Lessons from Nazi Medicine', *Institute of Medical Ethics Bulletin*, 47, 13–20.

International Stem Cell Forum Ethics Working Party (2006), 'Ethics Issues in Stem Cell Research', *Science*, 312, 366–7.

Isacson, O. and Deacon, T. (1997), 'Neural Transplantation Studies Reveal the Brain's Capacity for Continuous Reconstruction', *Trends in Neurosciences*, 20, 477–82.

Isacson, O. and Breakefield, X. O. (1997), 'Benefits and Risks of Hosting Animal Cells in the Human Brain', *Nature Medicine*, 3, 964–8.

Isacson, O., Pakzaban, P. and Galpern, W. G. (1998), 'Transplanting Fetal Neural Xenogenic Cells in Parkinson's and Huntington's Disease Models' in T. Freeman and H. Widner (eds), *Cell Transplantation for Neurological Disorders: Toward Reconstruction of the Human Central Nervous System* (Totowa, NJ: Humana Press), 189–210.

Isenmann, S., Brandner, S. and Aguzzi, A. (1996), 'Neuroectodermal Grafting: A New Tool for the Study of Neurodegenerative Diseases', *Histology and Histopathology*, 11, 1063–73.

Iserson, K. V. (1993), 'Postmortem Procedures in the Emergency Department: Using the Recently Dead to Practise and Teach', *Journal of Medical Ethics*, 19, 92–8.

— (1994), *Death to Dust: What Happens to Dead Bodies?* (Tucson, AZ: Galen Press).

— (2005), 'Teaching without Harming the Living: Performing Minimally Invasive Procedures on the Newly Dead', *Journal of Health Care Law & Policy*, 8, 216–31.

Israel, H. and Seidelman, W. (1996), 'Nazi Origins of an Anatomy Text: The Pernkopf Atlas', *Journal of the American Medical Association*, 276, 1633.

Jaul, E. and Calderon-Margalit, R. (2007), 'Persistent Vegetative State and Dementia in the Elderly', *International Psychogeriatrics*, 19, 1064–71.

Jennett, B. (2001), 'Brain Death and the Vegetative State', *Encyclopedia of Life Sciences* (updated 19 Apr 2001) <http://mrw.interscience.wiley.com/ emrw/9780470015902/els/article/a0002212/current/abstract>, accessed 4 Jul 2008.

— (ed.) (2005), 'Thirty Years of the Vegetative State: Clinical, Ethical and Legal Problems' in S. Laureys (ed.), *The Boundaries of Consciousness: Neurobiology and Neuropathology* (Oxford: Elsevier).

Jiang, N., Jiang, C. and Tang, Z. (1987), 'Human Foetal Brain Transplant Trials in the Treatment of Parkinsonism', *Acta Academiae Medicinae Shanghai*, 14, 1.

John Paul II (1995), *Gospel of Life* (Homebush, Australia: St Paul's).

Johnson, H. R. M. (1969), 'The Incidence of Unnatural Deaths Which Have Been Presumed to Be Natural in Coroners' Autopsies', *Medical Science and Law*, 9, 102–6.

Johnson, J., Bagley, J., Skaznik-Wikiel, M., Lee, H. J., Adams, G. B., Niikura, Y., Tschudy, K. S., Tilly, J. C., Cortes, M. L., Forkert, R., Spitzer, T., Iacomini, J., Scadden, D. T. and Tilly, J. L. (2005), 'Oocyte Generation in Adult Mammalian Ovaries by Putative Germ Cells in Bone Marrow and Peripheral Blood', *Cell*, 122, 303–15.

Johnstone, M.-J. (1989), *Bioethics: A Nursing Perspective* (London: W. B. Saunders).

Jonas, H. (1974), 'Against the Stream: Comments on the Definition and Redefinition of Death' in H. Jonas (ed.), *Philosophical Essays: From Ancient Creed to Technological Man* (Engelwood Cliffs, NJ: Prentice Hall).

Jones, D. G. (1987), *Manufacturing Humans: The Challenge of the New Reproductive Technologies* (Leicester, England: Inter-Varsity Press).

— (1989a), *Brain Grafts: Parkinson's Disease, Fetuses and Ethics* (Nottingham: Grove Books).

— (1989b), 'The New Zealand "Report of the Cervical Cancer Inquiry": Significance for Medical Education', *Medical Journal of Australia*, 151, 450–6.

— (1990), 'Contemporary Medical Scandals: A Challenge to Ethical Codes and Ethical Principles', *Perspectives on Science and Christian Faith*, 42, 2–14.

— (1991), 'Fetal Neural Transplantation: Placing the Ethical Debate within the Context of Society's Use of Human Material', *Bioethics*, 5, 23–43.

— (1994), 'Use of Bequeathed and Unclaimed Bodies in the Dissecting Room', *Clinical Anatomy*, 7, 102–7.

— (1998), 'The Problematic Symmetry between Brain Birth and Brain Death', *Journal of Medical Ethics*, 24, 237–42.

— (2002a), 'Re-Inventing Anatomy: The Impact of Plastination on How We See the Human Body', *Clinical Anatomy*, 15, 436–40.

— (2002b), 'The Use of Human Tissue: An Insider's View', *New Zealand Bioethics Journal*, June, 8–12.

— (2005a), 'Responses to the Human Embryo and Embryonic Stem Cells: Scientific and Theological Assessments', *Science & Christian Belief*, 17, 199–221.

— (2005b), *Designers of the Future* (Oxford: Monarch).

— (2006), 'Enhancement: Are Ethicists Excessively Influenced by Baseless Speculations?', *Medical Humanities*, 32, 77–81.

— (2007a), *Bioethics* (Hindmarsh, South Australia: ATF Press).

— (2007b), 'Anatomical Investigations and Their Ethical Dilemmas', *Clinical Anatomy*, 20, 338–43.

— (2008), 'Neuroethics: Adrift from a Clinical Base', *American Journal of Bioethics*, 8, 49–50.

Jones, D. G. and Fennell, S. (1991), 'Bequests, Cadavers and Dissections: Sketches from New Zealand History', *New Zealand Medical Journal*, 104, 210–12.

Jones, D. G. and Galvin, K. A. (2002), 'Retention of Body Parts: Reflections from Anatomy', *New Zealand Medical Journal*, 115, 267–9.

Jones, D. G. and Galvin, K. A. (2006), 'Neural Grafting in Parkinson's Disease: Scientific and Ethical Pitfalls on the Road from Basic Science to Clinical Reality', *Research Communications in Biology, Psychiatry and Neuroscience*, 30–31, 75–101.

Jones, D. G., Gear, R. and Galvin, K. A. (2003), 'Stored Human Tissue: An Ethical Perspective on the Fate of Anonymous, Archival Material', *Journal of Medical Ethics*, 29, 343–7.

Jones, D. G. and Harris, R. J. (1998), 'Archeological Human Remains: Scientific, Cultural and Ethical Considerations', *Current Anthropology*, 39, 253–64.

Jones, D. G. and Towns, C. R. (2006), 'Navigating the Quagmire: The Regulation of Human Embryonic Stem Cell Research', *Human Reproduction*, 21, 1113–6.

Jones, D. G. and Whitaker, M. I. (2007), 'The Tenuous World of Plastinates', *American Journal of Bioethics*, 7, 27–9.

— (2008), '*In Vitro* Fertilization and the Embryonic Revolution' in R. Luppicini and R. Adell (eds), *Handbook of Research on Technoethics* (London: Information Science Reference), 609–22.

Jones, J. H. (1981), *Bad Blood: The Tuskegee Syphilis Experiment* (New York: Free Press).

Jones, R. L. (2007), *Humanity's Mirror: 150 Years of Anatomy in Melbourne* (Victoria, Australia: Haddington Press).

Juengst, E. (1998), 'What Does Enhancement Mean?' in E. Parens (ed.), *Enhancing Human Traits: Ethical and Social Implications* (Washington, DC: Georgetown University Press), 29–47.

Junker-Kenny, M. (2006), 'Genetic Perfection, or Fulfilment of Creation in Christ?' in C. Deane-Drummond and P. Scott (eds), *Future Perfect? God, Medicine and Human Identity* (London: T&T Clark), 155–67.

Jussila, J. (2004), 'Preparing Ballistic Gelatine – Review and Proposal for a Standard Method', *Forensic Science International*, 141, 91–8.

Kadish, S. H. (1992), 'Letting Patients Die: Legal and Moral Reflections', *California Law Review*, 80, 857–88.

Kaiser, J. (2002), 'Population Databases Boom, from Iceland to the U.S.' *Science*, 298, 1158–61.

Kalia, M. (2003), 'Dysphagia and Aspiration Pneumonia in Patients with Alzheimer's Disease', *Metabolism*, 52, 36–8.

Kanelos, S. K. and McDeavitt, J. T. (1998), 'Neural Transplantation: Potential Role in Traumatic Brain Injury', *Journal of Head Trauma Rehabilitation*, 13, 1–9.

Kanitakis, J., Jullien, D., Petruzzo, P., Hakim, N., Claudy, A., Revillard, J. P., Owen, E. and Dubernard, J. M. (2003), 'Clinicopathologic Features of Graft Rejection of the First Human Hand Allograft', *Transplantation*, 76, 688–93.

Karpowicz, P. (2003), 'In Defense of Stem Cell Chimeras: A Response to "Crossing Species Boundaries"', *American Journal of Bioethics*, 3, 17–9.

Kass, L. R. (1971), 'Babies by Means of *In Vitro* Fertilization: Unethical Experiments on the Unborn?', *New England Journal of Medicine*, 285, 1174–9.

— (1985), 'Thinking About the Body', *Hastings Center Report*, 15, 20–30.

— (1997), 'The Wisdom of Repugnance', *The New Republic*, 216, 17–26.

— (2001), 'L'chaim and Its Limits: Why Not Immortality?' *First Things*, 113, 17–24.

Katches, M., Heisel, W. and Campbell, R. (2000), 'The Body Brokers: Part 1 – Assembly Line. Donors Don't Realize They Are Fuelling a Lucrative Business', *Orange County Register*, 16 Apr.

Katz, J. (1972), *Experimentation with Human Beings: The Authority of the Investigator, Subject, Professions, and State in the Human Experimentation Process* (New York: Russell Sage).

Katz, J. and Pozos, R. S. (1992), 'The Dachau Hypothermia Study: An Ethical and Scientific Commentary' in A. L. Caplan (ed.), *When Medicine Went Mad: Bioethics and the Holocaust* (New Jersey: Humana Press), 135–9.

Kaye, J. (2006), 'Do We Need a Uniform Regulatory System for Biobanks across Europe?' *European Journal of Human Genetics*, 14, 245–8.

Keene, C. D., Sonnen, J. A., Swanson, P. D., Kopyov, O., Leverenz, J. B., Bird, T. D. and Montine, T. J. (2007), 'Neural Transplantation in Huntington Disease: Long-Term Grafts in Two Patients', *Neurology*, 68, 2093–8.

Kemp, M. (2000), *Visualizations: The Nature Book of Art and Science* (Oxford: Oxford University Press).

Kennedy, I. (1988), *Treat Me Right* (Oxford: Clarendon Press).

Keyser-Tracqui, C. and Ludes, B. (2005), 'Methods for the Study of Ancient DNA', *Methods in Molecular Biology*, 297, 253–64.

Khachaturian, Z. (1992), 'The Five-Five, Ten-Ten Plan for Alzheimer's Disease', *Neurobiology of Aging*, 13, 197–8; discussion 9.

Khoshbin, L. S. and Khoshbin, S. (2007), 'Imaging the Mind, Minding the Image: An Historical Introduction to Brain Imaging and the Law', *American Journal of Law & Medicine*, 33, 171–92.

King, A. I., Viano, D. C., Mizeres, N. and States, J. D. (1995), 'Humanitarian Benefits of Cadaver Research on Injury Prevention', *Journal of Trauma*, 38, 564–9.

Kitwood, T. (1990), 'The Dialectics of Dementia: With Particular Reference to Alzheimer's Disease', *Ageing and Society*, 10, 177–96.

Kitwood, T. and Benson, S. (1995), *The New Culture of Dementia Care* (London: Hawker).

Kleinman, I. and Lowy, F. H. (1993), 'Ethical Considerations in Living Donation and a New Approach: An Advance-Directive Organ Registry', *Bioethics News*, 12, 16–24.

Klesert, A. L. and Powell, S. (1993), 'A Perspective on Ethics and the Reburial Controversy', *American Antiquity*, 58, 348–54.

Klimanskaya, I., Chung, Y., Becker, S., Lu, S.-J. and Lanza, R. (2006), 'Human Embryonic Stem Cell Lines Derived from Single Blastomeres', *Nature*, 444, 481–5.

Koch, E. and Sillen, A. (1996), 'Rights of Passage', *New Scientist*, 30–33.

Kohn, M. (2006), 'Grateful Dead', *New Statesman* (updated 6 Nov 2006) <http://www.newstatesman.com/200611060020>, accessed 8 May 2008.

Kontos, P. C. (2003), '"The Painterly Hand": Embodied Consciousness and Alzheimer's Disease', *Journal of Aging Studies*, 17, 151–70.

— (2005), 'Embodied Selfhood in Alzheimer's Disease', *Dementia*, 4, 553–70.

Kordower, J. H., Chu, Y., Hauser, R. A., Freeman, T. B. and Olanow, C. W. (2008), 'Lewy Body-Like Pathology in Long-Term Embryonic Nigral Transplants in Parkinson's Disease', *Nature Medicine*, 14, 504–6.

Kordower, J. H., Freeman, T. B., Chen, E. Y., Mufson, E. J., Sanberg, P. R., Hauser, R. A., Snow, B. and Olanow, C. W. (1998), 'Fetal Nigral Grafts Survive and Mediate Clinical Benefit in a Patient with Parkinson's Disease', *Movement Disorders*, 13, 383–93.

Kramer, P. D. (1993), *Listening to Prozac* (New York: Viking).

Kuliev, A. and Verlinsky, Y. (2005), 'Place of Preimplantation Diagnosis in Genetic Practice', *Journal of Medical Genetics*, 134A, 105–10.

Kuppers, P. (2004), 'Vision of Anatomy: Exhibitions and Dense Bodies', *Journal of Feminist Cultural Studies*, 15, 123–56.

Kuriyama, S. (1992), 'Between the Mind and Eye: Japanese Anatomy in the Eighteenth Century' in C. Leslie and A. Young (eds), *Paths to Asian Medical Knowledge* (Oxford: University of California Press), 21–43.

Kushner, T. and Belliotti, R. (1985), 'Baby Fae: A Beastly Business', *Journal of Medical Ethics*, 11, 178–83.

Labuschagne, B. C. and Mathey, B. (2000), 'Cadaver Profile at University of Stellenbosch Medical School, South Africa, 1956–1996', *Clinical Anatomy*, 13, 88–93.

Lachman, E. (1977), 'Anatomist of Infamy: August Hirt', *Bulletin of the History of Medicine*, 51, 594–602.

Lamb, D. (1985), *Death, Brain Death and Ethics* (London: Croom Helm).

Lancet (1832), 'Editorial', *Lancet*, 17, 243–5.

Lancet (2006), 'Striking the Right Balance between Privacy and Public Good' (editorial, 28 Jan), *Lancet*, 367, 275.

Langleben, D. D., Loughead, J. W., Bilker, W. B., Ruparel, K., Childress, A. R., Busch, S. I. and Gur, R. C. (2005), 'Telling Truth from Lie in Individual Subjects with Fast Event-Related fMRI', *Human Brain Mapping*, 26, 262–72.

Lanzetta, M., Petruzzo, P., Vitale, G., Lucchina, S., Owen, E. R., Dubernard, J. M., Hakim, N. and Kapila, H. (2004), 'Human Hand Transplantation: What Have We Learned?' *Transplantation Proceedings*, 36, 664–8.

Larriviere, D. and Bonnie, R. J. (2006), 'Terminating Artificial Nutrition and Hydration in Persistent Vegetative State Patients: Current and Proposed State Laws', *Neurology*, 66, 1624–8.

Lassek, A. M. (1958), *Human Dissection: Its Drama and Struggle* (Springfield, IL: Charles C. Thomas).

Latorre, R. M., Garcia-Sanz, M. P., Moreno, M., Hernandez, F., Gil, F., Lopez, O., Ayala, M. D., Ramirez, G., Vazquez, J. M., Arencibia, A. and Henry, R. W. (2007), 'How Useful Is Plastination in Learning Anatomy?', *Journal of Veterinary Medical Education*, 34, 172–6.

Laureys, S., Fayomonville, M. E., Luxen, A., Lamy, M., Franck, G. and Maquet, P. (2000), 'Restoration of Thalamocortical Connectivity after Recovery from Persistent Vegetative State', *Lancet*, 355, 1790–1.

Laureys, S., Giacino, J. T., Schiff, N. D., Schabus, M. and Owen, A. M. (2006), 'How Should Functional Imaging of Patients with Disorders of Consciousness Contribute to Their Clinical Rehabilitation Needs?', *Current Opinion in Neurology*, 19, 520–7.

Laureys, S., Lemaire, C., Maquet, P., Phillips, C. and Franck, G. (1999), 'Cerebral Metabolism During Vegetative State and after Recovery to Consciousness', *Journal of Neurology, Neurosurgery, and Psychiatry*, 67, 121.

Laureys, S., Owen, A. M. and Schiff, N. D. (2004), 'Brain Function in Coma, Vegetative State, and Related Disorders', *Lancet Neurology*, 3, 537–46.

Lawrence, A. A. (2006), 'Clinical and Theoretical Parallels between Desire for Limb Amputation and Gender Identity Disorder', *Archives of Sexual Behavior*, 35, 263–78.

Lee, S., Barton, E. R., Sweeney, H. L. and Farrar, R. P. (2004), 'Viral Expression of Insulin-Like Growth Factor-I Enhances Muscle Hypertrophy in Resistance-Trained Rats', *Journal of Applied Physiology*, 96, 1097–104.

Lemonick, M. D. (1996), 'Bones of Contention: Scientists and Native Americans Clash over a 9,300-Year-Old Man with Caucasoid Features', *Time*, 62.

Levy, N. (2007), *Neuroethics: Challenges for the 21st Century* (New York: Cambridge University Press).

Li, J. Y., Englund, E., Holton, J. L., Soulet, D., Hagell, P., Lees, A. J., Lashley, T., Quinn, N. P., Rehncrona, S. and Bjorklund, A. (2008), 'Lewy Bodies in Grafted Neurons in Subjects with Parkinson's Disease Suggest Host-to-Graft Disease Propagation', *Nature Medicine*, 14, 501–3.

Lifton, R. J. (1986), *The Nazi Doctors: Medical Killing and the Psychology of Genocide* (London: Macmillan).

Lin, Z., Chen, J. F., Wang, C. Y. and Jiang, J. M. (1994), 'Effect of Fetal Neural Transplantation on IQ of Patients with CNS Disease' in C. K. Tan and F. C. K. Chen (eds), *Singapore Neuroscience Association: First Asia-Pacific Colloquium in Neuroscience*, 144.

Linazasoro, G. (2006), 'Rate of Progression Determines the Clinical Outcome after Neural Transplantation in Parkinson's Disease', *Brain*, 129, E48; author reply E9.

Lindemann Nelson, H. (1994), 'The Architect and the Bee: Some Reflections on Postmortem Pregnancy', *Bioethics*, 8, 247–67.

Lindley, D. (1989), 'Remains Returned to Tribe', *Nature*, 340, 9.

Lindvall, O. (1997), 'Neural Transplantation: A Hope for Patients with Parkinson's Disease', *Neuroreport*, 8, 3–10.

— (1998), 'Update on Fetal Transplantation: The Swedish Experience', *Movement Disorders*, 1, 83–7.

Lindvall, O. and Bjorklund, A. (2004), 'Cell Therapy in Parkinson's Disease', *NeuroRx*, 1, 382–93.

Lindvall, O., Rehncrona, S., Brundin, P., Gustavii, B., Astedt, B., Widner, H., Lindholm, T., Björklund, A., Leenders, K. L., Rothwell, J. C., Frackowiak, R., Marsden, C. D., Johnels, B., Steg, G., Freedman, R., Hoffer, B. J., Seiger, A., Bygdeman, M., Stromberg, I. and Olson, L. (1989), 'Human Fetal Dopamine Neurons Grafted into the Striatum in Two Patients with Severe Parkinson's Disease: A Detailed Account of Methodology and a 6 Month Follow-Up', *Archives of Neurology*, 46, 615–31.

Linke, U. (2005), 'Touching the Corpse: The Unmaking of Memory in the Body Museum', *Anthropology Today*, 12, 13–19.

Lloyd, G. (1973), *Greek Science after Aristotle* (London: Chatto & Windus).

Lopez-Lozano, J. J., Bravo, G., Brera, B., Millan, I., Dargallo, J., Salmean, J., Uria, J. and Insausti, J. (1997), 'Long-Term Improvement in Patients with Severe Parkinson's Disease after Implantation of Fetal Ventral Mesencephalic Tissue in a Cavity of the Caudate Nucleus: 5-Year Follow up in 10 Patients. Clinica Puerta De Hierro Neural Transplantation Group', *Journal of Neurosurgery*, 86, 931–42.

Lundberg, G. D. (1984), 'Medicine without the Autopsy', *Archives of Pathology and Laboratory Medicine*, 108, 449–54.

Luyendijk-Elshout, A. M. (1970), 'Death Enlightened. A Study of Frederik Ruysch', *Journal of the American Medical Association*, 212, 121–6.

Macartney, J. (2006), 'Face Transplant for Bear Attack Victim', *The Times*, 15 Apr.

Macauley, S. L., Horsch, A. D., Oterdoom, M., Zheng, M. H. and Stewart, G. R. (2004), 'The Effects of Transforming Growth Factor-Beta2 on Dopaminergic Graft Survival', *Cell Transplantation*, 13, 245–52.

MacDonald, H. (2005), *Human Remains: Episodes in Human Dissection* (Carlton: Melbourne University Press).

Macklin, R. (1983), 'Personhood in the Bioethics Literature', *The Milbank Memorial Fund Quarterly. Health and Society*, 61, 35–57.

— (1999), 'The Ethical Problems with Sham Surgery in Clinical Research', *New England Journal of Medicine*, 341, 992–6.

— (2003), 'Dignity Is a Useless Concept', *British Medical Journal*, 327, 1419–20.

Macklon, N., Geraedts, J. and Fauser, B. (2002), 'Conception to Ongoing Pregnancy: The "Black Box" of Early Pregnancy Loss', *Human Reproduction Update*, 8, 333–43.

Maclaine, G. D. H., Macarthur, E. B. and Heathcote, C. R. (1992), 'A Comparison of Death Certificates and Autopsies in the Australian Capital Territory', *Medical Journal of Australia*, 156, 462–8.

Maddox, J. (1992), 'Genetics and the Public Interest', *Nature*, 356, 365–6.

Madrazo, I., Leon, V., Torres, C., Aguilera, M. C., Varela, G., Alvarez, F., Fraga, A., Drucker-Colin, R., Ostrosky, F., Skurovich, M. and Franco, R. (1988), 'Transplantation of Fetal Substantia Nigra and Adrenal Medulla to the Caudate Nucleus in Two Patients with Parkinson's Disease', *New England Journal of Medicine*, 318, 51.

Magee, W. L. (2005), 'Music Therapy with Patients in Low Awareness States: Approaches to Assessment and Treatment in Multidisciplinary Care', *Neuropsychological Rehabilitation*, 15, 522–36.

Magnier, M. and Zarembo, A. (2006), 'China Admits Using Organs from Executed Prisoners', *Los Angeles Times*, 17 Nov.

Maher, B. (2008), 'Poll Results: Look Who's Doping', *Nature*, 452, 674–5.

Mann, R. W., Bass, W. M. and Meadows, L. (1990), 'Time since Death and Decomposition of the Human Body: Variables and Observations in Case and Experimental Field Studies', *Journal of Forensic Sciences*, 35, 103–11.

Manninen, D. L. and Evans, R. W. (1985), 'Public Attitudes and Behavior Regarding Organ Donations', *Journal of the American Medical Association*, 253, 3111–15.

Marchione, M. (2006), 'Recent Body-Parts Scandals Prompt Review', (updated 23 Sep 2006), <http://www.washingtonpost.com/wp-dyn/content/article/2006/09/23/AR2006092300399.html>, accessed 3 Jul 2008.

Markesbery, W. R., Schmitt, F. A., Kryscio, R. J., Davis, D. G., Smith, C. D. and Wekstein, D. R. (2006), 'Neuropathologic Substrate of Mild Cognitive Impairment', *Archives of Neurology*, 63, 38–46.

Marks, J. H. (2007), 'Interrogational Neuroimaging in Counterterrorism: A "No-Brainer" Or a Human Rights Hazard?', *American Journal of Law & Medicine*, 33, 483–500.

Marks, S. C. and Bertman, S. L. (1980), 'Experiences with Learning About Death and Dying in the Undergraduate Anatomy Curriculum', *Journal of Medical Education*, 55, 48–52.

Marks, W. H., Wagner, D., Pearson, T. C., Orlowski, J. P., Nelson, P. W., McGowan, J. J., Guidinger, M. K. and Burdick, J. (2006), 'Organ Donation and

Utilization, 1995–2004: Entering the Collaborative Era', *American Journal of Transplantation*, 6, 1101–10.

Markus, A. (1990), *Governing Savages* (Sydney: Allen and Unwin).

Maslen, G. (1995), 'The Death of Archaeology', *Campus Review*, 7, 31.

Master, Z., McLeod, M. and Mendez, I. (2007), 'Benefits, Risks and Ethical Considerations in Translation of Stem Cell Research to Clinical Applications in Parkinson's Disease', *Journal of Medical Ethics*, 33, 169–73.

Matas, D. and Kilgour, D. (2007), 'Bloody Harvest: Revised Report into Allegations of Organ Harvesting of Falun Gong Practitioners in China', (updated 31 Jan) <http://organharvestinvestigation.net/report0701/report20070131-eng.pdf>, accessed 6 Sept 2007.

Matsuda, W., Matsumura, A., Komatsu, Y., Yanaka, K. and Nose, T. (2003), 'Awakenings from Persistent Vegetative State: Report of Three Cases with Parkinsonism and Brain Stem Lesions on MRI', *Journal of Neurology, Neurosurgery, and Psychiatry*, 74, 1571–3.

Mattern, R., Schueler, F. and Kallieris, D. (2004), 'Traumatology of the Traffic Accident – Dead People for the Safety in Traffic', *Forensic Science International*, 144, 193–200.

Max, B. (1989), 'This and That: The Ethics of Experimentation and the Legitimate Fear of Flying', *Trends in Pharmacological Sciences*, 10, 133–5.

May, J. (2007), 'Aboriginal Bones Coming Home', *Sydney Morning Herald*, May 12.

May, W. F. (1985), 'Religious Justification for Donating Body Parts', *Hastings Center Report*, 15, 38–42.

Mayhew, E. R. (2004), *The Reconstruction of Warriors: Archibald Mcindoe, the Royal Air Force and the Guinea Pig Club* (London: Greenhill Books).

McCall, B. (2006), 'Do You Want to Live to Be 800? This Man Says That You Can', *The Times Higher Education Supplement*, 10 Mar, 20.

McClure, S. M., Li, J., Tomlin, D., Cypert, K. S., Montague, L. M. and Montague, P. R. (2004), 'Neural Correlates of Behavioral Preference for Culturally Familiar Drinks', *Neuron*, 44, 379–87.

McCrummen, S. (2005), 'Brain-Dead Va. Woman Gives Birth; Baby Appears Healthy after 3-Month Ordeal', *Washington Post*, A1, A8.

McCullagh, P. (1993), *Brain Dead, Brain Absent, Brain Donors: Human Subjects or Human Objects?* (Chichester: John Wiley and Sons).

McDougall, E. M. (2007), 'Validation of Surgical Simulators', *Journal of Endourology*, 21, 244–7.

McGarvey, M. A., Farrell, T., Conroy, R. M., Kandiah, S. and Monkhouse, W. S. (2001), 'Dissection: A Positive Experience', *Clinical Anatomy*, 14, 227–30.

McKelvie, P. A. and Rode, J. (1992), 'Autopsy Rate and a Clinicopathological Audit in an Australian Metropolitan Hospital – Cause for Concern?', *Medical Journal of Australia*, 156, 456–62.

McKeown, T., Record, R. G. and Turner, R. D. (1975), 'An Interpretation of the Decline of Mortality in England and Wales During the Twentieth Century', *Population Studies*, 29, 391–422.

McLaren, A. (1986a), 'Prelude to Embryogenesis' in T. C. Foundation (ed.), *Human Embryo Research: Yes or No* (London: Tavistock Publications), 5–23.

— (1986b), 'Embryo Research', *Nature*, 320, 570.

McLean, S. A. (1999), 'Legal and Ethical Aspects of the Vegetative State', *Journal of Clinical Pathology*, 52, 490–493.

McMahan, J. (1995), 'The Metaphysics of Brain Death', *Bioethics*, 9, 91–126.

— (2002), *The Ethics of Killing: Problems at the Margins of Life* (New York: Oxford University Press).

McNeill, P. M. (1993), *The Ethics and Politics of Human Experimentation* (Hong Kong: Cambridge University Press).

Medawar, P. (1957), *Uniqueness of the Individual* (London: Methuen).

Medical Tribune and Medical News (1964), 'Hand Transplanted from Cadaver Is Reamputated', *Medical Tribune and Medical News*, 5, 23.

Meehan, B. (1984), 'Aboriginal Skeletal Remains', *Australian Archeology*, 19, 122–47.

Mehta, M. A., Owen, A. M., Sahakian, B. J., Mavaddat, N., Pickard, J. D. and Robbins, T. W. (2000), 'Methylphenidate Enhances Working Memory by Modulating Discrete Frontal and Parietal Lobe Regions in the Human Brain', *Journal of Neuroscience*, 20, RC65.

Meighan, C. W. (1992), 'Some Scholars' Views on Reburial', *American Antiquity*, 57, 704–10.

— (1993), 'The Burial of American Archeology', *Academic Questions*, 6, 9–19.

Mendez, I., Sanchez-Pernaute, R., Cooper, O., Vinuela, A., Ferrari, D., Bjorklund, L., Dagher, A. and Isacson, O. (2005), 'Cell Type Analysis of Functional Fetal Dopamine Cell Suspension Transplants in the Striatum and Substantia Nigra of Patients with Parkinson's Disease', *Brain*, 128, 1498–510.

Mendez, I., Viñuela, A., Astradsson, A., Mukhida, K., Hallett, P., Robertson, H., Tierney, T., Holness, R., Dagher, A., J.Q., T. and Isacson, O. (2008), 'Dopamine Neurons Implanted into People with Parkinson's Disease Survive without Pathology for 14 Years', *Nature Medicine*, 14, 507–9.

Menzel, P. T. (1991), 'The Moral Duty to Contribute and Its Implications for Organ Procurement Policy', *Transplantation Proceedings*, 2224, 2175–8.

Mepham, T. B., Moore, C. J. and Crilly, R. E. (1997), 'An Ethical Analysis of the Use of Xenografts in Human Transplant Surgery', *Monash Bioethics Review*, 16, 3–9.

Mertes, H., Pennings, G. and Van Steirteghem, A. (2006), 'An Ethical Analysis of Alternative Methods to Obtain Pluripotent Stem Cells without Destroying Embryos', *Human Reproduction*, 21, 2749–55.

Midgely, M. (2000), 'Biotechnology and Monstrosity', *Hastings Center Report*, 30, 7–15.

Mitchell, K. R., Kerridge, I. H. and Lovat, T. J. (1993), 'Medical Futility, Treatment Withdrawal and the Persistent Vegetative State', *Journal of Medical Ethics*, 19, 71–6.

Mitrani, V. B., Lewis, J. E., Feaster, D. J., Czaja, S. J., Eisdorfer, C., Schulz, R. and Szapocznik, J. (2006), 'The Role of Family Functioning in the Stress Process of Dementia Caregivers: A Structural Family Framework.' *Gerontologist*, 46, 97–105.

Mobbs, D., Lau, H. C., Jones, O. D. and Frith, C. D. (2007), 'Law, Responsibility, and the Brain', *PLoS Biology*, 5, e103.

Modi, S., Moore, C. and Shah, K. (2005), 'Which Late-Stage Alzheimer's Patients Should Be Referred for Hospice Care?' *Journal of Family Practice*, 54, 984–6.

Moe, K. (1984), 'Should the Nazi Research Data Be Cited?' *Hastings Center Report*, 14, 5–7.

Moll, J., Krueger, F., Zahn, R., Pardini, M., de Oliveira-Souza, R. and Grafman, J. (2006), 'Human Fronto-Mesolimbic Networks Guide Decisions About Charitable Donation', *Proceedings of the National Academy of Sciences of the United States of America*, 103, 15623–8.

Moll, J., de Oliveira-Souza, R., Moll, F. T., Ignacio, F. A., Bramati, I. E., Caparelli-Daquer, E. M. and Eslinger, P. J. (2005), 'The Moral Affiliations of Disgust: A Functional MRI Study', *Cognitive and Behavioral Neurology*, 18, 68–78.

Mollaret, P. and Goulon, M. (1959), 'Le Coma Dépassé (Mémoire Préliminaire)', *Review of Neurology*, 101, 3–15.

Molner, G. W. (1946), 'Survival of Hypothermia by Men Immersed in the Ocean', *Journal of the American Medical Association*, 131, 1046–50.

Monaghan, D. (1991), 'The Body-Snatchers', *The Bulletin*, 12 Nov, 30–8.

Montgomery, H., Marshall, R., Hemingway, H., Myerson, S., Clarkson, P., Dollery, C., Hayward, M., Holliman, D. E., Jubb, M., World, M., Thomas, E. L., Brynes, A. E., Saeed, N., Barnard, M., Bell, J. D., Prasad, K., Rayson, M., Talmud, P. J. and Humphries, S. E. (1998), 'Human Gene for Physical Performance', *Nature*, 393, 221–2.

Moore, C. M. and Brown, C. M. (2004), 'Gunther Von Hagens and Body Worlds Part 1: The Anatomist as Prosektor and Proplastiker', *Anatomical Record. Part B, New Anatomist*, 276, 8–14.

Moore, W. (2005), *The Knife Man: The Extraordinary Life and Times of John Hunter, Father of Modern Surgery* (London: Bantam Press).

Moreno, J. D. and Lederer, S. E. (1996), 'Revising the History of Cold War Research Ethics', *Kennedy Institute of Ethics Journal*, 6, 223–37.

Morenon, E. P. (2003), 'Nagged by NAGPRA: Is There an Archaeological Ethic?' in C. Fluehr-Lobban (ed.), *Ethics and the Profession of Anthropology, Second Edition* (Walnut Creek, CA: AltaMira Press), 107–40.

Morin, M. (2003), 'Former Autopsy Aide Held after Human Remains Found', *Los Angeles Times*, 20 Jul.

Morris, P., Bradley, A., Doyal, L., Earley, M., Hagen, P., Milling, M. and Rumsey, N. (2007), 'Face Transplantation: A Review of the Technical, Immunological, Psychological and Clinical Issues with Recommendations for Good Practice', *Transplantation*, 83, 109–28.

Müller-Hill, B. (1994), 'Human Genetics in Nazi Germany' in J. J. Michalczyk (ed.), *Medicine, Ethics, and the Third Reich: Historical and Contemporary Issues* (Kansas City: Sheed and Ward), 27–34.

Mulligan, C. J. (2005), 'Isolation and Analysis of DNA from Archaeological, Clinical, and Natural History Specimens', *Methods in Enzymology*, 395, 87–103.

Multi-Society Task Force on the Persistent Vegetative State (1994a), 'Medical Aspects of the Persistent Vegetative State (2)', *New England Journal of Medicine*, 330, 1572–9.

— (1994b), 'Medical Aspects of the Persistent Vegetative State (1)', *New England Journal of Medicine*, 330, 1499–508.

Mulvaney, D. J. (1989), 'Reflections on the Murray Black Collection', *Australian Natural History*, 23, 66–73.

— (1990), 'Bones of Contention', *The Bulletin*, 9 Oct, 104–7.

— (1991), 'Past Regained, Future Lost: The Kow Swamp Pleistocene Burials', *Antiquity*, 65, 12–21.

Murphy, D. and Buchanon, S. F. (1998), 'Community Guidelines for End-of-Life Care: Incremental Change or Significant Reform', *Bioethics Forum: Midwest Bioethics Center*, 14, 19–24.

Murray, J. E. (1992), 'Human Organ Transplantation: Background and Consequences', *Science*, 256, 1411–16.

Murray, T. (1996), 'Coming to Terms with the Living: Some Aspects of Repatriation for the Archaeologist', *Antiquity*, 70, 217–20.

Musaro, A., McCullagh, K., Paul, A., Houghton, L., Dobrowolny, G., Molinaro, M., Barton, E. R., Sweeney, H. L. and Rosenthal, N. (2001), 'Localized IGF-1 Transgene Expression Sustains Hypertrophy and Regeneration in Senescent Skeletal Muscle', *Nature Genetics*, 27, 195–200.

Myerson, S., Hemingway, H., Budget, R., Martin, J., Humphries, S. and Montgomery, H. (1999), 'Human Angiotensin I-Converting Enzyme Gene and Endurance Performance', *Journal of Applied Physiology*, 87, 1313–16.

Nachev, P. and Husain, M. (2007), 'Comment On "Detecting Awareness in the Vegetative State"', *Science*, 315, 1221; author reply.

Nash, L. G., Phillips, M. N., Nicholson, H., Barnett, R. and Zhang, M. (2004), 'Skin Ligaments: Regional Distribution and Variation in Morphology', *Clinical Anatomy*, 17, 287–93.

National Bioethics Advisory Commission (1999), *Research Involving Human Biological Materials: Ethical Issues and Policy Guidance* (Rockville, MD: National Bioethics Advisory Commission).

Nature (2007), 'A Sporting Chance', *Nature*, 448, 512.

Nau, J.-Y. (1988), 'Furore over Bodies "Shot" for Experiment', *The Guardian*, 13 Nov.

Neiburger, E. J. (1990), 'Profiting from Reburial', *Nature*, 344, 297.

Nelson, J. (1992), *The Rights and Responsibilities of Potential Organ Donors: A Communitarian Approach* (Washington, DC: The Communitarian Network).

New Zealand Press Association (2006), 'Maori Bones to Be Reburied', *New Zealand Herald*, 3 May.

Nicholls, E. H. (2002), 'Selling Anatomy: The Role of the Soul', *Endeavour*, 26, 47.

Nichols, L., Aronica, P. and Babe, C. (1998), 'Are Autopsies Obsolete?' *American Journal of Clinical Pathology*, 110, 210–18.

Nicholson, R. H. (1994), 'The Good Received, the Giver Is Forgot', *Hastings Center Report*, 24, 5.

Nie, J. B. (2006), 'The United States Cover-up of Japanese Wartime Medical Atrocities: Complicity Committed in the National Interest and Two Proposals for Contemporary Action', *American Journal of Bioethics*, 6, W21–33.

Nikkhah, G. (2001), 'Neural Transplantation Therapy for Parkinson's Disease: Potential and Pitfalls', *Brain Research Bulletin*, 56, 509.

Nolan, K. (1988), '*Genug Ist Genug:* A Fetus Is Not a Kidney', *Hastings Center Report*, 18, 13–8.

Nuffield Council on Bioethics (1996), *Animal to Human Transplants: The Ethics of Xenotransplantation* (London: Nuffield Council on Bioethics).

O'Malley, C. D. (1964), *Andreas Vesalius of Brussels 1514–1564* (Los Angeles: University of California Press).

O'Rourke, K. and deBlois, J. (1994), 'Induced Delivery of Anencephalic Fetuses: A Response to James L. Walsh and Moira M. Mcqueen', *Kennedy Institute of Ethics Journal*, 4, 47–53.

O'Sullivan, E. and Mitchell, B. S. (1995), 'Plastination for Gross Anatomy Teaching Using Low Cost Equipment', *Surgical and Radiologic Anatomy* 17, 277–81.

Office of the Health and Disability Commissioner (1996), 'Code of Health and Disability Consumers' Rights' (Wellington).

Okeroa, M. (2007), 'Maori Heads to Be Returned by Field Museum on Natural History', (updated 23 May 2007) <www.beehive.govt.nz/ViewDocument.aspx?DocumentID=28766>, accessed 23 Aug 2007.

Okun, M. S. and Vitek, J. L. (2004), 'Lesion Therapy for Parkinson's Disease and Other Movement Disorders: Update and Controversies', *Movement Disorders*, 19, 375–89.

Olanow, C. W. (2005), 'Double-Blind, Placebo-Controlled Trials for Surgical Interventions in Parkinson Disease', *Archives of Neurology*, 62, 1343–4.

Olanow, C. W., Freeman, T. B. and Kordower, J. H. (1997), 'Neural Transplantation as a Therapy for Parkinson's Disease', *Advances in Neurology*, 74, 249–69.

Olanow, C. W., Goetz, C. G., Kordower, J. H., Stoessl, A. J., Sossi, V., Brin, M. F., Shannon, K. M., Nauert, G. M., Perl, D. P., Godbold, J. and Freeman,

T. B. (2003), 'A Double-Blind Controlled Trial of Bilateral Fetal Nigral Transplantation in Parkinson's Disease', *Annals of Neurology*, 54, 403–14.

Oman, K. S., Armstrong, J. D. II and Stoner, M. (2002), 'Perspectives on Practicing Procedures on the Newly Dead', *Academic Emergency Medicine*, 9, 786–90.

Organ Procurement and Transplantation Network (2007a), 'Overall by Organ', <http://www.optn.org/latestData/rptData.asp>, accessed 20 Jun 2007.

— (2007b), 'Transplants by Donor Type', <http://www.optn.org/latestData/rptData.asp>, accessed 20 Jun 2007.

—(2007c), *2006 Annual Report of the U.S. Organ Procurement and Transplantation Network and the Scientific Registry of Transplant Recipients: Transplant Data 1996–2005* (Rockville, MD: Health Resources and Services Administration, Healthcare Systems Bureau, Division of Transplantation).

— (2007d), 'Organ by Age', <http://www.optn.org/latestData/viewDataReports.asp>, accessed 14 Jun 2007.

Orlowski, J. P., Kanoti, G. A. and Mehlman, M. J. (1990), 'The Ethical Dilemma of Permitting the Teaching and Perfecting of Resuscitation Techniques on Recently Expired Patients', *Journal of Clinical Ethics*, 1, 201–5.

Ornstein, C. and Zarembo, A. (2004), 'UCLA Suspends Body-Donor Program after Alleged Abuses', *Los Angeles Times*, 10 Mar.

Ortner, D. J. (1994), 'Scientific Policy and Public Interest' in T. L. Bray and T. W. Killion (eds), *Reckoning with the Dead: The Larsen Bay Repatriation and the Smithsonian Institute* (Washington, DC: Smithsonian Institution Press), 10–14.

Owen, A. M., Coleman, M. R., Boly, M., Davis, M. H., Laureys, S. and Pickard, J. D. (2006), 'Detecting Awareness in the Vegetative State', *Science*, 313, 1402.

Owen, A. M., Coleman, M. R., Menon, D. K., Berry, E. L., Johnsrude, I. S., Rodd, J. M., Davis, M. H. and Pickard, J. D. (2005), 'Using a Hierarchical Approach to Investigate Residual Auditory Cognition in Persistent Vegetative State', *Progress in Brain Research*, 150, 457–71.

Panush, R. S., Paraschiv, D. and Dorff, R. E. (2003), 'The Tainted Legacy of Hans Reiter', *Seminars in Arthritis and Rheumatism*, 32, 231–6.

Panush, R. S., Wallace, D. J., Dorff, R. E. and Engleman, E. P. (2007), 'Retraction of the Suggestion to Use the Term "Reiter's Syndrome" Sixty-Five Years Later: The Legacy of Reiter, a War Criminal, Should Not Be Eponymic Honor but Rather Condemnation', *Arthritis and Rheumatism*, 56, 693–4.

Pardoe, C. (1990), 'Sharing the Past: Aboriginal Influence on Archaeological Practice, a Case Study from New South Wales', *Aboriginal History*, 14, 208–23.

— (1991), 'Eye of the Storm', *Journal of Indigenous Studies*, 2, 16–23.

Parfit, D. (1984), *Reasons and Persons* (Oxford: Oxford University Press).

Park, K. (1995), 'The Life of the Corpse: Division and Dissection in Late Medieval Europe', *Journal of the History of Medicine and Allied Sciences*, 50, 111–32.

Parry, J. (2006), 'Chinese Rules on Transplantation Do Not Go Far Enough', *British Medical Journal*, 332, 810.

Peabody, J. L., Emery, J. R. and Ashwal, S. (1989), 'Experience with Anencephalic Infants as Prospective Organ Donors', *New England Journal of Medicine*, 321, 344–50.

Pearson, H. (2007), 'Infertility Researchers Target Uterus Transplant', *Nature*, 445, 466–7.

Peiris, J. S. (2003), 'Severe Acute Respiratory Syndrome (SARS)', *Journal of Clinical Virology*, 28, 245–7.

Pellegrino, E. D. (1991), 'Families Self-Interest and the Cadaver's Organs: What Price Consent?' *Journal of the American Medical Association*, 265, 1305–6.

Pels, P. (1999), 'Professions of Duplexity: A Prehistory of Ethical Codes in Anthropology', *Current Anthropology*, 40, 101–36.

Pentz, R. D., Flamm, A. L., Pasqualini, R., Logothetis, C. J. and Arap, W. (2003), 'Revisiting Ethical Guidelines for Research with Terminal Wean and Brain-Dead Participants', *Hastings Center Report*, 33, 20–26.

Peters, T. (2007), *The Stem Cell Debate* (Minneapolis: Fortress Press).

Peters, T. G. (1991), 'Life or Death: The Issue of Payment in Cadaveric Organ Donation', *Journal of the American Medical Association*, 265, 1302–5.

Pfaff, W. W., Patton, P. R., Howard, R. J., Ramos, E. L., Peterson, J. C., Fennell, R. S. and Scornik, J. C. (1994), 'Kidney Transplantation', *Journal of the Florida Medical Association*, 81, 332–4.

Phan, L. K., Wager, T., Taylor, S. F. and Liberzon, I. (2002), 'Functional Neuroanatomy of Emotion: A Meta-Analysis of Emotion Activation Studies in PET and fMRI', *NeuroImage*, 16, 331–48.

Phelps, E. A., O'Connor, K. J., Cunningham, W. A., Funayama, E. S., Gatenby, J. C., Gore, J. C. and Banaji, M. R. (2000), 'Performance on Indirect Measures of Race Evaluation Predicts Amygdala Activation', *Journal of Cognitive Neuroscience*, 12, 729–38.

Piccini, P., Brooks, D. J., Bjorklund, A., Gunn, R. N., Grasby, P. M., Rimoldi, O., Brundin, P., Hagell, P., Rehncrona, S., Widner, H. and Lindvall, O. (1999), 'Dopamine Release from Nigral Transplants Visualized *In Vivo* in a Parkinson's Patient', *Nature Neuroscience*, 2, 1137–40.

Piccini, P., Pavese, N., Hagell, P., Reimer, J., Bjorklund, A., Oertel, W. H., Quinn, N. P., Brooks, D. J. and Lindvall, O. (2005), 'Factors Affecting the Clinical Outcome after Neural Transplantation in Parkinson's Disease', *Brain*, 128, 2977–86.

Pitman, R. K., Sanders, K. M., Zusman, R. M., Healy, A. R., Cheema, F., Lasko, N. B., Cahill, L. and Orr, S. P. (2002), 'Pilot Study of Secondary Prevention of Posttraumatic Stress Disorder with Propranolol', *Biological Psychiatry*, 51, 189–92.

Polgar, S. and Ng, J. (2005), 'Ethics, Methodology and the Use of Placebo Controls in Surgical Trials', *Brain Research Bulletin*, 67, 290–7.

Post, S. G. (1991), 'The Echo of Nuremberg: Nazi Data and Ethics', *Journal of Medical Ethics*, 17, 42–4.

— (1995), *The Moral Challenge of Alzheimer Disease: Ethical Issues from Diagnosis to Dying* (Baltimore: The Johns Hopkins University Press).

— (2000), *The Moral Challenge of Alzheimer Disease: Ethical Issues from Diagnosis to Dying* (2nd edn; Baltimore: The Johns Hopkins University Press).

Potts, M. (2001), 'A Requiem for Whole Brain Death: A Response to D. Alan Shewmons the Brain and Somatic Integration', *The Journal of Medicine and Philosophy*, 26, 479–91.

Powell, J. W. (1981), 'A Hidden Chapter in History', *Bulletin of the Atomic Scientists*, October, 44–52.

Powell, S., Garza, C. E. and Hendricks, A. (1993), 'Ethics and Ownership of the Past: The Reburial and Repatriation Controversy' in M. B. Schiffer (ed.), *Archaeological Method and Theory* (Tucson: University of Arizona Press), 1–42.

Pozos, R. S. (1992), 'Scientific Inquiry and Ethics: The Dachau Data' in A. L. Caplan (ed.), *When Medicine Went Mad: Bioethics and the Holocaust* (New Jersey: Humana Press), 95–108.

President's Commission for the Study of Ethical Problems in Medicine and Biomedical and Behavioral Research (1981), *Defining Death: Medical, Legal and Ethical Issues in the Determination of Death* (Washington, DC: Government Printing Office).

President's Council on Bioethics (2002), *Human Cloning and Human Dignity: An Ethical Inquiry* (New York: Public Affairs).

— (2003), *Beyond Therapy: Biotechnology and the Pursuit of Happiness* (Washington, DC).

— (2005), *Alternatives Sources of Human Pluripotent Stem Cells* (New York: Public Affairs).

PRNewswire (2006), 'Anatomist Dr. Gunther Von Hagens Reiterates His Mission of Public Health Education to Press Corps in Guben, Germany', (updated 30 Nov) <www.prnewswire.co.uk/cgi/news/release?id=185453>, accessed 12 Oct 2007.

Proctor, R. N. (1992), 'Nazi Doctors, Racial Medicine, and Human Experimentation' in G. J. Annas and M. A. Grodin (eds), *The Nazi Doctors and the Nuremberg Code: Human Rights in Human Experimentation* (Oxford: Oxford University Press), 17–31.

— (1994), 'Racial Hygiene: The Collaboration of Medicine and Nazism' in J. J. Michalczyk (ed.), *Medicine, Ethics, and the Third Reich: Historical and Contemporary Issues* (Kansas City: Sheed and Ward), 35–41.

Pross, C. (1992), 'Nazi Doctors, German Medicine, and Historical Truth' in G. J. Annas and M. A. Grodin (eds), *The Nazi Doctors and the Nuremberg Code: Human Rights in Human Experimentation* (Oxford: Oxford University Press), 32–52.

Prottas, J. M. (1992), 'Competition for Altruism: Bone and Organ Procurement in the United States', *The Milbank Quarterly*, 70, 299–317.

Pullar, G. L. (1994), 'The Qikertarmiut and the Scientist: Fifty Years of Clashing World Views', in T. L. Bray and T. W. Killion (eds), *Reckoning with the Dead: The Larsen Bay Repatriation and the Smithsonian Institute* (Washington, DC: Smithsonian Institution Press), 15–25.

Purdy, L. M. (1990), 'Are Pregnant Women Fetal Containers?', *Bioethics*, 4, 273–91.

Puschban, Z., Scherfler, C., Granata, R., Laboyrie, P., Quinn, N. P., Jenner, P., Poewe, W. and Wenning, G. K. (2000), 'Autoradiographic Study of Striatal Dopamine Re-Uptake Sites and Dopamine D1 and D2 Receptors in a 6-Hydroxydopamine and Quinolinic Acid Double-Lesion Rat Model of Striatonigral Degeneration (Multiple System Atrophy) and Effects of Embryonic Ventral Mesencephalic, Striatal or Co-Grafts', *Neuroscience*, 95, 377–88.

Pustilnik, A. C. (2008), 'Violence on the Brain: A Critique of Neuroscience in Criminal Law', *Social Science Research Network*, (updated 30 Mar 2008) <http://ssrn.com/abstract=1114250>, accessed 17 Apr 2008.

Racho El-Akouri, R., Kurlberg, G. and Brannstrom, M. (2003), 'Successful Uterine Transplantation in the Mouse: Pregnancy and Post-Natal Development of Offspring', *Human Reproduction*, 18, 2018–23.

Ramachandran, A. C., Bartlett, L. E. and Mendez, I. M. (2002), 'A Multiple Target Neural Transplantation Strategy for Parkinson's Disease', *Reviews in the Neurosciences*, 13, 243–56.

Ramsay, S. (2001), '105,000 Body Parts Retained in the UK, Census Says', *Lancet*, 357, 365.

Randerson, J. (2007), 'Give Us Back Our Bones, Pagans Tell Museums', *The Guardian* (updated 5 Feb 2007) <http://www.guardian.co.uk/science/2007/feb/05/religion.artnews>, accessed 8 May 2008.

Rankinen, T., Bray, M. S., Hagberg, J. M., Pe´Russe, L., Roth, S. M., Wolfarth, B. and Bouchard, C. (2006), 'The Human Gene Map for Performance and Health-Related Fitness Phenotypes: The 2005 Update', *Medicine & Science In Sports & Exercise*, 38, 1863–88.

Rathgeb, S. (2002), 'New Generation of Whole Body Specimens Has Arrived in London's Body Worlds Anatomy Exhibition; or, Why It Is Ok to Laugh About Dead Bodies', <www.koerperwelten.de/Downloads/PM_HoffmanNewPlasti220702.pdf>, accessed 12 Oct 2007.

Reemtsma, K., McCracken, B. H., Schlegel, J. U., Pearl, M. A., Pearce, C. W. and DeWitt, C. W. (1964), 'Renal Heterotransplantation in Man', *Annals of Surgery*, 160, 384–410.

Reid, B. (1992), 'Death and Dignity', *Time*, 30 Mar, 57.

Reidenberg, J. S. and Latiman, J. T. (2002), 'The New Face of Gross Anatomy', *Anatomical Record. Part B, New Anatomist*, 269, 81–8.

Reiman, E. M. (2007), 'Linking Brain Imaging and Genomics in the Study of Alzheimer's Disease and Aging', *Annals of the New York Academy of Sciences*, 1097, 94–113.

Reinholt, F. P., Hultenby, K., Tibell, A., Korsgren, O. and Groth, C. G. (1998), 'Survival of Fetal Porcine Pancreatic Islet Tissue Transplanted to a Diabetic Patient: Findings by Ultrastructural Immunocytochemistry', *Xenotransplantation*, 5, 222–5.

Resnik, D. (2000), 'The Moral Significance of the Therapy-Enhancement Distinction in Human Genetics', *Cambridge Quarterly of Healthcare Ethics*, 9, 365–77.

Restall Orr, E. and Bienkowski, P. (2006), 'Respectful Treatment and Reburial: A Practical Guide', (updated 7 Nov 2006) <http://www.honour.org.uk/node/41>, accessed 8 May 2008.

Retained Organs Commission (2002), A Consultation Document on Unclaimed and Unidentifiable Organs and Tissue, a Possible Regulatory Framework (London: National Health Service).

Rich, V. (1995), 'Japanese War-Time Experiments Come to Light', *Lancet*, 346, 566.

Richardson, R. (1988), *Death, Dissection and the Destitute* (London: Penguin Books).

Richardson, R. and Hurwitz, B. (1995), 'Donors' Attitudes Towards Body Donation for Dissection', *Lancet*, 346, 277–9.

Riding In, J. (1992), 'Without Ethics and Morality: A Historical Overview of Imperial Archaeology and American Indians', *Arizona State Law Journal*, 24, 11–34.

Rifkin, B. A., Ackerman, M. J. and Folkenberg, J. (2006), *Human Anatomy, Depicting the Body from the Renaissance to Today* (United Kingdom: Thames and Hudson).

Riggs, G. (1998), 'What Should We Do About Eduard Pernkopf's Atlas?', *Academic Medicine*, 73, 380–6.

Roach, M. (2003), *Stiff. The Curious Lives of Human Cadavers* (London: Viking).

Robert, J. S. and Baylis, F. (2003), 'Crossing Species Boundaries', *American Journal of Bioethics*, 3, 1–13.

Robertson, J. A. (1988), 'Fetal Tissue Transplant Research Is Ethical', *IRB: A Review of Human Subjects Research*, 10, 5–8.

Rodino-Klapac, L. R., Chicoine, L. G., Kaspar, B. K. and Mendell, J. R. (2007), 'Gene Therapy for Duchenne Muscular Dystrophy: Expectations and Challenges', *Archives of Neurology*, 64, 1236–41.

Rodning, C. B. (1989), '"O Death, Where Is Thy Sting?" Historical Perspectives on the Relationship of Human Postmortem Anatomical Dissection to Medical Education and Care', *Clinical Anatomy*, 2, 277–92.

Rodriguez, W. C., 3rd and Bass, W. M. (1983), 'Insect Activity and Its Relationship to Decay Rates of Human Cadavers in East Tennessee', *Journal of Forensic Sciences*, 28, 423–32.

— (1985), 'Decomposition of Buried Bodies and Methods That May Aid in Their Location', *Journal of Forensic Sciences*, 30, 836–52.

Rogers, B. O. (1976), 'The Development of Aesthetic Plastic Surgery: A History', *Aesthetic Plastic Surgery*, 1, 3–24.

Rose, J. C., Green, T. J. and Green, V. D. (1996), 'NAGPRA Is Forever: Osteology and the Repatriation of Skeletons', *Annual Review of Anthropology*, 25, 81–103.

Rosen, J. (2007), 'The Brain on the Stand', *New York Times*, 11 Mar.

Rosenberg, R. N. (2001), 'Genomic Neurology: A New Beginning', *Archives of Neurology*, 58, 1739–41.

Ross, P. (1992), 'Eloquent Remains', *Scientific American*, 266, 73–81.

Roth, M. (1996), 'Euthanasia and Related Ethical Issues in Dementias of Later Life with Special Reference to Alzheimer's Disease', *British Medical Bulletin*, 52, 263–79.

Rousseau, M. C., Confort-Gouny, S., Catala, A., Graperon, J., Blaya, J., Soulier, E., Viout, P., Galanaud, D., Le Fur, Y., Cozzone, P. J. and Ranjeva, J. P. (2008), 'A MRS-MRI-fMRI Exploration of the Brain. Impact of Long-Lasting Persistent Vegetative State', *Brain Injury*, 22, 123–34.

Royal College of Physicians (2003), 'The Vegetative State: Guidance on Diagnosis and Management', (London: Royal College of Physicians).

Royal Liverpool Children's Inquiry (2001), *The Royal Liverpool Children's Inquiry Report* (London: House of Commons).

Rozga, J. (2006), 'Liver Support Technology – an Update', *Xenotransplantation*, 13, 380–9.

Sadongei, A. and Cash Cash, P. (2007), 'Indigenous Value Orientations in the Care of Human Remains', in V. Cassman, N. Odegaard and J. Powell (eds), *Human Remains: Guide for Museums and Academic Institutions* (Lanham, MD: AltaMira Press).

Sahakian, B. and Morein-Zamir, S. (2007), 'Professor's Little Helper', *Nature*, 450, 1157–9.

Saletan, W. (2008), 'Little Children', *New York Times*, 10 Feb.

Sances, A., Jr. and Kumaresan, S. (2001), 'Comparison of Biomechanical Head-Neck Responses of Hybrid III Dummy and Whole Body Cadaver During Inverted Drops', *Biomedical Sciences Instrumentation*, 37, 423–7.

Sandel, M. J. (2007), *The Case against Perfection: Ethics in the Age of Genetic Engineering* (Cambridge, MA: Belknap Press of Harvard University Press).

Sanfey, A. G., Loewenstein, G., McClure, S. M. and Cohen, J. D. (2006), 'Neuroeconomics: Cross-Currents in Research on Decision-Making', *Trends in Cognitive Sciences*, 10, 108–16.

Sanner, M. (1994a), 'Attitudes toward Organ Donation and Transplantation: A Model for Understanding Reactions to Medical Procedures after Death', *Social Science and Medicine*, 38, 1141–52.

— (1994b), 'A Comparison of Public Attitudes toward Autopsy, Organ Donation, and Anatomic Dissection: A Swedish Survey', *Journal of the American Medical Association*, 271, 284–8.

Santoro, A., Mancini, E., Ferramosca, E. and Faenza, S. (2007), 'Liver Support Systems', *Contributions to Nephrology*, 156, 396–404.

Sara, M., Sacco, S., Cipolla, F., Onorati, P., Scoppetta, C., Albertini, G. and Carolei, A. (2007), 'An Unexpected Recovery from Permanent Vegetative State', *Brain Injury*, 21, 101–3.

Sauer, I. M., Kardassis, D., Zeillinger, K., Pascher, A., Gruenwald, A., Pless, G., Irgang, M., Kraemer, M., Puhl, G., Frank, J., Muller, A. R., Steinmuller, T., Denner, J., Neuhaus, P. and Gerlach, J. C. (2003), 'Clinical Extracorporeal Hybrid Liver Support – Phase I Study with Primary Porcine Liver Cells', *Xenotransplantation*, 10, 460–9.

Savulescu, J. (2003), 'Human-Animal Transgenesis and Chimeras Might Be an Expression of Our Humanity', *American Journal of Bioethics*, 3, 22–5.

— (2005), 'New Breeds of Humans: The Moral Obligation to Enhance', *Reproductive Biomedicine Online*, 10, 36–9.

— (2006), 'Justice, Fairness, and Enhancement', *Annals of the New York Academy of Sciences*, 1093, 321–38.

Savulescu, J., Foddy, B. and Clayton, M. (2004), 'Why We Should Allow Performance Enhancing Drugs in Sport', *British Journal of Sports Medicine*, 38, 666–70.

Savulescu, J. and Sandberg, A. (2008), 'Neuroenhancement of Love and Marriage: The Chemicals between Us', *Neuroethics*, 1, 31–44.

Sawday, J. (1995), *The Body Emblazoned: Dissection and the Human Body in Renaissance Culture* (London: Routledge).

— (1997), 'Livid and the Dead', *The Times Higher Education Supplement*, 18 Apr.

Sazbon, L. and Groswasser, Z. (1991), 'Medical Complications and Mortality of Patients in the Postcomatose Unawareness (PC-U) State', *Acta Neurochirurgica*, 112, 110–12.

Schlesselman, J. (1979), 'How Does One Assess the Risk of Abnormalities from Human *In Vitro* Fertilisation?' *American Journal of Obstetrics and Gynecology*, 135, 135–48.

Schmidt, T. A., Abbott, J. T., Geiderman, J. M., Hughes, J. A., Johnson, C. X., McClure, K. B., McKay, M. P., Razzak, J. A., Salo, D., Schears, R. M. and Solomon, R. C. (2004), 'Ethics Seminars: The Ethical Debate on Practicing Procedures on the Newly Dead', *Academic Emergency Medicine*, 11, 962–6.

Schnakers, C. and Zasler, N. D. (2007), 'Pain Assessment and Management in Disorders of Consciousness', *Current Opinion in Neurology*, 20, 620–6.

Schneiderman, L. J., Jecker, N. S. and Jonsen, A. R. (1990), 'Medical Futility: Its Meaning and Ethical Implications', *Annals of Internal Medicine*, 112, 949–54.

Schuelke, M., Wagner, K. R., Stolz, L. E., Hubner, C., Riebel, T., Komen, W., Braun, T., Tobin, J. F. and Lee, S. J. (2004), 'Myostatin Mutation Associated with Gross Muscle Hypertrophy in a Child', *New England Journal of Medicine*, 350, 2682–8.

Schulte-Sasse, L. (2006), 'Advise and Consent: On the Americanization of Body Worlds', *BioSocieties*, 1, 369–84.

Scott, R. (2006), 'Choosing between Possible Lives: Legal and Ethical Issues in Preimplantation Genetic Diagnosis', *Oxford Journal of Legal Studies*, 26, 153–78.

Seidelman, W. E. (1988), 'Mengele Medicus: Medicine's Nazi Heritage', *The Milbank Quarterly*, 66, 221–39.

— (1989), 'In Memoriam: Medicine's Confrontation with Evil', *Hastings Center Report*, 19, 5–6.

Shames, J. L. and Ring, H. (2008), 'Transient Reversal of Anoxic Brain Injury-Related Minimally Conscious State after Zolpidem Administration: A Case Report', *Archives of Physical Medicine and Rehabilitation*, 89, 386–8.

Shannon, T. A. and Walter, J. J. (2003), *The New Genetic Medicine* (Lanham, MD: Rowman & Littlefield Publishers, Inc.).

Shavelle, R. M., Strauss, D., Whyte, J., Day, S. M. and Yu, Y. L. (2001), 'Long-Term Causes of Death after Traumatic Brain Injury', *American Journal of Physical Medicine & Rehabilitation*, 80, 510–16.

Shetty, A. K. and Turner, D. A. (1996), 'Development of Fetal Hippocampal Grafts in Intact and Lesioned Hippocampus', *Progress in Neurobiology*, 50, 597–653.

Shewmon, D. A. (2001), 'The Brain and Somatic Integration: Insights into the Standard Biological Rationale for Equating Brain Death with Death', *The Journal of Medicine and Philosophy*, 26, 457–78.

Shiel, A., Gelling, L., Wilson, B., Coleman, M. and Pickard, J. D. (2004), 'Difficulties in Diagnosing the Vegetative State', *British Journal of Neurosurgery*, 18, 5–7.

Shorter Oxford English Dictionary (2002), 5th edn (Oxford: Oxford University Press).

Shortridge, K. F., Zhou, N. N., Guan, Y., Gao, P., Ito, T., Kawaoka, Y., Kodihalli, S., Krauss, S., Markwell, D., Murti, K. G., Norwood, M., Senne, D., Sims, L., Takada, A. and Webster, R. G. (1998), 'Characterization of Avian H5N1 Influenza Viruses from Poultry in Hong Kong', *Virology*, 252, 331–42.

Shultz, S. (1992), *Body Snatching: The Robbing of Graves for the Education of Physicians in Early Nineteenth Century America* (Jefferson, NC: McFarland and Company).

Sieunarine, K., Zakaria, F. B., Boyle, D. C., Corless, D. J., Noakes, D. E., Lindsay, I., Lawson, A., Ungar, L., Del Priores, G. and Smith, J. R. (2005), 'Possibilities for Fertility Restoration: A New Surgical Technique', *International Surgery*, 90, 249–56.

Simon, J. (2002), 'The Theater of Anatomy: The Anatomical Preparations of Honoré Fragonard', *Eighteenth-Century Studies*, 36, 63–79.

Simpson, J. (2007), 'Causes of Fetal Wastage', *Clinical Obstetrics and Gynecology*, 50, 10–30.

Singer, C. (1957), *A Short History of Anatomy and Physiology from the Greeks to Harvey* (New York: Dover Publications).

Singer, P. (1975), *Animal Liberation* (New York: Random House).

— (1993), *Practical Ethics* (New York: Cambridge University Press).

Singh, R., McDonald, C., Dawson, K., Lewis, S., Pringle, A. M., Smith, S. and Pentland, B. (2008), 'Zolpidem in a Minimally Conscious State', *Brain Injury*, 22, 103–6.

Siraisi, N. G. (1990), *Medieval and Early Renaissance Medicine* (Chicago: University of Chicago Press).

Skegg, P. D. G. (1988), *Law, Ethics and Medicine – Studies in Medical Law* (New York: Oxford University Press).

— (2003), 'The Removal and Retention of Cadaveric Body Parts: Does the Law Require Parental Consent?', *Otago Law Review*, 10, 425–44.

Skulstad, K. (2006), 'Body Worlds Draws Large Crowds – and Controversy', (updated Nov 2006) <www.canadianchristianity.com/cgi-bin/bc.cgi?bc/bccn/1106/18body>, accessed 4 Jul 2008.

Sloane, P. D., Zimmerman, S., Suchindran, C., Reed, P., Wang, L., Boustani, M. and Sudha, S. (2002), 'The Public Health Impact of Alzheimer's Disease, 2000–2050: Potential Implication of Treatment Advances', *Annual Review of Public Health*, 23, 213–31.

Small, G. W., Rabins, P. V., Barry, P. P., Buckholtz, N. S., DeKosky, S. T., Ferris, S. H., Finkel, S. I., Gwyther, L. P., Khachaturian, Z. S., Lebowitz, B. D., McRae, T. D., Morris, J. C., Oakley, F., Schneider, L. S., Streim, J. E., Sunderland, T., Teri, L. A. and Tune, L. E. (1997), 'Diagnosis and Treatment of Alzheimer Disease and Related Disorders. Consensus Statement of the American Association for Geriatric Psychiatry, the Alzheimer's Association, and the American Geriatrics Society', *Journal of the American Medical Association*, 278, 1363–71.

Smith, R. D. and Zumwalt, R. E. (1984), 'One Department's Experience with Increasing the Autopsy Rate', *Archives of Pathology and Laboratory Medicine*, 108, 455–9.

Smith, S. (2007), 'I Won't Be Happy until I Lose My Legs', *The Guardian*, 29 Jan.

Smith, W. J. (2006), 'The Trouble with Transhumanism', *Center for Bioethics and Culture* <http://www.thecbc.org/redesigned/research_display.php?id=288>, accessed 18 Oct 2007.

Sommers, C. H. (1985), 'Tooley's Immodest Proposal', *Hastings Center Report*, 15, 39–42.

Song, R. J. (2003), 'To Be Willing to Kill What for All One Knows Is a Person Is to Be Willing to Kill a Person', in B. Waters and R. Cole-Turner (eds), *God and the Embryo: Religious Voices on Stem Cells and Cloning* (Washington, DC: Georgetown University Press), 98–107.

Sora, M. C. and Genser-Strobl, B. (2005), 'The Sectional Anatomy of the Carpal Tunnel and Its Related Neurovascular Structures Studied by Using Plastination', *European Journal of Neurology*, 12, 380–4.

Sora, M. C., Genser-Strobl, B., Radu, J. and Lozanoff, S. (2007), 'Three-Dimensional Reconstruction of the Ankle by Means of Ultrathin Slice Plastination', *Clinical Anatomy*, 20, 196–200.

Sørensen, A. T., Thompson, L., Kirik, D., Bjorklund, A., Lindvall, O. and Kokaia, M. (2005), 'Functional Properties and Synaptic Integration of Genetically Labelled Dopaminergic Neurons in Intrastriatal Grafts', *European Journal of Neuroscience*, 21, 2793–9.

Spence, S. A., Hunter, M. D., Farrow, T. F., Green, R. D., Leung, D. H., Hughes, C. J. and Ganesan, V. (2004), 'A Cognitive Neurobiological Account of Deception: Evidence from Functional Neuroimaging', *Philosophical Transactions of the Royal Society of London. Series B, Biological Sciences*, 359, 1755–62.

Spital, A. (1996), 'Mandated Choice for Organ Donation: Time to Give It a Try', *Annals of Internal Medicine*, 125, 66–9.

Starzl, T. E., Marchiero, T. L., Kirkpatrick, C. H., Wilson, W. E. C. and Porter, K. A. (1964), 'Renal Heterotransplantation from Baboon to Man: Experience with 6 Cases', *Transplantation*, 2, 752–76.

Stein, R. (2007), 'First U.S. Uterus Transplant Planned', *Washington Post*, 15 Jan.

Steinberg, L. (2008), 'A Social Neuroscience Perspective on Adolescent Risk-Taking', *Developmental Review*, 28, 78–106.

Steinbock, B. and Norcross, A. (eds) (1994), *Killing and Letting Die* (2nd edn; New York: Fordham University Press).

Steinke, H. and Spanel-Borowski, K. (2006), 'Coloured Plastinates', *Annals of Anatomy*, 188, 177–82.

Stepp, L. S. (2008), 'He's a Man, as Charged', *Washington Post*, 6 May.

Steppe, H. (1992), 'Nursing in Nazi Germany', *Western Journal of Nursing Research*, 14, 744–53.

Stern, M. (2003), 'Shiny Happy People: "Body Worlds" and the Commodification of Health', *Radical Philosophy*, 118 (March/April).

Stock, G. (2002), *Redesigning Humans: Our Inevitable Genetic Future* (New York: Houghton Mifflin Company).

Stoller, S. E. and Wolpe, P. R. (2007), 'Emerging Neurotechnologies for Lie Detection and the Fifth Amendment', *American Journal of Law & Medicine*, 33, 359–75.

Strom, C., Ginsberg, N., Applebaum, M., Bozorgi, N., White, M., Caffarelli, M. and Verlinsky, Y. (1992), 'Analyses of 95 First-Trimester Spontaneous Abortions by Chorionic Villus Sampling and Karyotype', *Journal of Assisted Reproduction and Genetics*, 9, 458–61.

Strous, R. D. and Edelman, M. C. (2007), 'Eponyms and the Nazi Era: Time to Remember and Time for Change', *Israel Medical Association Journal*, 9, 207–14.

Sullivan, D. A. (2001), *Cosmetic Surgery: The Cutting Edge of Commercial Medicine in America* (New Jersey: Rutgers University Press).

Sweeney, H. L. (2004), 'Gene Doping', *Scientific American*, 291, 62–9.

Swindell, J. S. (2007), 'Facial Allograft Transplantation, Personal Identity and Subjectivity', *Journal of Medical Ethics*, 33, 449–53.

Sykes, M., d'Apice, A. and Sandrin, M. (2003), 'Position Paper of the Ethics Committee of the International Xenotransplantation Association', *Xenotransplantation*, 10, 194–203.

Szreter, S. and Mooney, G. (1998), 'Urbanisation, Mortality and the Standard of Living Debate; New Estimates of the Expectation of Life at Birth in Nineteenth-Century British Cities', *The Economic History Review*, 50, 84–112.

Tabbal, S., Fahn, S. and Frucht, S. (1998), 'Fetal Tissue Transplantation in Parkinson's Disease', *Current Opinion in Neurology*, 11, 341–9.

Tackaberry, E. S. and Ganz, P. R. (1998), 'Xenotransplantation: Assessing the Unknowns', *Christian Medical Association Journal*, 159, 41–3.

Takahashi, K., Tanabe, K., Ohnuki, M., Narita, M., Ichisaka, T., Tomoda, K. and Yamanaka, S. (2007), 'Induction of Pluripotent Stem Cells from Adult Human Fibroblasts by Defined Factors', *Cell* 131, 861–72.

Takahashi, M., Ono, K., Wakakuwa, R., Sato, O., Tsuchiya, Y., Kamiya, G., Nitta, K., Tajima, K. and Weda, K. (1994), 'The Use of Human Dura Mater Allograft for the Repair of a Contaminated Abdominal Wall Defect: Report of a Case', *Surgery Today*, 24, 468–72.

Tallman, S. (1992), 'Kiki Smith: Anatomy Lessons', *Art in America*, 80, 147–75.

Tancredi, L. R. and Brodie, J. D. (2007), 'The Brain and Behavior: Limitations in the Legal Use of Functional Magnetic Resonance Imaging', *American Journal of Law & Medicine*, 33, 271–94.

Tarasenko, Y. I., Gao, J., Nie, L., Johnson, K. M., Grady, J. J., Hulsebosch, C. E., McAdoo, D. J. and Wu, P. (2007), 'Human Fetal Neural Stem Cells Grafted into Contusion-Injured Rat Spinal Cords Improve Behavior', *Journal of Neuroscience Research*, 85, 47–57.

Taylor, C. (1991), *The Ethics of Authenticity* (Cambridge, MA: Harvard University Press).

Taylor, D. O., Edwards, L. B., Boucek, M. M., Trulock, E. P., Deng, M. C., Keck, B. M. and Hertz, M. I. (2005), 'Registry of the International Society for Heart and Lung Transplantation: Twenty-Second Official Adult Heart Transplant Report – 2005', *Journal of Heart and Lung Transplantation*, 24, 945–55.

Teo, B. (1991), 'Organs for Transplantation: The Singapore Experience', *Hastings Center Report*, 21, 10–13.

— (1992), 'Is the Adoption of More Efficient Strategies of Organ Procurement the Answer to Persistent Organ Shortage in Transplantation?', *Bioethics*, 6, 113–29.

Ter Meulen, R. H. J., Nielsen, L. and Landeweerd, L. (2007), 'Ethical Issues of Enhancement Technologies' in R. E. Ashcroft, A. Dawson, H. Draper and J. R. McMillan (eds), *Principles of Health Care Ethics* (2nd edn; Chichester: John Wiley & Sons, Ltd), 803–9.

Thomson, J. A., Itskovitz-Eldor, J., Shapiro, S. S., Waknitz, M. A., Swiergiel, J. J., Marshall, V. S. and Jones, J. M. (1998), 'Embryonic Stem Cell Lines Derived from Human Blastocysts', *Science*, 282, 1145–7.

Thompson, P. B. (1997), 'Ethics and the Genetic Engineering of Food Animals', *Journal of Agricultural & Environmental Ethics*, 10, 1–23.

Thompson, R. V. (2001), 'Art Macabre: Is Anatomy Necessary?', *ANZ Journal of Surgery*, 71, 779; author reply 83–4.

Times of India (2008), 'Ministry Plans to Set up 10 Organ Banks', (updated 11 Mar 2008) <http://timesofindia.indiatimes.com/India/Ministry_plans_to_set_up_10_organ_banks/rssarticleshow/2853576.cms>, accessed 4 Jun 2008.

Tomlinson, T. (1984), 'The Conservative Use of the Brain-Death Criterion–a Critique', *Journal of Medicine and Philosophy*, 9, 377–93.

Tooley, M. (1983), *Abortion and Infanticide* (New York: Oxford University Press,).

Towns, C. R. and Jones, D. G. (2004), 'Stem Cells, Embryos, and the Environment: A Context for Both Science and Ethics', *Journal of Medical Ethics*, 30, 410–13.

Trigger, B. G. (1995), 'Review: Reckoning with the Dead: The Larsen Bay Repatriation and the Smithsonian Institute', *Journal of the Royal Anthropological Institute*, 4, 836–7.

Trouet, C. (2004), 'New European Guidelines for the Use of Stored Human Biological Materials in Biomedical Research', *Journal of Medical Ethics*, 30, 99–103.

Tsuji, S. (2001), 'Neurogenetics in the Postgenomic Era', *Archives of Neurology*, 58, 1758–9.

Tubbs, R. S., Salter, E. G. and Oakes, W. J. (2006), 'Artificial Deformation of the Human Skull: A Review', *Clinical Anatomy*, 19, 372–7.

Turner, D. C., Robbins, T. W., Clark, L., Aron, A. R., Dowson, J. and Sahakian, B. J. (2003), 'Cognitive Enhancing Effects of Modafinil in Healthy Volunteers', *Psychopharmacology*, 165, 260–9.

Ucko, P. (1991), 'Digging up with Dignity', *The Times Higher Education Supplement*, 18 Jan.

UK Transplant (2003), 'Survey Shows Huge Support for Organ Donation' [Press Release], (updated 25 Mar 2003) <www.uktransplant.org.uk/ukt/newsroom/news_releases/article.jsp?releaseId=47>, accessed 4 Apr 2008.

— (2006), *Transplant Activity in the UK, 2005–2006* (Bristol: NHS Blood and Transplant).

— (2008), 'Transplant Numbers at New Record – Thanks to Living Donors' [Press Release], (updated 11 Jul 2008) <http://www.uktransplant.org.uk/ukt/newsroom/news_releases/article.jsp?releaseId=213>, accessed 3 Sept 2008.

Uniform Law Commissioners (2002), 'A Few Facts About the Uniform Determination of Death Act', <http://www.nccusl.org/nccusl/uniformact_factsheets/uniformacts-fs-udda.asp>, accessed 23 May 2008.

Vaiva, G., Ducrocq, F., Jezequel, K., Averland, B., Lestavel, P., Brunet, A. and Marmar, C. R. (2003), 'Immediate Treatment with Propranolol Decreases Posttraumatic Stress Disorder Two Months after Trauma', *Biological Psychiatry*, 54, 947–9.

Valdes-Gonzalez, R. A., Dorantes, L. M., Garibay, G. N., Bracho-Blanchet, E., Mendez, A. J., Davila-Perez, R., Elliott, R. B., Teran, L. and White, D. J. (2005), 'Xenotransplantation of Porcine Neonatal Islets of Langerhans and Sertoli Cells: A 4-Year Study', *European Journal of Endocrinology*, 153, 419–27.

Valdes-Gonzalez, R. A., White, D. J., Dorantes, L. M., Teran, L., Garibay-Nieto, G. N., Bracho-Blanchet, E., Davila-Perez, R., Evia-Viscarra, L., Ormsby, C. E., Ayala-Sumuano, J. T., Silva-Torres, M. L. and Ramirez-Gonzalez, B. (2007), 'Three-Yr Follow-up of a Type 1 Diabetes Mellitus Patient with an Islet Xenotransplant', *Clinical Transplantation*, 21, 352–7.

van der Flier, W. M., Barkhof, F. and Scheltens, P. (2007), 'Shifting Paradigms in Dementia: Toward Stratification of Diagnosis and Treatment Using MRI', *Annals of the New York Academy of Sciences*, 1097, 215–24.

Vass, A. A., Bass, W. M., Wolt, J. D., Foss, J. E. and Ammons, J. T. (1992), 'Time since Death Determinations of Human Cadavers Using Soil Solution', *Journal of Forensic Sciences*, 37, 1236–53.

Vawter, D. E., Kearney, W., Gervais, K. G., Caplan, A. L., Garry, D. and Tauer, C. (1990), *The Use of Human Fetal Tissue: Scientific, Ethical and Policy Concerns* (Minneapolis, MN: University of Minnesota).

Veatch, R. M. (1973), 'The Whole Brain-Oriented Concept of Death: An Outmoded Philosophical Formulation', *Journal of Thanatology*, 3, 13–30.

— (1993), 'The Impending Collapse of the Whole-Brain Definition of Death', *Hastings Center Report*, 23, 18–24.

— (2005), 'The Death of Whole-Brain Death: The Plague of the Disaggregators, Somaticists, and Mentalists', *Journal of Medicine and Philosophy*, 30, 353–78.

Veith, F. J., Fein, J. M., Tendler, M. D., Veatch, R. M., Kleiman, M. A. and Kalkines, G. (1977), 'Brain Death. I. A Status Report of Medical and Ethical Considerations', *Journal of the American Medical Association*, 238, 1651–5.

Viano, D. C. and Lau, I. V. (1988), 'A Viscous Tolerance Criterion for Soft Tissue Injury Assessment', *Journal of Biomechanics*, 40, 387.

Vine, K. (2003), 'Used Body Parts; Little Shop of Horrors', *Texas Monthly*, 31, 90–102.

Voiglio, E. J., Frattini, B., Dorrzapf, J. J., Breteau, J., Miras, A. and Caillot, J. L. (2004), 'Ballistic Study of the SAPL GC27 Gun: Is It Really "Nonlethal"?', *World Journal of Surgery*, 28, 402–5.

Volicer, L., Berman, S. A., Cipolloni, P. B. and Mandell, A. (1997), 'Persistent Vegetative State in Alzheimer Disease. Does It Exist?', *Archives of Neurology*, 54, 1382–4.

Volkmann, J. (2007), 'Update on Surgery for Parkinson's Disease', *Current Opinion in Neurology*, 20, 465–9.

von Hagens, G. (1979), 'Impregnation of Soft Biological Specimens with Thermosetting Resins and Elastomers', *Anatomical Record*, 194, 247–55.

— (2000), 'Anatomy and Plastination' in G. von Hagens and A. Whalley (eds), *Anatomy Art – Fascination beneath the Surface* (Heidelberg: Institute for Plastination), 11–38.

— (2001), 'Gruselleichen, Gestaltplastinate Und Bestattungszwang (on Gruesome Corpses, Gestalt Plastinates and Mandatory Interment)' in F. J. Wetz and B. Tag (eds), *Schöne Neue Korperwelten: Der Streit Um Die Austellung*. (*Brave New Body Worlds—the Question of the Exhibition*) (Stuttgart: Klett-Cotta), 260–82.

— (2003), 'Gunther von Hagens' Statement About the ARD Programme "Dances with Corpses" on 12 March 2003, 11:30pm', <www.bodyworlds.com/downloads/stellungnahme_ard_en.pdf>, accessed 12 Oct 2007.

Wade, N. (1978), 'The Quick, the Dead and the Cadaver Population', *Science*, 199, 1420.

Waknine, Y. (2007), 'Provigil Linked to Risk for Serious Skin Rash, Psychiatric Symptoms', *Medscape Medical News*, 25 Oct.

Walker, B. (2001), *Inquiry into the Matters Arising from the Post-Mortem and Anatomical Examination Practices of the Institute of Forensic Medicine* (Sydney: The Government of the State of New South Wales).

Walker, K. (1959), *The Story of Medicine* (London: Arrow Books Ltd.).

Walter, M., Witzel, J., Wiebking, C., Gubka, U., Rotte, M., Schiltz, K., Bermpohl, F., Tempelmann, C., Bogerts, B., Heinze, H. J. and Northoff, G. (2007), 'Pedophilia Is Linked to Reduced Activation in Hypothalamus and Lateral Prefrontal Cortex During Visual Erotic Stimulation', *Biological Psychiatry*, 62, 698–701.

Walter, T. (2004a), 'Body Worlds: Clinical Detachment and Anatomical Awe', *Sociology of Health and Illness*, 26, 464–88.

— (2004b), 'Plastination for Display: A New Way to Dispose of the Dead', *Journal of the Royal Anthropological Institute*, 10, 603–27.

Walters, J. W. and Ashwal, S. (1988), 'Organ Prolongation in Anencephalic Infants: Ethical and Medical Issues', *Hastings Center Report*, 18, 19–27.

Walton, D. N. (1980), *Brain Death: Ethical Considerations* (Indiana: Purdue University Press).

Waltz, E. (2006), 'The Body Snatchers', *Nature Medicine*, 12, 487–8.

Wancata, J., Musalek, M., Alexandrowicz, R. and Krautgartner, M. (2003), 'Number of Dementia Sufferers in Europe between the Years 2000 and 2050', *European Psychiatry*, 18, 306–13.

Warner, J. H. and Rizzolo, L. J. (2006), 'Anatomical Instruction and Training for Professionalism from the 19th to the 21st Centuries', *Clinical Anatomy*, 19, 403–14.

Warren, P. M. (1999), 'Latest UCI Probe Targets Possible Sale of Body Parts', *Los Angeles Times*, 18 Sept.

Waterman, S. (2006), 'Variations on a Hebrew Theme: The Politics of Art Music in Israel', *GeoJournal*, 65, 113–23.

Waters, B. (2006), 'Saving Us from Ourselves: Christology, Anthropology and the Seduction of Posthuman Medicine' in C. Deane-Drummond and P. Scott (eds), *Future Perfect? God, Medicine and Human Identity* (London: T&T Clark), 183–95.

Watt, N. (2008), 'Transformed by a Face Transplant', (updated 24 Mar 2008) <http://abcnews.go.com/health/story?id=4511813&page=1>, accessed 3 Jun 2008.

Weimer, D. R. (2005), 'Native American Graves Protection and Repatriation Act (NAGPRA): Legal and Legislative Developments', *CRS Report for Congress*.

Weiss, J. (2006), 'Looking Death in the Face', *The Dallas Morning News*, 13 Dec.

Weiss, R. A. (1998a), 'Xenotransplantation', *British Medical Journal*, 317, 931–4.

— (1998b), 'Transgenic Pigs and Virus Adaptation', *Nature*, 391, 327–8.

Weitzman, M. (1990), 'The Ethics of Using Nazi Medical Data: A Jewish Perspective', *Second Opinion*, 14, 27–38.

Welch, H. G., Walsh, J. S. and Larson, E. B. (1992), 'The Cost of Institutional Care in Alzheimer's Disease: Nursing Home and Hospital Use in a Prospective Cohort', *Journal of the American Geriatric Association*, 40, 221–4.

Wendler, D. (2006), 'One-Time General Consent for Research on Biological Samples', *British Medical Journal*, 332, 544–7.

Wenk, G. L. (2003), 'Neuropathologic Changes in Alzheimer's Disease', *Journal of Clinical Psychiatry*, 64 Suppl 9, 7–10.

Wenning, G. K., Odin, P., Morrish, P., Rehncrona, S., Widner, H., Brundin, P., Rothwell, J. C., Brown, R., Gustavii, B., Hagell, P., Jahanshahi, M., Sawle, G., Bjorklund, A., Brooks, D. J., Marsden, C. D., Quinn, N. P. and Lindvall, O. (1997), 'Short- and Long-Term Survival and Function of Unilateral Intrastriatal Dopaminergic Grafts in Parkinson's Disease', *Annals of Neurology*, 42, 95–107.

Wertz, D. C. (1999), 'Archived Specimens: A Platform for Discussion', *Community Genetics*, 2, 51–60.

Wesslau, C., Grosse, K., Kruger, R., Kucuk, O., Mauer, D., Nitschke, F. P., Norba, D., Manecke, A., Polster, F. and Gabel, D. (2007), 'How Large Is the Organ Donor Potential in Germany? Results of an Analysis of Data Collected on Deceased with Primary and Secondary Brain Damage in Intensive Care Unit from 2002 to 2005', *Transplant International*, 20, 147–55.

Wetz, F. J. (2000), 'The Dignity of Man' in G. von Hagens and A. Whalley (eds), *Anatomy Art – Fascination beneath the Surface* (Heidelberg: Institute for Plastination), 239–58.

White, D. and Wallwork, J. (1993), 'Xenografting: Probability, Possibility, or Pipe Dream?', *Lancet*, 342, 879–80.

Whyte, J. (2007), 'Treatments to Enhance Recovery from the Vegetative and Minimally Conscious States: Ethical Issues Surrounding Efficacy Studies', *American Journal of Physical Medicine & Rehabilitation*, 86, 86–92.

Wicclair, M. R. (2002), 'Informed Consent and Research Involving the Newly Dead', *Kennedy Institute of Ethics Journal*, 12, 351–72.

Wiggins, O. P., Barker, J. H., Martinez, S., Vossen, M., Maldonado, C., Grossi, F., Francois, C., Cunningham, M., Perez-Abadia, G., Kon, M. and Banis, J. C. (2004), 'On the Ethics of Facial Transplantation Research', *American Journal of Bioethics*, 4, 1–12.

Wijdicks, E. F. (2002), 'Brain Death Worldwide: Accepted Fact but No Global Consensus in Diagnostic Criteria', *Neurology*, 58, 20–25.

Wikler, D. (1988), 'Not Dead, Not Dying? Ethical Categories and Persistent Vegetative State', *Hastings Center Report*, 18, 41–7.

— (1993), 'Brain Death: A Durable Consensus?' *Bioethics*, 7, 239–46.

Wikler, D. and Barondess, J. (1993), 'Bioethics and Anti-Bioethics in Light of Nazi Medicine: What Must We Remember?', *Kennedy Institute of Ethics Journal*, 3, 39–55.

Wild, J. (2005), 'Brain Imaging Ready to Detect Terrorists, Say Neuroscientists', *Nature*, 437, 457.

Williams, P. and Wallace, D. (1989), *Unit 731: Japan's Secret Biological Warfare in World War II* (New York: Free Press).

Wilson, F. C., Harpur, J., Watson, T. and Morrow, J. I. (2002), 'Vegetative State and Minimally Responsive Patients – Regional Survey, Long-Term Case Outcomes and Service Recommendations', *NeuroRehabilitation*, 17, 231–6.

Wilson, M. (2008), "Bodies' Exhibitors Admit Corpse Origins Are Murky', (updated 30 May 2008) <http://www.nytimes.com/2008/05/30/nyregion/30bodies.html>, accessed 3 Jun 2008.

Winkler, C., Kirik, D. and Bjorklund, A. (2005), 'Cell Transplantation in Parkinson's Disease: How Can We Make It Work?', *Trends in Neurosciences*, 28, 86–92.

Wojtas, O. (1994), 'Bank with Bones to Pick and Choose', *The Higher Education Supplement*, 7 Oct.

Wolf-Klein, G., Pekmezaris, R., Chin, L. and Weiner, J. (2007), 'Conceptualizing Alzheimer's Disease as a Terminal Medical Illness', *American Journal of Hospice & Palliative Care*, 24, 77–82.

Wolf, G. and Horger, E. (1995), 'Indications for Examination of Spontaneous Abortion Specimens: A Reassessment', *American Journal of Obstetrics and Gynecology*, 173, 1364–8.

Wolpe, P. R., Foster, K. R. and Langleben, D. D. (2005), 'Emerging Neurotechnologies for Lie-Detection: Promises and Perils', *American Journal of Bioethics*, 5, 39–49.

Working, R. (2005), 'Shock Value', *Chicago Tribune*, 31 July.

Wranning, C. A., El-Akouri, R. R., Lundmark, C., Dahm-Kahler, P., Molne, J., Enskog, A. and Brannstrom, M. (2006), 'Auto-Transplantation of the Uterus in the Domestic Pig (Sus Scrofa): Surgical Technique and Early Reperfusion Events', *Journal of Obstetrics and Gynaecology Research*, 32, 358–67.

Yamamoto, T. and Katayama, Y. (2005), 'Deep Brain Stimulation Therapy for the Vegetative State', *Neuropsychological Rehabilitation*, 15, 406–13.

Yang, Y. G., Wood, J. C., Lan, P., Wilkinson, R. A., Sykes, M., Fishman, J. A. and Patience, C. (2004), 'Mouse Retrovirus Mediates Porcine Endogenous Retrovirus Transmission into Human Cells in Long-Term Human-Porcine Chimeric Mice', *Journal of Clinical Investigation*, 114, 695–700.

Yesavage, J. A., Mumenthaler, M. S., Taylor, J. L., Friedman, L., O'Hara, R., Sheikh, J., Tinklenberg, J. and Whitehouse, P. J. (2002), 'Donepezil and Flight Simulator Performance: Effects on Retention of Complex Skills', *Neurology*, 59, 123–5.

Yu, J., Vodyanik, M. A., Smuga-Otto, K., Antosiewicz-Bourget, J., Frane, J. L., Tian, S., Nie, J., Jonsdottir, G. A., Ruotti, V., Stewart, R., Slukvin, I. I. and Thomson, J. A. (2007), 'Induced Pluripotent Stem Cell Lines Derived from Human Somatic Cells', *Science* 318, 1917–20.

Zeman, A. (1997), 'Persistent Vegetative State', *Lancet*, 350, 795–9.

Zhao, L., Duan, W., Reyes, M., Keene, C., Verfaillie, C. and Low, W. (2002), 'Human Bone Marrow Stem Cells Exhibit Neural Phenotypes and Ameliorate Neurological Deficits after Grafting into the Ischemic Brain of Rats', *Experimental Neurology*, 174, 11–20.

Zimmerman, A. (1991), 'Allowing the Unconscious to Depart', *Linacre Quarterly*, 58, 17–24.

Zimmerman, L. J. (1989), 'Made Radical by My Own: An Archeologist Learns to Accept Reburial', in R. Layton (ed.), *Conflict in the Archeology of Living Traditions* (London: Unwin Hyman), 60–7.

Index